D0204204

Database Security and Integrity

EDUARDO B. FERNANDEZ
RITA C. SUMMERS
CHRISTOPHER WOOD
International Business Machines Corporation

ADDISON-WESLEY PUBLISHING COMPANY
Reading, Massachusetts · Menlo Park, California
London · Amsterdam · Don Mills, Ontario · Sydney

This book is in the
Addison-Wesley Systems Programming Series

Consulting editors: IBM Editorial Board

Library of Congress Cataloging in Publication Data

Fernandez, Eduardo B 1936-
Database security and integrity.

(The Systems programming series)
Includes bibliographies and index.
1. Data base management. 2. Computers—Access control. I. Summers, Rita C., joint author. II. Wood, C., joint author. III. Title.
QA76.9.D3F47 001.64 80-15153
ISBN 0-201-14467-0

ISBN 0-201-14467-0
ABCDEFGHIJK-HA-8987654321

THE SYSTEMS PROGRAMMING SERIES

*The Program Development Process Part I—The Individual Programmer	Joel D. Aron
The Program Development Process Part II—The Programming Team	Joel D. Aron
*Mathematical Foundations of Programming	Frank Beckman
*Structured Programming: Theory and Practice	Richard C. Linger Harlan D. Mills Bernard I. Witt
*Coded Character Sets: History and Development	Charles E. Mackenzie
*The Structure and Design of Programming Languages	John E. Nicholls
*The Environment for Systems Programs	Frederic G. Withington
*Communications Architecture for Distributed Systems	R. J. Cypser

An Introduction to Database Systems, Third Edition	C. J. Date
*Database Security and Integrity	Eduardo B. Fernandez Rita C. Summers Christopher Wood
Interactive Computer Graphics	James Foley Andries Van Dam
*Compiler Design Theory	Philip M. Lewis II Daniel J. Rosenkrantz Richard E. Stearns
*Sorting and Sort Systems	Harold Lorin
*Operating Systems	Harold Lorin Harvey M. Deitel

*Recursive Programming Techniques	William Burge
*Modeling and Analysis: An Introduction to System Performance Evaluation Methodology	Hisashi Kobayashi
Conceptual Structures: Information Processing in Mind and Machines	John F. Sowa

*Published

Foreword

The field of systems programming primarily grew out of the efforts of many programmers and managers whose creative energy went into producing practical, utilitarian systems programs needed by the rapidly growing computer industry. Programming was practiced as an art where each programmer invented his own solutions to problems with little guidance beyond that provided by his immediate associates. In 1968, the late Ascher Opler, then at IBM, recognized that it was necessary to bring programming knowledge together in a form that would be accessible to all systems programmers. Surveying the state of the art, he decided that enough useful material existed to justify a significant codification effort. On his recommendation, IBM decided to sponsor The Systems Programming Series as a long term project to collect, organize, and publish those principles and techniques that would have lasting value throughout the industry.

The Series consists of an open-ended collection of text-reference books. The contents of each book represent the individual author's view of the subject area and do not necessarily reflect the views of the IBM Corporation. Each is organized for course use but is detailed enough for reference. Further, the Series is organized in three levels: broad introductory material in the foundation volumes, more specialized material in the software volumes, and very specialized theory in the computer science volumes. As such, the Series meets the needs of the novice, the experienced programmer, and the computer scientist.

Taken together, the Series is a record of the state of the art in systems programming that can form the technological base for the systems programming discipline.

The Editorial Board

ABOUT THE AUTHORS

Eduardo B. Fernandez

Eduardo B. Fernandez is an Advisory Industry-Specialist Scientific at the Hamden, Connecticut, Branch Office of IBM Corporation, where he deals with scientific and academic uses of computers.

Dr. Fernandez received a degree in Electrical Engineering from the Universidad Tecnica F. Santa Maria, Valparaiso, Chile, in 1960, followed by a Master's Degree in Electrical Engineering from Purdue University in 1963, and a Ph.D. in Computer Science from UCLA in 1972.

Between 1961 and 1965, he worked for the university of Chile at the NASA Satellite Tracking Station in Santiago, involved in maintenance and training. In 1966 he joined the Electrical Engineering and Computer Science Department of the University of Chile, where he taught and did research on circuit theory and digital systems. In 1973 he joined the Los Angeles Scientific Center of IBM Corporation, where he was involved in research on database systems, in particular on security and performance aspects.

He is the author or coauthor of 25 technical papers, several research reports, and 13 invention disclosures. He has lectured at places such as Stanford University, Yale University, Bell Labs, University of the Philippines, Politecnico di Milano, as well as in many conferences and symposia. He has taught at the University of Chile and Catholic University (Santiago, Chile), UCLA, Instituto Tecnologico de Monterrey (Mexico), and Asian Institute of Technology (Bangkok, Thailand).

Rita C. Summers

Rita Summers is a Senior Programmer at the IBM Los Angeles Scientific Center. Since joining IBM in 1964 she has designed and implemented systems for interactive applications, computer-assisted instruction, and numerical control, and has worked on multicomputer operating systems and language for database access. She received two IBM Outstanding Contribution Awards for her work on virtual memory systems. Her work in the area of database security includes leadership of a project that developed a design for a secure database system. She has participated in the development and teaching of courses on database security, both within IBM and in universities. She is the author of many technical reports, conference papers, and articles. Recent publications include "Data base security: Requirements, policies, and models" (with C. Wood and E. B. Fernandez), *IBM Systems Journal,* **19,** 2 (1980); "Authorization in multilevel database models" (with C. Wood and E. B. Fernandez), *Information Systems,* **4,** 2 (1979); and "A System Structure for Data Security" (with E. B. Fernandez), Report G320-2687, IBM Los Angeles Scientific Center, April 1977.

Before joining IBM Ms. Summers worked as a systems analyst and programmer at Ramo Wooldridge. She received B.A. and M.A. degrees from UCLA. She is a member of Phi Beta Kappa, the Association for Computing Machinery, and the Institute of Electrical and Electronics Engineers.

Christopher Wood

Christopher Wood is located at the Los Angeles Scientific Center, where he has been working in database security and performance since 1976. He joined IBM in 1970 as a systems engineer in London, England, specializing in the database area. In 1966 he obtained a B.S. in physics from Imperial College, London University, and in 1969 a Ph.D. from Balliol College, Oxford University, in theoretical physics. Dr. Wood is a member of the Association for Computing Machinery and the Institute of Electrical and Electronics Engineers.

Preface

This book is concerned with the security and integrity of information that is maintained in databases. Topics that are central to this concern are treated in depth, and important related topics are introduced. The book is aimed at a reader with some technical background in the computing field and with a serious interest in database security. Some background in database systems is also desirable; this could be a college course, experience in using or managing a database system, experience in designing or implementing a database management system, or a general cultural acquaintance with databases combined with other systems experience.

We have in mind three classes of readers:

- students
- system designers and programmers, and
- people responsible for managing and auditing the security of database systems.

The book may be used in different ways by these different groups of readers.

For the student

The book is designed to be useful for a senior level or graduate course in computer science or management science. All chapters are appropriate for study, but a shorter course can be obtained by skipping special topics, such as privacy (Chapter 2), distributed databases (Chapter 12), or statistical databases (Chapter 13). Integrity (Chapter 8) is a self-contained unit that could be omitted if the course is restricted to security.

For the system designer and programmer

For these readers the book provides a conceptual framework plus a comprehensive analysis of useful principles and techniques. The security designs of important database systems are covered. Again, special topics can be skipped.

For the security administrator or auditor

These readers can skip the more theoretical chapters and those dealing with design and programming technology. These are Chapters 6, 8, 10, 11, and 13. The remaining chapters should be useful for explaining why database security and integrity are important, creating an awareness of security and integrity threats and defensive measures, providing a conceptual framework, and relating auditing and control to that framework.

For all readers, and for the researcher as well, the references and the annotated bibliographies should be valuable.

Structure of the Book

Chapter 1 defines the topics of the book, argues for their importance, and introduces basic terminology. Chapter 2 reviews privacy concepts, privacy legislation, and current privacy issues. Chapter 3 summarizes the basic concepts and terminology of database systems. Chapter 4 is an overview of the entire computer security problem, showing where database security fits in. Chapter 5 discusses possible security policies, while Chapter 6 introduces models of database security. One of these models is used to structure some of the remaining chapters. The next chapter considers issues of authorization; that is, how users' rights to access the database are specified. Problems and techniques of integrity are described in Chapter 8. In Chapter 9 the topic of auditing and control is introduced and its relation to database security is discussed.

Chapter 10 introduces some basic design principles for systems that enforce security, discusses design choices, and describes the designs of a number of systems. Chapter 11 continues the treatment of security enforcement by describing operating-system and hardware mechanisms that support database security.

The special characteristics of security and integrity in distributed systems are considered in Chapter 12. The security of statistical databases is treated in Chapter 13. Finally, Chapter 14 speculates on the future of database security.

Acknowledgments

We gratefully acknowledge the help we have received from many sources. Encouragement and administrative support were provided by the editorial board of the Systems Programming Series and by the IBM Los Angeles Scientific Center. We especially would like to thank Kathy Hanson, Betsey Barnes, and Sal Matos, librarians at the Center, for their help in locating publications, and Roberta Tseng and Katy Piskur for their skilled use of a text-editing system. IBM's System Research Institute provided an opportunity to test the material of the book in a short course taught by the authors. A draft of the book was used in a longer course taught at California State University at Northridge. Marvin Schaefer, who taught that course, supplied valuable criticisms and references. A course based on sections of the book was taught at the Instituto Tecnologico de Monterrey, Mexico.

Our students in these courses helped us to clarify the presentation. Paula Newman and D. P. Beresford-Redman provided helpful comments on Chapter 9, Dick Attanasio on Chapter 11, Jim Gray on Chapter 8, and Patricia Griffiths on Chapters 10 and 12. Stan Kurzban read and commented on the entire manuscript. Tomas Lang supplied a detailed critique of an early version of the book.

We have been impressed by the skill of the editorial staff at Addison-Wesley, and by the care taken in the production of the book. We are grateful to IBM for supporting our work in many ways, but responsibility for the content of the book and for the views expressed is completely ours.

Hamden
Los Angeles
November 1980

E.B.F.
R.C.S.
C.W.

Contents

CHAPTER 1
INTRODUCTION

CHAPTER 2
PRIVACY REQUIREMENTS

CHAPTER 3
DATABASE CONCEPTS

CHAPTER 8
DATA INTEGRITY

CHAPTER 9
AUDITING AND CONTROLS IN A DATABASE ENVIRONMENT

CHAPTER 10
ENFORCEMENT DESIGN

CHAPTER 11
PROTECTION MECHANISMS

1
Introduction

1.1 THE NEED FOR DATABASE SECURITY AND INTEGRITY

Information is a critical resource in today's enterprises, whether they are industrial, commercial, educational, or civic. These organizations are now automating not only their basic operational functions, such as invoicing, payroll, and stock control, but also management-support functions such as sales forecasting, budgeting, and financial control. In order to support these functions, enterprises maintain more and more computerized information in databases, and they increasingly depend on that information for their correct functioning (Fig. 1.1). The continued successful operation of an enterprise demands that:

1. confidential data is available only to authorized persons, so that privacy requirements are satisfied and enterprise secrets guarded;
2. the data accurately reflects the state of the enterprise; that is, the data is protected against either malicious or accidental destruction or corruption.

These requirements are the concern of *database security* and *integrity*, the topics of this book.

1.2 THE VALUE OF INFORMATION

Information has been widely recognized as a resource of economic value to an enterprise. Indeed, in many enterprises a portion of the information is so crucial that its destruction could virtually paralyze the enterprise.

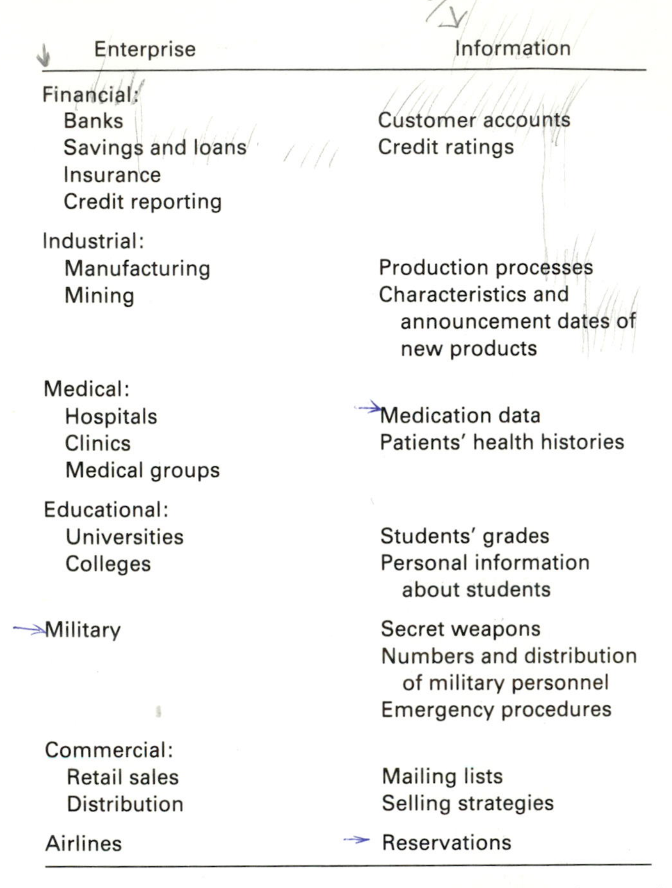

Enterprise	Information
Financial:	
Banks	Customer accounts
Savings and loans	Credit ratings
Insurance	
Credit reporting	
Industrial:	
Manufacturing	Production processes
Mining	Characteristics and announcement dates of new products
Medical:	
Hospitals	Medication data
Clinics	Patients' health histories
Medical groups	
Educational:	
Universities	Students' grades
Colleges	Personal information about students
Military	Secret weapons Numbers and distribution of military personnel Emergency procedures
Commercial:	
Retail sales	Mailing lists
Distribution	Selling strategies
Airlines	Reservations

Fig. 1.1 Examples of sensitive data in different types of enterprises.

Certain planning and operational information often falls into this category. Like other resources, information needs to be protected and managed to maximize its value to the enterprise. However, in contrast with the value of tangible assets, the value of information is often difficult to quantify.

For example, data corruption in a hospital database could result in patients receiving the wrong medication. Leakage or corruption of military information could endanger national security. Erroneous information in an airline database could threaten passenger safety. The effect depends not only on the information itself, but also on the type of improper action against it. Disclosing airplane maintenance schedules may be harmless, but altering them could cost lives.

Whether or not the value can be quantified, critical information can usually be identified and measures taken to protect it against unauthorized access and to ensure its accuracy and availability.

Just as important as the economic value of information is the privacy of individuals. The effect of disclosing or altering information about individuals ranges from annoyance to endangering their lives. Recognizing privacy rights, many countries have enacted laws to protect the privacy of their citizens. Privacy laws may require, for example, that personal information be used only for the original purpose for which it was collected, or that the accuracy of the information be maintained. Other laws are intended to protect customers and stockholders against loss due to lack of control of information resources. Thus there are also legal reasons for an enterprise to maintain the security and integrity of its information.

1.3 MISUSE OF COMPUTERS

The computer is now an integral part of many activities and operations that also include people and nonautomated procedures. This means that crime directed against these operations involves the computer in some way, either directly or indirectly. As the opportunity for more conventional crime decreases (because fewer procedures are manual, and because of computer-based checks on manual procedures), the opportunity for computer-related crime increases.

Many cases of misuse involving computers have been reported [2, 9, 10, 14, 19]. Examples of some possible types of misuse are:

- Theft of money (for example, by transferring it from the rightful owner to some real or fictitious agent of the criminal),
- Theft of material resources that are managed by computer-based systems,
- Access to proprietary information, such as trade secrets,
- Access to information that can be used for illegal purposes, such as blackmail or espionage,
- Disruption of operations such as chemical process control or computer-aided manufacturing, and

- Harmful or illegal revelation of personal data (in one case a young woman reportedly was rejected for a teaching job because her mother was under psychiatric care [18]).

These types of abuse are not unique to the computerized operation, but along with computer technology have come new types, such as:

- Theft of computer services [17], and
- Theft of proprietary software [12].

The extent of loss from computer-related crime is not known, but it is believed to be significant [4]. Even less is known about the total harm done to individuals or to society by improper access to personal records (damage awards for invasion of privacy have been reported [18]). Poor operating procedures, along with a lack of application controls, have left many organizations vulnerable to crime that does not require any computer expertise at all [1].

One view is that special laws are needed to successfully prosecute computer crime. Legislation has therefore been introduced to make it a federal crime to access a computer for fraudulent purposes, and several states have passed computer crime laws.

1.4 SECURITY AND INTEGRITY OF DATABASES

This book concentrates on security and integrity as they relate to databases. Why do databases warrant a separate treatment? The reason is that important additional security and integrity exposures arise in the database environment, as do opportunities for different and more effective solutions.

Typically a database contains data of various degrees of importance and levels of sensitivity. This data is shared among a wide variety of users with different responsibilities and privileges. It therefore becomes important to restrict users of the database to those portions of the total data that are necessary for their activities. Additionally, more control is needed over what changes a user can make to data because of the many ways these changes can affect other users of the database.

Another characteristic of databases is that a change to a data value destroys the old value. This means that new recovery techniques are needed to restore the database after system and program failures or errors.

Finally, many databases are online, accessed by multiple users concurrently. Special mechanisms are needed in this situation to maintain the integrity of the database and the consistency of information that is retrieved.

The emphasis of this book is on security and integrity measures of the database management system, but these alone are not sufficient. The underlying systems, such as the operating system and the computer hardware, must also be secure and reliable. The enterprise also needs security procedures external to the computer system, such as locks on the computer-room door and fireproof safes for storing copies of the database. Operating-system support for database security is covered in Chapter 11, and external procedures are surveyed in Chapter 4.

Many of the concepts and techniques discussed in this book are not yet implemented in commercial systems, although experimental systems have shown their feasibility. In this sense the book attempts to indicate the *requirements* for the next generation of database systems. In other cases the discussion points to unsolved problems and avenues for research.

1.5 DEFINITIONS

The terminology of database security varies a great deal, perhaps because several different areas are involved, each with its own terminology. We have tried to choose the most widely used definitions, as long as they are clear and consistent. The most central terms are defined here; other terms are introduced as used.

Information security is the protection of information against unauthorized disclosure, alteration, or destruction. It follows that *database security* is the protection of information that is maintained in a database. The need for database security derives in part from considerations of privacy. The term *privacy* is used broadly for all the ethical and legal aspects of personal data systems—systems that contain information about individuals. More specifically, privacy is the right of individuals to some control over information about themselves.

Since security has been defined in terms of protection against *unauthorized* actions, we must define what we mean by *authorization*. Authorization is the specification of rules about who has what type of access to what information. An authorized action abides by these *access rules*. The person who writes access rules is called an *authorizer*.

Since a database system is supported by a computing system, we need a set of terms for security within the computing system. The term *protection,* although sometimes used for any security mechanisms, refers primarily to techniques that control the access of executing programs to stored information [15]. These techniques include operating-system and hardware features. *System integrity* is the ability of a system to operate according to specifications even in the face of deliberate attempts to make it behave differently.

The process of ensuring that information and other protected objects are accessed only in authorized ways is called *access control.* Access control is one of several possible objectives for security within a computing system; it is schematically described in Fig. 1.2, where information from the database is transferred to and from the user's program according to the access rules. *Intentional resolution* aims at controlling the actions performed on the data once it is legally accessed. Intentional resolution can be represented by the diagram in Fig. 1.3, where now the system controls the user program's actions. *Information flow control* aims at preventing security leakage as information flows through the computer system.

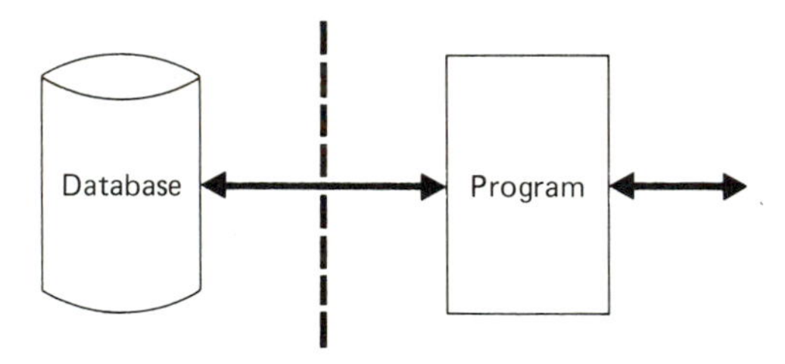

Fig. 1.2 Database access control.

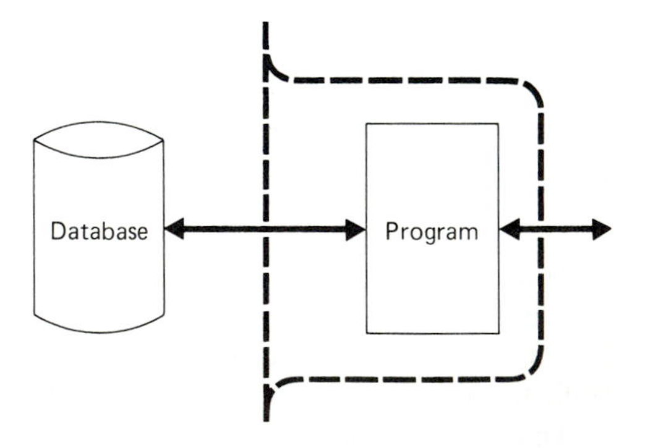

Fig. 1.3 Intentional resolution of program actions. [Figures 1.2 and 1.3 are adapted from Minsky, *Comm. ACM* **19,** 3 (March 1976), 148–159 (copyright 1976, Association for Computing Machinery, Inc.), by permission of the publisher.]

The term *integrity* is also applied to data and to the mechanisms that help to ensure its correctness. The part of data integrity concerned with the correctness of database information in the presence of user modifications is called *semantic integrity*. Semantic integrity constraints, which are either explicitly expressed or implicit in the data model, specify the correct states of the database. *Concurrency control* protects data integrity in the presence of changes coming from concurrent programs in execution. If these programs do not terminate normally—because of errors, system crashes, or security violations—a *recovery system* erases and reconstructs their changes so as to preserve data integrity. Figure 1.4 (taken from [16]) shows how a change to the database (possibly unauthorized or incorrect) can affect security or integrity or both. Data security and integrity are also objectives of *auditing*, which is the examination of information by persons other than those who produced the information. Closely related to auditing are *controls*—measures taken to ensure effec-

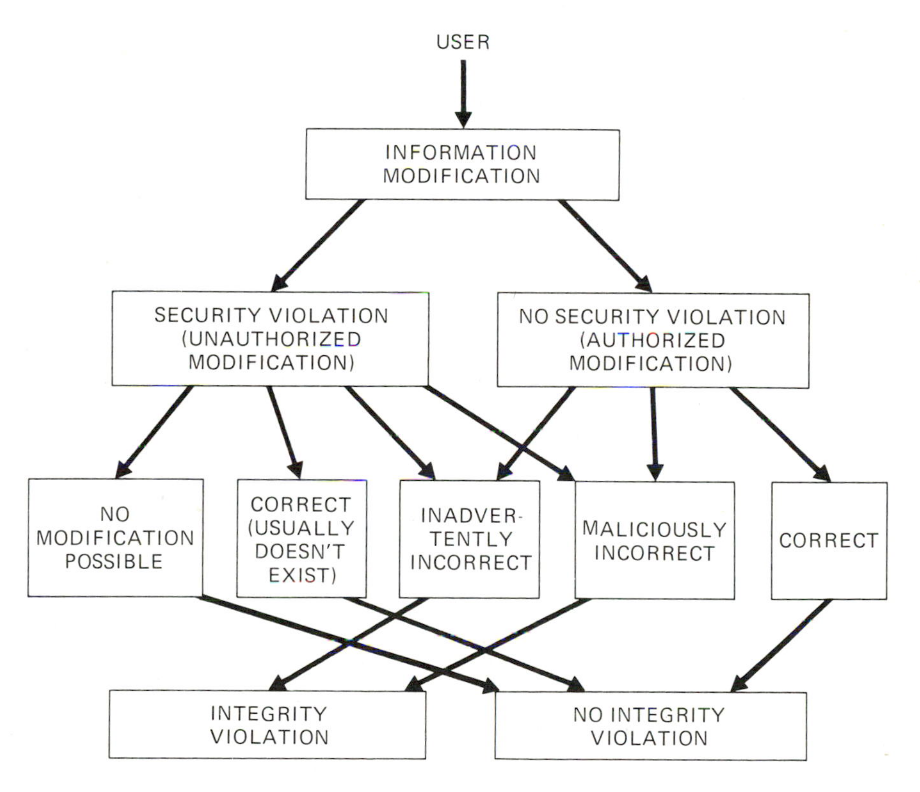

Fig. 1.4 Relationship between security and integrity. [Copyright 1977 IEEE. Reprinted, with permission, from Shanker [16].]

tive management control. Auditing and control practices of traditional accounting systems are being adapted for the database environment.

EXERCISES

1.1 Collect several examples of computer-related crime, real or imagined. These can be used later as test cases for the security measures discussed in the rest of the book. In other words, given the crime, could any of the known security measures stop it, or at least detect it?

REFERENCES AND BIBLIOGRAPHY

1. B. Allen, "Embezzler's guide to the computer." *Harvard Bus. Review* **53,** 4 (July–August 1975), 79–89.

A sample of security weaknesses in the operating procedures of typical enterprises, showing that computer-related crime requires no great cleverness or expertise.

2. B. Allen, "The biggest computer frauds: Lessons for CPAs." *Journal of Accountancy* **143,** 5 (May 1977), 52–62.

This article analyzes many computer fraud cases, trying to detect the conditions that allowed them to happen. It includes estimates of losses, methods of computer manipulation used to perpetrate the frauds, profiles of the perpetrators, and some measures that could have prevented these frauds. A table of fifteen long-running frauds is given as a summary and illustration.

3. J. J. Becker, "Demythologizing computer crime: The role of the National Center for Computer Crime Data." *Computer Security and Privacy Symposium Proc.,* 27–34, Honeywell Information Systems, 1979.

Describes a repository of information about cases of crime involving computers.

4. Committee on Government Operations, U.S. Senate. "Staff study of computer security in federal programs." U.S. Government Printing Office, Washington, D.C., 1977.

A comprehensive analysis of the security of federal computer installations. According to some testimonies, losses due to crime would be on the order of $100,000,000 per year.

5. A. D. Chambers, "Computer fraud and abuse." *Comp. Journal* **21,** 3 (August 1978), 194–198.

Extends study of [2], discussing categories of perpetrators, "way in," and other aspects of a set of reported crimes. Points out the value of segregation of functions and controls to prevent fraud.

6. "Guidelines for Automatic Data Processing Physical Security and Risk Management.'' Federal Information Processing Standards Publication No. 31, June 1974. U.S. Dept of Commerce, National Bureau of Standards. Available from Superintendent of Documents, U.S. Govt. Printing Office, Washington, DC 20402.

7. L. J. Hoffman, *Modern Methods for Computer Security and Privacy*. Prentice-Hall, Englewood Cliffs, N.J., 1977.

An overview of all aspects of computer data security. The treatment of most of these topics is sketchy, but a comprehensive list of references partially compensates. (See also Review No. 32551 in *ACM Computing Reviews,* Feb. 1978.)

8. D. K. Hsiao, D. S. Kerr, and S. E. Madnick, *Computer Security*. Academic Press, New York, 1979.

A survey of research in certain important areas of computer security.

9. L. I. Krauss and A. MacGahan, *Computer Fraud and Countermeasures*. Prentice-Hall, Englewood Cliffs, N.J., 1979.

10. *Los Angeles Times,* Feb. 10, 1977, p. 8. ''U.S. Guards Against Crime by Computer.''

11. J. Martin, *Security, Accuracy, and Privacy in Computer Systems*. Prentice-Hall, Englewood Cliffs, N.J., 1973.

A comprehensive and detailed discussion of technical, physical, administrative, and legal aspects of data security. While many of the topics are relevant to database security, there is no explicit and structured treatment of this subject. Due to the publication date, there is also no discussion of more recent developments.

12. S. H. Nycum, ''Anatomy of a computer crime.'' *AFIPS Conf. Proc.* **47,** 1978 NCC, 1151–1155. AFIPS Press, Montvale, N.J., 1978.

A description, written by a lawyer specializing in computer abuse, of a case of theft of proprietary software over telephone lines. The case showed the problems in applying the existing U.S. laws to such cases.

13. P. S. Browne, *Security: Checklist for Computer Center Self-audits*. AFIPS Press, Arlington, Va., 1979.

A detailed list of points to check in performing a self-assessment of an installation's security measures.

14. D. B. Parker, *Crime by Computer*. Charles Scribner's Sons, New York, 1976.

15. J. H. Saltzer and M. D. Schroeder, ''The protection of information in computer systems.'' *Proc. IEEE,* **63,** 9 (Sept. 1975), 1278–1308.

16. K. S. Shankar, ''The total computer security problem: an overview.'' *Computer* **10,** 6 (June 1977), 50–73.

17. B. Schultz, ''DP service theft case to test Canadian code.'' *Computerworld* **12,** 26 (June 26, 1978), 5.

A case involving three University of Alberta students who gained unauthorized access to the university computer and issued accounts to themselves. The case publicized the fact that Canada's criminal code had no section devoted to computer abuse, except in the area of privacy. The defendants were therefore accused of "theft of telecommunication services" (since they used a terminal connected by telephone lines).

18. *Time* **113,** 23 (June 4, 1979), p. 80. "Private Lives: Protecting Patient Records."

19. T. Whiteside, *Computer Capers: Tales of Electronic Thievery, Embezzlement, and Fraud.* T. Y. Crowell, New York, 1978.

A very readable and entertaining account of a wide variety of crimes perpetrated with the use of computers.

2 Privacy Requirements

2.1 INTRODUCTION

There is a growing interest in information privacy as computerized record-keeping increasingly affects the lives of individuals. In contrast to the situation only a few decades ago, today individuals obtain most of the services they need from large institutions. To make decisions about these services, the institutions rely on record-keeping rather than personal knowledge. This change has been tied to the development of automated systems, which have provided new support for fine-grained decisions. This leads in turn to demands for still more detailed information and to increased threats to privacy.

In this chapter we address the development of the privacy concept and review the history of privacy legislation. Some current privacy issues are then surveyed. Finally we consider what privacy requirements imply for the implementation of record-keeping systems and for database security.*

2.2 THE PRIVACY CONCEPT IN THE UNITED STATES

Information privacy is one aspect of a more general privacy concept that is an important tradition in a number of countries. We shall review its development in the United States, as surveyed in [17, 19, 31, and 32].

Although the Bill of Rights reflected concerns about privacy, the framers of those amendments chose to guard against specific abuses; they

* This chapter is intended as background only. We are not lawyers, and we have relied on the secondary sources cited.

did not explicitly state a general privacy concept. The legal concept of privacy that developed during the eighteenth and nineteenth centuries was based in part on constitutional protections such as freedom of speech and assembly, freedom from unreasonable searches and seizures, the right to due process, and freedom from self-incrimination, and in part on various common-law doctrines.

The late nineteenth century saw the introduction of new technology, such as the telephone, microphone, and candid camera, which could be used for surveillance. In 1890 Warren and Brandeis wrote: "Recent inventions and business methods call attention to the next step which must be taken for the protection of the person, and for securing to the individual . . . the right 'to be let alone' " [30, p. 195]. They urged the recognition of privacy as a separate and general right protected under the law. The right to privacy continued to develop in this century through a number of Supreme Court decisions and through recognition by nearly all the states of a common-law right to privacy, which means that individuals can seek legal redress for violations to their privacy.

The concept of due process is an important basis for information privacy with respect to government. Due process includes *procedural guarantees* and *substantive due process*. Both protect the individual against unfair government action. Rules set by authorities must be specified in advance and communicated to the persons affected by the rules; individuals must receive fair hearing before being penalized for violation of the rules; and appeal to higher authority must be available. Moreover, government decisions must not be arbitrary. There was, however, no due-process right of individuals to inspect or control records about themselves in government files, when these records were not being used in proceedings against them. A common-law tradition held that public records should be open, keeping government visible, and this tradition was reflected in specific laws and rules. With a few exceptions, such as labor unions, private institutions were excluded from this legal tradition.

The concept of *information* privacy is still evolving. The best-known definition was proposed by Westin [31, p. 7]:

> Privacy is the claim of individuals, groups, or institutions to determine for themselves when, how, and to what extent information about them is communicated to others.

During the 1960s, partly because of abuses resulting from the development of new technology and of the mass media, the Supreme Court invoked a constitutionally based right to privacy in a number of cases, but did not extend this right to the area of record-keeping. As recently as the 1950s and 1960s, the courts consistently held that the government could require citizens to furnish information and could allow information to be collected about them (by law-enforcement agencies, for example). On the other hand, a strong civil-liberties tradition opposed government disclosure of information about an individual's private life. In spite of this tradition, data was passed between different government agencies and even outside the government, in violation of confidentiality rules. Tax information, for example, has been widely used by agencies other than the Internal Revenue Service [17, p. 539]. As Westin and Baker summatize [32, p. 20], ". . . the reality of the 1960s was that civil liberties in record-keeping was an underdeveloped area of American law." In the 1970s a series of *fair information practices* laws (reviewed in the next section) began to change the situation.

In several cases during the 1970s the Supreme Court failed to state a right to information privacy. In 1976, for example, the court ruled that one Mitchell Miller, whose checks and bank statements had been shown to Treasury agents investigating an illegal distillery, had no legitimate expectation of privacy in his bank records.

Privacy is not the only ethical or legal concern about information. *Administrative secrecy* laws protect governments or other institutions. A good example is the British Official Secrets Act, which makes it a crime for a government servant to communicate official information. In contrast, the U.S. Freedom of Information Act of 1966 gives all persons the right to see the records of Federal government agencies. Although many agencies and many types of information are exempted, the law has been very heavily used.

2.3 THE HISTORY OF INFORMATION PRIVACY LEGISLATION

This section traces the history of privacy regulation and legislation. This legislation imposes significant requirements on database systems.

The very first regulation issued by the Social Security Administration (in 1937) allowed records to be released only to certain other agencies or to the person the records concerned (the *subject* of the records).[1] This confidentiality has been under continuing attack ever since.

The Fair Credit Reporting Act of 1971 was the first major U.S. law affecting information systems in the private sector. Credit bureaus must allow consumers to review their credit files, to request changes or deletions, or to include statements in their files. Several million requests are processed annually, and the law prohibits charging for this review if the consumer was recently refused credit through the bureau. This act represents one approach to privacy legislation in the private sector: the tailoring of legislation to specific industries.

---

1. This use of "subject" in privacy terminology conflicts with the use in security, where a subject is someone who *accesses* records.

The next significant event was the development in 1973 of a Code of Fair Information Practices [20], for the Department of Health, Education, and Welfare. According to the code,

- There must be no secret systems;
- Individuals must be able to find out what information is maintained about them and how it is used;
- They must be able to correct the information;
- Information obtained for one purpose must not be used for another without the individual's consent; and
- The organization maintaining the personal information must guarantee its reliability and take precautions to prevent its misuse.

(This last principle is the key one from the viewpoint of database security.)

The essence of the code was implemented in the Privacy Act of 1974 [18], whose intent was to protect individuals against invasion of privacy by the Federal government. As in the Freedom of Information Act, certain agencies are exempted; but in contrast to that act, the 1974 law puts an *active* responsibility on the federal agencies: they must initiate action, not merely respond to requests from individuals.

In Great Britain, the Younger Committee on Privacy, reporting in 1972, saw a potential threat to privacy from private-sector systems, and recommended creation of a standing commission to keep the problem under review. The Younger report was followed in 1975 by a White Paper proposing either a licensing agency or an agency to handle citizens' complaints [4].

The first national privacy law was the Swedish Data Act of 1973. It requires any record-keeping system to be licensed and inspected by a board, which may issue directives tailored specifically for that system. A federal privacy law went into effect in Germany in 1978, referring to all systems (federal, state, or private; automated or not) and imposing both technical and organizational requirements. It is not clear how strong this law will be, since it has two potential loopholes: the protection of data is to be appropriate to the type of data to be protected, and the cost has to be reasonable in relation to the desired level of protection. Both the German law and a French law passed in 1978 have provisions aimed at purging of obsolete information. National privacy laws are also in effect in Austria, Canada, Denmark, and Norway, and are under consideration in many other countries [23, 33]. Figure 2.1 summarizes some characteristics of the Swedish, German, and French laws.

In the meantime, the U.S. Privacy Protection Study Commission had

Attribute	Country: Sweden (1973)	Germany (1977)	France (1978)
Nonautomated records	—	(1)	(1)
Private sector as well as public	×	×	×
Prohibition on certain types of data (2)	×	—	×
Security requirements	(3)	×	×
Active notification of subject	—	×	×
Review/correction by subject	×	×	×
Cost of correction by subject paid by:			
Subject	—	×	×
Keeper	×	—	—
Correctness (Keeper's initiative)	×	—	—
Control of access and release	(3)	×	×
Data trespass punishable (4)	×	—	—
Penalties (Fine and prison)	×	×	×

1. Limited application.
2. For example, no racial origins or political, philosophical, or religious opinions (France).
3. Data Inspection Board empowered to require.
4. Penalty to trespasser as well as keeper.

Fig. 2.1 Attributes of some national privacy laws.

been considering the problem of legislation for the private sector. There were two possible paths: apply the provisions of the Privacy Act of 1974 to private industry, or treat the private sector differently from government. The Commission's report [17], issued in 1977, reflected its choice of the second alternative. This contrasts with the approach taken by most European countries. The Commission opted for laws tailored to specific industries, but based on common guiding principles [29]. It recommended three basic objectives of a national privacy protection policy:

- *To minimize intrusiveness.* That is, to create a proper balance between what an individual divulges and what he or she seeks in return. To create this balance the Commission recommended:

  more fully informing individuals about an organization's record-keeping practices;

  not collecting certain types of information at all (for example, arrest information for employment purposes);

  limiting the methods by which information is collected; and

  (as a last resort) complaints to governmental agencies.

- *To maximize fairness.* For most areas the Commission recommended that the subject be able to interact more easily with the record-keeper, to see records, to correct errors, and to authorize disclosure. A principle of *limited disclosure* was stated: Only the information specified in an authorized request should be disclosed. Fairness was also considered to imply reasonable procedures for ensuring that personal records are accurate, complete, and timely.

- *To establish obligations about using and disclosing personal data.* This means establishing a "legally enforceable expectation of confidentiality" in certain areas.

The Commission recommended national legislation to establish this expectation of confidentiality in records held by certain private-sector organizations—credit grantors, banks, insurance companies, doctors, and hospitals. The first legislation embodying Commission recommendations was passed in 1978 and amended in 1979 [8, 21]. This legislation, which deals with the issues of the Miller case, requires government authorities intending to access bank records to notify the subject of the records, and specifies steps the subject can take to prevent the access. The law also prevents one government agency from passing the records on to another. United States privacy history is summarized in Fig. 2.2. A number of states also have or are considering privacy laws [22].

2.4 CURRENT PRIVACY DEVELOPMENTS AND ISSUES

New privacy implications arise with every technological development that increases the potential for recording and searching information about individuals. Two such developments, *Electronic Funds Transfer (EFT)* and *transborder data flow (TDF),* are discussed in this section, along with

Year	Event
1890	Warren and Brandeis article
1929	Census Bureau Act privacy provision
1937	Social Security Administration regulation
1966	Freedom of Information Act
1971	Fair Credit Reporting Act
1973	HEW Code of Fair Information Practices
1974	Privacy Act
1977	Privacy Protection Study Commission Report
1978	Right of Financial Privacy Act

Fig. 2.2 History of U.S. privacy legislation.

two privacy issues: the use of universal identifiers, and the conflict of privacy with other objectives.

2.4.1 Electronic Funds Transfer

An EFT system is a computer-based network for automatically processing deposits, withdrawals, and transfers of money [2, 17, 28]. *Point-of-sale* EFT services include cash withdrawal (at a supermarket, for example) and also electronic movement of funds from a customer's account to a merchant's. The customer uses a plastic card and may also have a personal identification number (PIN) that serves as a password. *Automated clearinghouses* currently transfer funds between institutions, handling, for example, payrolls, insurance premiums, and Social Security benefits. *Remote banking* (Fig. 2.3) provides deposits, withdrawals, bill-paying, or other services from a terminal or a touch-tone telephone. *Automated check processing* (for transfers between individual accounts) is on the way. EFT may provide a way to reduce the high cost of payment transactions.

The expansion of EFT raises privacy questions because more details will be recorded, the records will be more centralized and easier to retrieve, and new kinds of information will be recorded. For example, benefit and tax information may accompany wage payments and could be recorded by the clearinghouse. Information about individuals or groups could be accumulated on a selective basis. Point-of-sale systems have been used to locate individuals, and potentially could trace a person's transactions and purchasing habits in detail. With automated check processing a great deal of personal data would be available to be searched economically. (Although most banks now microfilm all checks, the difficulty of searching the filmed record for specific information provides some protection.)

EFT may have other social effects not strictly related to privacy [13], and new potential opportunities for crime arise. The Privacy Protection Study Commission made several recommendations aimed at limiting the

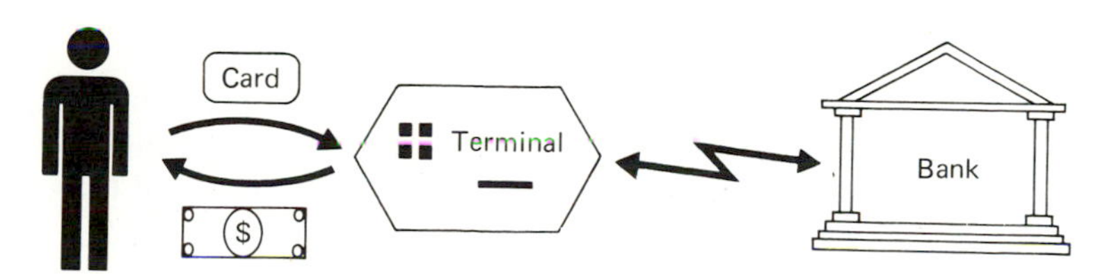

Fig. 2.3 Remote banking system.

information kept by EFT services, protecting individuals against inaccuracy, and keeping the government out of EFT. The Electronic Funds Transfer Act passed in 1978 and implemented in 1980 [7] gives consumers a number of protections against loss from erroneous or unauthorized transactions, and privacy legislation pertaining specifically to EFT has been proposed. Security and privacy issues in EFT are surveyed in [2, 12, 14, 16, and 19].

2.4.2 Transborder Data Flow

The amount of data flowing across national borders has been rapidly increasing. Such data flows in the private networks of multinational organizations or in public networks such as the Nordic Data Network and Euronet [3]. The protection of personal data that crosses borders is one of several TDF problems receiving much attention [26]. What happens when data originates in Country A, which has strong privacy laws, and then moves for processing to Country B, which has weak or nonexistent laws? Some European laws, for example, apply to all private sector records, while U.S. and Canadian laws do not. The laws of some countries apply to information about "legal persons" such as corporations. Some countries might even deliberately become "data havens," without strong privacy legislation, in order to attract data processing business. Other countries might use privacy regulations as a trade barrier, to protect their own data processing industries. Concern has been expressed in the United States that privacy arguments may be used to block free international flow of information [5, 6]. Transborder data flow is an area of great complexity and economic importance, involving not only privacy but also issues of national sovereignty, competition in data processing services, and telecommunications policy [26].

Among the principles proposed (by a member of the Swedish Data Inspection Board) for any *international* regulation are:

1. that information should be used only for the purposes decided in its country of origin,
2. that security measures be taken, and
3. that subjects have the right of inspection [3].

The OECD has recommended guidelines for its member countries, and the Council of Europe has drafted a data-protection convention with a "common core" based on principles common to the national laws of all the member nations. How the core is implemented would be left to the individual nations [10, 11, 25].

2.4.3 Universal Identifiers

The Privacy Commission found great public concern about the use of a "universal identifier," such as the Social Security number, to link personal records maintained in different databases, making it easier to maintain dossiers and thus tightening social control. The main concern is not the Social Security number as such, but the linkage and exchange, which can be (and is) achieved by using other identifiers and attributes. People are also concerned about the dehumanizing effect of a numerical identifier, as expressed in a letter asking the commission to "prevent us from becoming our Social Security numbers."

The Privacy Act of 1974 placed some restrictions on government use of the Social Security number, but these restrictions have had little practical effect. The Privacy Commission was concerned that a "standard universal label" would gradually evolve, and recommended positive steps to stop that evolution.

2.4.4 The Right to Privacy vs. the Right to Know

The potential conflict between privacy and other objectives can be seen clearly in the area of medical research. Researchers studying Lou Gehrig's disease, a progressive neurological disorder, were investigating links to patients' occupational and geographical histories [15]. They found their work to be hampered by the Privacy Act of 1974, since the Veterans' Administration and other federal agencies refused to release medical-record information. As this story reveals and as we can see from the Freedom of Information Act and the transborder data-flow issue, the right to privacy can conflict with society's need for free information flow. In the case of medical records, their confidentiality is limited in a number of ways. Communicable diseases and child abuse must be reported, for example. The emerging privacy policy appears to be to try to balance the power inherent in information: letting information flow more freely to the individuals that it concerns, but restricting powerful record-keepers, particularly governments.

2.5 IMPLEMENTATION OF SYSTEMS FOR PRIVACY

It is clear from even a brief review that privacy legislation has important implications for the design and implementation of record-keeping systems. The precise measures that will be required depend on the country, and (in the United States) on the industry. It is nevertheless useful to analyze what the principles behind privacy legislation may imply. Our discussion is based on Turn [24] and on Ware's discussion [29] of the technical consequences of the Privacy Commission recommendations. Some of these consequences carry significant costs, which have been analyzed in [9] and [19].

2.5.1 Notification

First, registers of databases must be maintained and published, to conform to the "no secret systems" requirement. Of more importance, however, is the subject's right to know about records. Usually the burden is placed on the subject to request records, but not necessarily to supply the same identifier used internally by the system (such as the Social Security number). This means that the system must be able to locate an individual's record using nonunique identifiers, such as name and birthdate.

2.5.2 Inspection and Review

Records must be provided to the individual in a form that is understandable and also complete. The subject may ask for corrections and, if they are refused, may submit a rebuttal statement, which must be included in reports.

2.5.3 Accounting Requirements

Records must be kept to support several types of auditing. Information sources must be recorded so that erroneous information can be traced. Recipients of reports must be listed, so that subjects can be notified of disclosures and so that the recipients can receive corrections. Information must be maintained to allow audit of compliance with privacy laws.

2.5.4 Data Quality

Quality is the degree to which records about an individual accurately reflect the individual. Technical measures can help by ensuring that the data is reasonable (obeys integrity constraints), that it is not compromised while in the system, and that it is timely. Obsolete information must be purged.

2.5.5 Data Security

One implication of privacy legislation is that access must be controlled on a need-to-know basis. Access must be given not to the individual's record as a whole, but to those parts relevant to the purposes of the requester.

This means either that different types of information about an individual must be physically separated, or that the database system must provide fine-grained access control to data elements or fields. Generalized database management systems appear to be the best means of providing this level of access control and of supporting the accounting and data-quality requirements.

More generally, data security must be maintained. The Privacy Act of 1974, for example, requires each federal record-keeping agency to ". . . establish appropriate administrative, technical, and physical safeguards to ensure the security and confidentiality of records and to protect against any anticipated threats or hazards in their security or integrity which could result in substantial harm, embarrassment, inconvenience, or unfairness to any individual on whom information is maintained." The computer specialists responsible for designing the *technical* safeguards also need an understanding of the goals of such measures. Privacy legislation does not always include detailed prescriptions for security. Its interpretation over the years will determine what level and type of security is needed to provide privacy.

REFERENCES AND BIBLIOGRAPHY

1. "The Analysis of Certain Potential Threats to EFT (Electronic Fund Transfer) System Sanctity." NTIS Report PB–279 985, U.S. Dept. of Commerce, Washington, D.C., Dec. 1976.

   A detailed study of the possible threats to an EFT system. Besides physical and administrative controls, the security measures that could be applied are basically encryption and network protocols, including authentication.

2. "Audit Considerations in Electronic Funds Transfer Systems." American Institute of Certified Public Accountants, New York, 1978.
3. R. Canning (Ed.), "The debate on transborder data flows." *EDP Analyzer* **16,** 4 (April, 1978).
4. A. S. Douglas, "The U.K. Privacy White Paper 1975." *AFIPS Conf. Proc.* **45,** 1976 NCC, 33–38. AFIPS Press, Montvale, N.J., 1976.
5. N. Dunn, "US vs. Them." *Computer Decisions* **11,** 2 (Feb. 1979), 24–30.
6. J. Eger, "Transborder data flow." *Datamation* **24,** 12 (Nov. 1978), 50–54.
7. "Electronic Fund Transfer Act." Title XX, PL 95-630 (Nov. 1978), 92 Stat 3728.
8. "Financial Institutions Regulatory and Interest Rate Control Act." PL 95-630 (Nov. 1978), 92 Stat 3641.
9. R. C. Goldstein, *The Cost of Privacy*. Honeywell Information Systems, Brighton, Mass., 1975.

10. P. Hirsch, "Europe's privacy laws—Fear of inconsistency." *Datamation* **25,** 2 (Feb. 1979), 85–88.

11. F. Hondius, "Council of Europe nearing completion of treaty on international data protection and privacy." *Computerworld* **14,** 3 (January 21, 1980), 18–19.

12. D. Kaufman and K. Auerbach, "A secure national system for electronic funds transfer." *AFIPS Conf. Proc.* **45,** 1976 NCC, 129–138. AFIPS Press, Montvale, N.J., 1976.

13. R. Kling, "Value conflicts and social choice in electronic funds transfer system developments." *Comm. ACM* **21,** 8 (August 1978), 642–656.

Pointing out that EFT systems are usually viewed as "'economic instruments' whose costs and benefits may be assessed adequately in dollars," this article views them also as political instruments. EFT developments are shown to raise different problems or provide different benefits for the holders of different *value positions* (such as private enterprise, statist, libertarian, neopopulist, and systems). The article emphasizes the importance of examining social impact *before* commitments to large-scale EFT are made. An extensive bibliography is provided.

14. K. L. Kraemer and D. W. Colton, "Policy, values, and EFT research: Anatomy of a research agenda." *Comm. ACM* **22,** 12 (Dec. 1979), 660–671.

15. *Los Angeles Times,* Aug. 22, 1976, Part 2, pp. 1, 4. "Privacy law slows medical hunt."

16. D. B. Parker, "Vulnerabilities of EFTs to intentionally caused losses." *Comm. ACM* **22,** 12 (Dec. 1979), 654–660.

17. *Personal Privacy in an Information Society*. Report of the Privacy Protection Study Commission. U.S. Govt. Printing Office, Stock No. 052–003–00395–3, July 1977.

An excellent source of information on record-keeping practices and the threats they pose for privacy. Surveys in some detail private- and public-sector areas (including consumer credit, banking, insurance, employer–employee relationships, medical care, education, government assistance, and taxpaying) and recommends legislation or other steps to correct the abuses in each area. The report also recommends establishment of an independent federal entity to monitor privacy matters.

18. "Privacy Act of 1974," Title 5, United States Code, Section 552a (Public Law 93–579), December 1974.

19. "Privacy Issues in Electronic Funds Transfer Systems: Recommendations for a Public Policy." NTIS Report PB–279 986, U.S. Dept. of Commerce, Washington, D.C., January 1978.

This report, prepared for the Electronic Industries Foundation, analyzes legal, economic, and technical aspects of privacy issues associated with future EFT systems.

20. *Records, Computers, and the Rights of Citizens*. U.S. Department of Health, Education, and Welfare Publication No. (OS) 73–94 (July 1973).

21. "Right of Privacy Act of 1979." PL 96-3 (March 1979), 93 Stat 5.

22. R. E. Smith, *Compilation of State and Federal Privacy Laws 1978–79*. Privacy Journal, Washington, D.C., 1978.

23. G. Stadlen, "Survey of national data protection legislation." *Computer Networks* **3,** 3 (June 1979), 174–186.
   Compares the data protection laws of eight countries, as well as two proposals, with respect to the following issues: coverage of the private sector, manual systems, and bodies or associations; communication of data to third parties; licensing of data keepers; enforcement through an ombudsman or through the courts; and transborder data flow.

24. R. Turn, "Implementation of privacy protection requirements." *Information Processing* **77,** Proc. IFIP, North-Holland, 1977, 957–962.

25. R. Turn, "Privacy protection and transborder data flows." *AFIPS Conf. Proc.* **49,** 1980 NCC, 581–586. AFIPS Press, Arlington, Va., 1980.

26. R. Turn (Ed.), *Transborder Data Flows: Concerns in Privacy Protection and Free Flow of Information*. Two volumes. AFIPS Press, Arlington, Va., 1980.

27. *United States v. Miller, United States Reports 425* (1976), 435–456. U.S. Government Printing Office, Washington, D.C., 1978.

28. "An update on corporate EFT." *EDP Analyzer* **18,** 5 (May, 1980).

29. W. Ware, "Handling personal data." *Datamation* **23,** 10 (Oct. 1977), 83–87.

30. S. D. Warren and L. D. Brandeis, "The right to privacy." *Harvard Law Review* **4,** 5 (Dec. 1890), 193–220.

31. A. F. Westin, *Privacy and Freedom*. Atheneum, New York, 1970.

32. A. F. Westin and M. A. Baker, *Databanks in a Free Society: Computers, Record-Keeping, and Privacy*. New York, Quadrangle Books, 1972.
   This is the influential report of the Project on Computer Databanks, which surveyed actual record-keeping practices in a broad sample of organizations. The survey failed to confirm some of the worst fears then commonly expressed. The report concludes "Computers are here to stay. So are large organizations and the need for data. So is the American commitment to civil liberties. . . . Our task is to see that appropriate safeguards for the individual's rights to privacy, confidentiality, and due process are embedded in every major record system in the nation, particularly the computerizing systems that promise to be the setting for most important organizational uses of information affecting individuals in the coming decades."

33. C. K. Wilk (Ed.), "Selected Foreign National Data Protection Laws and Bills." OT Special Publication 78–19, U.S. Dept. of Commerce, Washington, D.C., March 1978.

3 Database Concepts

3.1 WHAT IS A DATABASE?

In this chapter, we provide a foundation for the subject of database security by introducing the basic concepts and terminology of computerized databases. For more detail on databases, we refer our readers to the bibliography at the end of this chapter.

A *database* is a collection of interrelated data items that represent the information an enterprise needs in order to carry out certain functions. The database may be considered as consisting of information objects or *entities* and *relationships* between these entities; the entities and relationships are represented in some physical way in the database—by records and pointers, for example, depending on the DBMS. A software system, known as the *database management system,* or DBMS, provides access to the database for the user or the application program, and also provides such services as logging, recovery, and database reorganization. An essential characteristic of a database is that it supports a number of different applications, which can be batch or online or both. Often some of these applications must run concurrently.

As an example, let us consider a simplified bank where customers have only checking and savings accounts. The bank's database would then contain information related to the three *entity types:* customer, savings account, and checking account. Figure 3.1 shows some of the *attributes* associated with these entities, which might be stored as *fields*. The relationships between the entities are shown in Fig. 3.2. In general the relationships will be many-to-many; that is, a customer may have a

Entity type	Information
Customer	Name, address, type (individual or company), mailing instructions, Social Security number (if individual), company-related data . . .
Savings account	Account number, interest rate, conditions (e.g., minimum balance), current balance, transactions, opening date, closing date . . .
Checking account	Account number, overdraft conditions, standing orders, opening date, closing date . . .

Fig. 3.1 Data items in a banking database.

number of different accounts of the same type, and an account may have a number of joint owners.

In a simple database design we may have one *record type* for each entity type. Thus our banking database would contain customer, savings account, and checking account record types. We will see how relationships are represented when we look at some specific DBMSs later. In general there will be many *record occurrences* for each record type. For instance, the database contains a record occurrence for each customer. These customer records, although differing in content, all have the same format. When record occurrences are physically stored in the database they are known as *stored records*. A collection of occurrences of the same record type is known as a *stored file*.

A number of different *applications* supporting different functional areas of the bank can be processed against this database. For example:

- *Operational applications,* such as online and batch deposits and withdrawals.
- *Management information applications,* such as profitability analysis of accounts and long-range planning.

Application programs require their own tailored views of the common database because in general they use only a few of the entities, attributes,

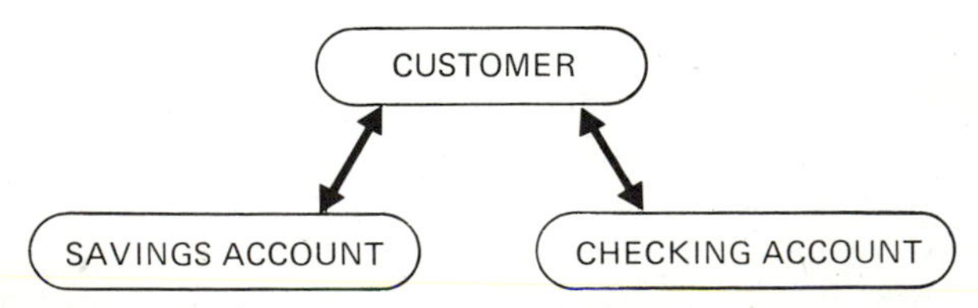

Fig. 3.2 Banking entities and relationships.

and relationships represented in the database. Therefore the program must be able to define record types that differ from the stored records and select a subset of the relationships. These application-oriented records are sometimes referred to as *logical records* or as *views*, since their definition determines the "view" the program has of the data in the database.

Consider the following questions concerning customer information:

- What are all the accounts associated with a particular customer?
- Who are all the customers related to a particular savings account?

A program that answers the first question requires a view of the database such as the one shown in Fig. 3.3. The program selects a particular customer logical record occurrence and then accesses the related account information. A program that answers the second question needs the view depicted in Fig. 3.4. This time the program selects a savings-account logical record occurrence and then accesses the related customer information. Note that the logical records can differ in format from the stored records.

One way to support this requirement for different but overlapping views is by duplicating data. This is in fact the traditional pre-database approach where each application has its own application file. However, a number of problems are caused by such data redundancy:

- It can be expensive to store multiple copies of the same data.
- It is wasteful of processing time to update duplicate copies.
- There may be inconsistencies between the multiple copies when different programs perform the updates.
- The most recent data is not available to all applications.

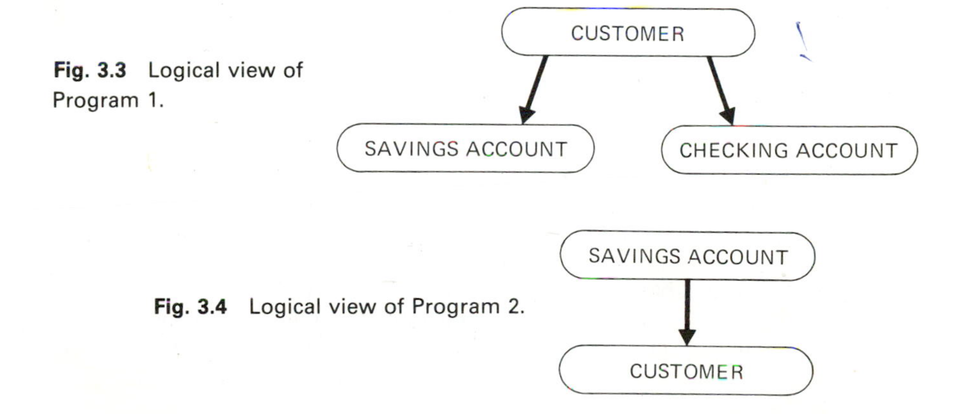

Fig. 3.3 Logical view of Program 1.

Fig. 3.4 Logical view of Program 2.

In controlling these problems, database management systems aim, first, to take over from the application program the responsibility for controlling redundancy and, second, to reduce the amount of redundancy to a minimum for performance and cost reasons. Data redundancy can never be totally eliminated; the amount required depends on the *data model* and *storage structures* used for the database. (In databases that are distributed among remote locations and used mainly for inquiry, redundancy is sometimes deliberately introduced for reliability and performance reasons. Most systems introduce redundancy to support recovery.)

An important part of the database is the *description* or *definition* of the data (as opposed to the data itself). A repository for this description is usually called the *data dictionary*. This dictionary may either be independent of the DBMS, in which case it is used only as a documentation tool, or it may be fully integrated into the DBMS. In this latter case it can also provide data definitions to the DBMS, to application programs, and to queries for access to the data.

3.2 DATA INDEPENDENCE

Data independence for the application program is an important requirement of database systems. Indeed a DBMS is often judged by the degree to which it provides data independence. Because of the cost of designing and developing application programs, it is desirable to extend their life as much as possible. The real world is continually changing and the database, as an abstraction of a part of that world, is consequently changing. New requirements are also placed upon the database because existing applications change and new ones are introduced. The degree to which application programs are shielded from all these changes is the measure of data independence provided by the system. The cost of maintaining application programs that are tightly bound to their data can be a considerable portion of a data processing department's budget.

Specifically, the requirements for data independence are:

- The ability to support new applications requiring new or existing data, without changing existing programs. This is sometimes known as *logical data independence*.
- The ability to change physical storage characteristics such as block size, access method, or devices, without changing any of the application programs. This is sometimes known as *physical data independence*.

3.3 DATABASE ARCHITECTURE

Data independence is achieved by describing data at a number of different *levels* and providing mappings between the levels. The data seen by the application program is mapped to its internal storage format and vice versa, so that the program is shielded from the lower-level details of the database. In order to perform this mapping, the DBMS needs descriptions, which are called *schemas*. Three levels of schema have been proposed by the ANSI/SPARC study group on database management systems [1, 2]; these are illustrated in Fig. 3.5. On the application side the *external schemas* describe each user's view of the data and define the *external data models*. On the database side, the *internal schema* describes how data is stored. Between the two is the single *conceptual schema* defining the *conceptual data model,* which is an abstract representation of the data in the database and its semantics. The conceptual schema may also be thought of as a description of enterprise information that is both implementation-independent and application-independent. For example, the description may be in terms of logical records and the relationships between them. Unfortunately there is no standard database terminology. In this book, for simplicity, we will speak of the *view* that the application program or user has of the database. In practice this may correspond to either an *external schema,* which is a *restructuring* of the conceptual schema, or a *subschema,* which is just a *subset* of the conceptual or external schema.

The DBMS must provide a language for describing the various schemas. In the CODASYL terminology [5], this language is known as the DDL—the *data description language*. A language is also required to allow a user to access the database. In the CODASYL report this is called the DML—*data manipulation language*. When access is by an application program written, for example, in PL/I or COBOL, the DML is sometimes embedded in that high-level language and is then known as a *data sublanguage*. Alternatively, the DML functions may be invoked by subroutine calls from the application program. End users who interact with the database directly via a terminal do so either through a high-level *query language* or through a "parametric" interface designed for a specific application. Operations that modify the database, such as DELETE, UPDATE, and INSERT, will be referred to as *maintenance* operations.

3.4 DATA MODELS

In this section we describe three common data models that are used by current database management systems: *hierarchical, network,* and *relational*.

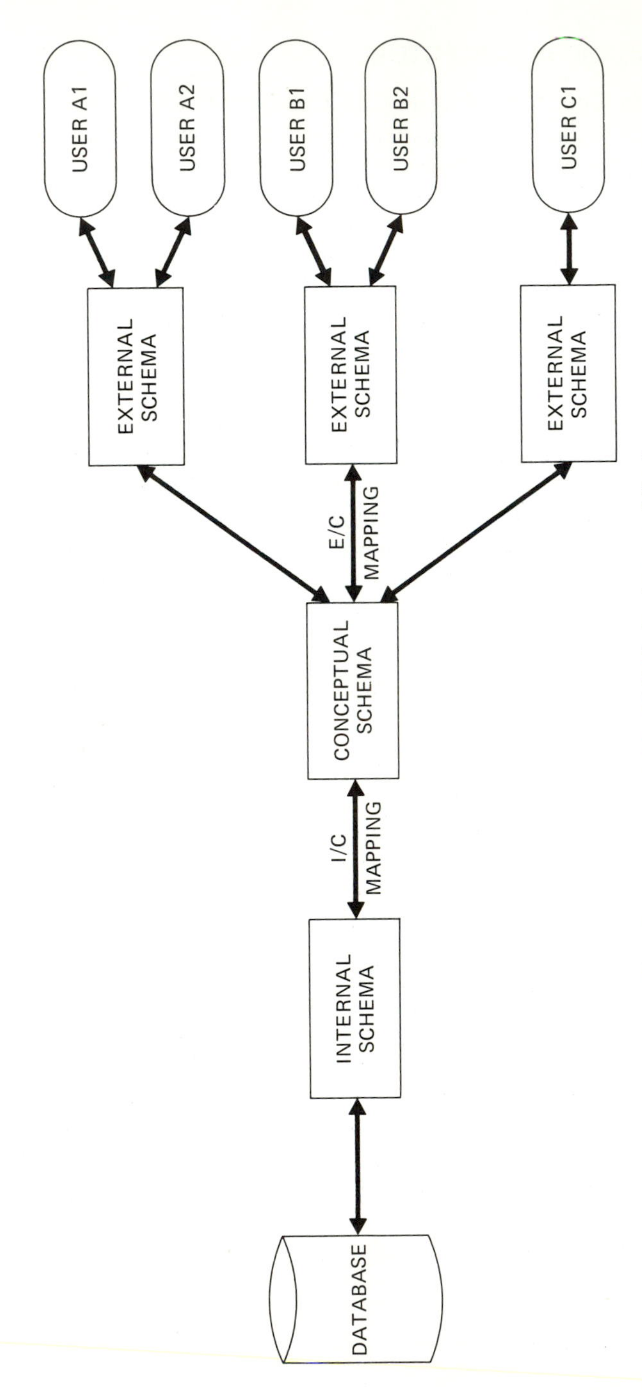

Fig. 3.5 Three-level ANSI/SPARC database architecture.

3.4.1 Hierarchical Data Model

A number of variations of the hierarchical model have been implemented in DBMSs. We restrict our discussion here to the model as implemented in IBM's Information Management System (IMS). Although the external level model is hierarchical, at the internal level the data model corresponds to linked hierarchies—a form of network. (This level serves also for the conceptual model.) Figure 3.6 depicts an internal schema (or *physical database description*) of a savings account and customer file linked by a "logical relationship." In each physical database, fields, or data items, are grouped into hierarchically arranged *segments*. A segment is the unit of access and control. Multiple hierarchical external views—known as *logical database descriptions*—can map to the same internal schema. Program views—described by *program communication blocks (PCBs)*—are hierarchies that are subsets of the logical database descriptions in the sense that certain segments in the hierarchy may be omitted. Figures 3.7 and 3.8 show two possible external views of data that map to the same internal schema of Fig. 3.6.

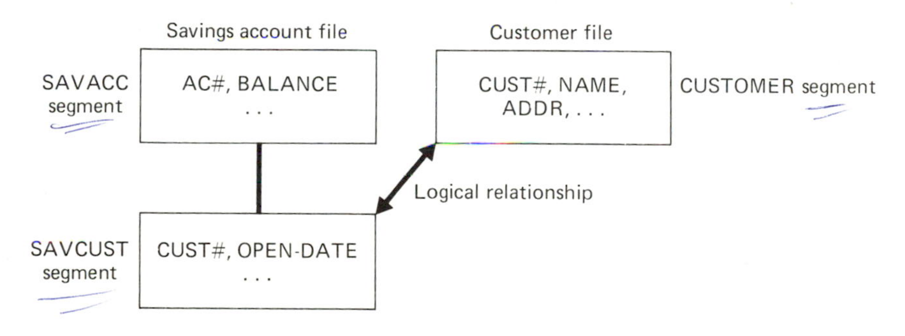

Fig. 3.6 IMS physical database description.

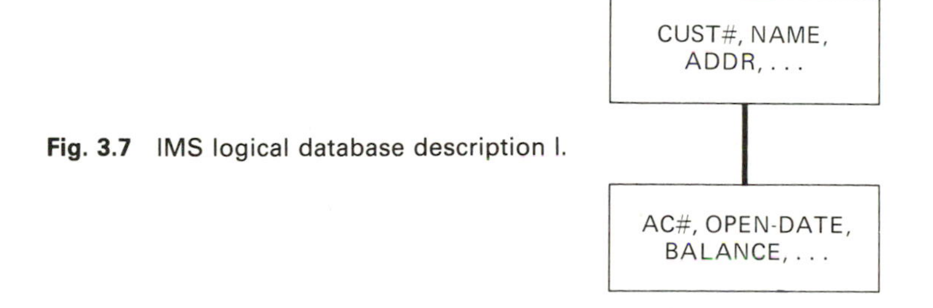

Fig. 3.7 IMS logical database description I.

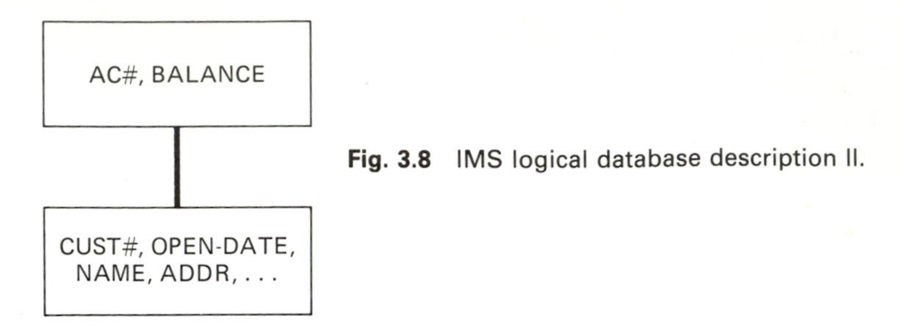

Fig. 3.8 IMS logical database description II.

3.4.2 Network Data Model

For network data models also, a number of variations have been implemented. We describe the network data model as specified by the CODASYL committee [5]. Although not a standard, this specification has been the basis for a number of implementations.

Figure 3.9 depicts the same account and customer data in a CODASYL network conceptual model. SAVACC, CUSTOMER, and SAVCUST are *record types,* which are groupings of related fields or *data items.* OWNS and IS_OWNED_BY are both *sets* (this usage differs from the normal mathematical use of the word set) of which SAVCUST is a *member* and CUSTOMER and SAVACC are the respective *owners.* A set represents a one-to-many relationship between record types. A record type may be a member and owner of a number of different sets, thus allowing a network to be constructed. The program view (called a *subschema*) specifies a conceptual network where data items, record types, and sets may be omitted, but no new records or sets defined. Figure 3.10 shows a subschema where only the fields AC# and CUST# have been included in the SAVCUST record.

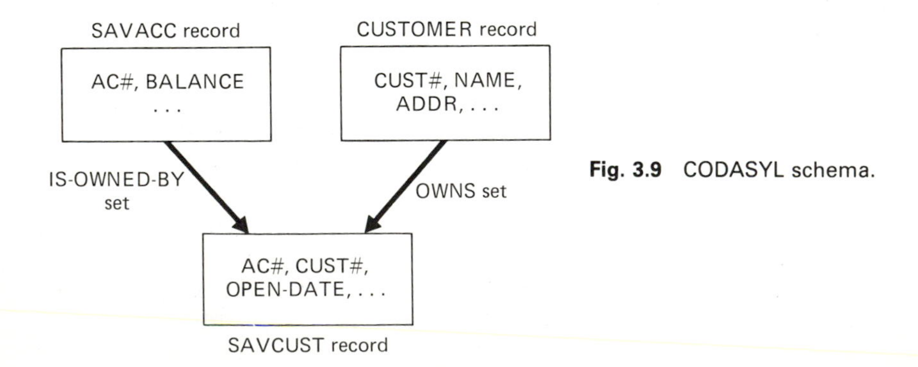

Fig. 3.9 CODASYL schema.

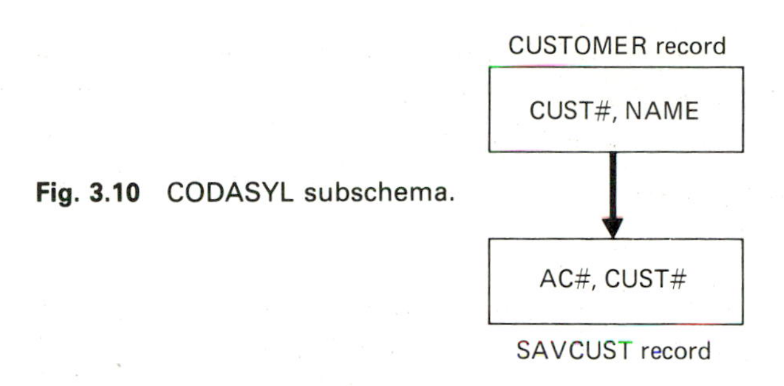

Fig. 3.10 CODASYL subschema.

3.4.3 Relational Data Model

Unlike the two previous models, the relational data model has a theoretical basis. It is based on the mathematical theory of relations. Specific implementations, however, may differ from the following description in various ways.

In the relational model, the banking data is represented at the conceptual level in Fig. 3.11 by *normalized relations,* together with the constraints that all values of CUST# and AC# in the SAVCUST relation also appear in the CUSTOMER and SAVACC relations. A normalized relation is basically a table of information consisting of a number of *columns* (attributes) and *rows* (tuples). For each row a column has a single value; the set of all possible values that the column may have is known as its *domain.* Each row may be uniquely identified by the values of one or more columns, collectively known as the *key.* The row order is not significant and thus the relation can be considered as a set of tuples. At the external level in most relational DBMSs, new relations called *views* may be defined on two or more existing relations. The views combine any of the columns and select any of the rows of the underlying "base" relations. For example, the relation in Fig. 3.12 is a combination of four columns of the conceptual level relations.

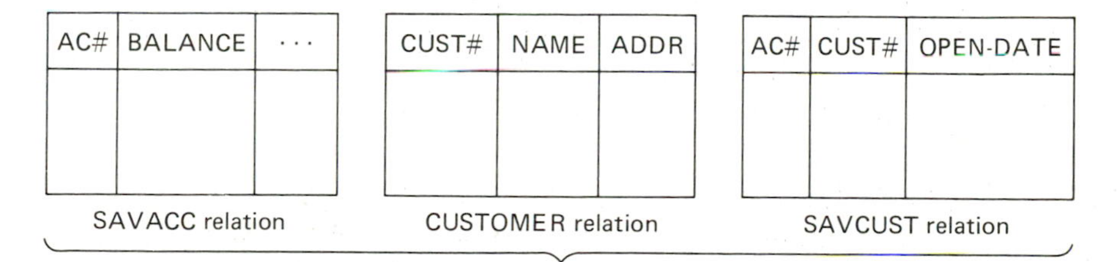

Fig. 3.11 Normalized relations.

CUST#	NAME	AC#	BALANCE

Fig. 3.12 A relational view.

The basic operators used to manipulate relations and define views are *selection, projection,* and natural *join*. Consider the relation R with columns $C_1, C_2, \ldots, C_r$ and the relation S with columns $D_1, D_2, \ldots, D_s$.

- *Selection*

  $R[C_i = x]$ is the set of rows whose column C has the value x.

- *Projection*

  $R[C_i, C_j, \ldots]$ is the relation obtained by dropping all columns except $C_i, C_j, \ldots$ and then dropping duplicate rows.

- *Natural join*

  $R[C_i = D_j]$ S is the join of relation R with relation S on the columns C_i and D_j. The domains of C_i and D_j must be the same. The resulting relation is the concatenation of rows of R with rows of S where the value of column D_j equals the value of C_i. The column C_i (or D_j) appears only once in the natural join. In the remainder of this book, the term *join* will be used to mean natural join.

3.5 ADVANTAGES OF THE DATABASE APPROACH

In this section we summarize some of the advantages to be gained from the database approach over the traditional application file approach. It should be noted that there are intermediate approaches that may achieve some but not all of the following benefits.

- *Centralized control:* Control over the integrity and security of data in the enterprise can be centralized. Centralization helps to ensure a consistent interpretation of the semantics of the data across the enterprise.
- *Multiple application use:* Unlike an application file, the data in the database are available for use by multiple applications, even though each program may require its own tailored view of the data.
- *Reduced data redundancy:* Multiple logical views of the same stored data are supported without the need for duplication. Thus each data item has only one place to be updated.

- *Data independence:* The DBMS shields application programs from changes in the way data are physically stored. The filtering effect of the subschema also shields programs from logical changes to data and relationships that they do not use.
- *Basis for growth:* New entities, attributes, and relationships may be added to the database in order to support new applications without affecting existing programs.
- *High-level query languages:* Many DBMSs support the use of high-level query languages, which can be used to obtain quick response to ad hoc queries, as well as for maintenance.
- *Batch or online support:* Online users and batch programs can access the database concurrently.
- *Direct and sequential access:* Databases can be designed to support both sequential and direct processing. This allows the efficient processing of large numbers of updates at one time while still providing good response for random retrievals or updates.

3.6 DATABASE SECURITY AND INTEGRITY

While the database approach brings advantages to the user, it also creates new, or more intense, problems in the areas of security and integrity. In the traditional approach, where each application system has its own files, a limited amount of data sharing is achieved by passing tailored files from one system to another. In a database environment, however, a multiplicity of users with differing security requirements—some of them online—access a common pool of data of varying sensitivity. This increased level of sharing means that access to the data must be controlled in order to ensure security and privacy.

In a traditional sequential update, an application program reads in a master file and creates a new updated version. Usually at least three generations of master files are retained for backup and recovery purposes. If an error in a program run is discovered, the corrected program need only be rerun using the old master file. Data redundancy between files also makes it easier to recreate corrupted or lost data.

In a database, since updates occur in place, old versions of data are automatically destroyed. There is also little or no data redundancy to aid the recreation of lost data. Thus special backup and recovery procedures are required to maintain the integrity of the database after data has been accidentally or maliciously corrupted.

It is also often more difficult to detect errors in the database. This is because in contrast to the sequential file approach, where the whole file is read during a processing run and unreadable records or incorrect data can easily be checked for, only a part of the database is typically accessed during any one program run. An error, either physical or semantic, can therefore exist for a long time before being discovered. Generally the longer any error has existed the more difficult it is to correct and, in the case of a semantic error, the more likely that the incorrect information has been used.

The very features of database systems that make them powerful and efficient also create new security and integrity problems. These same features also, however, provide a basis for systemwide solutions.

3.7 SAMPLE SYSTEMS

Throughout the book, aspects of database security will be illustrated by examples taken from the following DBMSs.

1. The *CODASYL* Data Description Language and Programming Language Committees have defined the specifications for a network database management system [5]. The DDL provides several integrity features, as well as a lock-and-key form of access control.

2. *IMS* is an IBM commercial database system, which provides a number of security and integrity features [9, 13]. *ADF* (Application Development Facility) is an IBM program product [10] that may be used in conjunction with IMS to expedite the development of application programs and provide a higher level of database security.

3. *INGRES* (Interactive Graphics and Retrieval System) is a relational database system developed at the University of California, Berkeley [16]. The query language QUEL is also used to specify security and integrity constraints.

4. *LASC* [8, 17] is a conceptual design (developed at the IBM Scientific Center in Los Angeles) for a secure database management system. Interaction with the database is provided through an extended PL/I. The application programmer uses predeclared logical views of the data. Enforcement of authorization is performed partly at compile time.

5. The *Query by Example System* (QBE) [18] allows users to define and access relational databases by manipulating tables on a display screen, without using a conventional query language.

6. *System R* is an experimental relational database system developed by IBM Research at San Jose [3]. The high-level language SQL (Structured English Query Language) [4] is used as the DML for System R. SQL is

also used for specifying data definitions, access rules, and integrity constraints.

Two file-control systems will also be used to illustrate data security at the file level.

7. *Multics* [15] is an operating system developed at MIT for Honeywell computers. It is designed to provide a high level of protection in a general-purpose time-sharing environment.

8. *RACF* is an IBM program product [11], which provides access control for files.

3.8 SUMMARY

The use of a DBMS provides many advantages, the most important being data independence. Data independence is achieved through multilevel data descriptions, with the DBMS performing data mapping between levels. At the external level the application program is provided with its own tailored view of the data in the database. Three data models are commonly used in current DBMSs: relational, network, and hierarchical. Because of the high level of sharing, lack of data redundancy, and update in place, DBMSs present new security and integrity problems. However, they also provide the opportunity for systemwide solutions.

REFERENCES AND BIBLIOGRAPHY

1. ANSI/X3/SPARC, "Study Group on Data Base Management Systems: Interim Report." *FDT (Bulletin of ACM SIGMOD)* **7,** 2 (1975).

   The generalized architecture described in this interim report is increasingly influential. The cover letter emphasizes the importance of the conceptual schema as a central repository for security statements. Section V is an overview of security functions, and Sections V and VI both address the place of security in the overall architecture.

2. ANSI/X3/SPARC, "DBMS Framework Report of the Study Group on Database Management Systems." D. Tsichritzis and A. Klug (Eds.), AFIPS Press, Montvale, N.J., 1977.

   This report is the result of the editing of the 1975 interim report by the Data Base Group at the University of Toronto. The result is a shorter, more cohesive, and consistent version, which reflects the thinking of the study group as it evolved after the publication of the interim report.

3. M. M. Astrahan *et al.*, "System R: Relational approach to database management." *ACM TODS* **1,** 2 (June 1976), 97–137.

4. D. D. Chamberlin *et al.*, "SEQUEL 2: A unified approach to data definition,

manipulation, and control." *IBM Journal Res. and Dev.* **20,** 6 (November 1976), 560–575.

5. CODASYL Data Description Language. NBS Handbook 113, Nat. Bureau of Standards, Washington, D.C., June 1973.
6. CODASYL Data Description Language Committee, "Report." *Information Systems* **3,** 4 (1978), 247–320.
7. C. J. Date, *An Introduction to Database Systems* (Second Edition). Addison-Wesley, Reading, Mass., 1977.
   This is an excellent basic course in database systems, covering the relational, hierarchical, and network approaches to database management, as well as the ANSI/SPARC architecture.
8. E. B. Fernandez, R. C. Summers, and C. D. Coleman, "An authorization model for a shared data base." *Proc. 1975 ACM-SIGMOD Int. Conference,* 23–31.
9. IBM Corporation, IMS/VS Version 1, General Information Manual, IBM Form No. GH20–1260–7. San Jose, Calif., October 1978.
10. IBM Corporation, IMS Application Development Facility Program Description/Operations Manual. IBM Form No. SH20–1931.
11. IBM Corporation, OS/VS2 MVS Resource Access Control Facility (RACF): Command Language Reference. IBM Form No. SC28–0733.
12. J. Martin, *Computer Data Base Organization* (Second Edition). Prentice-Hall, Englewood Cliffs, N.J., 1977.
13. W. C. McGee, "The Information Management System IMS/VS. Part V: Transaction processing facilities." *IBM Systems J.* **16,** 2 (1977), 148–168.
14. T. W. Olle, *The CODASYL Approach to Data Base Management*. J. Wiley and Sons, New York, 1978.
15. J. H. Saltzer, "Protection and the control of information sharing in Multics." *Comm. ACM* **17,** 7 (July 1974), 388–402.
16. M. Stonebraker *et al.*, "The design and implementation of INGRES." *ACM TODS* **1,** 3 (Sept. 1976), 189–222.
17. R. C. Summers and E. B. Fernandez, "A System Structure for Data Security." Report G320–2687, IBM Los Angeles Scientific Center, April 1977.
18. M. M. Zloof, "Query-By-Example: A data base language." *IBM Systems J.* **16,** 4 (1977), 324–343.

4 Database Security in Perspective

4.1 A FICTIONAL CASE OF COMPUTER MISUSE

4.1.1 Jack and Jill

Although a great deal of research has concentrated on the security of operating systems in the face of sophisticated attempts at penetration, simple subversion of applications by end users is probably more common. The following fictional story describes such an attempt.

Jack O'Verekstend is a teller at Anycity Security Bank, Suburbia branch, and Jack's good friend, Jill Abett, is a new, but clever, application maintenance programmer. Jack and Jill urgently need some extra cash, and Jill has discovered a flaw in the teller application. By making certain requests at his teller's terminal, requests that the application did not expect to come from a teller, Jack can cause the application to deduct small amounts from inactive customer accounts and add them to his own account.

Jack and Jill are unaware of some features of the DBMS supporting the flawed application. That system maintains a set of access rules; one of the rules states that tellers may not make deposits into their own accounts. The system logs Jack's attempt, and he is fired.

4.1.2 Jill Goes It Alone

Unfortunately for Anycity, its management does not know of Jack and Jill's friendship. Jill keeps her job and is promoted to a more responsible position.

Jack is no longer a teller and does not have an account, so Jill programs transfers to an account she opens under a fictitious name. The transfers are triggered by legitimate transactions requested by other tellers and occur on only a very small percentage of those transactions, randomly selected. Since Anycity exercises rather poor control over changes to application programs, Jill is able to install this change. This scheme succeeds for a time, until an auditor studying the log happens to notice the high activity on Jill's fictitious account. The application program is studied and the changes traced to Jill.

4.1.3 How Could Jack and Jill Succeed?

Jack and Jill exploited their employer's poor control over application programs. If that control had been tighter, a number of other paths were open: Jack might have saved his job if Jill had erased the log of his access (a possibility if she were a systems programmer). Jill could have used lower-level data management or I/O facilities to bypass the DBMS access rules and logging.

4.1.4 The Moral of the Story

A potential criminal can attack a database system at many levels. Many of the reported incidents have involved rather simple misuse of applications, typically by end users rather than by programmers. As better controls begin to prevent these simpler abuses, we can expect more complex attacks on the DBMS and the operating system, or attacks exploiting interactions between the different levels. *A database system must be secure as a total system.*

4.2 SECURITY THREATS AND DEFENSES IN COMPUTER SYSTEMS

4.2.1 Security Threats

A database security violation is the unauthorized reading, modification, or destruction of information that is stored in the database. Figure 4.1 indicates some of the possible threats to the security of a computer system. These threats may be broadly classified as either malicious or accidental. Under the category of malicious we include attempts to circumvent the security mechanisms protecting the database. Malicious attackers may exploit loopholes in the system, or may abuse positions of privilege and trust by using the data to which they have access in an illegitimate way—for example, by selling information to competitive enterprises.

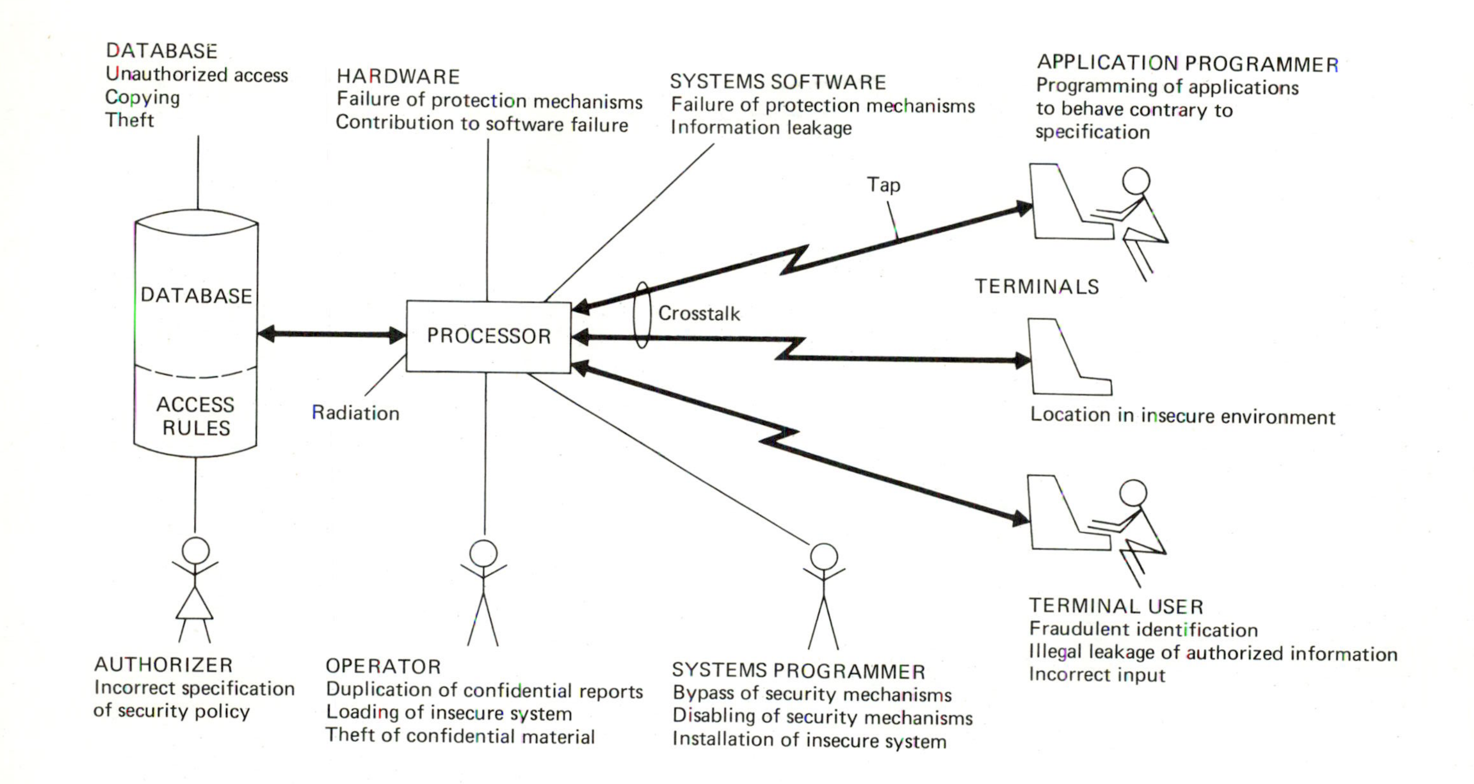
DATABASE
Unauthorized access
Copying
Theft
HARDWARE
Failure of protection mechanisms
Contribution to software failure
SYSTEMS SOFTWARE
Failure of protection mechanisms
Information leakage
APPLICATION PROGRAMMER
Programming of applications
to behave contrary to
specification
Tap
TERMINALS
DATABASE
ACCESS RULES
PROCESSOR
Crosstalk
Radiation
Location in insecure environment
TERMINAL USER
Fraudulent identification
Illegal leakage of authorized information
Incorrect input
AUTHORIZER
Incorrect specification
of security policy
OPERATOR
Duplication of confidential reports
Loading of insecure system
Theft of confidential material
SYSTEMS PROGRAMMER
Bypass of security mechanisms
Disabling of security mechanisms
Installation of insecure system
EXTERNAL ENVIRONMENT
Natural disasters
Malicious attacks
Unauthorized access to computer room

Fig. 4.1 Security threats. [Adapted from Ware [12], with permission of the Rand Corp.]

Nonmalicious threats include hardware and software failures, which cause the security policies of the installation to be incorrectly enforced. Such threats may also result from human errors, such as accidentally destroying information, or allowing it to be seen by the wrong people. Natural disasters such as flood or fire are also nonmalicious threats, which may destroy information or prevent access to it.

4.2.2 Security Procedures and Mechanisms

Because security threats arise from such a wide variety of sources, the procedures and mechanisms necessary to provide a secure environment must cover many areas of the enterprise. Some of the more important are listed in Fig. 4.2.

Procedures external to the computer system are necessary to create an environment where security mechanisms implemented within the system can be effective. If, for example, identification cards and passwords are used to gain access to the computer, then they must be controlled and protected. Personnel with access to highly secure information must be carefully selected. When the information involves national security or

Area	Procedures and Mechanisms
External procedures	Security clearance of personnel Protection of passwords Information classification and security policy formulation Application program controls Audit Periods processing
Physical environment	Secure areas for files/processors/terminals Radiation shielding
Data storage	Data encryption Duplicate copies
Processor software	Authentication of user Access control Threat monitoring Audit trail of transactions
Processor hardware	Memory protection States of privilege Reliability
Communication lines	Data encryption

Fig. 4.2 Security procedures and mechanisms.

military secrets, then security clearance procedures are used, along with procedures for classifying information and formulating security policies. Proper controls must be established for the development and maintenance of application programs, and for the use of transactions. Audits must be conducted to ensure that these controls are working properly.

Storage devices and other hardware must be physically protected against damage from natural disasters or malicious attacks. The protection of removable storage against theft is also necessary, and the protection of terminals may be necessary to control access to the computer. Backup copies of data files kept at different physical locations can also guard against information loss. The encryption of files, while not preventing their theft, at least prevents information disclosure. Encryption is also used to guard against wiretapping and crosstalk when information is sent across communication lines.

Computers and terminals are sources of electromagnetic radiation. With multiprogramming it is difficult to interpret the radiation from a computer. The danger from this type of electronic eavesdropping can be reduced by ensuring that eavesdropping equipment cannot be placed near the terminal.

Various software and hardware mechanisms are used to identify users of the computer system and to control and monitor the accessing and use of data within the system. These mechanisms are depicted in Fig. 4.3 and are described in more detail in later sections.

Once a program has been given access to the requested data, there is a danger that the program will convey that information not only to its lawful invoker but also (either deliberately or accidentally) to an unauthorized person, perhaps via another program active in the system at the same time. Preventing this is known as the *confinement problem* [8], which in practice is unsolved. Since information may leak via legitimate channels (for example, an interprocess message mechanism or a temporary storage file), confinement requires the monitoring and control of these channels. More difficult to control is flow along *covert* channels—that is, channels that are not intended for information transfer—where a process, by its use of a computer resource, transmits coded information to another process. (We use the term *process* for an execution of a program.) As an example, a process could convey information to other concurrent processes by altering its paging rate dynamically. Possible ways to block these covert channels are to introduce noise to reduce the bandwidth of the channel, or to dedicate a system to one kind of process at a time, a solution sometimes adopted in military systems and known as *periods processing*. Both solutions operate at the expense of efficiency.

A possible security strategy is to *verify* the correctness of all programs that access the database, to ensure that there are no malicious programs. (By verification we mean formal *proof* that a program meets security requirements.) Given the current state of the art in program verification, however, this is not a practical solution, especially when proprietary programs are used. A more reasonable task would be to verify those parts of the system that check the accesses of untrusted programs. This thwarts the so-called *Trojan horse* attacks in which clandestine security flaws are deliberately introduced into the software. Often, however, the security mechanisms are distributed throughout the code, so that all the code would have to be verified—an impossible task. An alternative approach is to design the software so that a limited portion contains all the basic security mechanisms. This portion, a *security kernel,* is then the only code that needs to be verified. With multilevel software (for example a DBMS executing on top of an operating system), a security kernel may be associated with each level. Thus the correct functioning of the database security mechanism depends only on the correctness of the DBMS kernel, which in turn depends only on the correct functioning of the OS security kernel. Even when the kernel approach has not been taken, it may be possible to identify a *security subsystem* that performs the security functions. In that case, however, verifying the subsystem is not sufficient to prove security.

In order for the software mechanisms to perform correctly, the underlying hardware must of course be reliable. The hardware also provides features such as memory protection and states of privilege. Direct hardware support for some of the security functions can reduce their overhead.

In summary, the security of a database depends on a complex set of protective measures: human, software, and hardware. One weak link in the chain of security measures can threaten the security of the whole system. In this book we concentrate on that part of security most directly associated with the control and monitoring of access to information in the database. We assume that the underlying hardware is reliable and correct. Hardware reliability is excluded from detailed treatment here only because it is a major topic in its own right, and not for lack of importance.

4.2.3 An Overview of Database Security

Figure 4.3 shows some of the safeguards that can be built into a database system and Fig. 4.4 indicates where in this book these countermeasures are discussed. Referring to Fig. 4.3, *authentication* (1) is a way to verify the identity of a user at log-on time. The most common authentication method uses *passwords,* which are combinations of characters known only to the user. Another common method requires the user to insert a machine-readable badge. More elaborate techniques depend on sensing

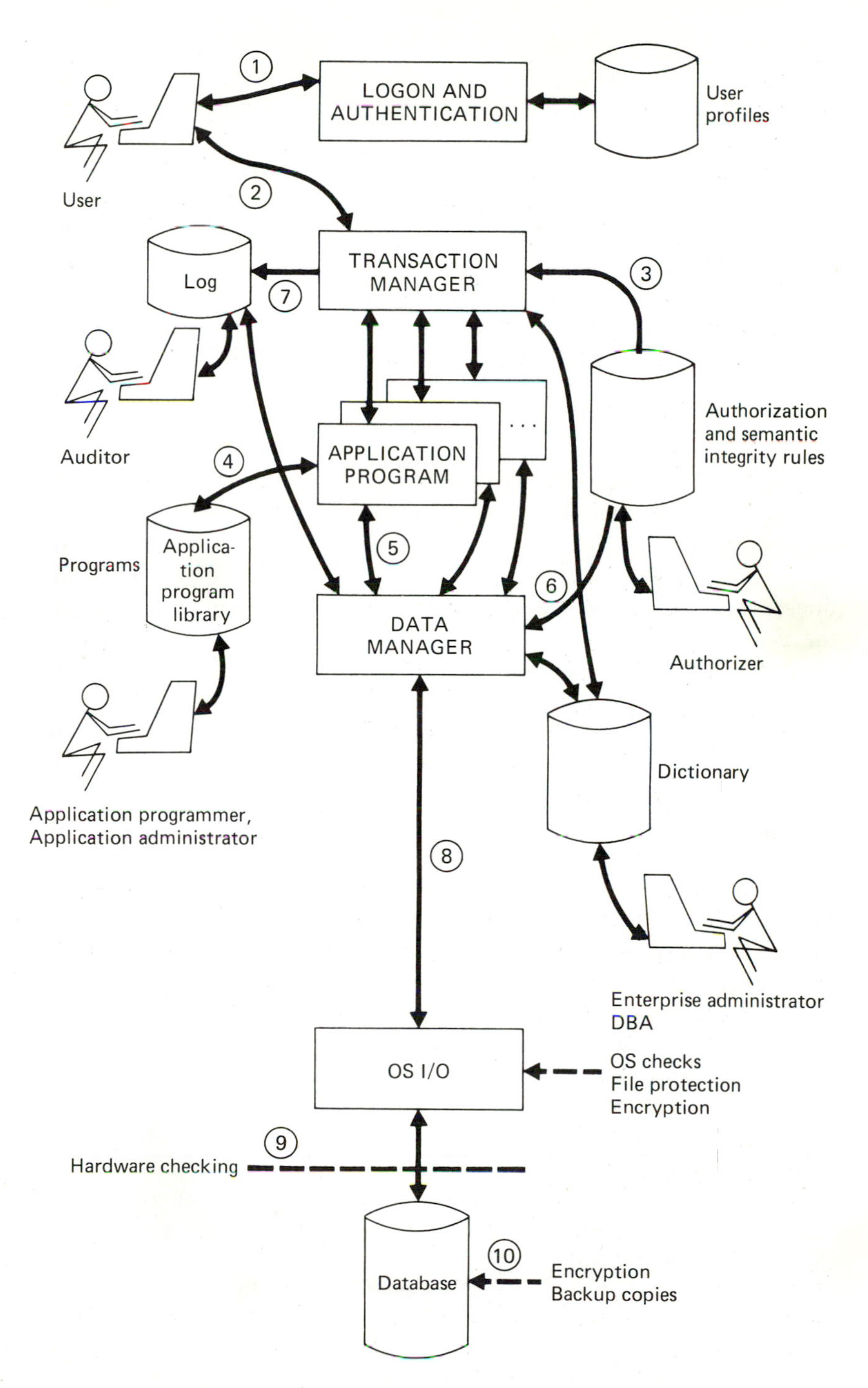

Fig. 4.3 Security checking for database transactions.

Safeguard	Where discussed:
User authentication	Section 11.8
Transaction access checking	Chapter 10
Definition of authorization rules	Chapter 7 and Section 12.3
Request validation	Chapters 6 and 10
Semantic integrity checking	Section 8.3
Logging of accesses	Section 8.5, Section 9.5
Audit trail	Chapter 9
Operating-system checking	Chapter 11
Hardware checking	Sections 11.5, 11.6, 11.9.1
Physical volume protection	Section 9.4.3, Section 11.9
Concurrency control	Section 8.4, Section 12.6.1
Recovery	Section 8.5, Section 12.6.2
Statistical database security	Chapter 13
Distributed database security	Chapter 12

Fig. 4.4 Database security safeguards.

fingerprints, the size of the hand, or some other physical characteristic of the user.

Once the user is authenticated and attempts a transaction (2), the user's authorization to use this transaction is checked (3). Execution of the transaction may involve several application programs, which are stored in a program library (4). *Application programmers* build and maintain this library, while an *application administrator* controls the development and use of the programs. The database is described at different levels of the multilevel architecture introduced in Chapter 3. High-level descriptions, defining the conceptual schema, are designed by an *enterprise administrator,* while lower-level descriptions, such as the internal schema, are built by the *database administrator* (DBA).

Access rules control access to the objects in the database and to specific portions of the program library. These rules are written by a *security administrator* or *authorizer* using some appropriate language. A *security monitor* or *security officer* checks the day-to-day application of the rules.

When application programs execute, their requests for data go to the DBMS (5). The DBMS has access to the database descriptions needed to organize data access, and performs the necessary checking of authorization (6). Also, if the transaction attempts to modify the contents of the database, the proposed changes are checked for compliance with semantic integrity assertions, which specify the correct states of the database.

Updates provided by concurrent users are also synchronized by the DBMS to avoid inconsistencies in the changes to the database. The

DBMS keeps a log or audit trail of accesses to the database (7). A *security auditor* checks the audit trail for compliance with security policies. The audit trail (or a separate log) also contains information to allow the database to be restored to a correct state if a failure occurs (in the transaction or in the system). This is the process of *recovery*.

Database access requests, once validated, are translated into I/O requests, which are passed to the operating system (8). Additional checks are possible here, for proper use of files or of operating-system functions. The hardware can provide additional protection (9), such as transferring data only to memory that belongs to the DBMS. The physical volumes on which the database is stored can be protected by encryption and by backup copies (10).

4.3 ESTIMATING THE COSTS AND BENEFITS OF SECURITY MEASURES

How does one decide what security measures to implement? If the security measures are too elaborate, they can be an economic and administrative burden. A lack of the right security measures, on the other hand, can be more costly if, for example, attempts at fraud succeed. To help answer the question of what and how much security is required, a cost/benefit analysis of possible security measures can be performed.

4.3.1 Cost Estimates

Additional functions in any system, computerized or not, involve additional cost. Security is no exception. Additional cost for security comes from performance loss, increased complexity (which could lead to more frequent errors), loss of system flexibility, human resources to administer and maintain the security system, and additional hardware (if special security hardware is used). In general, the higher the degree of security desired, the higher the cost of providing that security.

The cost of security measures can be broadly classified as:

- *Startup costs*. These include procedure and program development, hardware and software acquisition, and personnel training.
- *Operational costs*. These include salaries and equipment usage.

There has been little systematic study of the cost of providing a given degree of security or implementing a given security policy. There are, however, analyses of the performance overhead incurred by some specific security mechanisms. The cost of security measures required by certain legislation was studied by Goldstein [5], who concluded that a generalized data management system can significantly reduce these costs. This conclusion is shared by other studies [3].

4.3.2 Benefit Estimates

The benefits that can result from security measures include risk reduction. *Risk analysis* can help to quantify the benefits obtained from risk reduction.

Risk analysis

The goal of one risk-analysis approach [2] is to arrive at a quantitative estimate of the risk associated with each specific *loss event*. Examples of such events are "disclosure of nonexempt employee data" or "destruction of payroll file." Using this estimate, the enterprise can decide what course to follow, such as simply accepting the risk, or taking protective measures costing less than the risk.

For each loss event *E*, two parameters are estimated:

1. the economic *impact, v,* of the loss, and
2. the *probability, p,* of the event.

It is recommended that these estimates be made by a team including data processing managers, auditors, programmers, and department managers. The estimates are used to arrive at the risk per unit of time, such as dollars per year. A risk-analysis example is shown in Fig. 4.5.

This approach has been criticized [4] because (1) it is difficult to estimate even rough values for *p* and *v*, and (2) no methodology is provided for choosing risk-reducing measures and estimating their impact on *E*. Subsequent studies have tried to quantify *p* and *v* more finely [9]. Project SECURATE [6] *does* consider security measures. It considers a system as consisting of

- objects, each with a loss value,
- threats, each with a probability, and
- security features.

A user of SECURATE provides the loss values and probabilities, and rates the features. The user also provides a set of triples (object, threat, feature), specifying which threats apply to which objects and which features can resist the threats (Fig. 4.6). The system performs various analyses, such as looking for the weakest link in the security features.

Not all risks can be reduced to economic terms. This is true for certain military information, for example, and where loss of privacy is involved. An approach proposed by Turn [11] is to classify data in

RISK ANALYSIS WORK SHEET

SYSTEM/ DATA SET NAME	ACCIDENTAL			INTENTIONAL			Exposure if unable to process for: HOURS					COMMENTS
	Disclosure	Modification	Destruction	Disclosure	Modification	Destruction	2	4	8	12	18	
					V p E							

Fig. 4.5 Risk-analysis worksheet. [From Courtney [2], with permission.]

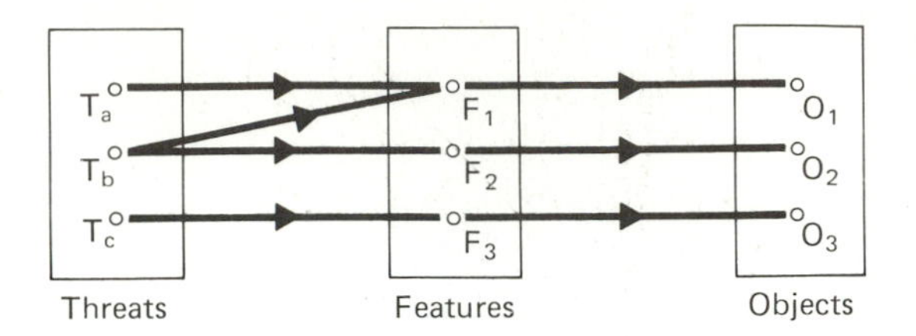

Fig. 4.6 SECURATE security-analysis model.

sensitivity levels according to its impact on an individual's life. Seven sensitivity levels are proposed, which range from "no appreciable adverse effects" to "loss of life or physical safety." A combination of these sensitivity levels with the approach using p and v estimates is possible and may be of value in institutions dealing with large amounts of personal data [9]. An aspect not considered in the basic risk model is the set of *realization costs,* the costs and exposure incurred by the perpetrator of the attack [1].

Finally, we would like to emphasize that risk analysis as applied to security should be approached with caution. Much guesswork is involved, since appropriate statistical information hardly ever exists.

Other benefits

Usually security measures provide multiple benefits. They either protect against more than one security exposure or they provide other kinds of benefits. For example, a secure system implies a more disciplined use of resources, access to only the data needed for a given application function, and clear, controlled interfaces between different levels of the system. Application development in this environment should be simpler, and the resultant programs more reliable and easier to maintain. In other words, security implies improved control, which in turn implies a more efficient and productive system. These advantages, in the long range, could offset the cost of security.

4.4 SECURITY EVALUATION OF A DATABASE SYSTEM

It is also useful to introduce at this point some qualitative criteria for evaluating security. For the present, these evaluations may have to be quite subjective, but the criteria are nonetheless useful guidelines for those who must build or choose a new system or add new security features to an existing system.

- *Completeness*. Completeness is measured by the variety of possible attacks that the system is intended to defend against. The required completeness depends on the value and sensitivity of the information.

- *Confidence*. Confidence refers to trust that the system actually protects against the types of attacks that it is designed to protect against. Confidence is attained by means of analysis, proofs, testing, and penetration studies. In some environments (e.g., the military), provable security is valuable. In general, proof is a very difficult task, and systems that strive for provable security are currently limited with respect to the type of policies they support. For other systems an alternative is to show that there is some defense against generic types of attacks that are known to occur frequently.

- *System flexibility*. The system should be able to implement a wide variety of security policies (some common policies are discussed in Chapter 5). If a policy is built into the original design, it may be very difficult to adapt the system to enforce a different policy.

- *Ease of use for security administrators*. A simple interface is needed for the people in charge of security functions. A complex interface will result in frequent errors, which could hamper work (if users are denied rights they need) or allow improper actions (if users are given rights they should not have).

- *Flexibility for the users*. The system should not impose unnecessary or cumbersome restrictions, such as complex protocols for authentication or rigid rules for writing applications. Flexibility can be estimated by studying how the installation of security features affects users, existing programs, and the writing of new programs. The property of not interfering with ongoing work is sometimes called *user transparency*.

- *Tamperproofness*. If a security mechanism is protected from unauthorized modification, then this mechanism is said to be *tamperproof*. This is an essential characteristic, since even if a security mechanism were proved to be correct, any later modifications to it would destroy its security.

- *Low overhead*. The performance overhead of some specific features, such as encryption, has been measured or estimated. In a given installation, it may also be possible to directly measure the total security overhead, but more studies are needed to *predict* this overhead. Qualitative analyses of different approaches (for example, compile-time vs. execution-time access decisions) can also be useful for selecting the best implementation of a given security policy.

- *Low operating cost.* This includes the cost of special hardware or software, salaries of security administrators and other people who perform security-related functions (such as notifying individuals about the use of personal information), and cost of security audits.

The relative weight of these criteria depends on the objectives of the enterprise, the laws that apply to it, the variability of the environment in which it operates, and other less important factors. For example, a credit reporting agency will not give great weight to user flexibility, since its procedures are usually standard and are performed by specialized personnel. Completeness of security, however, is very important to the agency because of the sensitivity of the information it handles. System flexibility is also important, since privacy laws may change, and low performance overhead could be crucial to economical operation of the agency.

4.5 SUMMARY

We have tried to convey in this chapter some feeling for the global nature of the database security problem—the variety of sources of threats and the many types of defenses. Mechanisms for computer security range from careful personnel selection to hardware memory protection. The roles of people involved in database security have been described in the context of basic security procedures, such as authentication, authorization, and logging. We have described ways of analyzing the costs and benefits of security measures, as well as criteria by which an enterprise can evaluate these measures.

REFERENCES AND BIBLIOGRAPHY

1. D. A. Bonyun, "Realization costs: A forgotten element of risk analysis." *Comp. Security and Privacy Symposium Proc.,* Honeywell Information Systems, 1979.
2. R. H. Courtney, Jr., "Security risk assessment in electronic data processing systems." *AFIPS Conf. Proc.* **46,** 1977 NCC, 97–104. AFIPS Press, Montvale, N.J., 1977.

   Describes a methodology for risk analysis. This consists of determining the expected loss per year for each loss event (E) as a function of the impact of the loss (v) and the probability of its occurrence (p). Guidelines and examples to help in the selection of p and v are given, as well as practical hints about how to proceed in a real situation.
3. E. Fong, "A Data Base Management Approach to Privacy Act Compliance." NBS Special Publication 500–10, U.S. Dept. of Commerce, June, 1977.

4. S. Glaseman, R. Turn, and R. S. Gaines, "Problem areas in computer security assessment." *AFIPS Conf. Proc.* **46,** 1977 NCC, 105–112. AFIPS Press, Montvale, N.J., 1977.

5. R. C. Goldstein, *The Cost of Privacy.* Honeywell Information Systems, Brighton, Mass., 1975.

6. L. J. Hoffman, E. H. Michelman, and D. Clements, "SECURATE—Security evaluation and analysis using fuzzy metrics." *AFIPS Conf. Proc.* **47,** 1978 NCC, 531–540. AFIPS Press, Montvale, N.J., 1978.

7. IBM Corporation, "Data Security—Threats and Deficiencies in Computer Operations—A Report on a Completed Study—A translation from an IBM Svenska AB publication." Form No. G320–5646–0 (October 1975).

   A detailed catalog of threats and the deficiencies that allow them. The list was obtained from the study of nine computer installations in Sweden, including equipment from IBM, Honeywell–Bull, and Univac.

8. B. W. Lampson, "A note on the confinement problem." *Comm. ACM* **16,** 10 (October 1973), 613–615.

9. J. Lobel, "Risk analysis in the 1980's." *AFIPS Conf. Proc.* **49,** 1980 NCC, 831–836. AFIPS Press, Arlington, Va., 1980.

10. O. G. Selfridge and R. T. Schwartz, "Telephone technology and privacy." *MIT Technology Review* **82,** 6 (May, 1980), 56–65.

    Surveys the status of the security of telephone communications, pointing out that electronic switching systems have made telephone security dependent on computer security.

11. R. Turn, "Classification of personal information for privacy protection purposes." *AFIPS Conf. Proc.* **45,** 1976 NCC, 301–307. AFIPS Press, Arlington, Va., 1976.

    Surveys proposed sensitivity classifications for personal information. A new classification is proposed that consists of six sensitivity levels. The degree of security required for each level is discussed. There is also a discussion on how to classify personal information.

12. W. H. Ware (Ed.), "Security Controls for Computer Systems." Report R–609–1, The Rand Corporation, Santa Monica, Calif., reissued October 1979.

    Reprint of an influential classified 1970 report. A comprehensive and still relevant discussion of security problems, policies, and techniques.

5
Policies for Database Security

5.1 INTRODUCTION

For a systematic approach to database security, it is important to distinguish between security policies and security mechanisms. *Security policies* are high-level guidelines concerning information security, selected from among alternatives. These policies are dictated by user needs, installation environment, institution regulations, and legal constraints. *Security mechanisms,* on the other hand, are sets of functions that are used to implement and to enforce the various security policies. The functions can be implemented in hardware, software, or firmware, or by administrative procedures.

At each level of an enterprise information system, from management actions to protection hardware, security decisions are made. These decisions constitute the set of data security policies of the enterprise. We can then talk of enterprise policies, administrative policies, data processing installation policies, DBMS policies, and operating-system policies. (This classification is a simplification, since some policies apply to several of these levels.) As an example of enterprise policy, a hospital may allow patients to see their medical records. An administrative policy might be that employee performance records are retained for no more than three years. An example of installation policy is that at least two people must agree on changes to application programs used in the installation. An operating-system policy might be to protect storage in units of 2048 bytes.

Different types of enterprises (such as military, commercial, or educational) may have quite different security policies. Legal considerations also play a role. For example, legislation dictates certain policies for government agencies and credit bureaus. The policies of a computer installation are directed by the higher-level policies of the enterprise and also depend on the type of hardware and software available. In general, policies at the lower levels are driven by those at higher levels. For example, a high-level policy of decentralization requires lower-level mechanisms that support decentralized operation. Conversely, the lower levels affect the higher levels. For example, it may not be practical to choose a given high-level policy if low-level mechanisms cannot support it adequately.

This chapter, after discussing the relationship between policy and mechanism, considers some of the most important database secruity policies.

5.2 POLICIES AND MECHANISMS

Considering system structure, we can view policies as implemented by lower-level mechanisms. If ability to change policies is needed, separating mechanisms from policies becomes a requirement. In other words, the policy should not be built into the mechanism. This separation allows the same mechanism to implement different policies. The advantages of this strategy have been demonstrated in the design of operating systems [2]. The environments of an enterprise and of a database system inevitably will change, and changes in the chosen security policies will follow. These changes should not require a redesign or replacement of the security mechanisms, but should be "programmable" using the existing mechanisms.

The design and construction of the mechanisms in turn imply lower-level policy decisions, so that the system involves a hierarchy of policy–mechanism relationships. For example, suppose a decision has been made to support an authorization structure where data objects appear as nodes of a tree, and where access to any node implies access to all nodes below it. The designers of the mechanism to support this policy must make a lower-level decision. Does the system assume this tree structure in the way it organizes the data and the directories, or does it, at greater cost, support other possible authorization structures?

Some mechanisms are capable of implementing a number of alternative policies, while other mechanisms are tailored to specific policies. Access rules, for example, can provide a very general mechanism for implementing a number of different access-control policies. A password field in a file label, along with procedures that check the password each time the file is opened, provides a mechanism tailored to the policy that passwords are required for file access. General-purpose mechanisms are clearly valuable in systems (such as the DBMS or the operating system) that are used in many different environments with differing security policies. Special-purpose mechanisms have the advantage of being simpler to implement and therefore are more likely to be implemented correctly. They may allow proof that the system as a whole exhibits certain security properties. Furthermore, they may perform better because they are tailored to meet specific needs.

Some policies are implemented by automatic procedures, others by administrative controls, and many by a combination of the two. For example, a bank may have the policy that any change to an application program must be approved by two persons other than the person making the change. The nonautomated mechanism could be a form to be signed by the approvers. Time-sharing systems often require passwords to be changed periodically, and they enforce this policy automatically by making the password invalid after the specified time interval has passed. Implementing policies administratively carries the risk that they will not in fact be enforced. One theft of proprietary software [1] was accomplished over telephone lines by the use of a legitimate user's password. Testimony at the trial indicated that passwords were rarely changed. Although the company's policy dictated frequent change, that policy was implemented by an inadequate mechanism.

A policy is of little value if it is *incorrectly* implemented, either because the access rules are wrong or because the rules or mechanisms cannot fully support the policy. Two types of errors may then result:

1. an access is denied which, according to the policy, should have been allowed;
2. an access is allowed which, according to the policy, should have been denied.

In many situations it is preferable to choose a simpler policy that is more apt to be correctly stated and that is well supported by the underlying mechanisms.

5.3 POLICIES FOR DATABASE SECURITY

We now look at some of the more important security policies. In general, these are high-level policies, although their level is not uniform. Some can be seen as subpolicies to be used when implementing higher-level policies.

Most of the *low-level* policies that we will describe concern the selection and use of the security features provided by the DBMS. Of course the designers of the DBMS also make policy decisions about which security features are included. In practice, the security features provided by commercial DBMSs are currently very limited, thus restricting the choice of policies.

5.3.1 Policies about Security Administration

Centralized or decentralized control

A fundamental security choice is between *centralized* or *decentralized control*. With centralized control, a single authorizer (or group) controls all security aspects of the system. INGRES is an example of a system that has adopted this type of policy. In other environments, a decentralization of these functions may be required for either efficiency or convenience. In a decentralized system different administrators control different portions of the database, normally following guidelines that apply to the whole database.

Ownership vs. administration

A related policy concerns the concepts of *ownership* and *administration* of databases in the enterprise. The owner of a database is sometimes considered to be the person who is responsible for creating the data. For example, a payroll database exclusively updated by the payroll department may be considered as being owned by the manager of payroll. However, with many shared databases it is difficult to identify a unique owner. For example, a stock-control database may be updated by production, sales, purchasing, and shipping departments. While there may or may not be the concept of ownership, there is always the need for an administration function, whose objective is to define the data shared by the users and to control its use. This function may be performed by the owner, if one exists, or by a database administrator. The basic distinction between those two policies lies in the fact that, while the owner is allowed every possible type of access, the administrator possesses only the rights that *control* the data.

5.3.2 Policies for Access-control Specification

The need-to-know policy

One very important high-level policy restricts information to those people who really need the information for their work. This policy is especially important for databases subject to privacy legislation, and is a sound principle for any system, since it restricts the number of possible sources for information leaks and minimizes the possibility that the integrity of the database will be compromised. This *need-to-know policy* is sometimes called the *policy of least privilege,* because all users and programs operate with the smallest set of privileges necessary to perform their functions.

Maximized sharing

An alternative policy is that of *maximized sharing,* where the intention is to make maximum use of the information in the database. This does not necessarily mean that everyone is allowed to access all the information, because there may still be privacy requirements and sensitive data. However, within these constraints, sharing is maximized. An example is a medical research database containing information about certain diseases. The main objective is to allow researchers maximum access to the information. However, any data that can be related to a specific patient has to be protected. Another example is a library where maximum access is allowed to everything but very valuable or scarce books, which require special permission.

Open and closed systems

In a *closed system* access is allowed *only if* explicitly authorized. In an *open system* access is allowed *unless* explicitly forbidden. A closed system is inherently more secure and is the basic support for a need-to-know policy; but it may have more overhead if the system attempts to maximize sharing. A clear reason for the greater security of closed systems is the fact that inadvertent deletion of an access rule restricts access, while a missing rule in an open system allows unauthorized access.

Name-dependent access control

The policy of least privilege has varying implications for the types of access rules that are required, depending on how strictly it is interpreted. At a minimum, we should be able to specify the data objects a user can access. (A data object is a group of occurrences of data items and relationships that has a name known to the DBMS. For example, in a relational DBMS, a data object might be a relation or an attribute, and in a CODASYL DBMS a set or record type.) The *granularity* of the data objects in the access rules is another policy decision. A strict interpretation of the policy of least privilege requires that the objects have the finest granularity allowed by the DBMS. With relational systems this is the column or attribute; with CODASYL the data item or field. Consider the employee relation EMP with attributes NAME, SAL, MGR, and DEPT, represented in Fig. 5.1. A personnel manager might need access to the complete relation, while the mailroom clerk would need access only to the NAME and DEPT attributes. This type of control we call *name-dependent* access control. It is sometimes referred to as *content-*

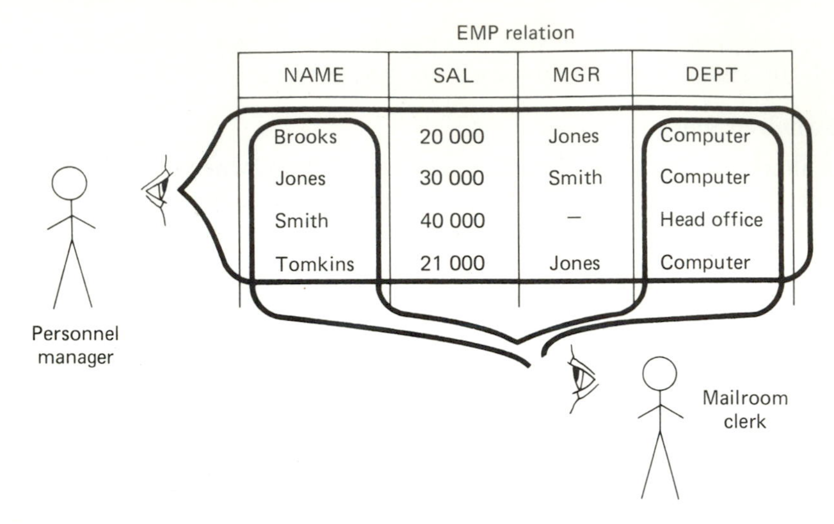

EMP relation
NAME
SAL
MGR
DEPT
Brooks
20 000
Jones
Computer
Jones
30 000
Smith
Computer
Smith
40 000
–
Head office
Tomkins
21 000
Jones
Computer
Personnel manager
Mailroom clerk

Fig. 5.1. Name-dependent access control.

independent access control, because a decision on whether or not to allow a data access can be made without using data values from the database.

Content-dependent access control

The policy of least privilege may be extended even further by specifying access rules that *do* refer to the content of data item occurrences (as well as to their names). This *content-dependent* access control results in finer granularity of control. For example, managers may be allowed to see the salaries of the employees they manage, but not the salaries of any other employees. For this type of control, data values must first be retrieved from the database in order to determine whether or not the access request should be satisfied.

Access types

So far our security policies have allowed users either no access or any type of access to specified data objects. More control over the use of data is achieved by specifying the types of access the user may have to the data object, such as READ, UPDATE, INSERT, DELETE, or some combination. Thus, while the personnel manager may have access to EMP for all types of operations, the mailroom clerk might be allowed only to READ the NAME and DEPT attributes (Fig. 5.2). These users therefore have the minimum set of access rights they need to do their jobs. Some simplification in the use of this policy can be obtained by *ordering* the

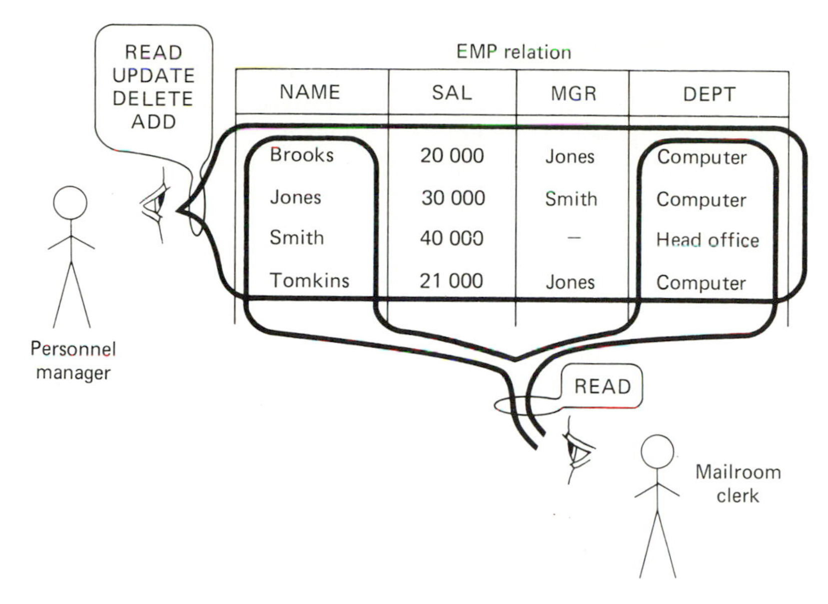

Fig. 5.2. Access-type-dependent access control.

access types, so that access of a higher type *implies* access of a lower type. For instance, UPDATE access may imply READ access.

When users need only summary or statistical data, the policy of least privilege requires that they do not have access to the underlying detailed data. (We assume here that mathematical functions, such as average, sum, and standard deviation, are supported by the DBMS at the user interface.) For this *functional* access control, the concept of access types may be extended to include functional access types. Thus we can specify that a user has access to the average salary but not to the individual salary values. While this is not enough to guarantee the security of the individual values (as discussed in Chapter 13), it is an important support for more elaborate methods.

Context-dependent control

The policy of *context-dependent* access control refers to combinations of items. One facet of this policy restricts the fields that can be accessed together. For example, if we have a relation containing employee names and salaries, we may wish to prevent some users from learning the salaries of particular employees. One approach would be to prevent any access by those users to the relation. To maximize sharing, however, we would allow separate access to names and salaries while preventing users from accessing them together in the same request or in a specific set of requests (for example, all the requests of a program). Thus salary statistics could be computed, and employee names accessed without correlations being made between the two. Another aspect of this policy is the *requirement* that certain fields appear together. For example, information about a person being arrested could be given only if the disposition of the arrest is also included.

History-dependent control

In general it is not sufficient to control only the context of the immediate request if users are to be prevented from making certain deductions. For example, if the employee relation also contained a project-identifier attribute, a user could list first all names and projects and then salaries and projects. Some correlation between names and salaries could then in general be made. Preventing this kind of deduction requires *history-dependent* control, which takes into account not only the context of the immediate request but also all past requests. That is, we restrict the current access of a user because of accesses that the user has made in the past. As another illustration of where history-dependent control is useful, consider a confidential engineering plan partitioned into subsets. We may wish to ensure that no one accesses all the parts, thus gaining complete knowledge of the plan. One way to enforce this is by keeping a record of each user's access, which conditions any new request that user makes.

5.3.3 Policies to Control Information Flow

The policies we have described control access to data but not how a program uses the data once it is accessed. Control over the program's use of data is necessary to prevent, for example, the *leakage of information* from an authorized program to an unauthorized one.

We have implicitly assumed that some authorizer can give access rights to other users. This is known as *discretionary access control.* A simpler but less flexible approach is to compartmentalize the enterprise's use of the system and follow the fixed policy that data belonging to one compartment or category cannot be accessed by users assigned to another category. This is an example of *nondiscretionary* access control. An extension to the *compartmentalization policy* is the *multilevel control policy,* which is often used in military installations. Besides having categories, information is also classified (according to its sensitivity) into levels such as unclassified, confidential, secret, and top secret (Fig. 5.3). Users are also assigned levels and categories. A security level is then defined as a classification and a set of categories. One security level is

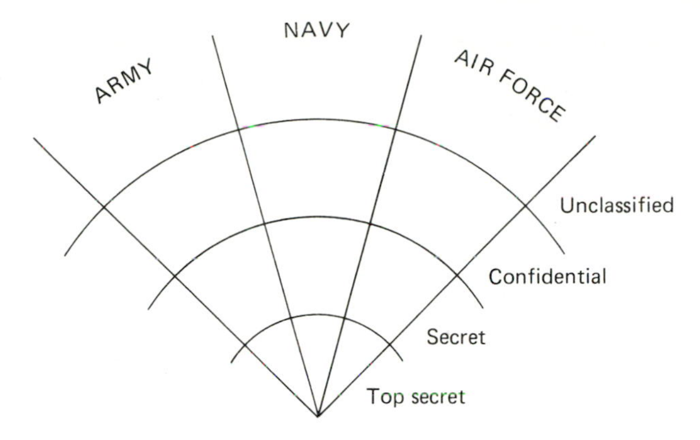

Fig. 5.3. Combination of compartments and levels.

considered greater than or equal to a second security level if the classification of the first is greater and the set of categories of the first includes the set of categories of the second. The policy then states that a user cannot read data unless the user's security level is greater than or equal to the security level of the data, and that writing must not cause information to flow from a higher to a lower security level.

It is possible to combine discretionary and nondiscretionary access-control policies. For instance, discretionary access rules may be specified for personnel within a department, while a nondiscretionary policy prevents access of the department's data by people outside the department. The relation of the various policies supporting least privilege is shown in Fig. 5.4.

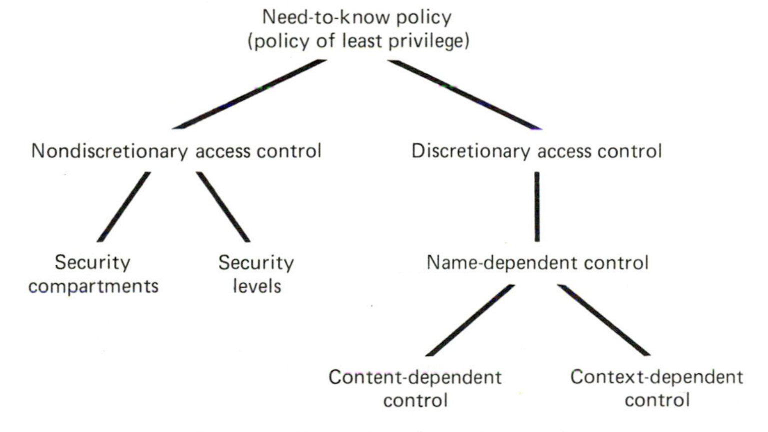

Fig. 5.4. Examples of security policies.

5.3.4 Policies for Enforcing Control

We have discussed policies associated with the *specification* of access control and information-flow control. Another class of policies is concerned with how this control is *enforced*. For example, there is a choice of using *preventive* mechanisms or only *detective* mechanisms. If the latter policy is chosen, a system may allow all access requests to be satisfied but will also log them. The log may be audited at a later time to determine whether any users violated security policy. Other policies, which can be seen as design principles for DBMSs, operating systems, and hardware, are discussed in Chapters 10 and 11.

5.4 SUMMARY

We have reviewed the most significant policies concerned with database security. Other policies are relevant to privacy, integrity, and auditing; and they are discussed when we deal with these subjects. The models discussed in the next chapter formalize these policies.

EXERCISES

5.1. Select a specific enterprise and define a set of data security policies for it.

5.2. A library's handling of rare books was used as an example of the policy of maximized sharing. What other policy is exemplified?

5.3. Describe a possible use for a policy that allows users to insert records but does not allow them to fill in certain of the field values.

5.4. Assume a given type of enterprise, e.g., educational, insurance, etc. Define a policy to handle personal information in this enterprise. Use, for example, R. Turn's concept of sensitivity levels (Chapter 4).

REFERENCES

1. S. H. Nycum, "Anatomy of a computer crime" *AFIPS Conf. Proc.* **47**, 1978 NCC, 1151–1155. AFIPS Press, Arlington, Va., 1978.

2. W. Wulf *et al.*, "HYDRA: The kernel of a multiprocessor operating system." *Comm. ACM* **17**, 6 (June 1974), 337–345.

HYDRA is the kernel of the operating system for C.mmp, the Carnegie-Mellon University Multi-Mini-Processor. The paper describes and justifies the decisions made in the design of this kernel, one of which is the separation of mechanism and policy. This separation was needed to provide a flexible kernel that could support a family of operating systems.

6 Models of Database Security

6.1 INTRODUCTION

In experimental disciplines, theories concerning the behavior of complex systems are often presented in the form of mathematical models. In order to test the validity of a theory, the behavior of the model is compared with experimental observations. The main usefulness of these theories or models is in predicting system behaviors that have not yet been observed. While some areas of information processing have been treated experimentally (for example, software physics [5]), models in this discipline serve primarily to aid in the design and understanding of complex systems rather than as prediction tools. Our treatment of models of database security is prompted by the following important purposes that a model can serve.

1. *A design tool.* A model can embody the design objectives of a system being built and serve as a structure to guide the design.
2. A *framework for researchers*. A model can provide a basis for theoretical studies of security, allowing researchers to concentrate on the salient features of a problem without considering the details involved in specific implementations.
3. *A tool* for proving correctness of design or implementation. A formal model allows formal assertions to be made and proved.
4. *An educational tool.* The description of a complex system can be simplified, since details are omitted. The formal quality of the model prevents many of the ambiguities of a purely verbal description.

5. *A comparison and evaluation tool.* The functional capabilities of different systems can be compared and evaluated by analyzing their models. Even a system that was not designed by using a model can be evaluated by means of a model of its features.

In this book we use a model as a framework for presenting database security in a structured way. For this purpose the following attributes of a model are valuable.

- *Simplicity.*
- *Generality.* The ability to incorporate different policies and apply to a wide variety of implementations.
- *Precision.* The ability to faithfully represent the policies and behavior of a system.
- *Data model independence.* Freedom from the peculiarities of specific data models.

This chapter describes several significant models of database security. We start by defining a basic model, which is then extended. This model, which applies to access control, is based on the concept that an access request is validated against a set of access rules. Other models go further, trying to control the *use* of accessed data objects. We discuss the most significant models in this latter group.

6.2 A BASIC MODEL OF DATABASE ACCESS CONTROL

Models of database access control have grown out of earlier work on protection in operating systems. One of the most influential protection models was developed by Lampson [10] and extended by Graham and Denning [6]. This model has three components: a set of *objects,* a set of *subjects,* and a set of *rules* defining what *types of access* a subject has for an object. Objects are those entities known to the operating system to which access must be controlled, such as pages of memory, programs, auxiliary storage devices, and files. Subjects are the entities that request access to objects, such as *processes,* which are programs in execution. Access types might be EXECUTE, ALLOCATE, READ. The set of all access rules can be thought of as forming an *access matrix A,* where columns $o_1, o_2, \ldots, o_n$ represent objects and rows $s_1, s_2, \ldots, s_m$ represent subjects. The entry $A[s_i, o_j]$ contains a list of access types, $t_1, t_2, \ldots$, specifying the access privileges held by subject s_i for object o_j. Figure 6.1 shows part of an access matrix for an operating system. The list of objects a subject may access, together with the mode of access, is sometimes called the *capability list* of the subject.

		OBJECTS					
		Subjects		Files		Devices	
		S1	S2	F1	F2	D1	D2
SUBJECTS	S1		CALL	READ WRITE		SEEK	
	S2				READ		SEEK

Fig. 6.1. Portion of an access matrix for an operating system.

This model treats the security of all system objects in a uniform way; and therefore one approach to database security is to consider it as just an extension of operating-system security. Thus the objects in the access matrix would be not only resources such as memory pages, devices, and files, but also database objects. The operating system could then be extended to handle all security within the system. However, there are some fundamental differences between operating-system and database-system security.

- More objects must be protected in a database.
- The lifetime of the data is normally longer in a database.
- Database security is concerned with differing levels of granularity, such as file, record, or field.
- Operating systems protect real resources. In database systems the objects can be complex logical structures, a number of which can map to the same physical data objects.
- The different architectural levels—internal, conceptual, and external—have different security requirements.
- Database security is concerned with the semantics of data as well as with its physical representation.

An operating system extended to handle these differences would become highly complex. It therefore seems a good design principle to treat database security as a responsibility of the DBMS rather than the operating system. The DBMS uses the basic security services provided by the operating system, and operating systems may indeed provide services primarily intended for DBMS use. As a further justification, most

DBMSs in practice are built to run on existing operating systems. It is then justifiable to develop models specifically for database security.

In such a model we can again use the concepts of access rules and access matrix, but objects are now sets of data item occurrences. The names of these sets must be known to the DBMS. We use the variable O (capital letters indicate set variables) to represent data objects. For a given database, O may take on any of a finite set of values $\{O_1, \ldots, O_j, \ldots, O_n\}$. In a relational DBMS, for example, the possible values of O would be the names of all the relations and attributes. Subjects are now end users (the people who request database access), groups of them, or programs executing on their behalf. In a given installation there will be a set of potential subjects $\{s_1, \ldots, s_i, \ldots, s_m\}$. The variable s is defined over this set. Access types are operations such as READ, WRITE, UPDATE, ADD, and DELETE (the particular set depends on the data model). For a given DBMS a set of legal types is defined, $\{t_1, \ldots, t_k, \ldots t_\ell\}$. The variable t may take on any of these values.

Note that the database access matrix is more static than the operating-system access matrix. It is modified explicitly only when an authorizer specifies a new access rule or revokes an old one; the matrix does not change dynamically during process execution, as in operating systems. Figure 6.2 shows part of an access matrix that represents the rules governing access to the EMPLOYEE relation. The attributes of the EMPLOYEE relation are EMP_NAME, PERS_NO, ADDRESS, TEL_NO, and SALARY. From the figure we see that the personnel manager has unrestricted access (indicated by the ALL entry) to all attributes, while the administration clerk has READ access to all attributes except SALARY. A null entry implies no access is allowed to that object (i.e., a closed system is assumed).

It is worth emphasizing here that the model does not imply any particular implementation. Thus we do not require access rules to be actually stored in matrix form. In fact this would be an inefficient way of

OBJECT / SUBJECT	EMP-NAME	PERS-NO	ADDRESS	TEL-NO	SALARY	
PERSONNEL_ MANAGER	ALL	ALL	ALL	ALL	ALL	
ADMIN_CLERK	READ	READ	READ	READ	–	

Fig. 6.2. Portion of a database access matrix.

storing them because, in general, the access matrix is very sparse: any given subject has access to only a small subset of the database. We will see in Chapter 11 more efficient ways of representing access rules.

The model should be general enough to represent the security policies described in Chapter 5. The access matrix is capable of modeling name-dependent access control down to any level of granularity supported by the DBMS. In order to represent access rules that are content-dependent, the model needs to be extended so that the access rule contains a *predicate* p. A predicate is an expression that defines the members of a set, for example, by describing a condition for membership or by enumerating these members.

We can consider the predicate as allowing us to define an arbitrary set O′ of data item occurrences as the effective object of the access rule. That is, O′ is the subset of O for which the predicate p is true, or :

$$O' = O : p$$

The predicate may also be used to state additional constraints (such as allowing access at only a certain time of the day) by referring to system variables. The predicate in this case may be considered as being composed of a data predicate, p_d, and a system predicate, p_s, connected by a boolean operator. The data predicate p_d should then strictly be substituted for p in the above expression for O′.

We can now represent an access rule by the tuple (s, O, t, p), which specifies that subject s has access t to those occurrences of O for which predicate p is true. The data that must be retrieved in order to evaluate the predicate is known as *protection data*. Figure 6.3 shows a simple example of an access rule giving the payroll clerk READ access to all the attributes in the EMPLOYEE relation for those employees who earn less than $20,000. By using suitable predicates, certain context-dependent access control may also be specified. For example, a predicate could enumerate fields that should not appear together in a query.

Access control involves more than just specifying access rules. There

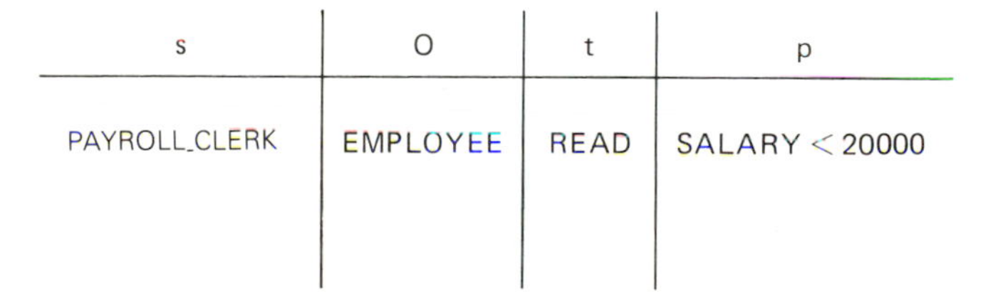

s	O	t	p
PAYROLL_CLERK	EMPLOYEE	READ	SALARY < 20000

Fig. 6.3. An access rule.

must also be a *validation process,* which ensures that all accesses to the database are authorized by access rules. A possible model of the validation process is indicated in Fig. 6.4. All database *access requests* are intercepted and passed to the validation process in the form (s, O, t, p′) indicating that user s has requested access t to the set of data item occurrences defined by O : p′.

We assume here that the identity s of the requesting user has been previously authenticated. If the access matrix contains a rule with the same (s, O, t), protection data to evaluate the access rule predicate is retrieved; otherwise the request is denied. (If a rule does not exist, it effectively means that for the (s, O, t) of the request, the access rule defines a *null* access type.) If the predicate in the access request refers to data items not included in the requested object, it is necessary to check

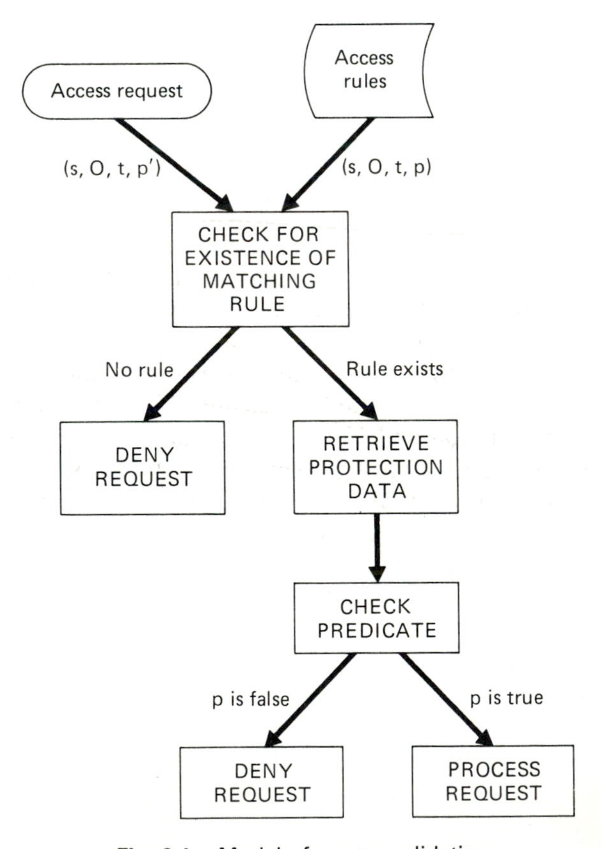

Fig. 6.4. Model of access validation.

that the subject also has READ access to these data items. For example, a query may request a list of the names of employees who earn over $100,000. It is not sufficient that the requester has access to employee names, because the inference can be made that the salary of every employee listed is over $100,000. It is therefore necessary to check that the subject also has READ access to salary information. If any of the relevant access rules do not exist, the request is denied. If they do exist the predicates in the rules must then be evaluated; if any are false, the request is denied; otherwise the request is allowed to proceed.

Note that we have assumed, for simplicity, that the request is either completely satisfied or denied. This would always be the case if the request was for a specific field occurrence. When the request is for a record occurrence then, if some of the fields in that record are authorized and some are not, the enforcement process could allow the authorized fields to be passed to the user, rather than denying the whole request. This is a policy decision that must be made by the designer of the security procedures. Likewise, a request for a set of records may be modified so that only the subset satisfying the predicate is returned to the user. The technique of partially satisfying a user request is known as *query modification* [13].

6.3 EXTENSIONS TO THE BASIC MODEL

By defining the access rule as (s, O, t, p) we have left unexpressed some important requirements of authorization and request validation. We now extend the model by introducing three new components of the access rule, rules for validating authorizations and requests, and additional interpretations of subject, object, and predicate. The extensions are based on the model of Hartson and Hsiao [8] and on the LASC system [14].

One requirement is for control over the set of access rules. The model as specified so far does not allow for some important policies about who may write access rules. One such policy permits only the authorizer who wrote the rule to change it. For this purpose, the access rule specifies the authorizer, a, so that the rule becomes (a, s, O, t, p). The model must also cover important policies for *delegation of rights*. By a *right* we mean a certain kind of access to an object; a right is the (O, t, p) of the access rule. A subject s_1 who holds the right (O_1, t_1, p_1) may be allowed to delegate that right to another subject s_2; this delegation is equivalent to inserting a new access rule (s_1, s_2, O_1, t_1, p_1). Since a portion of the rule is "copied," we add a *copy flag,* f, to the access rule specifying whether s_2 is (in turn) allowed to delegate the access right. To express policy choices (such as how to control delegation) in the model, we speak of *validation rules*. Some validation rules govern changes to access rules; others govern the way requests are validated.

We extend the access rule further by also specifying *auxiliary procedures* to be performed when the rule is used during request validation. These procedures can be used either *before* or *after* the access decision is made; and their use after the decision can be contingent on what decision was made. One use of this contingency is for actions to be taken when the request is denied, such as notifying a security monitor or logging the request. (Usually, these enforcement procedures reflect a systemwide policy that applies to all subjects and objects, or a policy that applies to an object regardless of subject. For complete flexibility, however, we include auxiliary procedure specifications in the access rule.) We introduce a list of pairs: $(c_1, ap_1), \ldots, (c_n, ap_n)$ specifying auxiliary procedures to be invoked and their *conditions* of invocation. The *extended access rule* now becomes $(a, s, O, t, f, p, [(c_1, ap_1), \ldots, (c_n, ap_n)])$. For most purposes of this book, however, the *basic access rule* (s, O, t, p) is sufficient. Figure 6.5 summarizes the elements of this model.

Programs or applications can appear in access rules as subjects. Sometimes we wish the program's rights to *amplify* the user's rights, allowing for example sorting of a file that the user cannot read. In the Hartson and Hsiao model, each rule may have "extensions," which specify the rights of programs. In some other cases *restrictions* are

Element		Interpretation
Basic access rule (s, O, t, p)		Controls access to protected objects
Extended access rule (a, s, O, t, f, p, $[(c_1, ap_1) \ldots (c_n, ap_n)]$)		
* Authorizer	a	Person who writes access rules
* Subject	s	User, application, transaction, terminal, . . .
* Object	O	Data, program, application, . . .
* Access type	t	READ, UPDATE, APPEND, AUTHORIZE, . . .
* Copy flag	f	Control for delegation of rights
* Predicate	p	Condition for access
* Auxiliary procedure	ap	Rule-specific extension to validation process
* Condition	c	Condition for auxiliary procedure invocation
Request (s, O, t, p)		Specification of access event
Validation process		Checking of requests against rules
Validation rules		Control of validation process and of access rules

* Components of access rule.

Fig. 6.5. Elements of the security model.

needed, as with the policy that users' rights are *limited* by the rights of the applications they are using [4]. Programs and applications can also appear as objects. The relevant access types then include EXECUTE or USE.

Validation rules govern the interpretation of access rules. There is not always a single obvious way to make an access decision. For example the policy of query modification can be expressed by a validation rule. As another example, suppose we allow the subject in a rule to be a user *group*. Then if two groups have different access predicates for (O, t), we need a policy to determine the predicate for a user belonging to both groups. A validation rule might specify the OR of the two predicates.

6.4 MULTILEVEL MODELS

The models described provide for an arbitrary assignment of access rights to subjects. *Multilevel* security models differ in several respects. As indicated earlier, they deal with nondiscretionary access control. One reason for the importance of nondiscretionary models is that certain formal statements about system security can be made that cannot be made for discretionary systems. Multilevel models differ as well in treating not only *access* to information, but also the *flow* of information within a system. Like discretionary models, multilevel models were first developed for operating systems (the early work was specifically influenced by the Multics system) and later applied to database systems.

6.4.1 Basic Features of Multilevel Models

In this section we describe a simplified version of the model developed by Bell and LaPadula [1]. This model introduces the concepts of *level* and *category*. Each subject is assigned a *clearance level*, and each object a *classification level*. For the military environment, these levels might be Top Secret, Secret, Confidential, and Unclassified. A subject generally represents a process executing on behalf of a user and having the same clearance level as the user. The objects can be areas of storage, program variables, files, I/O devices, users, or anything else that can hold information. Each subject and each object also has a set of categories, such as Nuclear or NATO. A *security level* is a composite:

(classification level, set of categories).

One security level is said to *dominate* another if and only if:

1. its classification or clearance level $\geq$ the other, *and*
2. its category set contains the other.

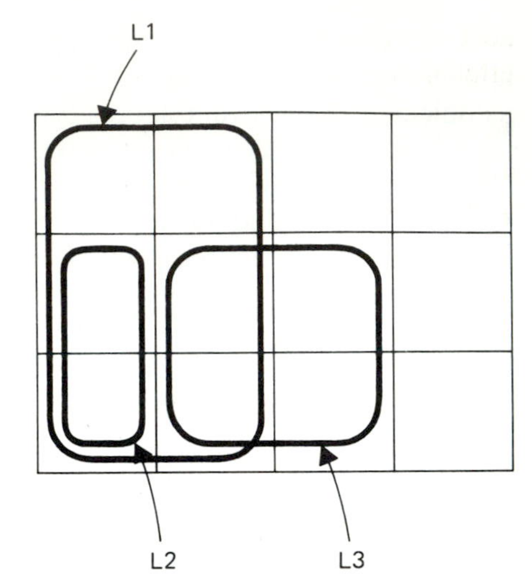

Fig. 6.6. Ordering of security levels.

Clearance and classification levels are ordered (for example, Secret > Confidential > Unclassified), but security levels are only partially ordered, so that some subjects and objects are not comparable. For example in Fig. 6.6 security level L1 dominates security level L2 since its classification level is higher and its set of categories includes the set of categories of L2. Security levels L1 and L3, on the other hand, are not comparable. The elements of the model are summarized in Fig. 6.7.

An access of an object can either *observe* the object (extract information from it) or *alter* the object (insert information into it). The set of

Element	Interpretation
Subject s	Process
Object o	Data, files, . . .
Classifications	Clearance level of subject, classification level of object
Categories	Access privileges
Security level	(Classification, category set)
Access attribute t	No observe, no alter; observe only; observe and alter; alter only
Access matrix	Discretionary security
Request	Changes current access or other aspects of system state
(s, o, t)	Current access
Decision	Yes, no, error, or ?
Rules	Determine decision, next state

Fig. 6.7. Elements of the multilevel model.

access types is determined then by all the possible combinations of these effects. The access types are:

- neither observe nor alter,
- observe only (READ),
- alter only (APPEND),
- observe and alter (WRITE).

The model considers the *states* of a secure system, which are described by:

- the *current access set,* which is a set of triples (subject, object, access type), or (s, o, t),[1]
- an access matrix,
- the security level of each subject, and
- the *maximum* and *current* security levels of each subject.

(Note that the system state for these models does *not* include the *values* in the database.)

6.4.2 Changing System State: Requests, Decisions, and Rules

Any change to the system's state is caused by a *request*. Requests can be for access to objects, for changes to security levels or to the access matrix, or to create or destroy objects. The system's response to a request is called a *decision*. Given a request and a current state, the decision and the new state are determined by a *rule*. (Rules here correspond to the validation rules of the discretionary models, not to the access rules.) These rules of operation of the system prescribe how each type of request is to be handled. Proving that a system is secure involves proving that each rule is security-preserving. Then, if the system state is secure, any request will result in a new secure state.

6.4.3 Secure System States

A secure state is defined by two properties: the *simple security property* and the *-*property*. (The *-property has also been called the *confinement property*.) The simple security property is: for every current access (s, o, t) with an "observe" access type, the level of the subject dominates the level of the object. This condition can be expressed as "no reading upward in level."

---

1. Bell and LaPadula use different symbols: (s, O, a).

The simple security condition does not prevent a combination of accesses, each secure in itself, from providing a *potential* for compromise. As can be seen from Fig. 6.8, a malicious subject could extract information from a Top Secret object and put it into a Confidential object. The *-property is defined as follows: a current access (s, o, t) implies:

if t = READ: level (o) is dominated by current level (s);
if t = APPEND: level (o) dominates current level (s);
if t = WRITE: level (o) equals current level (s).

The simple security and * properties represent nondiscretionary security, where access is governed by the level of the subject and object. The *discretionary security property* is satisfied if every current access is authorized by the current access matrix.

6.5 AN INFORMATION-FLOW MODEL

D. Denning [3] has treated information-flow aspects of the multilevel models in a more general way. The concepts of class and category are subsumed under a single concept of security class, and a variable *class-combining operator* is introduced in place of a fixed one. An information-flow model describing a specific system is defined by five components: (1) a set of objects, (2) a set of processes, (3) a set of security classes, (4) a class-combining operator, and (5) a *flow relation*. The class-combining operator $\oplus$ specifies the class of the result of any operation. For example, if we concatenate two objects, a and b, whose classes are a and b, the class of the result is $a \oplus b$. A flow relation between two classes, for

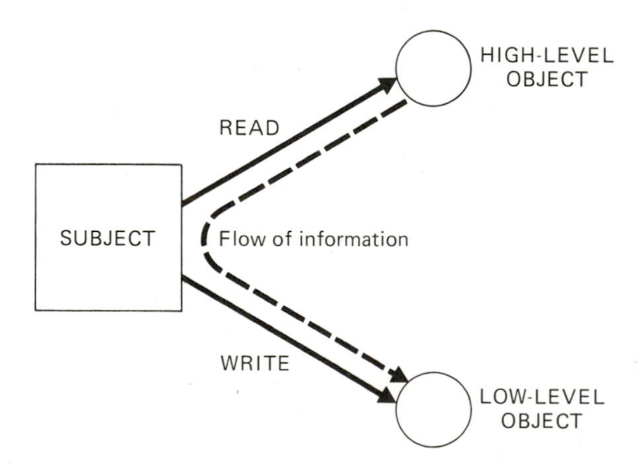

Fig. 6.8. Information flow showing need for the *-property. [From Bell and LaPadula [1], with permission of the authors.]

example A → B, means that information in class A is permitted to flow into class B. A flow model is *secure* if a flow relation cannot be violated.

Denning has shown that, if certain reasonable assumptions are made, three components of the model (classes, ⊕, and →) form a mathematical structure called a *lattice*. (These three components embody the authorization structure or flow policy represented by the model.) A lattice consists of a partially ordered set, plus least upper bound and greatest lower bound operators. The lattice shown in Fig. 6.9 represents a system containing personal data of three types: medical (m), financial (f), and criminal (c). The classes shown are all the possible subsets of {m, f, c}; they represent combinations of the data types. Information flows (as shown by the arrows) only into classes at least as inclusive. Thus for this lattice the class-combining operator ⊕, which is the least upper bound operator, yields the union of the two classes. A flow violation would occur, for example, on an attempt to move information produced from combining medical and financial data into the class designated medical only.

How can we guarantee that programs are secure, that they do not violate the information-flow requirements expressed by a lattice model? We must consider both *explicit* and *implicit* flows. Consider the statement *if* a = 0 *then* b = c. The statement produces an explicit flow from c to b when a = 0, but *always* causes an implicit flow from a to b, since we can discover whether a = 0 by examining b after execution of the statement. A program is secure if all explicit and implicit flows are secure.

Proposed mechanisms to enforce secure information flow are discussed in Chapter 11. They involve compile-time certification of programs

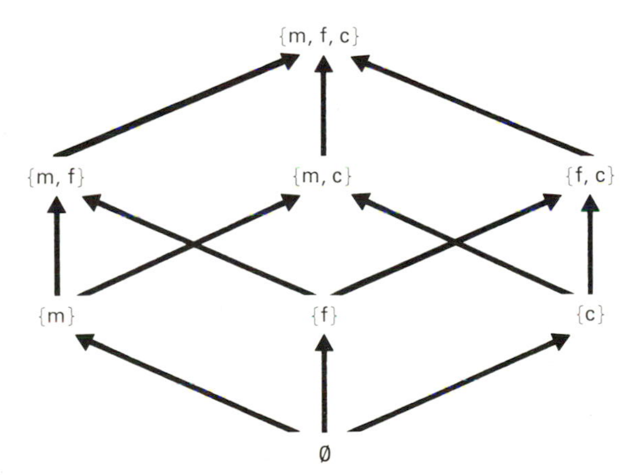

Fig. 6.9. Lattice of subsets of {m, f, c}. [From Denning [3]. Copyright 1976, Association for Computing Machinery, Inc., reprinted by permission.]

or run-time enforcement (which may be supported by hardware) or combinations of the two.

6.6 COMPARISON OF MODELS

We can classify models broadly into two categories, those that control access to objects and are extensions of the access matrix approach, and those that control information flow. An advantage of models based on the access matrix is their flexibility in allowing a wide range of security policies to be easily specified. For example, access-type-dependent and content-dependent access rules may be simply represented. The main disadvantage is that the flow of information is not controlled. As an illustration, suppose the security policy of an enterprise allows user A to READ object O_2 and WRITE object O_1, and user B only to READ object O_1 (Fig. 6.10). While this policy may be represented by an access matrix (Fig. 6.11), there is nothing to prevent A from copying O_2 into O_1 and thus allowing B access to the information of O_2.

This illegal flow of information is prevented in the second category of models. However, because of the structuring of the multilevel model, it cannot represent arbitrary security policies. For example, the simple policy that allows A to access objects O_3 and O_2, B to access O_2 and O_1, and C to access O_1 and O_3 can be handled only through the addition of an access matrix. The lattice model, with its more general approach of

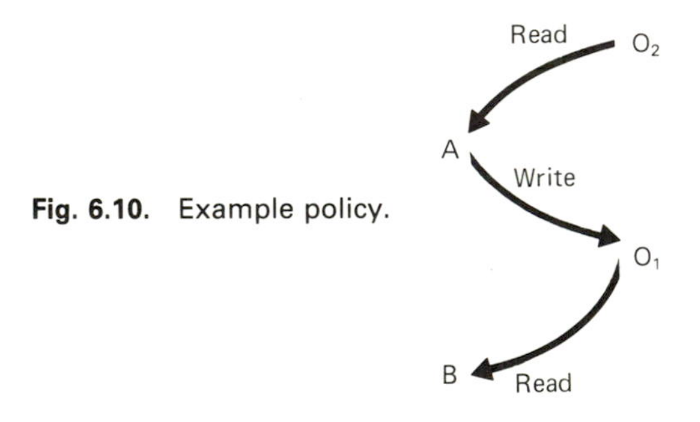

Fig. 6.10. Example policy.

s	O	t	p
A	O_2	Read	—
A	O_1	Write	—
B	O_1	Read	—

Fig. 6.11. Example access matrix.

partially ordering classes, can handle this situation. However, the creation of new database objects with new security requirements may require a complete restructuring of the class lattice. Moreover, access-type-dependent and content-dependent access rules cannot be simply represented by the lattice itself. Control of information flow also requires execution-time checks, which may cause unacceptable overhead. In summary, the two approaches represent different compromises among efficiency, flexibility, and security.

EXERCISES

6.1. Give an interpretation of query modification in an *open* system.

6.2. Basic access-control models have been proposed where there is no concept of subject, i.e., the type of access is defined by the security of the data and applies to *all* the users. The access rule is then (O, t, p). In other cases there is no concept of object, i.e., there are READ users, UPDATE users, etc.; this means that a READ-user, for example, can read everything. Now the rule is (s, t, p). Discuss the power of these simpler models. (What policies can or cannot be implemented?)

6.3. Assume the following relation R (Registration) with fields C# (Course Number), S# (Student Number), and DEPT:

R	C #	S #	DEPT
	100	10	S
	100	12	S
	120	10	S
	120	18	S
	140	20	M
	140	18	M
	200	10	P
	200	12	P
	250	12	S
	250	18	S
	300	28	P
	320	30	M
	320	35	M
	320	21	M

with the following access rules:

(U, R, READ, where C# = 120),
(U, R, UPDATE, where C# = 200),
(U, C#, UPDATE, where S# = 35),
(U, S#, READ, where S# = 35).

Assume that the access types are ordered such that UPDATE implies READ.

An application program request on behalf of user U is: READ C#, S# from R where DEPT ≠ 'S'. Which values are delivered to this program?

6.4 Give a validation model (in the style of Section 6.2) for the extended model of Section 6.3.

6.5 Design a lattice to represent a military system with four levels and two categories (NATO and Nuclear). What is the class-combining operator?

6.6 Build a lattice to represent personal data of different levels of sensitivity, where the data can be accessed by the departments Health, Personnel, and Headquarters.

REFERENCES AND BIBLIOGRAPHY

1. D. E. Bell and L. J. LaPadula, "Secure Computer System: Unified Exposition and Multics Interpretation." Report ESD–TR–75–306, MITRE Corp., Bedford, Mass., March 1976.

2. R. W. Conway, W. L. Maxwell, and H. L. Morgan, "On the implementation of security measures in information systems." *Comm. ACM* **15,** 4 (April 1972), 211–220.

A "security matrix" is proposed, which is equivalent to the access matrix of the basic model. This is used as a functional model of a security system, which separates data-dependent and data-independent access decisions. This is the first paper to propose compile-time access decisions.

3. D. E. Denning, "A lattice model of secure information flow." *Comm. ACM* **19,** 5 (May 1976), 236–243.

4. E. B. Fernandez, R. C. Summers, and C. D. Coleman, "An authorization model for a shared data base." *Proc. 1975 ACM-SIGMOD Int. Conference,* 23–31.

The authorization model for the LASC system. The model includes (1) the use of applications as context for user rights, (2) the use of predicates that can depend on any data in the system as part of the access rules, and (3) the use of ordered access types. Enforcement of this model at compile time is discussed.

5. A Fitzsimmons and T. Love, "A review and evaluation of software science." *ACM Comp. Surveys* **10,** 1 (March 1978), 3–18.

6. G. S. Graham and P. J. Denning, "Protection: Principles and practice." *AFIPS Conf. Proc.* **40,** 1972 SJCC, 417–429. AFIPS Press, Montvale, N.J., 1972.

Lampson's model is interpreted in more detail. In particular, creation and deletion of objects, granting of access to objects, and sharing by untrustworthy subsystems are considered. An argument for the correctness of the model is also given, and ways of implementing it are discussed. This paper is also a good example of the use of a model in comparing and evaluating existing systems.

7. M. A. Harrison, W. L. Ruzzo, and J. D. Ullman, "Protection in operating systems." *Comm. ACM* **19,** 8 (August 1976), 461–471.

8. H. R. Hartson and D. K. Hsiao, "A semantic model for data base protection languages." *Proc. 2nd Int. Conf. on Very Large Databases,* North-Holland, 1976.

   In this paper the authors develop a model of database protection capable of supporting a wide range of security policies. The model is based on the concept that an access request is validated against a set of access rules. The basic model provides for data-dependent field-level access control. Extensions allow for history-dependent control, auxiliary procedure invocation, and extended authorization.

9. A. K. Jones, R. J. Lipton, and L. Snyder, "A linear time algorithm for deciding security." *Proc. 17th Annual Symp. on Foundations of Computer Science,* 1976, 33–41. Available from IEEE.

10. B. W. Lampson. "Protection." *Proc. 5th Annual Princeton Conf. on Info. Sciences and Systs.,* 1971, 437–443. Reprinted in *ACM Operating Systems Review* **8,** 1 (January 1974), 18–24.

    This is the basic exposition of the access-matrix concept, which is developed starting from a fundamental protection system based on processes that have sets of rights and communicate only through messages in order to share data. The access-matrix model is applied to explain some existing protection systems and possible implementations are suggested.

11. J. K. Millen, "Security kernel validation in practice." *Comm. ACM* **19,** 5 (May 1976), 243–250.

12. P. G. Neumann *et al.*, "A Provably Secure Operating System: The System, its Applications, and Proofs." SRI, Menlo Park, Calif., Feb. 1977.

13. M. Stonebraker and E. Wong, "Access control in a relational database management system by query modification." *Proc. 1974 ACM National Conference,* 180–186.

14. R. C. Summers and E. B. Fernandez, "Data Description for a Shared Data Base: Views, Integrity, and Authorization." Report G320–2671, IBM Scientific Center, Los Angeles, Calif., August 1975.

7
Authorization

7.1 INTRODUCTION

Chapter 5 discussed some database security policies. Putting these policies to work in a discretionary system requires:

1. the translation of the policies into access rules, and
2. the enforcement of these access rules by the system—ensuring that every access complies with the rules.

This chapter deals with the first of these aspects, authorization. Enforcement is discussed in later chapters.

Security policy is likely to be formulated in terms of the knowledge that users can gain or the facts they can manipulate, whereas access rules must be written about the objects known to the DBMS. A good authorization system will help to bridge the gap between these two ways of thinking by providing:

- A simple and clear interface for defining rules.

  As Saltzer and Schroeder state, ". . . to the extent that the user's mental image of his protection goals matches the mechanisms he must use, mistakes will be minimized. If he must translate his image of his protection needs into a radically different specification language, he will make errors" [24, p. 1283].

- Facilities for changing the authorization state.

  Policies change. New users are given access to the system, other users leave, the functions of the users change and therefore their access rights change. Objects are created for the needs of new applications, and other objects are destroyed when they are no longer needed.

- Ways to analyze the effect on the policy objectives of the current authorization state or of a proposed change.

We would like to be able to ask questions such as "Starting from the current authorization state, what facts can be inferred by a specific user, or what functions performed?"

One aspect of this goal is for the system to determine what inferences can be made on the basis of accessible data. The other aspect has been expressed as the *safety* question [12, 19]: Given an access matrix, if we grant subject S_1 access of type t_1 to object O_1, what other subjects can thereby obtain that same right, or (more generally) what changes will be produced in the authorization state? The safety question has been shown to be undecidable for arbitrary systems with no restrictions on how rights can be granted or how new objects are created, but is potentially answerable for restricted systems.

For the present neither safety nor inference questions can be answered for most systems, so we must be content with good tools for displaying and analyzing access rules and with subjective evaluations of how well they express policy.

- Ways to exploit the information in access rules to better understand and control the information system.

The set of access rules provides a great deal of information of the sort typically maintained in data dictionaries about how various entities of the information system relate to one another. For example, a DBA planning to delete some object would want to know which users have access to the object.

In this chapter we consider various issues in authorization, organizing the discussion around the access-rule concept. We have defined a basic access rule as a 4-tuple (s, O, t, p) that describes the access t of a subject s to an object O, under conditions expressed by a predicate p. It is useful to think of a complete set of rules, with a unique rule corresponding to each possible combination of (s, O, t) and therefore to each possible access request. We shall show, however, that many of these rules do not have to be written or stored. Although different predicates could be defined for the same (s, O, t), these can be combined into a single predicate, preserving (s, O, t) as a unique identifier for a rule.

Some of the examples in this chapter are taken from systems (Multics and RACF) that control access to *files*. The principles behind these systems, however, apply equally well to database systems. The authorization schemes of several DBMSs are described in Chapter 10.

7.2 THE AUTHORIZER

Someone must maintain the set of access rules which at a given instant describe the rights of all the users. *Authorizers* are the users who have this function.

The rights of the authorizer can be viewed in two different ways. In the first approach, the creator of an object becomes its *owner* and receives all rights on it, including the right to define access rules. The second approach gives the authorization function to persons with global system responsibility, such as the Enterprise Administrator, DBA, or Security Administrator. This means that ownership is separated from authorization, and special administrative access types define authorization rights. In an environment with a large number of unrelated databases, such as a computer utility, the ownership approach is more appropriate. In the case of a corporate database, the second approach is more suitable. It supports the least-privilege policy better, since authorizers do not automatically receive access to the objects they administer, as is the case in ownership systems.

7.3 SUBJECTS

We saw in Chapter 6 that a subject is any person or other entity that can request access to a protected object. The most important subjects are the *users,* particularly the end users, of the database system. Usually there is a directory of users, which may also contain *user profiles* that describe attributes of users. Such attributes can define access rights or default authorization characteristics, such as the status of new files created by the user, or can simply be used as data for evaluation of content-dependent access rules.

The authorizer's job can be simplified by the definition of *groups* or *classes* of users. When a user group is given access rights, all users belonging to the group receive those rights. Subsequently a user who joins a group automatically receives all the rights of the group. Administrators and application developers are also subjects, but they have special types of access to data objects, or access to special kinds of objects, as we shall see in the next section.

We can also treat transactions or application programs as subjects and control their access to data. In IMS, for example, a *program's* access to databases is controlled. An *application* is a set of transactions or programs that accomplish related functions. If users belong to more than one group or use more than one application, their rights at any moment may depend on both their identity and the group or application. One way of expressing this requirement is to use the group name or application name in the predicate of an access rule. For example, JOAN may be allowed access to ADDRESS only when using the MAILROOM application. Another way is to make the subject a *composite,* such as (user, group), or (user, application). The composite's rights can be granted explicitly or can be calculated from individual and group rights.

In LASC, for example, users always interact with the database through applications, and authorizers explicitly grant rights to a (user class, application) composite. These rights cannot exceed the rights of the application. In Multics [6, 23] a subject identifier has three parts: individual, project, and compartment. Projects are groups of users who work together in some activity and therefore share certain rights. Users may also designate personal compartments in order to restrict their own rights. (This is useful to confine the effects of errors or to prevent borrowed programs from gaining unintended access.) The user specifies which project and compartment apply for any session.

7.4 OBJECTS

The most crucial issues in authorization have to do with the choice of objects to protect. Some of these issues are:

- The level of the objects to be protected (external schema, conceptual schema, or internal schema).
- The size of the unit of protection (file, record, field).
- Protection through views. In systems where a view concept exists, should the view be the protected object or should the components of the view be controlled directly?
- Protection of data descriptions. Some systems separate data from descriptions of that data. Should these descriptions be protected differently?

Primarily we are concerned here with data objects, although application programs and various database system components usually are also protected objects.

7.4.1 Level of Objects

Are the protected objects at the external level, the conceptual-schema level, or the internal level? The answer is *at all of these levels,* but the fundamental access rules should apply to the conceptual level. The reason is that the conceptual level provides a global view of the data, where their semantics are explicit. Access rules specified for conceptual objects apply regardless of how those objects are viewed or used by different applications. In System R the definer of a view receives access to it based on his or her access to the view components, which can be *base relations* (the relations defined in the conceptual schema) or other views. In this way, rules about the conceptual schema propagate to the external schema.

Another approach is to write rules about the external schema, but to require their consistency with rules about the conceptual schema, as is discussed in Section 7.10.2. Conceptual-level rules then are written by authorizers with global database responsibility, while external-level rules may be written by application administrators. The CODASYL approach is to allow access-control clauses on both schema and subschema, but not to allow the subschema to bypass schema controls.

7.4.2 Granularity

A commonly used level of granularity is the *file* level, which corresponds to the relation level, or to the record-type level in CODASYL databases. Sometimes a coarser granularity suffices, and groups of files are protected as a single object. The groups can be defined in various ways, such as: storage in the same physical area, common name portions in a multipart name, a subtree of a hierarchical directory structure, or explicit naming of group members.

File-level control does not always suffice, however. As shown in Chapter 5, there is a clear need in many situations for policies of field-level control and content-dependent control.

One possible approach to field-level access control is to write rules about *domains* or *field types,* and to derive from them the rules about columns or fields. The problem with that approach is that the same domain may have a different meaning in different relations, and automatic derivation would be inappropriate. For example, suppose that a SALARY domain appears in two relations: EMPLOYEE(NAME, SALARY) and LIMIT(JOBNAME, SALARY). A personnel department employee might need access to SALARY in the LIMIT relation but have no reason to know individual salaries. Field-level access rules therefore must have as their objects the fields of a file or relation. Among the systems we are considering, INGRES, QBE, and LASC support complete field-level access rules. The CODASYL DDL allows access-control clauses to be associated with any level of the schema description, down to the data item (field) level. IMS, with field-level sensitivity, provides a form of field-level access control, in that a program can be given access to a subset of fields of a segment. System R provides field-level control of *update* access but only record-level control of read access, although complete field-level control is possible through the view mechanism.

7.4.3 Views as Objects

One way of providing fine-grained authorization is to define tailored views for different users according to their access needs and then control access to the views. If a powerful query language is used to define the views, the granularity can be as fine as desired.

One of the first explicit recognitions of the view concept for security was in the DBTG report [7]. In that report and in the CODASYL reports [1, 2], a subschema is defined as a description of those database objects known to a specific program or set of programs. The subschema is a way of limiting the rights of a program to a subset of the schema. Schema data objects at various levels (such as record-type, set or data-item) in the description can be omitted from the subschema. Since the subschema can omit specific data items and since data items can have their own access-control locks (which may differ from the schema locks), the result is field-level access control. Since the subschema can define only limited transformations from the schema, Manola [20] has suggested extensions to the CODASYL DDL to allow other kinds of subschema restriction, such as *derived fields,* which could provide statistical access. (Derived fields *can* be specified for the schema.)

IMS also restricts program rights through views. The IMS view is a *logical database record,* which is based on one or more *physical* database records. Both physical and logical database records are hierarchical arrangements of segment types, but the logical record can omit some segments or fields of the physical records. A program has no access of any type to the omitted segment types (except that, when an accessible segment is deleted, its inaccessible dependent segments are also deleted). An application program specifies its database usage through its *PSB* (Program Specification Block). The PSB contains one or more *PCBs,* one for each logical database record the program uses.

Views in System R can eliminate or reorder columns, combine two or more base relations or views, and eliminate certain rows on the basis of their content. System R, therefore, in effect provides field-level and content-dependent access control.

7.4.4 Data Descriptions as Objects

An important special type of data object is data description or *metadata.* The description of an object and the *values* of that object are conceptually distinct, and access to them can be separately controlled. Data descriptions can be manipulated either implicitly through commands or explicitly as data objects. In the former case, the commands reflect special *control* access types, such as ADMINISTER. In the latter case, appropriate access to the control data objects must be granted. A good example is the CODASYL schema description. Access-control locks can be associated with any of the access types (such as COPY, ALTER, DISPLAY) that apply to the description. Even where this distinction between objects and descriptions is made, however, the access-control *mechanisms* can be the same.

7.4.5 Transactions and Programs as Objects

Transactions and programs can be subjects, receiving access rights according to their purposes. It is necessary then to control access to them, since they indirectly provide access to data objects.

In IMS (Fig. 7.1), users or logical terminals receive access to transactions (which may be further protected by passwords). In System R also, end users can receive RUN access to application programs. While application programmers are authorized to perform the operations of the programs they write, end users are authorized only to RUN the programs. For example, there is no reason to give tellers general authorization to update the ACCOUNTS relation when they must use a specific program for updating accounts.

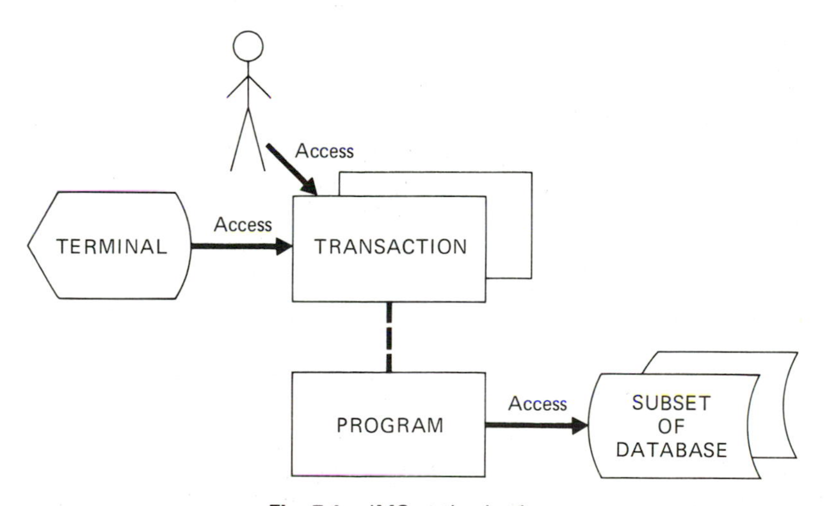

Fig. 7.1. IMS authorization.

7.5 ACCESS TYPES

Any database system provides a set of operations for each category of object recognized by the system. These allowable operations form the set of possible access types, and access rules grant a subset to specific subjects. The exact set of access types depends on the data model, but it often includes: READ, WRITE or UPDATE, INSERT, DELETE. It may also include special access types, such as CREATE, DESTROY, and ADMINISTER. Of course the set of access types depends on the category of object; for a transaction, the only possible access may be USE or RUN.

Access types are sometimes ordered, so that access of a higher type implies access of a lower type. Such an ordering can simplify the writing and storing of access rules. WRITE access often implies READ access. In many situations, however, we wish to allow users to add things to a file but not to read the file. Distinguishing INSERT or APPEND access from WRITE access can solve this problem, but a more general solution is to use a partial ordering rather than a total ordering. To that end, access types for data objects can be divided into categories which are concerned with:

- retrieval only,
- maintenance (changes to database values), and
- control (actions on metadata).

Access types are then ordered within each category [9]. Figure 7.2 is an example of such an ordering.

7.6 SPECIFYING SUBSETS AND CONDITIONS

So far we have seen how to control access to data objects which, at the finest granularity, may correspond to fields or columns in a relation. Finer control can be specified through predicates in access rules or in views.

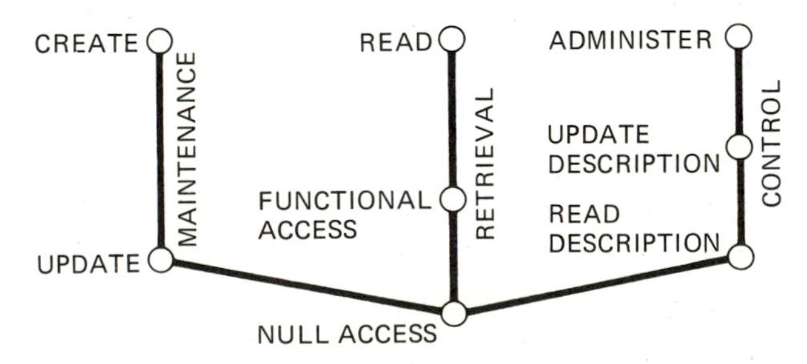

Fig. 7.2. Ordering of access types for data objects.

7.6.1 Predicates in the Access Rule

Content-dependent access control

For content-dependent access control the authorizer defines predicates whose evaluation depends on the contents of the database or on system variables such as time of day, terminal ID, or event occurrences. The predicate

```
DEPT = 'MATH' AND TIME-OF-DAY > '1200'
```

would allow access only to the MATH department records and only after noon.

Context-dependent access control

Suppose we wish to restrict a certain set of users from accessing the attributes EMPNO together with SALARY. In other words, although the users have separate access to both attributes, they should not be able to deduce the salaries of individual employees. We could write this constraint as

```
¬ (EMPNO, SALARY)
```

in the rule specifying access to the EMPLOYEE relation. Any access rules defined for views defined on the EMPLOYEE relation can then be checked for consistency with this constraint.

Since NAME also uniquely identifies the employee, we should add a second restriction, and the predicate becomes

```
¬ (EMPNO, SALARY) AND ¬ (NAME, SALARY)
```

The situation becomes more complex if we add the attribute PROJECT_NO to the relation. Two separate queries that are consistent with the constraints above allow unauthorized inferences to be made. First EMPNO and PROJECT_NO can be listed and then PROJECT_NO and SALARY. The precision with which a correlation between EMPNO and SALARY can be made depends on factors such as the number of employees working on a project. The number of different ways of making an unauthorized correlation increases rapidly when there are multiple relations containing some common attributes.

Ideally the authorizer would only have to specify which correlations are prohibited, leaving the problem of enforcement to the system. This places two requirements on the system. The first is for history-dependent control; that is, the system must remember what accesses have been made in the past and use this information to determine whether or not the current access request should be allowed. The other requirement is for the ability to determine what inferences can be made from a sequence of requests. No existing system provides these features but a design has been proposed [3]. A system has been implemented [18] which supports inference planning by the user of a relational DBMS. The inference-generating techniques used may well be applicable to the context-control problem in database security. The problem of inference is treated in Chapter 13.

Access path control

With some data models, such as networks or hierarchies, it is not sufficient to specify the fields that can be accessed. It is also necessary to control the paths that are used to gain access to fields, because the semantics of the retrieved data depends on the access path used. One way to specify path control would be to list the relationships that can be used to access the required data. As an example, consider the CODASYL network in Fig. 7.3. The access rule

```
JOHN CAN READ (TNAME, SNAME, GRADE) BY (ADVISE, GIVE)
```

would prevent JOHN from correlating GRADE and SNAME. Another approach is to treat the relationship as an object, as in

```
JOHN CAN USE ADVISE.
```

7.6.2 Predicates in Views

In a DBMS that uses the view mechanism for fine-grained access control, predicates can be specified in the view definition instead of in access rules. Content-dependent, history-dependent, and access-path control can be specified using the same predicate forms we have just described. For views, control of the immediate context does not require a predicate, because the view itself expresses the context. Access-rule predicates have the advantage that the same view can be used for different subjects

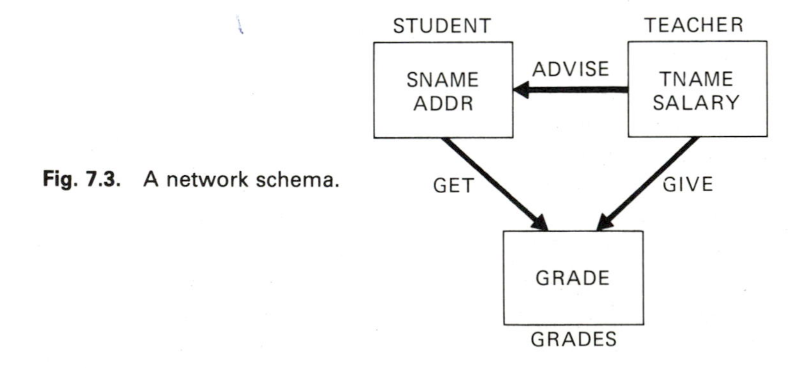

Fig. 7.3. A network schema.

who need to perform the same function, but for a different set of data occurrences.

7.7 AUXILIARY PROCEDURES

We complete our discussion of access-rule components by considering auxiliary procedures. These are system-defined or authorizer-defined procedures that may be invoked when the access rule is used, if their associated conditions hold. Auxiliary procedures allow the authorizer to specify more detail about authorization requirements than the authorization language can convey. This detail can apply to the validation of requests or to the treatment of rule violations. Examples of procedures that could be built into a system are "log," "alert the authorizer," and "prevent access and log." Auxiliary procedures have been proposed in other contexts and have been called "triggers" [8], "formularies" [15], "surveillance programs" [4], "actions" [26], and "database procedures" [2]. In systems with very limited authorization language, auxiliary procedures provide the *only* way to specify authorization criteria. One problem, however, is that, if these criteria are buried in a procedure, they are less understandable and more difficult to audit and modify.

7.8 AUTHORIZATION LANGUAGE AND DISPLAYS

We have described what kinds of information access rules convey. The same basic semantics can be expressed in various possible forms of *authorization language*. As authorization is performed in the context of other functions, it is worth considering the different ways that the authorization language can relate to the languages used for these other functions. The functions of interest are:

- data description,
- query, and
- operating-system commands.

A somewhat independent issue is whether authorization is written as a component of an object description, or in the user profile, or as an access rule.

Authorization in the DDL

This is the CODASYL approach, which allows an access-control clause in any category of description (such as schema, area, record, or data item). For example,

```
RECORD NAME IS DEPT;
  . . .
ACCESS-CONTROL LOCK FOR GET IS 'OPEN-SESAME'.
```

The run-unit must supply a *key* that matches the lock; the run-unit might, for example, obtain the key from the user as a password. The lock is not necessarily a constant, but can be a variable or an auxiliary procedure (called a Database Procedure) that is to be passed the key. The procedure could converse with the user to get further evidence of the user's right to perform the access.

Authorization by the query language

Another approach is to use the *same* language structure for query and authorization. In fact, some systems use the same type of language for query and all aspects of data definition and control, thus exploiting the power of the query language. A good example of this approach is QBE, which provides a uniform way of manipulating information on a screen for data description, queries, and authorization. Assume, for example, a table named EMP with fields NAME and MGR. To insert a new row into EMP, the user enters the row under the displayed column headings:

```
EMP                   NAME        MGR
I.                    ALEX        JOHN
```

("I" is the INSERT command.) Giving user JOHN print (P) access to the table is done similarly:

```
   EMP                NAME        MGR
I.AUTH(P.)JOHN        N           M
```

The underlines indicate *example* elements, meaning here *any* name or manager. To give JOHN access to only his employees the authorizer would enter

```
   EMP                NAME        MGR
I.AUTH(P.)JOHN        N           JOHN
```

The QBE authorization language has essentially the power of the QBE query language, since authorization and queries are expressed in the same way.

Authorization through the command language

If the underlying operating system has an appropriate control language, the authorization language can be integrated into it, so that a user does not need two different control languages. This practice is followed in RACF, which can be used with the TSO system [16] and uses TSO commands for its authorization language.

Authorization through user profiles

In ADF a "Sign-on Profile" database associates each user with a profile segment that lists allowable transactions and access types. Authorizers use the generalized ADF facilities to directly manipulate these associations and profiles.

Authorization expressed as rules

In a number of systems, authorizers explicitly write access rules or issue commands granting or revoking rights. In LASC, authorization statements are direct expressions of rules, as in:

```
JOHN CAN READ EMPLOYEE.
```

In System R, GRANT and REVOKE commands are used:

```
GRANT INSERT, SELECT ON EMPLOYEE TO JOHN;
REVOKE INSERT ON EMPLOYEE FROM JOHN;
```

Commands are also used in RACF:

```
PERMIT EMPLOYEE ID (JOHN).
```

7.8.1 Description of Views

In System R, any legitimate SQL query can define a view, since the result of any query is itself a table. Suppose there exists a table named EMP containing five columns: EMPNO, NAME, DNO, JOB, SALARY. The following sequence defines a view called D50 containing the number, name, and job title of employees in Department 50.

```
DEFINE VIEW D50 (EMPNO, NAME, JOBTITLE) AS
     SELECT EMPNO, NAME, JOB
     FROM EMP
     WHERE DNO = 50;
```

A user who needs to know about Department 50 employees (but not their salaries) can be given access to view D50.

```
GRANT READ ON D50 TO JOHN;
```

A CODASYL COBOL subschema could be declared as

```
SS NOSAL WITHIN SCHEMA PERSONNEL . . .
AD JOB FIELD-NAME BECOMES JOBTITLE . . .
RECORD SECTION.
01 EMP.
```

```
02 EMPNO; PICTURE 9(6).
02 NAME; PICTURE A(20).
02 JOBTITLE; PICTURE A(15).
```

Note, however, that the subschema cannot select specific record occurrences by value, such as those for Department D50. The same is true of the IMS logical database record. In LASC [26], views (called templates) are declared very much like PL/I structures, with the addition of predicates to define joins and to select record occurrences. The D50 view would be defined as:

```
DECLARE 1 D50 TEMPLATE
     WHERE (EMP.DNO = 50),
   2 EMPNO,
   2 NAME,
   2 JOBTITLE LIKE JOB;
```

7.8.2 The Authorizer's Picture of Access Rules

Authorizers need a clear picture of the system's current authorization status, as well as convenient ways of interrogating that status. In a number of systems, that picture is provided by the database or file or catalog that contains access rules or other protection information. In IMS, a library containing the PSBs for all programs is maintained through utility programs. However, it is usually more convenient to use a dictionary to display and manipulate these descriptions. In RACF, a data set profile contains a list of all authorized users and groups, and a LISTDSD command can be used to display that information. In QBE and System R, all the access rules are stored in system tables to which administrators can be given access. These tables can be queried and manipulated like any user-defined table.

In file systems controlled by *directories,* the authorizer's picture includes the directory structure. In Multics, the directory structure is hierarchical, and directories fit into it very much like ordinary files. Figure 7.4 shows such a tree-structured directory. Associated with each file is an *access control list* listing users and their permitted access types, which are granted independently. Multics associates with each directory an "initial access control list," which is copied into the list of any new file created under that directory. A summary of these different pictures is given in Fig. 7.5.

Displays for authorizers should include at least the ability to display all rules pertaining to specific subject or a specific object. Query-type systems can handle this requirement directly if the access rules are maintained as part of the database. Other systems typically provide special commands, such as the LISTDSD command of RACF. Changing

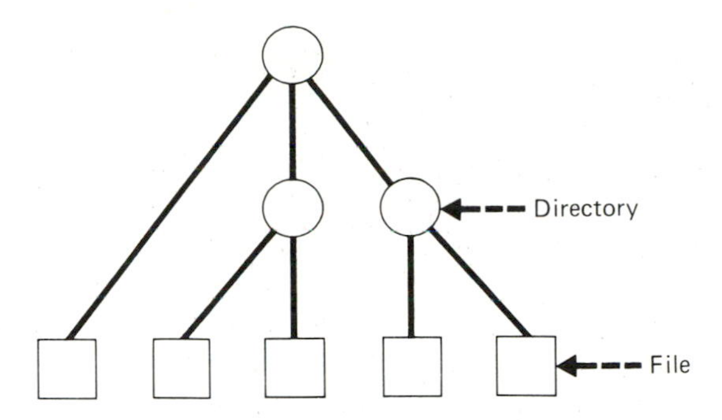

Fig. 7.4 Hierarchical directory structure.

of access rules can have dramatic effects on system operation, changing the availability of transactions or applications. Good displays can help the authorizer to study the impact of contemplated changes. Since access rules are extremely sensitive objects, an authorizer's own rights should determine what displays are available. For example, the LISTDSD command is available only to the data set's owner and certain privileged users.

7.8.3 The User's Picture of Access Rules

It is generally agreed that access rules should not be visible to the user, since knowledge of a rule can enable the user to make inferences about

System	Authorizer's picture
CODASYL	Data descriptions
IMS	PSB Library Data dictionary Sign-on profile database (ADF)
INGRES	PROTECTION relation
Multics	Directory structure and access control lists
QBE	AUTHORITY table
RACF	Data set access control lists
System R	Several authorization tables

Fig. 7.5. The authorizer's picture of access rules.

inaccessible data. A good principle is *inaccessible data should be indistinguishable from nonexistent data.*

7.9 THE USE OF CLASSES

If users and objects are not grouped in any way, the authorizer has to explicitly define access rules for each object that can be accessed by each user. Groups or classes may be used to improve this situation. Consider a simple case where a number of different users have the same access rights. If the group of users is defined as a class, only one access rule per object need be specified and stored for the entire group. Similarly, data objects may also be grouped into classes. Although classes can simplify authorization they can also complicate it (with a resulting loss of security) if used in a complex or unconstrained way.

To illustrate the use of classes, let us consider a medical database. Let RECORDS be a data class containing patient records. Let this data class contain two subclasses: TESTS, specifying the results of laboratory tests, and MEDICATION, describing prescriptions. Let the users also be grouped into classes EMERGENCY_ROOM and PHARMACY. The set of access rules stored by the system might be as follows.

User class	Data class	Access type
EMERGENCY_ROOM	RECORDS	WRITE
PHARMACY	MEDICATION	WRITE
PHARMACY	TESTS	READ

To validate a request for EMERGENCY_ROOM to WRITE MEDICATION, the system would have to understand the structuring of the classes and apply some policy about how class rules are used. A reasonable policy here is that WRITE access to RECORDS implies WRITE access to its subgroups. The following sections consider different types of class structuring and how they are used in various systems.

7.9.1 Structuring of Classes

The simplest type of structure simply partitions the database into a set of disjoint classes and partitions the users in exactly the same way. A service bureau, for example, might use this type of structure. If a second independent partitioning is superimposed on the first, the result is something like the multilevel authorization scheme discussed in Chapter 6, where every subject and object is classed in two ways, by level and by compartments. (Note, however, that in the multilevel scheme the *access rules* are built in.)

With a *hierarchical* structuring, each class includes all the classes below it in the hierarchy. The Multics system provides a hierarchy of data classes through its directory structure. This hierarchy is used only to determine the *default* access rules for a new object, and these can be replaced by explicit rules. A more general structuring described in [10] corresponds to a directed graph, where an object or group can have more than one parent. These various types of structure are illustrated in Fig. 7.6.

The data classes and user classes are not necessarily structured the same way. In the medical-record example, the data classes are hierarchical, but the user classes are partitioned. Even if both types of classes have the same type of structure, such as hierarchical, the specific hierarchies can differ.

7.9.2 Interpretation of Class Structuring

If each object and each user belongs to exactly one class, the interpretation is straightforward. A user has all the rights of his or her class. If any of these rights applies to an object class, the user has the rights for all objects in that class.

With hierarchical structures, an access rule is specified at the highest

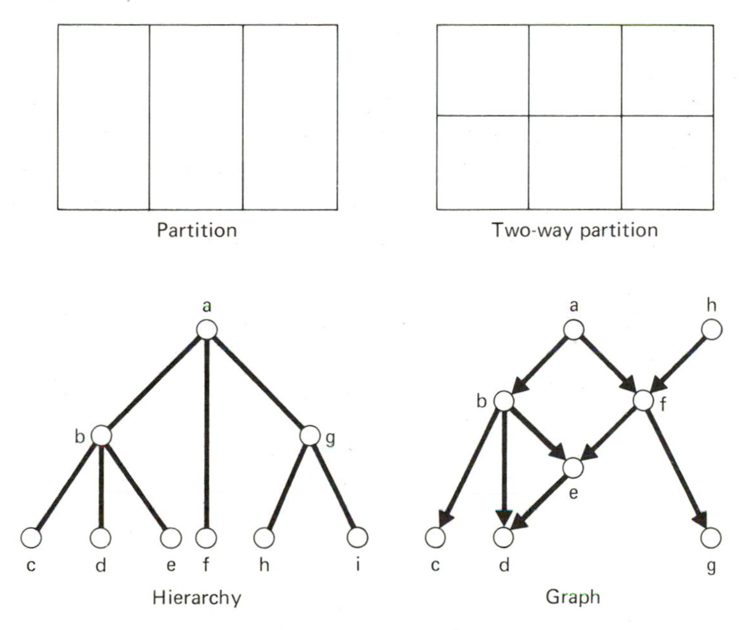

Fig. 7.6. Structuring of classes.

subject and object levels to which it applies. In the hierarchy of Fig. 7.6, for example, a rule that applies to g, h, and i is specified only for g. Some issues in the interpretation of these structures are discussed in Section 7.9.3.

In the graph structure, if we interpret nodes as object classes, each class inherits the rules that apply to all of its parents. Class e, for example, inherits the rules written for b and f. It also inherits (through b and f) the rules written for classes a and h.

Certain naming conventions can simplify the authorizer's job further. For example, the object name can be considered as a concatenation of the class names. Thus the name A.B.C indicates that the object is a member of class B, which in turn is a member of class A. Access rules specified for class A automatically apply to a new object A.B.C. In RACF the first portion of a file name is either the user ID of the creator or the class name. When a user requests access, RACF first checks if the user ID or user class name equals the first portion of the file name. Thus many access rules need not ever be written or stored.

7.9.3 Issues in Interpretation of Classes

In this section we consider some policy issues that arise when a subject or object belongs to more than one class [14]. In a sense this is always so, since a subject always belongs to a class consisting only of that subject and also to a GENERAL or PUBLIC class consisting of all subjects (although such a GENERAL class may not be explicit).

When user or subject classes are allowed to overlap, more than one access rule may be applicable to a given access request. For example, given a request by subject s, who belongs to classes S_1 and S_2, for access t to object O, there may be two candidate rules:

r_1: (S_1, O, t, p_1) and r_2: (S_2, O, t, p_2).

What does the system do? We consider some possible policies.

1. *The user chooses.* Some systems require a user to specify which class applies for a particular session. For example, a Multics user who works on several projects, or an RACF user who belongs to several groups, chooses one to provide the authorization context for a session.

2. *The rules have an ordering.* In Multics, rules for a specific user or project are used in preference to rules for the GENERAL (*) user or project. The rule (Smith.Inventory.*, F1, NULL) would be used rather than (*.Inventory.*, F1, READ) (so that Smith would be denied access to F1, although it would be accessible to all other members of the inventory

project). With this policy, more specific rules take precedence over less specific ones.

3. *The rules are combined.* A user can receive the union of the rights of the classes. This allows, for example, an overall minimum level of rights to be specified for the GENERAL user class. (This class has access to an UNPROTECTED class of objects.) These GENERAL rights are combined with each user's more specific individual rights. In our example, the request is valid if it is authorized by *either* r_1 or r_2. (This amounts to an OR of the predicates.)

Now suppose that O belongs to two *data* classes, O_1 and O_2, and that we have the candidate rules

r_1: (s, O_1, t, p_1) and r_2: (s, O_2, t, p_2).

Under the policy proposed in Reference 10, the rules would be combined by OR'ing the predicates (since a class receives the maximum of the rights of its parents). A policy of ANDing the predicates would be more restrictive, making it possible to specify maximum rights for objects in a class. Any access rules later specified for parents of the class could then only have the effect of further restricting access to the common objects. However, *removal* of a rule could then *increase* access, which might be dangerous.

Similar issues apply to hierarchical structures of object classes. Some possible policies are:

1. Rules for a class establish a *ceiling* for descendants of the class. Any rules for the descendants must be more restrictive. Such a policy might be appropriate where authorization rights were delegated, and different authorizers controlled subtrees of the hierarchy, since an authorizer could never grant access exceeding that for his or her highest level class. This policy again raises the danger that deletion of a lower-level rule may increase access.

2. Higher-level rules establish a *floor,* and lower-level rules may grant additional access. Although this policy is less appropriate for delegation, it may be very useful in simplifying authorization.

7.9.4 Built-in Structures and Rules

Hierarchical or graph-form class structuring reduces the number of decisions authorizers must make but still retains the flexibility (and complexity and lack of safety) of a discretionary access control mechanism. It is also possible to simplify authorization by reducing the number of security policies that the system supports. With a multilevel security policy, for example, the authorizer's job is reduced to specifying the security classifications and categories of the users and data. The allowed accesses are then calculated automatically by the system, using built-in rules.

7.10 CONSISTENCY AND EFFECT OF NEW RULES

An authorizer who is defining new rules should be able to determine their consistency with existing rules and their effect on the authorization state of the system. This is especially important when rules apply to classes or when rules are written for different architectural levels, as the effect of a new rule may not be immediately apparent.

7.10.1 Types of Access Rules

It is useful to distinguish three forms of access rule [10].

- *Stored access rule,* which is explicitly stored in the system.
- *Effective access rule,* which is actually applied to validate a request. This rule is not necessarily stored; it may be deduced from some of the stored rules. An effective rule exists for every possible (s, O, t).
- *Defined access rule,* which is specified to the system by the authorizer. The authorization policies of the system may cause that rule or other rules to be modified. A new state of stored rules is reached.

When the authorizer defines a new rule, the system must determine its effect on the authorization state. If the new rule is ambiguous, the authorizer should be given an opportunity to resolve the ambiguity.

Case 1

First, consider a defined rule r_d and assume that an existing effective rule, r_e, has the same (s, O, t) as r_d. Then, if $p_d \neq p_e$, the system must determine whether the authorizer's intention is to combine the predicates or to replace the existing predicate. The boolean connective used to combine the predicates may also need to be specified, although some systems have a predetermined way of connecting predicates.

If a new auxiliary procedure is defined for an existing condition, then the rule is inconsistent, since we allow for only one procedure per condition in an access rule. A system can remove this inconsistency either by always overriding the existing rule or by asking the authorizer to resolve the inconsistency.

Case 2

If there is no effective rule with a matching (s, O, t), normally the system can simply accept the new rule. In a system where access types are ordered, however, if there is a rule with the same subject and object, further ambiguities may have to be resolved.

7.10.2 Consistency between Levels

As indicated earlier, basic access rules should be specified at the conceptual level. A view defines how external data objects are structured from the underlying conceptual objects. In addition, views may also specify the operations that can be performed on the view. For example, in IMS different access types can be specified for each segment of a logical database record. When a new view is defined, the authorizer should examine the effective access rules for the view, which are derived from the underlying conceptual-level access rules. Depending on the functions to be performed using that view, the authorizer may wish to specify additional external access rules. A sensible policy is that these rules should be consistent with, that is, *more restrictive* than, the rules derived from the conceptual-level access rules. In general, it is not a trivial task to map rules from one level to another. Not only can the external *objects* have a complex structure but the external-level *operations* may map to different operations at the conceptual level [27].

7.11 SUMMARY

This chapter describes authorization from the viewpoint of the authorizer. Issues relating to each component of the access rule are discussed. Authorizers also need a set of facilities to make their work simpler in large and complex database systems. These facilities are for expressing access rules, displaying existing rules, determining the consistency and impact of new rules, and reducing the number of rules that have to be specified.

EXERCISES

7.1. A database contains the following relations:

```
ENROLLMENT (C#, S#, GRADE),
STUDENT (S#, NAME, ADDRESS, LEVEL), and
COURSE (C#, TEACHER, DESCRIPTION).
```

Indicate how to express in SQL and QBE a policy that allows the teacher of a course to give grades to his or her own students. Assume that a given course is taught by only one teacher, that one student can take several courses, and that a teacher can teach several courses.

7.2. Consider a database containing the table EMPLOYEE (NAME, MANAGER, SALARY, . . .). The policy of Company X is that managers can see the salary of any of their subordinates, including those who report to lower-level managers. Try to express this policy in access rules for QBE and SQL.

7.3. Design an authorization database, with relations to store the components of the extended access rule. Give an algorithm to expand a high-level command that gives a DBA the right to create, delete, and modify authorization rules. This command could be of the form "GRANT AUTHORIZATION TO dba_name" and should be reflected in access rules that apply to the authorization database.

7.4. Consider a request (s, O, t, p), where O belongs to multiple classes, and multiple access rules therefore apply. Do we have to combine the access types from the different rules to validate this request?

7.5. Consider the lattice of Fig. 6.9, which refers to medical, financial, and criminal data. How does it relate to the class-structuring concepts of this chapter? Considering only access control (ignoring information-flow control), set up some reasonable data classes and user classes for a public hospital, and write access rules.

REFERENCES AND BIBLIOGRAPHY

1. CODASYL Data Description Language. NBS Handbook 113, Nat. Bureau of Standards, Washington, D.C., June 1973.
2. CODASYL Data Description Language Committee, "Report." *Information Systems* **3**, 4 (1978), 247–320.
3. D. Cohen, "Design of Event-Driven Protection Mechanisms." Ph.D. Thesis, Computer Science Dept., Ohio State University, 1977.
4. R. W. Conway, W. L. Maxwell, and H. L. Morgan, "A technique for file surveillance." *Information Processing* **74** (Proceedings of the 1974 IFIPS Conference), 988–992. North-Holland, Amsterdam, 1974.
5. R. C. Daley and J. P. Donohue, "Security and Authorization—Semantics and Examples." *Data Security and Data Processing,* Vol. 4, IBM Corp. Form No. G320–1374 (June 1974), 135–149.

   Results of an MIT study on the security facilities of IBM's RSS (Resource Security System). Discusses need for decentralization of authorization functions, grouping of users and data, program-to-file authorization, relevant access types for this environment, and a list of suggestions on how to improve that system.
6. R. C. Daley and P. G. Neumann, "A general-purpose file system for sec-

ondary storage." *AFIPS Conf. Proc.* **27,** Part 1, 1965 FJCC, 213–229. AFIPS Press, Montvale, N.J., 1965.

7. Data Base Task Group. *Report* (April 1971). Available from ACM.

8. K. P. Eswaran, "Specifications, Implementations, and Interactions of a Trigger Subsystem in an Integrated Database System." Report RJ 1820, IBM Research Laboratory, San Jose, Calif., August 1976.

9. E. B. Fernandez, R. C. Summers, and C. D. Coleman, "An authorization model for a shared database." *Proc. 1975 ACM-SIGMOD Int. Conference,* ACM, New York, 1975, 23–31.

10. E. B. Fernandez, R. C. Summers, and T. Lang, "Definition and evaluation of access rules in data management systems." *Proc. 1st Int. Conf. on Very Large Data Bases,* Boston (1975), 268–285; available from ACM.

11. P. P. Griffiths and B. W. Wade, "An authorization mechanism for a relational database system." *ACM TODS* **1,** 3 (Sept. 1976), 242–255.

The authorization system for System R. The paper discusses authorization commands, representation of the authorization information, granting and revocation of rights, authorization checking, and the use of views for authorization.

12. M. A. Harrison, W. L. Ruzzo, and J. D. Ullman, "Protection in operating systems." *Comm. ACM* **19,** 8 (August 1976), 461–471.

13. H. R. Hartson, "Languages for Specifying Protection Requirements in Data Base Systems." Ph.D. Thesis, Computer Science Dept., Ohio State University, August 1975.

Develops a model of access control which is then used to define requirements for a family of authorization languages that can express different security policies. The model includes access specifications and request validation. History-keeping and auxiliary procedures are also considered (here and in Reference 14).

14. H. R. Hartson and D. K. Hsiao, "Full protection specifications in the semantic model for database protection languages." *Proc. ACM 1976 Annual Conference,* 90–95; available from ACM.

15. L. J. Hoffman, "The Formulary Model for flexible privacy and access controls." *AFIPS Conf. Proc.* **39,** 1971 FJCC, 587–601. AFIPS Press, Montvale, N.J., 1971.

16. IBM Corporation, "OS/VS2 TSO Command Language Reference." IBM Form No. GC28–0646.

17. IBM Corporation, "Query-by-Example: Terminal User's Guide." IBM Form No. SH20-2078-1. June, 1980.

18. C. Kellogg, P. Klahr, and L. Travis, "Deductive Planning and Pathfinding for Relational Data Bases." In *Logic and Data Bases,* J. Minker and H. Gallaire (Eds.). Plenum Press, 1978, 178–200.

19. R. J. Lipton and T. A. Budd, "On Classes of Protection Systems." In R. A.

DeMillo *et al.* (Eds.). *Foundations of Secure Computation.* Academic Press, New York, 1978, 281–296.

20. F. A. Manola and S. H. Wilson, "Data Security Implications of an Extended Subschema Concept." Report No. NRL 7905, Naval Research Laboratory, Washington, D.C. (July 1975). [Also in *Proceedings of the 2nd USA-Japan Computer Conf.,* 1975, 481–487.]

The security implications of the schema/subschema architecture are analyzed here, and some extensions are proposed. These include the ability to specify the legal operations on a subschema; facilities to support compile-time checking of these operations; and more powerful transformations from schema to subschema that allow application-oriented abstract objects to be defined.

21. F. A. Manola, "The CODASYL Data Description Language: Status and Activities, April 1976." Report No. NRL 8038, Naval Research Laboratory, Washington, D.C. (November 1976).

22. W. C. McGee, "The Information Management System IMS/VS. Part IV: Data communication facilities." *IBM Systems J.* **16,** 2 (1977), 136–147.

23. J. H. Saltzer, "Protection and the control of information sharing in Multics." *Comm. ACM* **17,** 7 (July 1974), 388–402.

24. J. H. Saltzer and M. D. Schroeder, "The protection of information in computer systems." *Proc. IEEE* **63,** 9 (Sept. 1975), 1278–1308.

25. M. Stonebraker and P. Rubinstein, "The INGRES protection system." *Proc. of the 1976 ACM Annual Conference,* 80–84; available from ACM.

The design decisions for the security system of INGRES are justified. In particular, the paper discusses the role and power of the DBA, the protection language, reasons for a centralized DBA, the policy about access violations, and the reason for not having auxiliary procedures.

26. R. C. Summers and E. B. Fernandez, "Data Description for a Shared Data Base: Views, Integrity, and Authorization." Report G320–2671, IBM Scientific Center, Los Angeles, Calif., August 1975.

This report specifies a DDL, with particular emphasis on the security aspects. Among the objects and facilities that can be described in the DDL are views, access rules, user classes and data classes, actions to enforce security, and administrative control over data.

27. C. Wood, R. C. Summers, and E. B. Fernandez, "Authorization in multilevel database models." *Information Systems* **4,** 2 (1979), 155–161.

8
Data Integrity

8.1 INTRODUCTION

An important complement to database security is database *integrity,* which is concerned with the correctness of the contents of the database. The integrity of the data can be compromised due to *failures*—events at which the system fails to provide normal operation or correct data. Failures are caused primarily by errors, which may originate in user programs, their interactions, or the system. In this chapter we discuss three main facets of integrity:

- semantic integrity,
- concurrency control, and
- recovery.

8.2 TRANSACTIONS

The concept of *transaction* plays a crucial role in integrity. The idea of a transaction as seen by an end user is familiar to the reader. An IMS user, for example, enters a transaction code to initiate a transaction, which terminates when the response is sent. A transaction usually results in a set of actions on the database that form a meaningful unit of work, such as reserving a seat on a flight or opening a new savings and loan account.

A transaction as seen by the user may involve more than one transaction from the system viewpoint. In this chapter we consider primarily the *system* meaning of transaction. A transaction should be designed and executed so that it either completes satisfactorily or makes no change to the database. If this practice is observed, a transaction is *atomic* when viewed from outside the transaction.

Now let us give a somewhat idealized definition of a transaction from the viewpoint of the *transaction management* component of a hypothetical DBMS [27]. The transaction manager makes use of a set of operations that can be performed on data objects. (These operations are provided by a data management component of the DBMS.) An instance of such an operation is called an *action*. A transaction is then a sequence of actions. Either the entire sequence completes successfully or the transaction has *no effect* on the database.

A transaction can fail to complete for various reasons, such as:

- An action violates a security or integrity constraint (for example, the initial balance in the new savings and loan account is less than the minimum balance needed for that type of account).
- The user cancels the transaction.
- An unrecoverable I/O error occurs (because of damaged media, for example).
- The system backs out the transaction to resolve a deadlock.
- The application program fails.
- The system crashes.

The essential points in the life of any transaction are *begin* and *commit* (or end). Until the transaction commits, none of its changes is seen by other transactions. If it never reaches the commit point, the transaction should have no effect on the database. A transaction may also *abort* (terminate without committing), *save* (save transaction status without committing), or *back up* (to a save point). If a failure occurs, the recovery procedure may have to *undo* or *redo* the transaction.

Although some systems (INGRES, for example) do not explicitly define transactions, the transaction concept still applies. In the case of INGRES, each command is treated as a transaction.

The concepts of atomicity and commitment also apply to much larger units of processing than the typical transaction [14]. Consider the sequence of Fig. 8.1, for example. Holding the paychecks (not committing them) until the audit and stock-purchase programs have been run makes it possible for them to be easily redone if those programs discover errors. The boundary around these programs establishes a *sphere of control*. Unfortunately, current operating systems and DBMSs provide little support for these larger spheres of control, which are typically managed by manual or application-specific procedures.

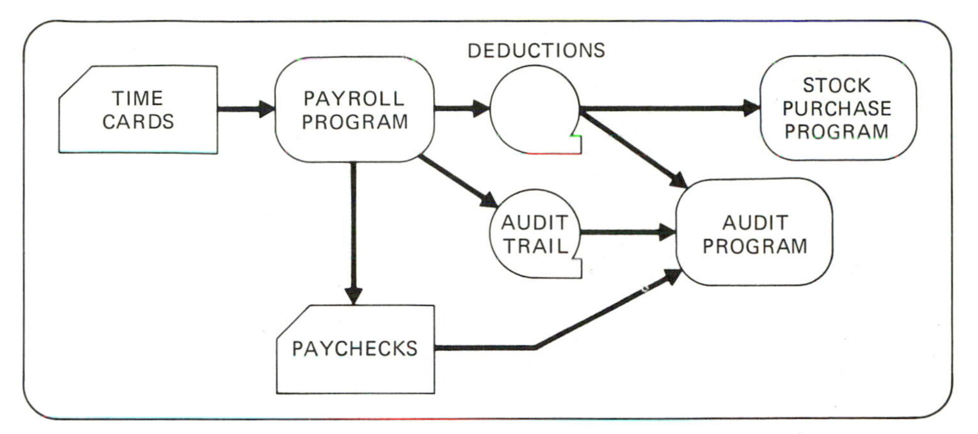

Fig. 8.1. A sphere of control.

8.3 SEMANTIC INTEGRITY

8.3.1 Basic Concepts

Semantic integrity is concerned with ensuring that the database is correct even though users or application programs try to modify it incorrectly. We use the generic term *maintenance operation* for any operation that can modify the state of the database, such as UPDATE, INSERT, or DELETE. Assuming that the database security system prevents unauthorized access and hence malicious attempts to corrupt data, most potential errors will be caused by incorrect input, incorrect programs, or lack of understanding on the part of the user. Traditionally, most integrity checking has been performed by the application programs and by periodic auditing of the database. Some of the problems of relying on application programs for integrity checking are:

- Checking is likely to be incomplete because the application programmer may not be aware of the semantics of the complete database;
- Each application program must *trust* other programs that modify the database—one rogue program could corrupt the whole database;
- Code to enforce the same integrity constraints occurs in a number of programs, wasting programming effort and risking inconsistencies;
- The criteria for integrity are buried in procedures and are therefore hard to understand and control;
- Maintenance operations performed by users of high-level query languages cannot be controlled.

Most of these errors could be detected by auditing. However, the time lag in detecting errors by auditing can also cause problems, because:

- It may be difficult to trace the source of an error and hence correct it;
- The incorrect data may have been used in various ways, causing errors to propagate through the database and into the environment.

As the database has a meaning independent of any specific use, a better approach is for the DBMS to perform that part of integrity checking which is independent of the application. Those aspects that refer to the semantics of individual applications can be dealt with separately (see Section 8.3.10). Although current DBMSs provide little support for semantic integrity, some valuable work has been done on specifying the nature of such support, and we describe that work in this section.

The semantics or meaning of a database is in part a matter of shared understandings among the users, in part implied by the data structures used, and in part expressed as *integrity constraints*. These constraints are explicitly stated by persons with data-control responsibility. Examples of constraints in an educational database might be:

- Student identifiers are six-digit numbers;
- Course grades are A, B, C, and D;
- Students can be enrolled only in courses that are scheduled;
- Only one class may be scheduled in a room at a time.

A *validation mechanism* checks changes to the database for compliance with these constraints, and predefined procedures are performed when a potential violation of one or more of the integrity constraints is detected. Note however that the correctness of the database is still not guaranteed. For instance, a teacher might incorrectly specify a student grade but, as long as it was a legal one (i.e., A through D), it would still be accepted by the DBMS. Integrity mechanisms can only ensure that the data in the database is reasonable.

8.3.2 Types of Integrity Constraints

Integrity constraints may be classified in a number of different ways [12, 17].

- *Record or set.* One classification concerns whether a constraint applies to an individual record (or tuple) or to a set of records. An example of a *record constraint* is:

All salaries must be less than $100,000.

Examples of *set constraints* are:

a) The set of managers must be contained in the set of employees; and

b) The average salary of professors must be less than $20,000.

- *Static or transitional.* Constraints can specify either correct states of the database (*static constraints*) or correct transitions. The previous examples are all static. An example of a *transitional constraint* is:

  A new salary must exceed an old salary.

- *Selective or general.* Constraints may be enforced only upon the occurrence of certain maintenance operations (for example, only after a deletion), or at any time.

- *Immediate or deferred.* A user will often make a sequence of related changes to the database. The database is in a legal state at both the start and end of such a transaction, but certain constraints are necessarily violated at points within the sequence. For example, consider a transaction that transfers money from one account to another. Once the first account is debited, certain control balances may be incorrect until the second account is credited. Constraints that hold after any maintenance operation are known as *immediate constraints.* Those that hold only after the completion of a transaction are known as *deferred constraints.*

- *Unconditional or conditional.* Finally, constraints may be enforced only when a certain condition is true. For example:

  The salaries of all clerks must be less than $20,000.

  This constraint is enforced on only those employee records where the employee is a clerk.

Figure 8.2 summarizes this classification of constraints. A further distinction discussed below is between explicit and implicit constraints. Constraints may also be classified [12] as *range* (values in a particular attribute must fall within certain bounds), *format,* and *statistical* (using statistical functions).

Classification of constraints
1. Single record or set.
2. Static or transitional.
3. General or selective.
4. Immediate or deferred.
5. Unconditional or conditional.

Fig. 8.2. Classification of integrity constraints.

8.3.3 Validation of Database Maintenance Operations

Validation may be performed at different times depending on the type and specification of the integrity constraints. The possible times are:

T1: after a primitive database maintenance request,
T2: at specific points within a transaction,

T3: after the completion of a transaction,
T4: on request from the DBA or auditor.

Transitional constraints must be checked at T1 unless a generalized audit trail (discussed in Chapter 9) makes it possible to check at T4. Enforcement at T2 can be used, for example, to prevent a long transaction being backed out because some integrity failure is detected only at the end of the transaction.

8.3.4 Violation of Integrity Constraints

If the integrity constraint being checked is not satisfied by the intended changes to the data, we say an *integrity violation* has occurred. A number of corrective actions are possible depending on when the violation is detected.

- If the check is made at time T1, the request is rejected and a message is returned to the program indicating that the request was in error. If the request implies changes for a *set* of values, it may be useful for the system to return a list of the values that violated some integrity assertion. This is done, for example, in INGRES, where a relation ERRORS stores all the tuples that failed the integrity constraints; this relation is accessible to the user's program for inspection.
- If the check is made at time T2, only that part of the transaction after the previous integrity check need be repeated. The source of error is then restricted to the set of maintenance operations after that point.
- If the check is made at time T3, the whole transaction is backed out, returning the database to its initial state. In this case it may be impossible to determine which individual maintenance request is in error.
- If the check is performed at time T4, it may not even be possible to determine which transaction caused the error. Automatic correction is in general not possible. The best action is probably a warning message to the DBA, accompanied by reports on the current state of the database and on the transactions that have been processed since the previous check. A generalized audit trail could provide this information about transactions and could help determine what corrections are necessary.

8.3.5 Model of Integrity

We can define a simple model for integrity that parallels the access-control model described in Section 6.2. In both cases we have rules or constraints that need to be checked when the database is accessed. The main difference is that the rules in the case of integrity apply independently of the subject making the request. We can define an integrity rule as a tuple (O, t, c, p, ap), where O is the *data object* to which the rule applies, t indicates for which *access type* the rule will be invoked, c is a predicate expressing a *condition* that must be true in order for p to apply to O, p is an *assertion* (semantic constraint) that must be true for an occurrence of the object O, and ap is an auxiliary procedure that specifies what the system will do if p is not true.

This model allows us to specify the different types of integrity constraints described above. For example, an integrity constraint referring to sets, such as "Enrolled students must be registered students," would be expressed as two rules. In one a predicate, specifying "the set of enrolled students is included in the set of registered students," is associated with the object "enrolled students." In the other the predicate "the set of registered students includes the set of enrolled students" is associated with the object "registered students." For transitional constraints the predicate would refer to "old values" and "new values." Specifying the appropriate access type in the rule allows the constraint to be checked only for specific types of maintenance operations. The condition c can be used to specify whether the constraint is to be applied immediately or deferred to the end of a transaction or to a periodic audit. It also allows constraints to apply only to certain data occurrences. The condition EMP.DEPT = '60G', for example, would make the constraint apply only to the employees of department 60G. The auxiliary procedure can specify, for example: deny the request, back out the transaction, or log the request and notify the DBA.

8.3.6 Auxiliary Procedures

The auxiliary procedure component of the rule suggests the possibility of specifying a procedure (sometimes known as a *triggered action* [17]) to be invoked whenever a specified maintenance operation is executed, or whenever a certain state of the database is reached. Some possible uses of auxiliary procedures are:

- To perform integrity checks, either because the system does not support integrity assertions or because the checks are too complex to be written as assertions;
- To log selectively; and
- To allow the database to maintain itself automatically.

As an example of this third use, if a new employee tuple is inserted, a triggered procedure could automatically increase the count of employees in the department. In the rule to specify such action:

O = employee relation
t = INSERT
c = true
p = false
ap = procedure to increment and decrement appropriate counts.

Auxiliary procedures may be invoked either synchronously with the maintenance request or asynchronously (running as a separate transaction, for example). In the synchronous case the system must be prepared to handle a failure of the procedure to complete normally. While auxiliary procedures provide a very general integrity mechanism, they also raise a number of problems, not all of which have satisfactory solutions. Some of these problems are:

1. Integrity or security violations within auxiliary procedures could result in a never-ending sequence of procedures invoking procedures.
2. The proper access rights of the invoked procedures are an issue: Should these be the rights of the invoker of the triggering maintenance operation or the rights of the DBA who specified the auxiliary procedure?
3. Triggering of maintenance procedures results in a somewhat confusing division of responsibility between the user (or programmer) and the DBA. The user has to be aware in general of the procedures that will be invoked by a maintenance operation. For instance, in the previous example, the user might be unaware that the employee count had been automatically updated, and might update it a second time.

CODASYL systems such as IDMS implement auxiliary procedures (called database procedures) with the equivalent of c = true and p = false.

8.3.7 Implicit Integrity Constraints

Some integrity constraints need not be explicitly stated because they are built into the data structures themselves. For example, in record-based DBMSs each record occurrence must conform to the record-type specification. Thus all fields specified in the type description must be present in each record occurrence (assuming that null values are not allowed). In most DBMSs that support the concept of a key, an inserted record is checked for a unique key value, thus preventing duplicates. On update, changing the value of the key is not allowed.

Data structures also implicitly enforce constraints between record types. For example the hierarchical data structure in IMS enforces a one-to-many relationship between parent and dependent segments. This means that, if a root segment representing teachers has dependent segments representing courses, the system automatically enforces the constraint that every course has one and only one teacher.

In the relational model a fundamental kind of integrity constraint between sets of attributes is *functional dependency*. (An attribute Y of a relation R is functionally dependent on attribute X of R if and only if each X-value in R determines exactly one value for Y.) While most relational DBMSs do not support the explicit specification of functional dependencies, the relational schema can be designed so that many functional dependencies are implicitly represented. The DBMS can then preserve these constraints by ensuring that all keys within a relation are unique. There are in general many other integrity constraints applicable to relations besides functional dependencies. System R, which does not have the concept of keys, requires all integrity constraints to be explicitly specified. Explicit constraints can often clarify the semantics of the database.

Since a database is a model of some real-world system, it would be convenient to be able to specify constraints in terms of those real-world structures rather than in terms of the record-oriented structures of the hierarchical, network, and relational data models. In order to do this we need a data model that can more directly represent the real world. Many different models have been proposed [47], although usable systems seem some way off. Codd, for example, has proposed some extensions to the relational model that allow more semantics to be captured [9]. In particular, the proposals support:

1. Meaningful units that are as small as possible—*atomic semantics*; and
2. Meaningful units that are larger than the usual n-ary relation—*molecular semantics*.

Support for atomic semantics includes the ability of the DBMS to represent the existence of an entity even if a key has not been assigned or after it has ceased to have one (for example, it may be necessary to start storing information about a new employee before an employee number is assigned).

Support for molecular semantics includes two kinds of *abstraction: generalization* and *aggregation* [48]. In generalization, a set of similar objects is regarded as a generic object. For example, trucks and cars are both considered types of motorized vehicles although they do not necessarily have identical sets of attributes. In aggregation, a relationship between objects is regarded as a higher-level object. For example, a reservation is a relationship between a person, a hotel, and a date. A generic object is specified as simultaneously an aggregation and a generalization (see Fig. 8.3). Since the relations in the database now fit together

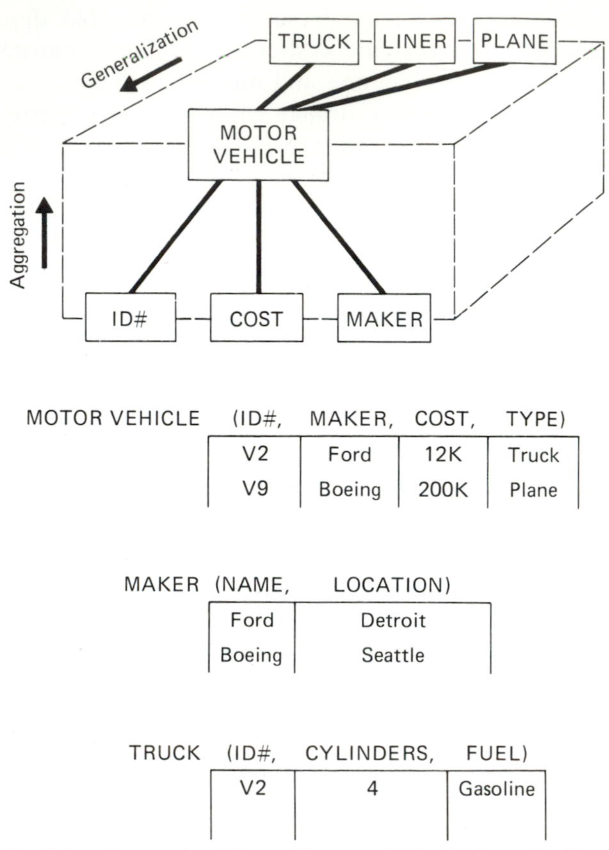

MOTOR VEHICLE

ID#	MAKER	COST	TYPE
V2	Ford	12K	Truck
V9	Boeing	200K	Plane

MAKER

NAME	LOCATION
Ford	Detroit
Boeing	Seattle

TRUCK

ID#	CYLINDERS	FUEL
V2	4	Gasoline

Fig. 8.3. A generic object—Motor vehicle. [Adapted with permission from course materials of J. Smith and D. C. P. Smith.]

in a meaningful way, there is a set of fundamental, implicit, integrity constraints called *relational invariants*. These apply to all relations and constrain them according to their roles as generic objects. In Fig. 8.3, for example, inserting a new motor vehicle that is a Ford truck would require the same individual to occur in the TRUCK relation and Ford to appear in the MAKER relation.

There are some advantages in incorporating constraints as part of the data model since, if all integrity constraints are made explicitly, then typically:

- There will be a large number of constraints;
- It will be difficult to ensure that the constraints are consistent;
- There may be a large performance overhead associated with the enforcement of the constraints.

The DBMSs of the future are likely to support richer data structures (such as generalization), allowing the more complex integrity constraints to be built into the data model. Even simpler integrity constraints such as range limitations could become part of the definition of data abstractions [53].

8.3.8 Expression of Integrity Constraints

Some means of specifying explicit integrity constraints to the DBMS is required. In IMS, data descriptions provide this means. Thus the DBDs contain, for example, the specifications of which keys are unique and rules concerning the deletion and creation of logical parents [34]. CODASYL also uses the DDL to specify values and formatting for data items in the CHECK clause. Checking is performed whenever a value is changed or added. These *item* constraints may specify that:

- The data value is (or is not) equal to some prespecified value, or falls (or not) within some range of permissible values;
- Data item value is not NULL;
- A procedure is to be invoked, which can do additional checking of any kind.

A CALL clause on the description of a schema, area, record, or set can specify a user-written procedure to be invoked for checking either before or after the request is executed. The STRUCTURAL CONSTRAINT clause on a set description can constrain owner and member record occurrences to have the same value in specified fields [36].

Integrity constraints have been proposed for QBE [55] but not implemented in its first commercial version. These constraints are specified in a way similar to authorization rules. If the employee relation EMP has attributes NAME, JOB, and SALARY, then the constraint that all salaries must be less than $100,000 is specified as follows:

EMP	NAME	JOB	SALARY
I.CONSTR. I.			< 100000

The constraint that upon update the new salary value must be greater than the old is specified by:

EMP	NAME	JOB	SALARY
I.CONSTR(U.) I.	JONES		> S1
I.	JONES		S1

The full range of integrity constraints described earlier can be expressed, except that there is no explicit distinction between immediate and deferred constraints. The constraints are always applied after completion of all the operations that have been specified on the screen. (This set of operations thus forms a transaction.) The same constraint may therefore sometimes be applied immediately and sometimes be deferred, depending on the particular query being executed. A problem in the formulation of integrity assertions in QBE is the fact that if a constraint applies to several relations, it must be split among them. This might confuse someone trying to inspect the set of assertions that apply to some data item.

Use of the SQL query language to specify integrity constraints has also been proposed [17]. As an example, the assertion that all employee salaries are less than $100,000 is written:

```
ASSERT A1 ON EMP: SALARY < 100000
```

where A1 is the name of the assertion and EMP is the name of the relation containing the attribute SALARY. The assertion that whenever an employee's salary is updated the new salary must be larger than the old is specified by:

```
ASSERT A2 ON UPDATE OF EMP (SALARY):
          NEW SALARY > OLD SALARY
```

Conditions can also be included, as shown in the following example:

```
ASSERT A3 ON EMP: IF JOB = 'CLERK' THEN
          SALARY < 15000
```

Transitional integrity constraints are always checked immediately. Static constraints are checked at the completion of a transaction unless the word IMMEDIATE is specified or the command ENFORCE INTEGRITY is given.

Other languages to express semantic integrity constraints are proposed in [26] for a COBOL-like syntax, in [19], in [30], and in [49], where the INGRES approach is presented.

8.3.9 Efficient Validation of Integrity Constraints

Efficient techniques for integrity checking are badly needed if we are to have commercial systems that support integrity assertions. We discuss here the results of some research in this area. Hammer and Sarin [31] propose a compile-time assertion processor that analyzes each database request in conjunction with the applicable static integrity assertions. An *error predicate* is defined as the complement of the assertion predicate; if it is true, the assertion is violated. The *error set* is the set of object occurrences that violate the assertion, and the integrity mechanism must identify this set.

The assertion processor analyzes the predicate together with the request and sets *goals* that it tries to prove. For example, consider the

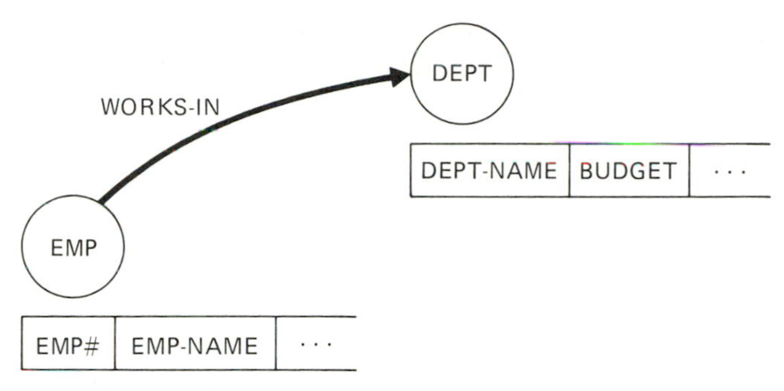

Fig. 8.4. Sample database for assertion processor.

database of Fig. 8.4 and the assertion "an employee's salary cannot exceed 1/10 the budget of the department he or she works in" with the request "set employee e1's salary to S." The assertion processor will try to prove for each employee that (1) budget is nondecreasing and (2) salary is nonincreasing.

The first goal is always true, since the request does not affect budget and since the assertion is always assumed to be true before the request is executed. The second goal can be proved about every employee except e1. So the processor generates a test to be performed at execution time: new salary is less than old salary. If this is true, it has been proved that salary is nonincreasing and no further test is needed. In this case it is not necessary to access the DEPT entity, since the test can be performed on one occurrence of EMP. Only if the goal is not proved is it necessary to evaluate the error predicate.

Other work taking a similar approach is described in [22], and the different approach used by INGRES is described in [49].

8.3.10 Application-dependent Integrity

So far we have been concerned with integrity constraints that are purely dependent on the semantics of the database. We now turn our attention to integrity considerations that are dependent on the application program or, more precisely, on the mapping between the application semantics and the database semantics.

Maintenance operations through views

An application program specifies operations on data structures defined in the program view. These operations are translated by the DBMS to operations applied to the *schema*. In this section we are concerned that the semantics of the application are correctly preserved in this translation. Two alternative approaches to this problem are: (1) restrict maintenance operations on views to those that are simple and unambiguous to translate, and (2) define the operations and their translations as part of the view.

Implemented systems take the first approach. System R, for example, disallows updates on views involving joins. Dayal and Bernstein also take the first approach in their analysis of the problem for relational database systems [15]. Their criteria for a maintenance operation on a view to be correctly translatable are:

- There is a unique set of operations on the schema that produces the desired effect;
- There are no extraneous operations on the schema;
- There are no side effects on the view; and
- The semantic integrity of the database is preserved.

(An earlier discussion of these criteria is found in Reference 5.) As an illustration, consider the two relations LECTURER and COURSE depicted in Fig. 8.5. A view COURSE_LECT can then be defined that is the equijoin of these two relations.

As an example of an extraneous update, consider the insertion into COURSE_LECT of the tuple < C4, L1, SMITH >. This translates to an insertion < C4, L1, – > into the COURSE relation (where – stands for undefined). If, instead, the tuple < C4, L1, MATH > were inserted, there would be an extraneous update to the COURSE_NAME field. Such

LECTURER RELATION

LECT #	LECT_NAME
L1	SMITH
L2	JONES

COURSE RELATION

COURSE #	LECT #	COURSE_NAME
C1	L1	MATH
C2	L3	PHYSICS
C3	L2	CHEMISTRY

COURSE_LECT VIEW

COURSE #	LECT #	LECT_NAME
C1	L1	SMITH
C3	L2	JONES

Fig. 8.5. Lecturer and course relations and their join.

updates are undesirable because they are not required for the view update.

Now consider the insertion of the tuple < C4, L3, DOE >. This translates to the insertion of two tuples: < C4, L3, – > into the COURSE relation and < L3, DOE > into LECTURER. However, a new tuple now appears in the COURSE_LECT view: namely < C2, L3, DOE >. This is a side effect on the view, which may be undesirable because it is not requested by the user.

In the following example from Reference 8, there is no possible operation on the schema that produces the right effect. A deletion or insertion operation on a view formed by the join of some base relations cannot be reflected back to those relations. For example, let the relations R(A, B) and S(B, C), be equijoined on the common attribute B to produce T(A, B, C). If at a given moment the values for R and S are:

R(A B)	S(B C)
s a	a u
t a	a v
. . .	. . .

then, T must be

T(A B C)
s a u
s a v
t a u
t a v
. . .

If a user wants to delete row (t, a, v) from T there is no way to reflect this to R and S without producing a side effect on T, such as also deleting (t, a, u).

Dayal and Bernstein argue for the uniqueness criterion because of the difficulty of choosing between ambiguous alternatives, although integrity constraints sometimes will permit some alternatives to be discarded. They conclude that maintenance operations through views are possible in only a very few situations. These possibilities are likely to be even fewer when the data models used at the external level differ from that used at the conceptual level.

In many situations, however, these restrictions may be considered unacceptable by users of the database [1, 7]. If an operation on a view is meaningful to a user, there should be some way to unambiguously convey the intention of that operation to the DBMS. One approach, which overcomes the uniqueness problem, is to include a functional definition of all allowed maintenance operations in the definition of the view. An additional benefit of this approach is that the user need no longer be constrained to use the low-level maintenance operations defined in the data model. More meaningful operations can be defined that are tailored to the specific application.

As a simple example consider a stock-control database, which contains for each part the quantity received and the quantity shipped. A warehouse controller has a view of the database that contains a quantity-on-hand field; this field is materialized by the DBMS by subtracting the quantity received from the quantity shipped. An update to quantity-on-hand may therefore have two intentions: to update quantity received or to update quantity shipped. Thus two update functions can be defined for the view and given meaningful names such as RECEIPT and SHIP.

The use of these operational mapping functions may be considered as an application of abstract data types to database processing [53]. Abstract data types have been supported by some programming languages such as SIMULA 67 [11] and CLU [35] for a number of years. They allow data structures and associated operations to be defined so that the underlying representation of the structure is hidden from the user of the abstract data type.

Input validation

Input data can be edited for correctness at a number of different times. If the input is entered at an intelligent terminal, simple editing can often be performed by the terminal; for example, checking that fields are all numeric and the correct length. More complex editing (discussed in Chapter 9) may be performed by the application program. Finally, if the input data is used to update the database, the relevant integrity constraints will be enforced.

Although some of this editing may be redundant, in general it is not desirable to eliminate terminal and application program editing. For example, in a data-entry application the terminal user may need immediate notification of typing errors and there may well be a significant time lag before the data fields are entered into the data base. However, it should be possible for systems software to eliminate the need for the redundant *specification* of the editing rules.

8.4 CONCURRENCY CONTROL

Even if the database served only a single user at a time, its semantic integrity would have to be protected. In this section we turn to some problems that arise because a number of users access data concurrently.

We consider both integrity of applications and the more crucial integrity of the database itself. In order to discuss concurrency, we must first introduce an operating system concept: the *process*. For our purposes, it is sufficient to think of a process as a stream of activity (a program in execution) that proceeds in parallel with other such streams. A transaction may be represented by a single process or by a set of processes all working on behalf of the transaction.

The classical example of integrity loss due to concurrency is the "lost update" problem. Suppose that airplane seats are being reserved without any special provision for concurrency. Assume also the following actions:

- A_1: Read the number of available seats
- A_2: Write the number of available seats

Each transaction, T, reads the number of seats, decrements it, and then writes the number of seats. The concept of a *schedule* is useful in studying the effects of concurrency when the actions of several transactions can be interleaved in various ways. A schedule is a specific ordering of these actions. If actions A_1 and A_2 are done by transactions T_1 and T_2 according to the following schedule, no updates are lost:

- T_1, A_1
  T_1, A_2
  T_2, A_1
  T_2, A_2

This is a *serial* schedule, but for performance reasons we often wish to interleave the actions of different transactions. With the following interleaved schedule, the update of T_1 is lost.

- T_1, A_1
  T_2, A_1
  T_1, A_2
  T_2, A_2

A good concurrency facility attempts to solve more than this problem, however. It also ensures that one user does not see inconsistent data as a result of concurrent updating by other users. Consider, for example, a report produced for a medical clinic. The report has a heading giving the number of clinic patients, followed by the names of the patients. It would be inconsistent to print the number 55 followed by 56 names. This problem is sometimes called *inconsistent analysis*.

Another requirement of the concurrency facility is to provide information for recovery.

It is important to meet these requirements—data integrity, consistency of analysis, and recovery support—in a way that is easy to use and that performs well.

We assume here that a transaction, when successfully executed by itself, preserves integrity; that is, it does not violate either the semantic integrity constraints or the implicit assumptions that systems often rely on (such as the summary total number of clinic patients is equal to the number of patient names). We concentrate on what is needed to ensure that a *set* of such transactions, run concurrently, also preserves integrity. This has been called the *correct synchronization* problem [46]. A system of concurrent transactions is defined to be correctly synchronized if it is equivalent to a system where the transactions run *serially*—equivalent in the sense that the same final state is reached and the same outputs are produced. Such a system is *integrity-preserving.*

8.4.1 Concurrency Problems

Three forms of inconsistency can result from concurrency: *lost updates, dirty read,* and *unrepeatable read* (see Fig. 8.6). An example of lost update has been given. Lost updates can also result from backing up or *undoing* a transaction. If transactions T_1 and T_2 have both updated the same data object, and T_1 is undone, then the update of T_2 is lost.

If T_2 reads a value that has been changed by T_1, and T_1 then aborts, T_2 will have read *dirty data*—data not yet committed.

An *unrepeatable read* occurs if T_2 reads the same item both before and after T_1 changes the item. Inconsistent analysis is a result of unrepeatable read.

We can now define three different *levels of consistency,* corresponding to which types of consistency are guaranteed, or (to put it differently) which consistency problems are prevented.

Lost update	T_1:	Update X
	T_2:	Update Ⓧ . . . . lost
	T_1:	Backup
Dirty read	T_1:	Update X
	T_2:	Read Ⓧ . . . . "unreal"
	T_1:	Abort
Unrepeatable read	T_2:	Read X
	T_1:	Update Ⓧ . . . . inconsistent
	T_2:	Read X

Fig. 8.6. Types of inconsistency due to concurrency.

- Level 1 prevents lost updates;
- Level 2 also prevents reading dirty data;
- Level 3 also prevents unrepeatable reads.

Some DBMSs allow users to *select* a consistency level for specific data applications. The main argument for allowing lower levels of consistency is to increase concurrency, thereby increasing throughput.

The approach most commonly used to eliminate consistency problems is *locking*.

8.4.2 Locking

The DBMS can use the locking facilities that the operating system provides so that multiple processes can synchronize their concurrent access of shared resources. A lock is associated with each shared object (Fig. 8.7). An *exclusive* lock can be granted to only one process at a time; a *shared* lock may be granted to multiple processes, but a given object cannot be locked in shared and exclusive *mode* at the same time: that is, shared and exclusive modes are *incompatible*; they *conflict*. (Some systems provide other locking modes as well.) The operating system usually provides *Lock* and *Unlock* commands for requesting and releasing locks. If a lock request cannot be granted, the process is *suspended* until the request can be granted. In general, a shared lock is requested for reading an object and an exclusive lock for writing.

If transactions do not follow very restrictive locking rules, *deadlock* can occur. Consider the following schedule of exclusive locks (where each transaction is represented by one process):

Step 1: Transaction 1: Lock A
Step 2: Transaction 2: Lock B
Step 3: Transaction 1: Lock B
Step 4: Transaction 2: Lock A

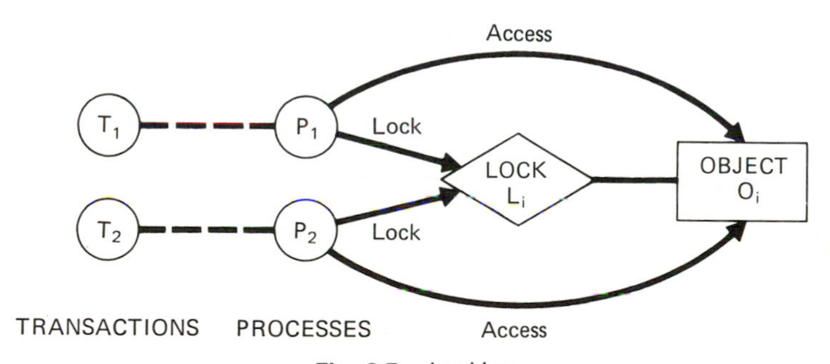

Fig. 8.7. Locking.

At Step 3 Transaction 1 is suspended (since Transaction 2 holds the lock on B). At Step 4 Transaction 2 is suspended (since Transaction 1 holds the lock on A). Both transactions are now suspended, neither can release its lock, and a deadlock exists. This is sometimes called "deadly embrace."

The deadlock problem can be solved either by *preventing* deadlocks or by *detecting* them after they occur and taking steps to resolve them. Deadlock can be prevented by placing restrictions on the way locks are requested. For example, if a transaction requests all its locks at once and obtains either all or none, no deadlock can occur. This restriction may be too severe, however, in situations where a transaction must lock some items before it can determine which other items it needs.

If deadlocks occur rarely, deadlock detection may be a better approach. Deadlocks can be detected by examining the status of locks, and algorithms to do this efficiently have been developed [27]. (A cruder technique is to observe activity coming to a halt at terminals.) Once detected, the deadlock can be resolved by aborting a transaction and rescheduling it. Methods for selecting the best transaction to abort have also been developed. The fact that deadlock has occurred should be transparent to the user except for perhaps a lengthening of the response time.

8.4.3 Integrity-preserving Schedules

If transactions follow certain rules, integrity can be preserved, and recovery from deadlock can be simplified. Let us define a schedule as the actions of a set of transactions, with an *ordering* of all conflicting actions (Fig. 8.8). (Two actions conflict if they act on the same object and are not

Schedule 1	Schedule 2
T_1: A_1 (r)	T_1: A_1 (r)
T_1: A_2 (w)	T_2: A_1 (r)
T_2: A_1 (r)	T_1: A_2 (w)
T_2: A_2 (w)	T_2: A_2 (w)

Ordering "conflicting" actions:

Schedule 1: T_1/r → T_1/w → T_2/r → T_2/w

Schedule 2: T_1/r → T_1/w; T_2/r → T_1/w; T_1/w → T_2/w

Fig. 8.8. Partial ordering of schedules.

Example Transactions

T_1 A: = A + 100 T_2 A: = A * 2
B: = B + 100 B: = B * 2

Example Schedules

S_1:

T_1 A: = A + 100
T_2 A: = A * 2
T_1 B: = B + 100
T_2 B: = B * 2

$T_1 \longrightarrow T_2$
A,B
Consistent

S_2:

T_1 A: = A + 100
T_2 A: = A * 2
T_2 B: = B * 2
T_1 B: = B + 100

T_1 ⇄ T_2 (A from T_1 to T_2; B from T_2 to T_1)
Inconsistent

S_3:

T_1 A: = A + 100
T_1 B: = B + 100
T_2 A: = A * 2
T_2 B: = B * 2

$T_1 \longrightarrow T_2$
A,B
Serial

Fig. 8.9. Three schedules for two transactions. [From Eswaran *et al.* [18]. Copyright 1976, Association for Computing Machinery, Inc., reprinted by permission.]

both reads.) Figure 8.9 shows three possible schedules for transactions T_1 and T_2. The transactions can serialize their actions through locking.

A *dependency graph* can be used to determine whether a schedule preserves integrity. Nodes of the graph represent transactions, and an edge from T_a to T_b means that T_b *depends* on T_a; that is, some action of T_b takes some of its inputs from an *earlier* action of T_a. Figure 8.9 gives the graphs for the three schedules. It can be shown that a schedule is integrity-preserving if the graph contains no cycles. This means that, for any transaction T_i, all the transactions that T_i depends on precede it in the graph, and all those that depend on T_i follow it. The graph for such a schedule is the same as the graph for an equivalent *serial* schedule—one where the transactions run one at a time. (Certain schedules whose graph contains a cycle may also be integrity-preserving [3, 42], and it is necessary to preserve any inherent time-ordering among the transactions.)

8.4.4 Lock Protocols to Preserve Integrity

A *lock protocol* is a set of rules to be followed by transactions in locking and unlocking objects. One such protocol, called the *two-phase* lock protocol, has been shown to be integrity-preserving [18]. If all transactions follow this protocol, only integrity-preserving schedules can occur. The protocol requires (1) that each object be locked before access, and (2) that once the first Unlock is issued, no Lock be issued. The transaction

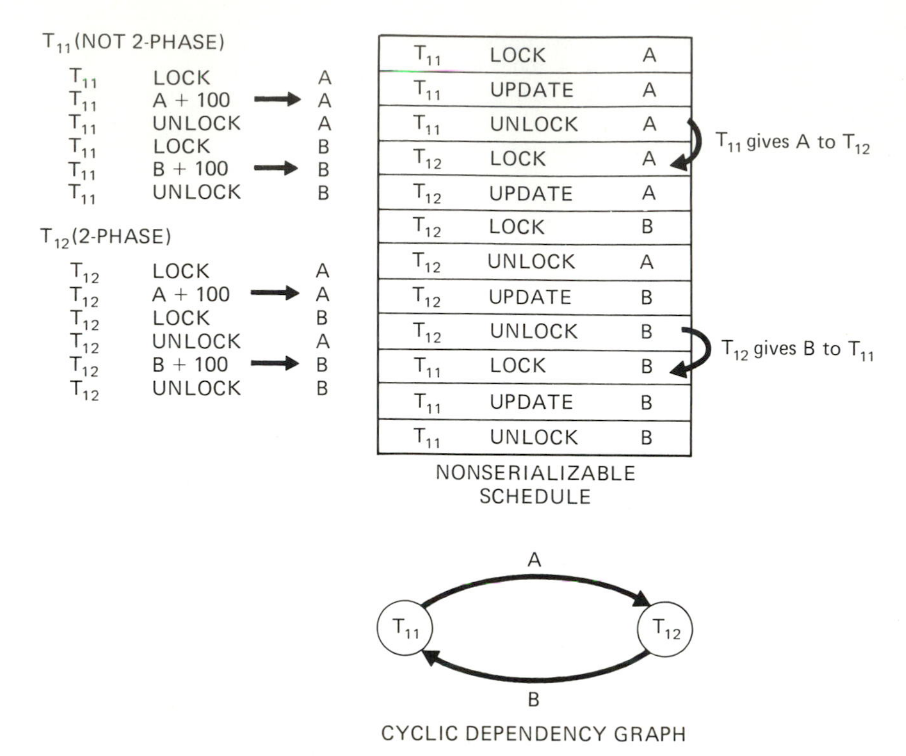

Fig. 8.10. Two-phase lock protocol. [From Eswaran *et al.* [18]. Copyright 1976, Association for Computing Machinery, Inc., adapted by permission.]

thus has two phases: a *growing* phase, during which locks are acquired, and a *shrinking* phase, during which locks are released. To see that rule 2 is necessary, consider Fig. 8.10. T_{11} is a version of T_1 that does not obey rule 2 (it locks B after unlocking A). T_{12} *is* two-phase. In a possible schedule, T_{12} depends on T_{11} for A, and T_{11} depends on T_{12} for B. The dependency graph contains a cycle. The schedule is not equivalent to any serial schedule and is therefore not integrity-preserving.

In practice exclusive locks are usually held to the commit point. This stricter protocol simplifies recovery by preventing dependencies among transactions; then, if a transaction does not successfully complete, undoing it does not require the undoing of other transactions that have used its results. (This propagation of backing out is sometimes called a *cascading* or *domino* effect.)

8.4.5 Granularity of Locking

An important issue is how large a unit should be locked at one time. At one extreme there is only one unit—the entire database—and transactions run serially. At the other extreme, the unit could be a field of a record.

SYSTEM	UNITS OF LOCKING
IMS/VS (with program isolation)	Segment type Segment instance
DMS1100	Area Page within area
System R	Segment Page Record
CODASYL	Area

Fig. 8.11. DBMS locking granularity.

Intermediate examples are a DBTG area, a file, or a column of a relation. Small units imply fewer incompatible lock requests and therefore greater concurrency. Since there are many such units, however, a cost is paid in lock management overhead—in both storage and processing time. Figure 8.11 summarizes the *locking granularity* provided by several DBMSs—that is, how small a unit of locking is supported.

There is evidence from simulation experiments [44, 45] that a rather coarse granularity (such as 10 granules for a 5000-item database) is best for large transactions (accessing 5 to 10% of database items) or for transactions performing mainly sequential access. For other cases, finer granularity was found to be superior. The choice of granularity depends on the type of applications and the way they use the database. Simulation results depend on the number of different database items used by transactions and the locking strategy (whether locks are acquired in advance or as needed).

To allow a DBMS to support a *range* of granularities, Gray *et al.* [28] have proposed a *hierarchical lock* scheme. In this scheme, the various levels of granularity correspond to levels in a hierarchy. A lock request can refer to any level. In Fig. 8.12, for example, the vertices of the hierarchy represent database, area, file, and record. When a vertex instance is locked, all its descendants are locked in the same mode (exclusive or shared). The main problem here is to prevent a vertex locked in one mode from later becoming locked in an incompatible mode when one of its ancestors is locked. The solution involves locking all ancestors in *intention* mode, to indicate intent to lock descendants. Intention mode conflicts with all other modes, so that the vertex cannot later be locked in shared or exclusive mode. In the example of Fig. 8.12, locking of a record must be preceded by intention-locking of the database, area, and file. The order of release if the locks are not to be held until the end of transaction must be record, file, area, database.

Fig. 8.12. A locking hierarchy.

8.4.6 Predicate Locks

A transaction may need to access in a consistent state all objects for which a certain predicate is true. For a relational database this would mean locking those tuples of a relation that satisfy the predicate [18]. A predicate lock allows more concurrency than locking the entire relation. However, the system must determine the set of tuples to be locked (by examining all the tuples one at a time, for example), and while this is happening other transactions may insert or change tuples that may satisfy the predicate. These potential tuples are called *phantoms*. Consistency can be maintained by comparing predicate lock requests to determine whether they potentially conflict. However, if predicates are arbitrarily complex it is not possible to decide whether two distinct predicates conflict. It is therefore necessary to restrict the form of predicate allowed. For example, there is a straightforward decision procedure to determine whether *simple predicates* conflict, a simple predicate being defined as a boolean combination of predicates of the form:

$< \text{field name} > \{ < | = | \neq | > \} < \text{constant} >$

Currently no system implements predicate locking.

8.4.7 Locking and Information Leakage

In systems that control information flow, locks can provide a covert channel for illegal flow. Suppose a higher-level process has read access to some object, and a lower-level process has update access to the same object. By locking the object (even in shared mode), the higher-level reader process can pass information to the lower-level writer process, thus violating the *-property. A different type of mechanism, the *event-count,* can be used to solve this *secure readers–writers problem* [43]. An eventcount is a nondecreasing integer variable. Three indivisible operations are defined on an eventcount E: *advance* (E), which adds one to the value of E, *read* (E), which returns the value, and *await* (E, v), which blocks the process until the eventcount reaches the value v. These operations are strictly separated into observe-only (*read, await*) and write-only (*advance*). Another type of nondecreasing integer variable, the *sequencer,* is used to *order* events. Each use of the operation *ticket*(S)—inspired by the ticket machines used in busy stores—returns a different value, with the ordering of the values corresponding to the time ordering of the executions of the *ticket* operations.

These constructs are used in the following programs in Reference 43.* (A similar solution was earlier given in [32, pp. 119–125].)

Two eventcounts, IN and OUT, are defined, and a sequencer T. The eventcounts are used by both programs, but the reader only reads them, and the writer only writes them, so they cannot be used to violate the *-property.

```
procedure writer ( )
    begin integer t;
        advance (IN);
        t := ticket (T);
        await (OUT, t);
        . . . update the data . . .
        advance (OUT);
    end
procedure reader ( )
    begin integer w;
        abort: w := read (IN);
        await (OUT, w);
        . . . read the data . . .
        if read (IN) ¬= w then goto abort;
    end
```

Note that the reader must repeat the operation (by going to "abort") if it determines, after rereading IN, that a writer has intervened.

8.4.8 Concurrency in Some Systems

In this section we summarize several systems with respect to (1) what application programs or queries must do to ensure that they preserve integrity in a concurrent environment, and (2) what the effect is.

---

*Copyright 1979, Association for Computing Machinery, Inc.; reprinted by permission.

CODASYL

An area is opened for processing in one of three concurrency modes (NONEXCLUSIVE, EXCLUSIVE, or PROTECTED) and for one of two usage modes (RETRIEVAL or UPDATE). EXCLUSIVE prevents any other run-unit from opening the area for any usage mode. PROTECTED conflicts with UPDATE. This means that PROTECTED prevents any other run-unit from opening for UPDATE. Figure 8.13 summarizes compatible and conflicting usage modes.

These area options provide a very coarse locking granularity. At the record level, CODASYL uses *monitored mode* rather than locking. If a run-unit has placed a record in monitored mode and then attempts to change the record, the attempt fails if another run-unit has changed the record since it entered monitored mode. The application program is responsible for taking appropriate action. By issuing REMONITOR, the application program can clear the error condition and then may even proceed to change the record.

This scheme has been criticized because it does not protect against unrepeatable reads [16]. Even with "good behavior" by all application programs, monitored mode provides only Level 2 consistency. The only way to achieve Level 3 consistency is by opening in PROTECTED or EXCLUSIVE mode.

		N		P		E	
		R	U	R	U	R	U
N	R	Y	Y	Y	Y	X	X
	U	Y	Y	X	X	X	X
P	R	Y	X	Y	X	X	X
	U	Y	X	X	X	X	X
E	R	X	X	X	X	X	X
	U	X	X	X	X	X	X

USAGE-MODE Options
R Retrieval
U Update
P Protected
E Exclusive
N Nonexclusive

Fig. 8.13. CODASYL concurrent scheduling of run-units according to usage mode.

System R

In System R the user of the SQL language [6] simply specifies the beginning and end of a transaction, as well as save points. The system automatically generates Lock and Unlock requests for the database objects and may also generate other save points. (Explicit locking is also available; it allows the user to achieve more efficient locking in some circumstances.) The SQL user can specify in the BEGIN TRANSACTION command the level of consistency (1, 2, or 3) required for the transaction. The lock granularity is also selectable; the definer of a segment (file) specifies that the locking unit for that segment is a record, a page, or the entire segment. If the chosen granularity results in too many locks, the system automatically "escalates" to a coarser granularity.

IMS

Concurrency in IMS [33, 38] is controlled by three kinds of specifications: processing options in the PCB, DL/I operations that result in automatic locking, and explicit locking. The PCB specifies which DL/I commands are used by the program; it also can specify *exclusive* use of a segment *type* (PROCOPT = E). An exclusive option conflicts with any other option for the same segment type, and IMS will not initiate a program with any such conflicts. Without the Program Isolation feature, IMS will schedule only one program at a time that updates a segment type; any number of read-only programs can execute concurrently. (This type of strategy, called *intent scheduling,* prevents deadlock.)

With Program Isolation, multiple updating programs can execute concurrently, as long as the PCB does not specify exclusive use. Locking for these programs is normally automatic. A GET HOLD operation (which indicates intent to update) results in a "single-update" lock on the segment *occurrence*. The system changes this to an exclusive lock if the segment is replaced. The single-update lock, which is essentially a shared lock (it allows other users to read but *not* to GET HOLD), is released when the program moves away from the locked occurrence (by a GET NEXT, for example). Exclusive locks, however, are held until the program reaches a commit point or *synchronization point*. Deadlock can occur.

IMS also allows programs to explicitly lock a retrieved segment and to associate it with a lock *class*. Locks obtained in this way are also single-update locks, but in this case they are held until the program explicitly releases the entire class. (These locks may also be converted to exclusive mode, in which case they too are retained to a synchronization point.) This type of locking is useful for holding a number of segments unchanged while they are being examined. It provides Level 3 consistency if done by the examining program, whereas the single-update lock provides only Level 2. The exclusive option in the PCB provides Level 3.

8.5 RECOVERY

Recovery is the restoration of the database after a failure, to a state that is acceptable to the users. What is "acceptable" may vary from situation to situation, but it generally means at least a *consistent state* with no erroneous data. The database is in a consistent state if its data values are those that would result if some set of transactions had completed and no transactions were in progress, and if its information satisfies the semantic integrity constraints (explicit or implicit). It may be acceptable to lose some data, that is, to lose the results of some transactions.

Failures may be caused by hardware malfunctions, software errors, or human errors. Following Gray [27], we can list different types of failures, according to how generally and permanently they affect the database system.

- *Action failure.* If a single database operation fails (for example, because the requested data is not found, or because of an integrity violation), the action is simply undone and an error indication is returned to the requesting program, which can correct the request and continue the transaction.
- *Transaction failure.* If a transaction fails (for example because of deadlock), it must be backed out (undone) to an appropriate point. Besides being a unit of consistency as described earlier, a transaction is also a unit of recovery.
- *System failure.* A system failure, or *crash,* which may be detected in the DBMS, the operating system, or the hardware, requires stopping and restarting the system. The media on which the database is stored usually survive a system failure.
- *Media failure.* Nonrecoverable errors on storage, such as permanent parity failure, or a lost tape, require the most complex recovery procedures.

A recovery system provides two types of functions: those that prepare for possible failures, and those that restore the database after a failure. The system prepares for failure by (1) being *failure-resistant* (sometimes called crash-resistant), and (2) maintaining *recovery data* that can be used after a failure. A failure-resistant system performs maintenance operations so as to leave the database in a correct state in the event of a failure.

A good recovery system should do the following:

- *Minimize lost work.* Users should not have to restart transactions or reenter data.

- *Allow recovery on a transaction basis.* It should be possible to undo and redo single transactions, as opposed to restoring an entire database or entire file.

- *Provide fast recovery.* Since at least part of the database is unavailable to users during recovery, the procedure should take a minimum of time. The system can speed up recovery by generating recovery data frequently, and by periodically consolidating the recovery data, so that less data has to be scanned during recovery.

- *Minimize manual bookkeeping.* If users must keep records about what recovery data has been generated, and then make complex decisions about what recovery procedures to take, they are likely to make costly errors. The recovery system should be as automatic as possible.

- *Ensure the safety of recovery data.*

Note that recovery procedures in general only repair the *effect* of failures; it is left to other techniques (such as hardware diagnosis or program testing) to discover and repair the *causes.* Comprehensive surveys of recovery can be found in [25] and [52].

8.5.1 Preparatory Recovery Functions

Recovery log

A *recovery log* is the most comprehensive way of maintaining recovery data. It records each maintenance action, keeping:

- A "before image," a copy of the information before the action; and
- An "after image," a copy of the information after the action.

The recovery log can be kept on tape or disk or on some type of mass storage system. The log must of course be highly reliable. For this reason it is often "dual-recorded" on two separate devices. The log should be kept on one or more dedicated devices, which could have special hardware features, such as "write once" to prevent overwriting the log, at least while it is on that device.

A typical log (IMS, for example) keeps before and after images, the identity of the program that made the change, the data and time of entry, and the identity of the database, data set, and record being modified. Often, as in IMS, the recovery log is combined with logging that serves more general purposes. It then may be called a system log, or audit trail or journal.

In most systems, modifications to the database are first made in *buffers* in main memory and only later written to secondary storage. A buffer is an area of memory where database files are temporarily mapped. Usually this buffer is shared by all the users, filled on demand, and replaced using a least-recently-used strategy. In some systems the buffers are written out whenever updates are committed. The use of buffers causes problems in keeping the log consistent with the database. If the system crashes after the buffers are written but before the log is written, there is no way to undo the changes. One solution to this problem is to write the log *before* writing the buffers.

Save points

A *save point* is a user-defined position in a transaction. At a save point the status of the transaction environment is saved, so that it is possible to resume processing from that point on. Save points avoid the need to undo a complete transaction when a failure occurs. A complex operation can be implemented as an atomic unit by enclosing the component operations within save points.

Image copies

An *image copy* or *backup dump* saves the contents of the database on removable media that can be stored away from the machine room. Copies can be made for the whole database or for specific parts; they can be made at predefined intervals, after the occurrence of some event (such as the end of a job), when the system is not busy, or at the user's request. Taking a dump is a time-consuming process; in some systems all transaction processing must be stopped while the dump is taken, and in other systems there may be a noticeable effect on response time.

System checkpoints

A *system checkpoint* saves the status of processing, so that it can be resumed after a normal or abnormal stop. Information typically saved includes the list of the programs active at the checkpoint, status of variables, positions in sequential files, pointers to message queues, and status of temporary working files. Frequent checkpoints save work at restart but they imply more overhead. There is an optimum checkpoint interval for a given system that considers the cost of taking checkpoints against the cost of restart [24]. Unless all transaction activity is quiesced, the checkpoint does not record a consistent state. Quiescing all activity is generally not acceptable to users, however, so systems often take a nonconsistent checkpoint that can be used at restart in conjunction with the recovery log to reconstruct a consistent state.

Differential files

With this technique, all changes to a file are kept in a separate *differential file,* which is periodically merged with the main file. A differential file is thus similar to a recovery log, but the actual updates have not yet occurred. Since the main file is never altered except during merging, it becomes feasible to keep two copies of the main file. Moreover, the last version of the main file becomes a backup file. Of course, retrieval must be done differently if differential files are used. The differential file must be searched first for the most recent entry for a particular item. If no entry is found, the main file is searched. Differential files are especially useful where the organization of the main file makes changes very expensive. One binary relational system [50] uses differential files and combines them with the main files only when the database is reorganized. INGRES uses differential files for all updating, but for a much shorter time period. The main file is modified at the end of a query.

Backup and current versions

This technique differs from the differential technique in that changes are made to the current version rather than being saved in a differential file. The current version is copied into the backup version at a commit point. A variation of this technique is used in System R in conjunction with a log.

Updating a copy

The objective of this technique, also called "careful replacement," is to avoid update in place as much as possible, so as to minimize the time the object is in an inconsistent state. The object is copied just before updating, and changes are made to the copy. This copy replaces the original only after the alteration completes successfully. This technique can be applied to small components of the database, as well as to entire files.

8.5.2 Procedures for Recovery after Failure

We turn now to recovery procedures that are used after a failure.

Backward recovery

If the system crashes (without damaging secondary storage) or a transaction fails, the database objects affected by the transactions running during

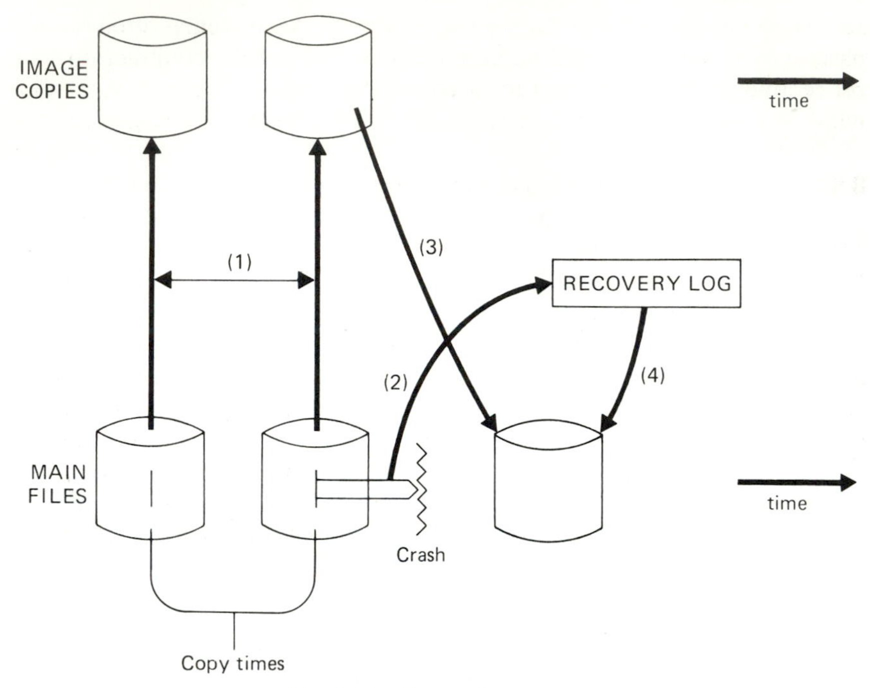

Fig. 8.14. Forward recovery.

the failure can be restored to their states before those transactions started. This requires processing the recovery log backward to undo the changes made by these incomplete transactions.

Forward recovery

Image copies are made ((1) in Fig. 8.14), and a recovery log records all changes to the current files (2). If there is a media failure the database is restored from the latest image copy (3). The recovery log is then used to redo all the changes since the last image copy (4).

Compensation

Instead of undoing and redoing erroneous changes, it is sometimes more efficient to compensate for their effects. For example, an update that incorrectly gives an employee a salary X dollars too much could be compensated for by decreasing the salary by X dollars. Compensation may be the only way to undo the effect of a committed transaction.

Salvation

In some cases—for example if the log has been damaged—it may be impossible to recover by the usual procedures. Special routines (called *salvation programs*) can then be used to check consistency of suspect parts of the database, and to correct errors by patching. Nonautomatic procedures such as compensation and salvation should be used rarely and with great care, since they run the risk of introducing new errors.

8.5.3 Recovery in IMS and System R

IMS

Figure 8.15 provides a simplified overview of IMS recovery. IMS logging writes the before and after image of each updated segment onto a log tape (1). The "log tape write ahead" protocol ensures that no change to database storage occurs before the corresponding log record is written to storage. Image copies of databases are made periodically (2), and system checkpoints (3) are taken at frequent intervals such as every five minutes. In addition to the system log, IMS maintains (4) a "dynamic log," containing the before images for all changes each active program has made since its last synchronization point. (These images are used to automatically back out uncommitted changes of a failing program; they are erased

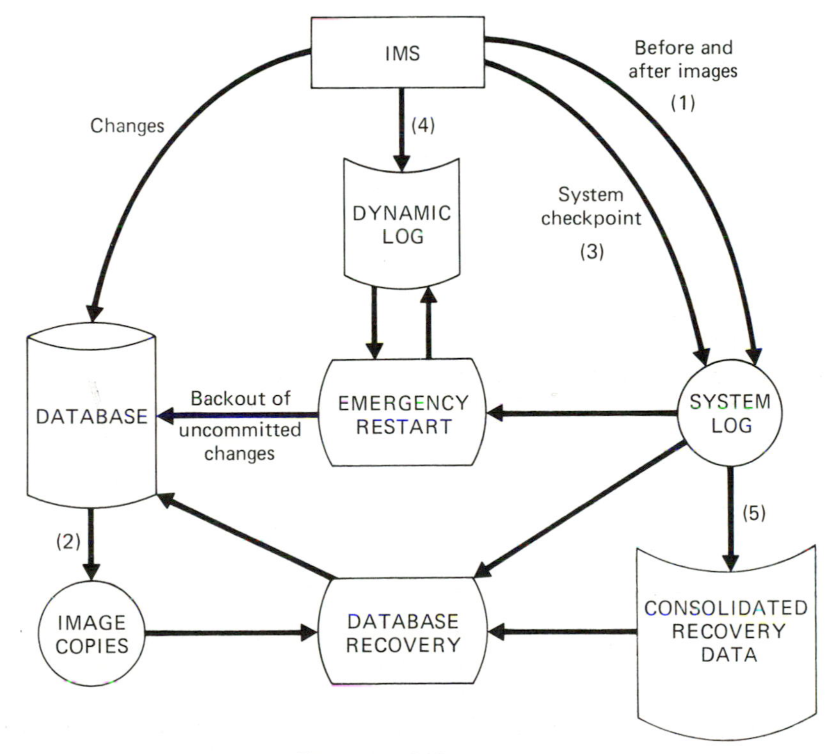

Fig. 8.15. IMS recovery.

when a synchronization point is reached.) The information needed to restart the system (such as the most recent checkpoint) is kept in a restart data set on disk.

The restart data set and the log are used for restarting after a system failure with no media failure. The system locates on the log tape the last checkpoint or one specified by the operator and restores the status information that was saved at the checkpoint. The log is processed forward from the checkpoint to restore the system to its state at the time of failure. Then the log is processed backwards, and the log records for updates are copied to the dynamic log, which is then used to back out the uncommitted changes. Each program is now restored to its state at its last synchronization point; it will be rescheduled to redo its uncommitted work. It is not necessary to redo any committed updates, since IMS always forces writing of the buffers at a commit point.

Several procedures are used to prepare the log data for fast recovery after media failure (5). A special feature can be used to periodically reorganize the data by data set; that is, all the before/after images for a particular data set are together. Second, a "change accumulation" data set is produced, which contains only the information that is still needed for recovery, sorted so that it can be used sequentially during recovery.

If the database storage *has* been damaged, the damaged data sets must be restored from image copies. It is then necessary to redo (from log tapes and change accumulation data sets) all updates made after the image copy was made.

Although we have described here only database recovery, an equally important IMS function is recovery of input and output messages. Complete integrity requires both database and message recovery.

System R

System R [29, 37] uses a recovery log in conjunction with the backup/current version technique that was introduced earlier. System R data is stored in files (also called *segments*), which are linear spaces divided into pages. A dual mapping is maintained between pages of memory and their locations on disk. One mapping represents the current state of a segment; the other (called a *shadow* version) represents a previous state.

System R keeps a log of all maintenance actions. For each action the log records before and after images, object and transaction identifiers, time stamps, length of the log record, and a pointer to the previous log record for this transaction (since one log is used for all the concurrent transactions). Undoing transactions requires a directly addressable log; for this and other reasons the log is kept on disk, and acts as a buffer for a more permanent tape log. Dual logging for extra reliability is optional. System checkpoints are taken periodically, their frequency depending on

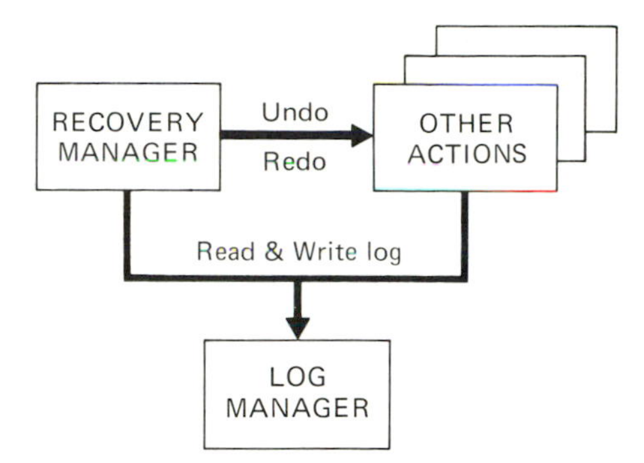

Fig. 8.16. System R recovery and log management. [From Gray [27].]

log activity. Checkpoints are taken with transactions in progress, but *no actions*. At checkpoint time all current versions become the shadow versions.

To protect against media failure, backup dumps to tape are also taken at longer intervals; these dumps are taken with no transactions in progress. The log is maintained by a log manager program using the Write Ahead Log protocol. A recovery manager sets up the data structures needed for recovery and is responsible for shutdown, startup, checkpoints, and dumps. Figure 8.16 shows how these programs fit together.

The basic design of System R allows transactions to have numbered save points (although these have not been exposed at the SQL interface) and commit points. If a transaction fails, its uncommitted changes are undone by traversing the log backwards.

After a crash the system uses the shadow versions that were recorded at the last checkpoint. The system thus restarts in an *action-consistent state* (since no actions were in progress at checkpoint time). Using the log, all transactions uncommitted at the time of the crash are undone, and the changes of all committed transactions are preserved. This implies redoing any transactions that committed after the checkpoint, as System R does not force out the buffers at commit points. (See Fig. 8.17.)

Transactions that are performing undo have priority for deadlock handling; that is, these transactions are never preempted in order to resolve a deadlock. The idea is never to undo undo's. Unbreakable

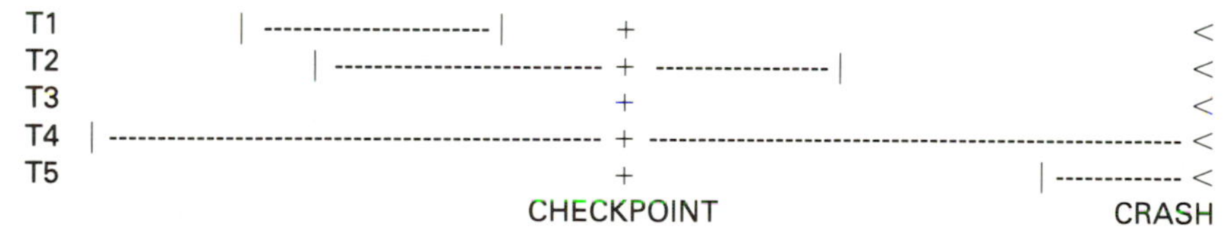

Fig. 8.17. Possible states of transactions with respect to checkpoint and crash. [From Gray *et al.* [29].]

deadlocks are prevented by the protocol that only one transaction at a time performs an undo action.

To recover from media failure, the most recent dump tape is loaded into the database, and forward recovery is performed.

8.5.4 Security Issues in Recovery

- *Protection of recovery data.* This is critical because the recovery from a system crash bypasses the usual security measures. A doctored recovery log could be used to make unauthorized changes. The log can be protected with the same mechanisms used for other files, and can have additional protection from special hardware and from the operating system.

- *Opportunity for system penetrations.* A system restart after a crash provides an opportunity to use a subverted version of the operating system (by loading from the wrong device, for example).

- *Recovery utilities.* Because of their very general rights, these programs threaten security unless their use is carefully controlled.

- *Salvation programs.* These often operate stand-alone, thus bypassing all protection. A good recovery system should make it possible to avoid using salvation programs.

EXERCISES

8.1. The authorization and semantic-integrity models could be combined into a ''data-control model'' that subsumes both models. Indicate the components and the interpretation of such a model.

8.2. Consider the database of Exercise 6.3. Using QBE syntax, give an assertion so that no student can take more than two courses in the same department unless the course number is greater than 200. Give also an assertion that all students in the registration table must exist in the student table.

8.3. Build a dictionary or catalog for this database in the syle of System R (see [12, Section 8.6]) and give assertions using SQL such that, when the name of an object is changed or new objects are defined, the new names are different from existing names.

8.4. For the two schedules given for the ''lost update'' example of Section 8.4, (a) draw graphs representing the (partial) ordering of the actions, and (b) draw dependency graphs.

8.5. Four transactions, T_1 to T_4, contain the following actions:

$\underline{T_1}$	T_{11}: A := A + 1	$\underline{T_2}$	T_{21}: A := A * 2
	T_{12}: B := B * 2		T_{22}: D := D − 1
	T_{13}: C := C: ** 2 − C		
$\underline{T_3}$	T_{31}: B := B ** 2	$\underline{T_4}$	T_{41}: C := C ** 3
	T_{32}: D := D + 5		T_{42}: E := E * 3
	T_{33}: E := E − 1		

Determine whether the following two schedules preserve integrity or not.

S_1: T_{11}, T_{21}, T_{12}, T_{22}, T_{13}, T_{31}, T_{32}, T_{41}, T_{33}, T_{42}
S_2: T_{31}, T_{11}, T_{12}, T_{21}, T_{32}, T_{33}, T_{41}, T_{13}, T_{22}, T_{42}

8.6. Provide a simpler solution to the secure readers-writers problem for the case where there is only one writer but multiple readers.

REFERENCES AND BIBLIOGRAPHY

1. F. Bancilhon and N. Spyratos, "Update Semantics of Relational Views." IRIA Research Report No. 329, Le Chesnay, France, October 1978.

    Another approach to maintenance through views is developed. A view is defined as a mapping function and the *complement* of the view as another mapping function. The "whole data base" can be derived from the view and its complement. A view can have *multiple* complements. The criterion for a valid update is: only the view is changed, and the complement is not changed. The choice of a complement thus determines the update policy.

2. P. A. Bernstein *et al.*, "The concurrency control mechanism of SDD–1: A system for distributed databases (The fully redundant case)." *IEEE Trans. on Software Eng.* **SE–4,** 3 (May 1978), 154–168.
3. P. A. Bernstein, M. A. Casanova, and N. Goodman, "Comments on 'Process synchronization in database systems.' " *ACM TODS* **4,** 4 (Dec. 1979), 545–546.
4. R. G. Canning (Ed.), "Recovery in database systems." *EDP Analyzer* **14,** 11 (Nov. 1976).
5. D. D. Chamberlin, J. N. Gray, and I. L. Traiger, "Views, authorization, and locking in a relational database system." *AFIPS Conf. Proc.* **44,** 1975 NCC, 425–430. AFIPS Press, Montvale, N. J., 1975.
6. D. D. Chamberlin *et al.*, "SEQUEL 2: A unified approach to data definition, manipulation, and control." *IBM J. Res. and Dev.* **20,** 6 (Nov. 1976), 560–575.
7. E. K. Clemons, "An External Schema Facility to Support Data Base Update." In *Databases: Improving Usability and Responsiveness,* B. Schneiderman (Ed.). Academic Press, New York, 1978, 371–398.
8. E. F. Codd, "Recent investigations in relational database systems." *Information Processing* **74,** North-Holland, 1974, 1017–1021.

9. E. F. Codd, "Extending the database relational model to capture more meaning." *ACM TODS* **4,** 4 (Dec. 1979), 397–434.

10. R. M. Curtice, "Integrity in data base systems." *Datamation* **23,** 5 (May 1977), 64–68.

11. O. J. Dahl and C. A. R. Hoare, "Hierarchical Program Structures." In *Structured Programming,* Dahl, Dijkstra, and Hoare (Eds.), Academic Press, 1972.

12. C. J. Date, *An Introduction to Database Systems* (Second Ed.). Addison-Wesley, Reading, Mass., 1977.

13. C. J. Date, "Locking and recovery in a shared database system: An application programming tutorial." *Proc. 5th Int. Conf. on Very Large Data Bases,* Rio de Janeiro, 1979, 1–15.

    Presents concurrency control features of a proposed Unified Database Language. The term *recoverable unit* is proposed for an atomic transaction, and five different levels of consistency (*isolation level*) are defined.

14. C. T. Davies, "Data processing spheres of control." *IBM Sys. J.* **17,** 2 (1978), 179–198.

    The general model on which transaction-oriented recovery is based. Its basic concept is the sphere of control, discussed in Section 8.2. The model is concerned with the relationship between resources and spheres of control, the types of resource status that must be maintained, and the effects that dependency and commitment have on process scheduling and recovery. While no system implements this model completely, recovery in IMS and System R has been strongly influenced by this philosophy.

15. U. Dayal and P. Bernstein, "On the updatability of relational views." *Proc. 4th Int. Conf. on Very Large Data Bases,* Berlin, 1978, 368–377. Available from ACM.

16. R. W. Engles, "Currency and Concurrency in the COBOL Database Facility." In [41], 339–363.

17. K. P. Eswaran, "Specifications, Implementations, and Interactions of a Trigger Subsystem in an Integrated Database System." Report RJ1820, IBM Research Laboratory, San Jose, Calif., August 1976. A shorter version, under the name "Aspects of a Trigger Subsystem in an Integrated Database System," appeared in *Proc. 2nd Int. Conf. on Software Engineering,* 1976, 243–250; available from ACM and IEEE.

    Discusses use of auxiliary procedures (called there "triggers") as extended semantic integrity assertions and as a means of materializing views. The paper also studies the level of authorization and the locking mode of these procedures, as well as some implementation issues in the context of System R.

18. K. P. Eswaran *et al.,* "The notions of consistency and predicate locks in a database system." *Comm. ACM* **19,** 11 (November 1976), 624–633.

    Defines the concepts of transaction, consistency, and schedule, introduces two-phase transactions, argues for predicate locks, and suggests ways to implement them.

19. E. B. Fernandez and R. C. Summers, "Integrity aspects of a shared data base." *AFIPS Conf. Proc.* **45,** 1976 NCC, 819–827. AFIPS Press, Montvale, N. J., 1976.
    Proposes the integrity model used here. Also a language to express semantic integrity assertions.

20. J. J. Florentin, "Consistency auditing of databases." *The Comp. J.* **17,** 1 (Feb. 1974), 52–58.
    The first paper to point out the need to use mathematical logic to deal with integrity constraints. It also introduces the concepts of static and transitional (called dynamic) constraints, and analyzes the effort required for validation in terms of the number of sequential file searches needed to evaluate the assertion predicates.

21. A. L. Furtado, K. C. Sevcik, and C. S. dos Santos, "Permitting updates through views of data bases." *Inform. Systems* **4,** 4 (1979), 269–283.
    The authors propose considering views as "screens" that prevent the violation of integrity constraints. They introduce the notion of an *assumption constraint,* which expresses user (application) assumptions about the database. The following criterion is used: when a change is made through one view, the resulting changes to the database as seen through other views should not violate any assumption constraint. The paper presents methods of applying updates through relational views defined by the various relational operators, as well as alternative approaches to maintaining assumption constraints.

22. G. Gardarin and M. Melkanoff, "Proving consistency of database transactions." *Proc. 5th Int. Conf. on Very Large Data Bases,* Rio de Janeiro, 1979, 291–298.
    Introduces formal language for specifying transactions and integrity constraints and shows how a "transaction consistency verifier" could prove at compile time that a transaction cannot violate a constraint.

23. G. Gardarin and S. Spaccapietra, "Integrity of Data Bases: A General Lockout Algorithm with Deadlock Avoidance." In [41], 394–411.

24. E. Gelenbe, "On the optimum checkpoint interval." *Journal of the ACM* **26,** 2 (April 1979), 259–270.
    A theoretical analysis (using a queuing model) of the problem of the time interval between successive checkpoints that maximizes system availability (excluding the unpredictable intervals of time when the system is recovering from a failure). This analysis shows that this interval must be deterministic and a function of the system load.

25. T. K. Gibbons, *Integrity and Recovery in Computer Systems.* Hayden Book Co., Rochelle Park, N.J., 1976.
    The only book dedicated exclusively to recovery. It discusses errors and failures, basic strategies for recovery, recovery in batch and real-time

systems, and calculation of optimal dumping frequency. It is, however, oriented to file systems.

26. R. W. Graves, "Integrity control in a relational data description language." *Proc. ACM'75 Pacific,* 108–113; available from ACM.

27. J. N. Gray, "Notes on Data Base Operating Systems." In *Operating Systems—An Advanced Course,* R. Bayer *et al.,* (Eds.), Springer-Verlag, 1978, 393–481.

Excellent discussion of operating-system support for DBMSs, in particular transaction management, concurrency, and recovery. The recovery section discusses the protocols needed for recovery in a system executing a set of concurrent transactions. Reference 29 describes the application of these ideas to System R.

28. J. N. Gray *et al.,* "Granularity of Locks and Degrees of Consistency in a Shared Data Base." In [41], 365–394.

29. J. N. Gray *et al.,* "The Recovery Manager of a Data Management System." Report RJ2623, IBM Research Laboratory, San Jose, Calif., August 1979.

30. M. Hammer and D. J. McLeod, "A framework for data base semantic integrity." *Proc. 2nd Int. Conf. on Software Eng.,* 1976, 498–504; available from ACM.

Identifies three aspects of integrity constraints: the assertion, the validity requirement (equivalent to the concept of condition), and the violation action (equivalent to the auxiliary procedure). Extensive discussion of the possible types of assertions, in particular the predicates used to identify constrained data and to state its properties in the context of a relational database.

31. M. Hammer and S. K. Sarin, "Efficient monitoring of database assertions." *Suppl. to Proc. 1978 ACM-SIGMOD Int. Conference on Management of Data,* 38–49; to appear in *ACM TODS.*

32. T. H. Hinke and M. Schaefer, "Secure Data Management System." Report TM-(L)-5407/007/00, System Development Corporation, Santa Monica, Calif., June 1975.

33. IBM Corporation, IMS/VS Version 1 Application Programming Reference Manual. Form No. SH20–9026–6, 1978.

34. IBM Corporation, IMS/VS System/Application Design Guide. Form No. SH20–9025–6, 1978.

35. B. H. Liskov, A. Snyder, R. Atkinson, and C. Schaffert, "Abstraction mechanisms in CLU." *Comm. ACM* **20,** 8 (August 1977), 564–576.

36. M. E. S. Loomis, "The 78 CODASYL database model: A comparison with preceding specifications." *Proc. ACM-SIGMOD 1980 Int. Conf. on Management of Data,* 30–44.

37. R. A. Lorie, "Physical integrity in a large segmented database." *ACM TODS* **2,** 1 (March 1977), 91–104.

38. W. C. McGee, "The Information Management System IMS/VS. Part V: Transaction processing facilities." *IBM Systems J.* **16,** 2 (1977), 148–168.

39. D. J. McLeod, "High-level domain definition in a relational data base system." *ACM FDT* **8,** 2 (1976), *Proceedings of Conf. on Data: Abstraction, Definition and Structure,* 47–57; available from ACM.

40. R. Munz, H. J. Schneider, and F. Steyer, "Application of sub-predicate tests in database systems." *Proc. 5th Int. Conf. on Very Large Data Bases,* Rio de Janeiro, 1979, 426–435.

41. G. M. Nijssen (Ed.), *Modeling in Data Base Management Systems.* Proc. IFIP Working Conference on Modelling in Data Base Management Systems. North-Holland, Amsterdam, 1976.

42. C. H. Papadimitriou, "The serializability of concurrent database updates." *Journal of the ACM* **26,** 4 (October 1979), 631–653.

43. D. P. Reed and R. K. Kanodia, "Synchronization with eventcounts and sequencers." *Comm. ACM* **22,** 2 (Feb. 1979), 115–123.

44. D. R. Ries and M. Stonebraker, "Effects of locking granularity in a database management system." *ACM TODS* **2,** 3 (Sept. 1977), 233–246.

45. D. R. Ries and M. Stonebraker, "Locking granularity revisited." *ACM TODS* **4,** 2 (June 1979), 210–227.

46. G. Schlageter, "Process synchronization in database systems." *ACM TODS* **3,** 3 (Sept. 1978), 248–271.

47. M. E. Senko, "Conceptual schemas, abstract data structures, enterprise descriptions." *Proc. Int. Computing Symp.,* Liege, Belgium, April 1977, 85–107.

48. J. M. Smith and D. C. P. Smith, "Database abstractions: Aggregation and generalization." *ACM TODS* **2,** 2 (June 1977), 105–133.

49. M. Stonebraker, "Implementation of integrity constraints and views by query modification." *Proc. 1975 ACM-SIGMOD Int. Conf. on Management of Data,* 65–78.

    Semantic integrity in INGRES. The enforcement of semantic constraints follows the same approach as authorization and uses query modification. Examples of integrity assertions using QUEL are given, as well as four algorithms (for different types of assertions) to enforce integrity.

50. P. J. Titman, "An Experimental Data Base System using Binary Relations." In *Data Base Management,* J. W. Klimbie and K. L. Koffeman (Eds.), Elsevier North-Holland, New York, 1974, 351–361.

51. S. Todd, "Automatic constraint maintenance and updating defined relations." *Information Processing* **77,** North-Holland, 1977, 145–148.

    A study of the problem of updating views using an approach based on magnitudes of changes. The effect of update is the minimal change satisfying the update and the constraints. The theory could be used as a tool for application designers.

52. J. S. M. Verhofstad, "Recovery techniques for database systems." *Comp. Surveys* **10,** 2 (June 1978), 167–195.

A comprehensive survey that tries to establish common principles for the heterogeneous variety of existing recovery mechanisms. Includes detailed discussions of the recovery features of System R, Multics, IMS, and other systems.

53. H. Weber, "The D-Graph Model of Large Shared Data Bases: A Representation of Integrity Constraints and Views as Abstract Data Types." Report RJ1875, IBM Research Laboratory, San Jose, Calif., Nov. 1976.

54. K. C. Wong and M. Edelberg, "Interval hierarchies and their application to predicate files." *ACM TODS* **2,** 3 (Sept. 1977), 223–232.

Describes methods for maintaining files of predicates and for determining whether predicates overlap. These methods apply only to limited forms of predicates, but are potentially useful for predicate locking, semantic integrity, and authorization enforcement. See also Reference 40.

55. M. Zloof, "Security and Integrity within the Query-by-Example Data Base Management Language." Report RC6982, IBM Research Laboratory, Yorktown Heights, N.Y., February 1978.

9 Auditing and Controls in a Database Environment

9.1 INTRODUCTION

Many of the principles developed by auditors over the years for traditional accounting systems remain highly relevant for today's database systems. These principles have important implications for the design and use of database systems, but they are too often neglected by system designers. In practice there is a good amount of overlap in the *objectives* of auditors and system designers, but their points of view are different. In this chapter we describe the principles and practices of audit and control from a database security viewpoint. The chapter should also provide some insight into the auditor's view of security and integrity.

9.2 BASIC CONCEPTS

9.2.1 The Objectives of Auditing and Controls

Auditing is the examination of information by someone other than the persons who produced it or who use it. The goal is to establish the reliability of the information and thus to make it more useful. The best-known use of auditing is by certified public accountants, who conduct an audit so that they can *attest* to financial statements (that is, assume responsibility for the fairness of the statements). This *independent* or *external* audit, conducted by objective outside persons, examines not only the financial statements but also accounting records and other relevant information. The auditors write a report based on the audit, expressing their opinion of the financial statement.

Internal audit is carried out *within* an enterprise, usually by an internal audit group that reports to a high level in the enterprise or to an audit committee of the board of directors. Internal auditors are therefore independent of the audited function or department. One of the main purposes of internal audit is to monitor and evaluate the system of *internal control,* which includes a wide variety of measures taken to promote effective operation of the enterprise. It is the goal of internal control to ensure that management policy is carried out, that various kinds of exposures are prevented, and that the enterprise operates efficiently. An adequate system of internal control is required by U.S. law for all companies that report to the Securities and Exchange Commission [5]. The Foreign Corrupt Practices Act of 1977 requires such a company to maintain an internal control system to ensure that:

- Transactions are executed in accordance with management authorization;*
- Transactions are recorded in order to prepare an accurate financial statement and to account for assets;
- Access to assets is permitted only in accordance with management's authorization.

When the enterprise relies on a computerized information system, the objectives of internal control encompass those of database security and integrity.

9.2.2 Effect of the Database Environment

Although the goals remain the same, some dramatic differences are apparent when we consider auditing and controls in a computer environment.

- Because the more technical steps are now automated, the remaining manual procedures are often performed by people who are unfamiliar with the data and with accounting practices and are therefore less able to review or check.
- The elimination of manual steps has also eliminated both visual

* The term "transaction," as used in auditing standards (and in this chapter), refers to an *enterprise* transaction, such as an exchange with another enterprise, or a transfer of assets within the enterprise. Often such a transaction is implemented as a database transaction in the sense of Chapter 8.

checking and traditional paper audit trails. As EFT systems grow in usage, visible audit trails will become even more rare.

- Perpetrators of fraud can copy information or destroy evidence extremely rapidly and less visibly. (Compare erasing a tape with burning a bushel of documents.)
- Human beings cannot directly see the data. This means that error or fraud is less likely to be detected by chance. It also means that the auditor either must use independent programs to examine data, or must rely on the audited system's programs.

A database environment implies further differences:

- Functions and data previously separated (operating data and financial data, for example) are being integrated. While this is a positive step in most respects, one result is that redundancy and independent sources for comparison are lost. A single program may perform a combination of tasks that would be considered incompatible (for control purposes) if performed by a human being.
- Today's database and application systems span many different functional areas of the enterprise. The complexity of these integrated systems makes it difficult for the auditor to understand them.
- The sheer size of many databases makes it difficult to scan them for irregularities.

When the database system also processes online transactions still other differences appear:

- Often the user who initiates a transaction also enters the data, so there is less opportunity for checking.
- Transactions are initiated from remote terminals, which may be outside the administrative control of the computer installation or even the enterprise.
- The sequence of processing is less repeatable, because transactions arrive randomly.
- Transactions are processed singly rather than in batches, so various batch controls cannot be used.
- Continuous operation makes auditing more difficult, since activity on the database cannot be stopped while auditing is done.
- Update in place eliminates the automatic creation of generations of files that formerly served as useful controls. It also means that a

complete file is rarely processed at one time, so there is no occasion to check control information.

On the other hand, the database environment makes it possible to *improve* audit and control. The computer itself is a valuable tool. For example, the auditor can perform sophisticated statistical sampling of records to be examined, scan complete databases, or calculate relationships among different records. A number of the traditional controls can be supported by the DBMS, and new types of control are possible using DBMS features. Online inquiry restores the visibility of data, making it easier to detect errors. The increased use of distributed processing is making it possible to reintroduce some traditional controls. A node in a distributed system can collect a batch of transactions and compute control information before passing the batch to another node for processing. In an EFT system, for example, both the terminal device and the central system can maintain control totals and transaction logs.

9.2.3 Control Principles

A thorough survey [41] turned up numerous control practices, but nearly all of them reflect a very few basic principles or policies:

1. *Establish separation of responsibility*. This is always good practice. For example, one person authorizes paychecks, and another person prepares them. One person changes a program, a committee approves the change, and someone else installs it. Responsibility should also be rotated. The data processing department should be independent of users.

2. *Prevent errors and violations*. Errors are prevented by various types of "passive" controls, such as the careful design of display screens and input forms to reduce input errors. A more "active" measure is to restrict the portion of the database a program can access.

3. *Check validity of processing and data*. Checking of validity while a process is being performed (sometimes called *in-process audit*) is exemplified by the checking of semantic integrity constraints. Redundant information may be entered or kept in the database to support this checking, which is done at *control points*. When a problem is found, it is important to *follow up* to determine the cause and to correct both the cause and its effects. *Editing* of input data detects errors that passive controls did not prevent.

4. *Produce an audit trail*. An audit trail is a history of the activities of a system. It is produced during processing and used for *post-process audit*.

This audit can be more global than in-process audit, reviewing transactions and their results over a long period of time. More complex analysis is possible.

9.2.4 The Audit Process

In this section we first summarize the major steps in *independent* audits. These steps are followed whether or not computers are involved, but computer-based systems require new methodology in each step.

1. *Review internal control.* In this step the auditor obtains an understanding of the system of internal control (through interviews, observation, and studying documentation) and writes a description that is used in other steps of the audit.

2. *Test the system.* The auditor determines, through *tests of compliance,* whether the internal control system actually behaves according to its description. One type of compliance test, called a *transaction test,* follows specific transactions through the system. For example, the auditor might follow a sample of sales orders through all of their processing. In *functional tests* the auditor concentrates on whether a single procedure has been performed consistently and effectively on all transactions. Other tests trace actions back to the transactions that caused them.

3. *Evaluate the system.* The results of the first two steps determine (a) whether the auditors recommend improvements to the internal control system, and (b) how much the remainder of the audit can rely on data produced by that system.

4. *Conduct substantive tests.* Substantive tests are directed at the values of specific items of the financial statement. Such a test might check, for example, that the accounts receivable amount is correct.

9.2.5 Audit of Computer-based Systems

Because of the technical knowledge required for auditing computerized systems, there is now an auditing specialty known as *EDP audit,* and the American Institute of Certified Public Accountants has published a statement on standards for the independent audit of these systems [18, 38], as well as guidelines for study and evaluation of the internal controls [4]. The auditor's responsibilities have been interpreted for a computer environment as:

- understanding the system,
- verifying the phases of processing, and
- verifying the results of processing.

Techniques to help the auditor carry out each of these responsibilities are described in Section 9.6.

9.2.6 Types of Audits

Audits—outside or internal—of computer-based systems can have varying objectives [17, 25]. Some examples are:

- *Installation security audit.* The focus here is on computer assets, including hardware, software, and data. Examples of the items covered are: access to the media library, casualty insurance, and disaster recovery plans.
- *Operation audit.* This is an audit of the operation of a computer installation.
- *Application system audit.* The term *application system* refers to an integrated set of programs, such as those that make up a billing system. This type of audit (also called the "*postinstallation audit*") reviews the entire application system, including controls, program logic, and data.
- *Fraud audit.* An audit to determine whether fraudulent manipulation has occurred will tend to be more complete (and more costly) than an audit with more general goals.

9.3 COMMON FORMS OF COMPUTER FRAUD

It is useful to consider which types of computer fraud occur most frequently. Most of the cases fall into three general categories [1, 20], where the fraud is perpetrated either by manipulating input transactions, by modifying programs, or by altering files. We briefly describe each of these techniques in turn.

Input manipulation schemes

These schemes, which showed up most frequently in a study of 150 fraud cases, may be categorized further as follows:

- An extra transaction is entered that benefits the perpetrator in some way. This might be, for example, a phony purchase order.
- A valid transaction is not entered. An example is the failure to record the death of a pensioner, thus allowing payments to continue.
- An authorized transaction is modified so that incorrect information is placed in the database.

- Error-correction procedures are misused. These procedures are often vulnerable to fraudulent use, especially if they bypass the normal security measures.

Program modification schemes

Programs can be modified to perform or aid many different types of fraudulent action. For example, undocumented transactions can be included in the code, control totals can be incorrectly maintained, and files incorrectly modified. These modifications can be made when the program is initially written, when authorized changes are made, or at any other time, if access to the program library can be obtained.

File alteration schemes

While many file alteration schemes are really variants of the two previous types of schemes, there are some specific techniques, such as:

- Use of a utility or special-purpose program to modify a master file, or
- Substitution of an alternative file for the real file.

We will discuss in the following sections controls that can be used to prevent these types of fraud.

9.4 CONTROL PRACTICES

In auditing standards, controls are classified as "general" or "application." Figures 9.1 and 9.2 list the controls according to this classification, and Fig. 9.3 lists some additional database considerations used by auditors in reviewing general controls. Since the distinction between general and application controls is less relevant in a database environment, we group control practices here as they pertain to:

- transaction initiation and data entry,
- database content, processing, and access, and
- database storage.

Although we concentrate on controls *within* the automated system, *external* controls and procedures are equally important, as is the relationship between the two kinds of controls.

9.4.1 Controls on Transaction Initiation and Data Entry

It is important to limit (if possible through access rules) who can initiate each type of transaction. This type of control supports a least-privilege "need-to-do" policy. Controls on transaction initiation also enforce

GENERAL CONTROLS

Organization and Operation Controls

1. Segregation of functions between EDP department and users.
2. Authorization over execution of transactions.
3. Segregation of functions within EDP.

Systems Development and Documentation Controls

4. Active participation by users, accounting department, and internal auditors in system design and software acquisition.
5. Written specifications, reviewed by management and user departments.
6. Testing a joint effort of users and EDP, including manual and computerized parts of system.
7. Final approval from management, users, and EDP before placing system in operation.
8. Control of the file conversion to prevent unauthorized changes.
9. Approval of all changes to the operational system.
10. Formal documentation procedures.

Hardware and Systems Software Controls

11. Maximal utilization of control features of hardware, operating system, and other software.
12. Change control for systems software.

Access Controls

13. Need-to-know access to program documentation.
14. Need-to-know access to data files and programs.
15. Control of access to hardware.

Data and Procedural Controls

16. Controls on data receipt and recording, error followup, and distribution of output.
17. Written manual for computer operations.
18. Review and evaluation of systems by internal auditors at critical stages of development.
19. Continuing review and test by internal auditors.

Fig. 9.1. Categories of general controls.

separation of responsibility. An organization may draw up a "transaction-conflicts matrix," specifying which combinations of transactions should not be available to the same person. For example, a cash refund transaction may conflict with a transaction that alters customer records. In the matrix of Fig. 9.4, transactions T_1 and T_2 conflict.

Additional control is achieved by authorizing only certain terminals for a transaction, and by restricting the people who can use a terminal.

APPLICATION CONTROLS

Input Controls

1. Only authorized and approved input accepted by EDP.
2. Verification of all codes used to represent data.
3. Control of conversion of data into machine-sensible form.
4. Control of movement of data between processing steps, or between departments.
5. Control of error correction and resubmission of corrected transactions.

Processing Controls

6. Control totals produced during processing reconciled with input control totals.
7. Controls to prevent processing the wrong file, detect file manipulation errors, and highlight operator-caused errors.
8. Limit and reasonableness checks.
9. Verification of control totals at appropriate points in the processing cycle.

Output Controls

10. Output control totals reconciled with input and processing controls.
11. Output tested by comparison to original source documents.
12. Output distributed only to authorized users.

Fig. 9.2. Categories of application controls.

This can be done by access rules, by keeping the terminal in a controlled area, or through a lock on the terminal. It is also important to log *unsuccessful attempts* to initiate a transaction.

When a transaction is started, it can be assigned a unique identifier, such as a sequence number, which is displayed to the user. The user and the system use this identifier to ensure that no transaction is lost and that no transaction is processed more than once. It is often desirable, for both efficiency and control, to collect a *batch* of transactions, which are then processed as a group. The collection is done either manually, by a central processor, or by a cluster controller or distributed processor. Certain *control totals* are computed for the batch and checked against the results.

AUDITORS' CRITERIA

Adequacy of database administration
Control functions performed by DBA
Separation of data control from application development
DBMS used
Number of databases and their usage
Adequacy of database documentation
Access control for database documentation

Fig. 9.3. Database considerations in review of general controls.

	T_1	T_2	T_3
T_1		X	
T_2	X		
T_3			

Fig. 9.4. Transaction-conflicts matrix.

For example, suppose a branch office authorizes payroll checks for its staff and specifies their amounts, and a central office prepares the checks. The branch can compute the number of checks and the dollar total, for comparison against the returned checks.

Some application systems automatically generate transactions. For example, when the quantity of an item in stock reaches the order level, a replenishment transaction may be generated. It is essential to produce a visible log or report of such system-generated transactions.

A number of control techniques are aimed at accurate data entry [30, 41]. Since error is always possible in any manual data entry, the amount of data to be entered should be kept to a minimum. Techniques to reduce data entry include preformatted display screens and menus, default responses, and *turnaround documents,* such as a utility bill, which is returned with the payment and which contains a machine-readable account number. Appropriate design of identifiers allows the system to detect data entry errors.

Account numbers usually include one or more check digits, which are a function of all the other digits. (This is just one example of redundancy as a control technique.) Applications can be programmed to expect certain data (such as a time card for each employee) and to produce exception reports about missing data.

Input can be edited for appropriate formats: alphabetic or numeric, proper number of fields and characters. Input editing also uses criteria that play the same role as database semantic integrity constraints. *Reasonableness checks* compare the input value against preestablished criteria. A value for a person can be tested for extreme deviation from a group average, or from that person's own past history. (Did the customer's electricity utilization for March differ greatly from that of the previous March?) One user response can be tested for consistency with others, for example, the answers to "How many persons in your family?" and "Name the persons." More complex checks use statistical properties of the database to determine what is reasonable [21].

The *database* integrity constraints potentially could be used for input editing. What is needed is a specification to the input-editing program of what database item corresponds to an input item, and a way for the editor to invoke the DBMS constraint-checking mechanism.

Interactive data entry has the advantage that the system can detect errors immediately. If the system uses display screens the erroneous information can be highlighted and the correct information protected from change until the user corrects the error. If a batch transaction is rejected because of invalid data, there must be logging and follow-up to ensure that the corrected transaction eventually is performed. Otherwise the execution of transactions could be prevented simply by creating errors. Error-correction transactions are often quite complicated and may introduce additional errors. An error should be corrected by the group that introduced it, and not by the data processing department. Corrections need the same editing checks as the original transaction, as well as additional controls, including authorization by someone other than the person who made the original error.

9.4.2 Controls on Data Content and Access

Control information in the database

Special information can be kept in the database specifically for control purposes. Since an application system may involve checking at various stages and by a number of different programs, an item sometimes carries a *data quality flag* indicating what checks it has passed. It may have an *expiration date,* which can be used to periodically purge obsolete data.

Redundancy that exists in the database for efficiency reasons may also be used for control. *Item counts,* for example, should be maintained whenever random updating occurs and checked whenever the set of items is processed sequentially. (This checking should always be done when the set of items is copied.) Periodic scanning of a database to check controls of this type is useful. Unfortunately, it is difficult for designers to select a good time in the processing cycle for checking. For one thing, the database may rarely be free of update activity and therefore available for checking control information. This problem can be alleviated somewhat by partitioning a file or database into sections, each of which has its own control data. Then only one section at a time has to be locked for auditing. Control totals can also reduce the level of concurrency in the system if many different update transactions have to increment the same controls.

Cross-footing balance checks (Fig. 9.5) involve categorizing items in different ways, computing totals for each category, and comparing the grand totals for the different categorizations. *Hash totals* are meaningless totals used to verify that all items are correctly transmitted, processed, or stored. A hash total might be computed, for example, by summing all the

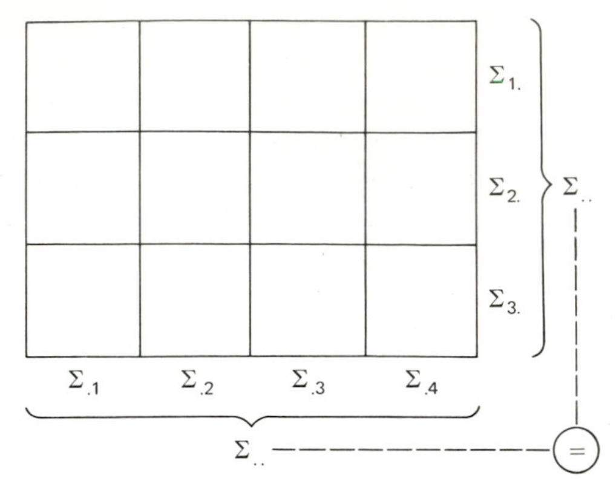

Fig. 9.5. Cross-footing balance controls.

customer numbers in a batch of sales orders. A *control total* is some meaningful total, such as the dollar total of a batch of paychecks.

Labels on storage volumes should be checked by the operating system to ensure that the right data is processed, and any bypass of this checking should be logged.

Semantic integrity constraints (whether implemented by application programs or by the DBMS) also depend on special control information.

Controls on database access

Need-to-know access control supports the principle of separation of responsibility, and flexible authorization facilities make it possible to rotate responsibility frequently.

Coadministration, which spreads the data control and authorization function among several administrators, is a useful control because it makes collusion necessary to grant access improperly. Different types of coadministration policies can be specified [9], such as:

- all the coadministrators must agree,
- the majority of the coadministrators must agree,
- at least a specified number of coadministrators must agree.

In another possible approach to separation of responsibility [13, 26], sometimes called "cooperative authorization," the actual access of some object by a subject requires the approval or cooperation of other subjects. Subjects receive rights that are conditional or incomplete; they must be complemented with other subjects' rights to perform some action. This contrasts with coadministration, where only the *granting* of a right by an administrator requires approval from other administrators.

Authorizing programs to access specific data, as in IMS, is a good control practice, as is control of program-to-program linkage.

Most systems exhibit regular patterns of usage of programs and data. Deviations from these patterns, such as great increases or decreases in activity on particular parts of the database, can be detected by operators or by analysis of logs, and should result in exception reports. Periodic reports on dormant data may reveal irregularities. If the dormant data is obsolete it should be purged, both to comply with privacy standards and to conserve resources.

Program library

As a particularly critical component of the database, the program library needs special controls. The system's production load modules should be kept in separate libraries, to which access is strictly limited. Strict control of access to source programs and documentation is equally important. A change to a production program normally must be approved by several independent groups or individuals. It is good practice to maintain a log of these changes and approvals. Changes that are not emergency fixes are best saved in batches for "block cut-in" (analogous to a software vendor's release), rather than being applied one at a time. Versions should be clearly identified, and old versions retained. Vendor-supplied software sometimes includes control features to identify modules that have been changed from the shipped version. (This is part of a more general need to verify the authenticity of software.) Other useful controls include hash totals and comparing modules for differences.

9.4.3 Controls on Database Storage

The online access control of a DBMS must be supplemented by control over the storage media such as disks, tapes, diskettes, and hard-copy documents. The media library should be a separate function, with its own authorized personnel in organizations that are large enough, and with a separate space to which access can be controlled. The library maintains inventory records and media-use records, and controls the retention and release of media. Encryption (treated in Chapter 11) can be used to protect storage media against unauthorized reading and to reduce the gain from theft. Storage of copies off-site is also valuable. (A practical set of guidelines for control of the media library is given in [20].)

9.5 THE AUDIT TRAIL

The audit trail serves as a bridge between controls (which produce the audit trail) and auditing (which uses it). It provides the information that allows auditors to verify the system of controls and the results of processing. The audit trail must be complete, or at least must select what to record in a way that cannot be predicted and that covers all actions that may later have to be audited. The audit trail then becomes a significant deterrent to fraud. The audit trail allows post-process auditing to reconstruct a sequence of actions: who initiated them, the time, and the results.

Bjork [6] has provided an excellent summary of audit-trail requirements for transaction-oriented database applications. The audit-trail function has three main aspects:

- detection of the actions to be recorded,
- the actual recording, and
- support for auditing.

Some desirable features in a generalized audit-trail function are:

- It is transparent to the process being audited.
- It is a generalized facility supporting *all* applications.
- It allows the real sequence of events to be reconstructed.
- Recording can be selectively and dynamically started and stopped.
- Events to be recorded can be specified in terms of: the process (or application) to be audited, time, data objects and their values, database operations, transaction type, or combinations of these criteria.
- What to record for each event can be specified.

We mentioned earlier that database systems, with their destructive updating, lose certain advantages of older systems, which retained generations of files. A generalized audit trail would allow these advantages to be regained by adding a time dimension to the database. An earlier version of a data item could be accessed; an earlier version could even be *corrected,* in the sense that all its uses would be recorded and could be "undone." Suppose, for example, that an error were found in the records about an individual. All uses of the erroneous data could be traced. If erroneous reports had been sent, corrections could be mailed. The propagation of the error through the database could also be traced.

Some of the items to be included in the audit-trail entry are:

- operation or event that caused the entry to be made,
- time of the event,
- application program,
- transaction sequence number,
- user,
- terminal (or line or port),

- name of the data object (if one is involved),
- some means of identifying the *occurrence** of the object,
- new value and old value.

(Some of these items can be factored out so that they need not appear in each entry.) In terms of the model of Chapter 6, an audit-trail entry describes a specific execution of a request. However, the audit trail need not be limited to *database* requests; it can also include user and operator commands.

Although it is common practice to combine the audit trail and the recovery log, they are conceptually distinct. Each needs data not needed for the other, one major difference being that a recovery log does not usually record *read* operations. (See Fig. 9.6.) There is therefore some argument for physically separating the recovery log and the audit trail. Processing of the recovery log should not be slowed by the need to pass over audit data. The recovery procedure itself must appear in the audit trail. A separate audit trail is more secure, since access can be restricted to the auditor. However, maintaining separate logs is undoubtedly more expensive.

A number of issues remain to be resolved for a generalized audit trail. For example, we would like it to be valid "forever." But will the entries remain meaningful after the structure of the database changes? What *level* of event or operation is recorded? If higher-level events are recorded the audit must "trust" the system's mapping of these to lower-level events. Is there one audit trail or several? Some ways to distribute the audit trail would be: by data class, by user class, by type of database operation, by application system, or by transaction type. Another issue is the privacy question raised by auditors' examination of the audit trail.

9.6 COMPUTER AUDITING TECHNIQUES

In this section we turn to the topic of auditing techniques. The literature on EDP auditing, including a comprehensive survey of the practices of many organizations [41], reveals that auditing practices lag far behind advances in database art. Auditing tends to be file-oriented and to take little account of continuous online operation. Fortunately, the cultural gap between auditors and database practitioners is rapidly narrowing. There is increasing agreement that the DBMS can be used as an audit tool.

---

* This is by no means trivial, since in a complex database it may be necessary to record the object's relationship to other objects.

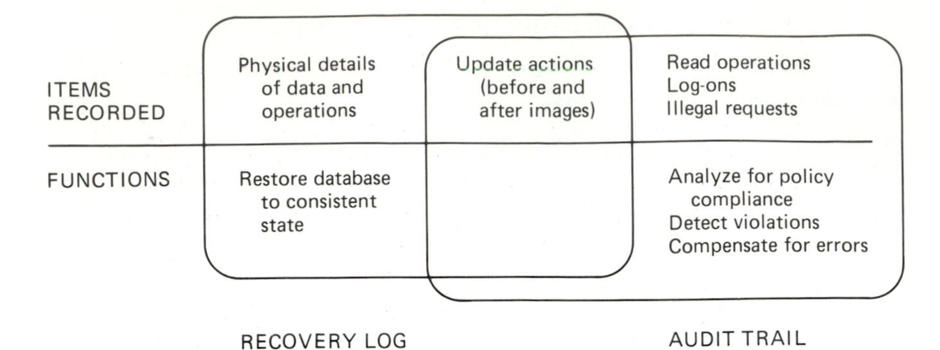

Fig. 9.6. Relationship between recovery log and audit trail.

Descriptions of auditing techniques and tools can be found in many textbooks, reports, and articles. A number of Generalized Audit software packages are available, but they are designed primarily for use with sequential file structures. Their value has therefore declined with the growing use of DBMSs, and there is no comprehensive tool to replace them. However, many of the techniques used with these packages also apply in a database environment. Our purpose here is to convey some flavor of the techniques, which in many cases are the same ones used by software developers, but with different names. As shown in Fig. 9.7, we organize the techniques into three major categories, corresponding to the auditor's responsibilities of "understanding the system," "verifying phases of processing," and "verifying results of processing."

Understanding the system	Verifying phases of processing	Verifying results of processing
Documents: Program listings Flowcharts HIPO charts Narrative Interviews Questionnaires Control flowcharting System description tools	Test data Base-case system evaluation Integrated test facility Tagging Tracing Mapping Transaction selection Parallel simulation	*Data selection and extraction:* Embedded audit-data collection Extended records Backup dumps Audit package record extraction DBMS facilities *Data examination:* Control verification Semantic integrity Independent source comparison

Fig. 9.7. Auditing techniques.

9.6.1 Techniques for Understanding the System

Gaining understanding is an organizational and behavioral problem as well as a technical one. The tools are much the same as those used for understanding any complex system. The auditor reviews documentation, such as program listings, flowcharts or HIPO charts [39], and narrative descriptions. System designers and programmers are interviewed, and questionnaires can supplement these interviews. Auditors have also developed a set of analytical auditing symbols for flowcharting the controls of a system. An example control flowchart is shown in Fig. 9.8. Although the symbols and method are file-oriented, the concepts apply to database systems. Automated system-description tools, described in Section 9.7.3, are also becoming available.

9.6.2 Techniques for Verifying Processing

Techniques in this category have the objective of ensuring that all processing is being carried out properly and that controls are working correctly. The techniques apply to both substantive tests and tests of compliance.

1. *Transaction selection.* A sample of transactions can be selected for detailed analysis, according to criteria established by the auditor. The sample can be random or can include, for example, all payment transactions involving over $1,000. The selection software either scans a batch of input transactions, or is invoked by the system's transaction-management component.

2. *Test data.* This technique is an extension of program testing. The auditor prepares transactions to be processed by the system being audited. The correct results are predicted by some independent method and are compared with the actual results. When the test-data method is extended to provide a comprehensive and continually maintained set of test transactions, plus efficient ways of comparing the expected and actual results, it is sometimes called *base case system evaluation.*

The major problem with this technique is the difficulty of preparing sufficiently comprehensive inputs. Test-data generators can help. The test transactions also need a database to run against, so that the real database is not affected; copies or backup versions can sometimes be used. With this and other techniques the auditor must determine that the test data is processed by the programs normally used on real data. This is particularly a problem for outside auditors who audit a company only once or twice a year.

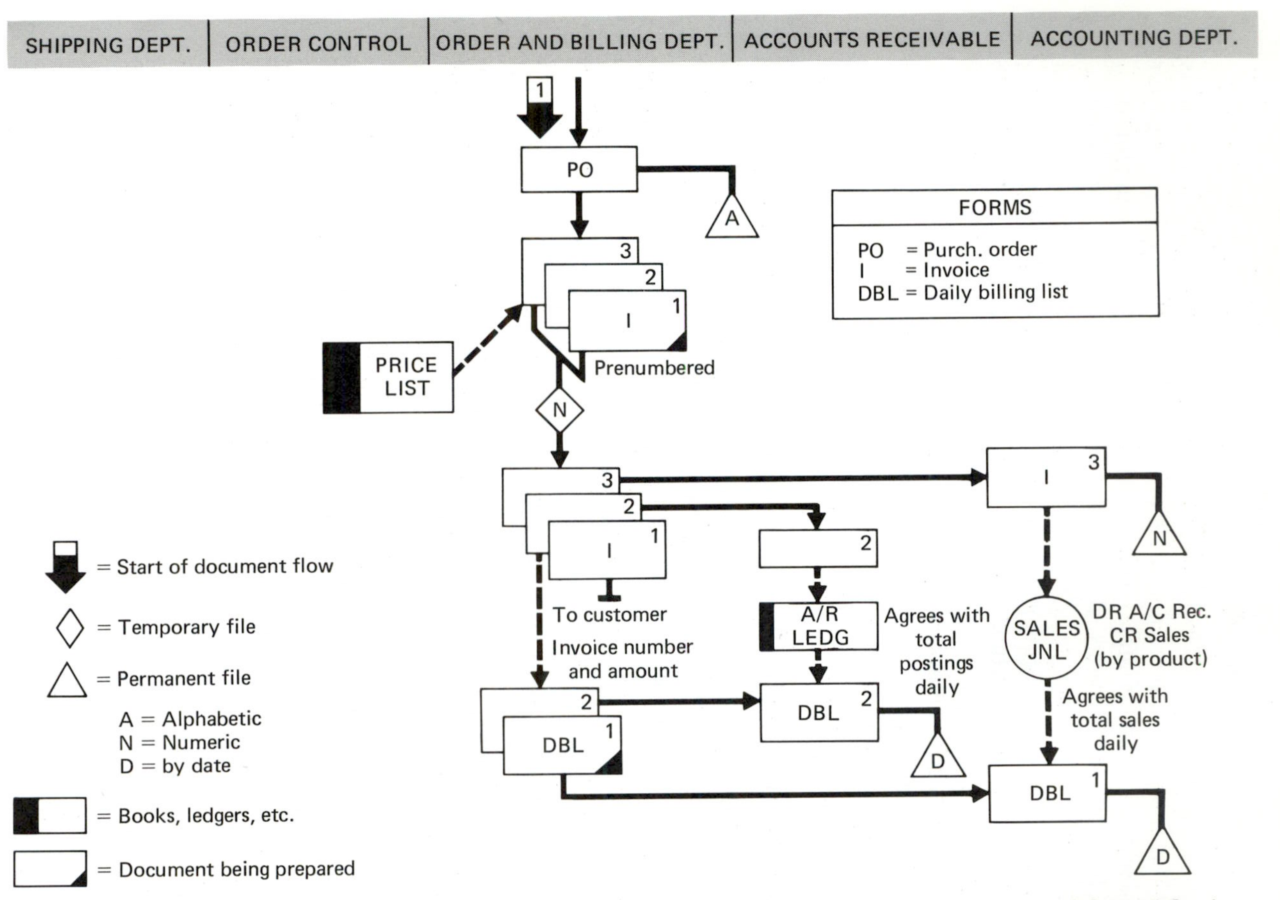

Fig. 9.8. Control flowcharting (from Institute of Internal Auditors [41]). [From Systems Auditability and Control Study, Data Processing Audit Practices Report. Copyright 1977 by the Institute of Internal Auditors, Inc.; reprinted with permission.]

3. *Integrated test facility*. This technique extends the test-data approach by embedding in the database some dummy entities against which to run tests. These entities are there all the time and sometimes form a "mini-company" whose data is processed along with the real company's data. This technique is more realistic, since it uses the normal procedures for system operation.

Tests can be made all through the year, thus increasing confidence that the audited programs are indeed the ones regularly used. The test data must be removed from the system, however, or its effects undone, so that real results are not affected. (The real company does not want to issue paychecks to employees of the minicompany.) Removing the test data may endanger real data. Care must be taken to guard against this.

4. *Transaction tagging* (*snapshot*), *tracing, and mapping*. Special logic is sometimes added to programs at key points to display or record relevant information when processing "tagged" test data (Fig. 9.9). (This auditor manipulation of application code is itself an exposure, however.) Detailed tracing of program execution is occasionally used by internal auditors on complex and critical programs. "Mapping" techniques determine how often sections of code are executed, or which sections are never executed.

5. *Parallel simulation*. With this technique the auditor creates application programs that simulate key functions of the operational system. When the real and simulated systems are given the same data, their results can be compared. The input to the simulation can be taken from the audit trail of the real system (see Fig. 9.10). The simulation is costly to prepare, but special high-level languages can help reduce this cost. Also, the simulation is typically simpler than the real application. For example, simulating the interest computation for a savings account is much simpler than doing the complete account update. Parallel simulation is a promis-

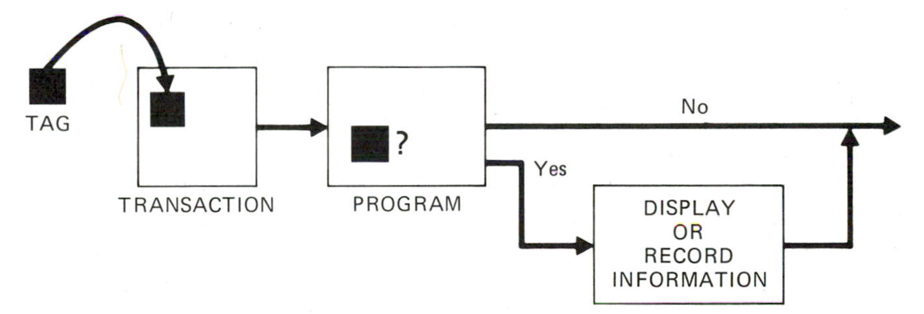

Fig. 9.9. Transaction tagging.

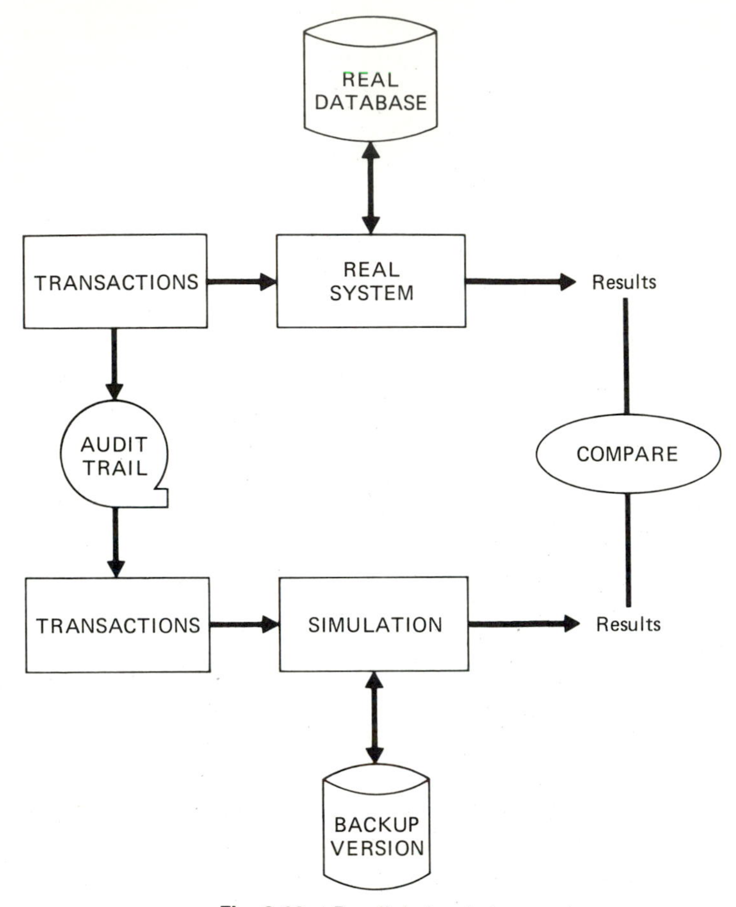

Fig. 9.10. Parallel simulation.

ing tool, especially for substantive tests [41], and it remains applicable in a database environment.

9.6.3 Techniques for Verifying Results of Processing

In these techniques, the auditor focuses on the data rather than on the processes. We discuss two problems here:

- how to select and extract the data, and
- what to look for in the data.

Selecting and extracting data

1. *The embedded audit data collection* technique inserts into application programs audit modules that collect data according to criteria specified by

the auditor. Exception conditions can thus be monitored. This technique could be replaced by a generalized audit trail function.

2. *The extended records* technique establishes a complete audit trail for a transaction, including application-oriented items. The technique requires a substantial amount of application programming, which could be reduced if a generalized audit-trail function allowed the application to augment the general items with its own information.

3. *Backup dumps* that are taken for recovery purposes are also useful for auditing. For example, where an audit trail is available, two successive dumps can be compared to determine whether all differences are accounted for by transactions. As database storage structures grow more complex, however, the use of dumps becomes more difficult, since the software required to analyze them becomes more complex.

4. The *record extraction* facilities of generalized audit packages have been used widely. They allow records of files to be selected on the basis of combinations of attribute values, or randomly, and placed in work files for further analysis.

5. The *query facilities of the DBMS* can be used to extract the data. These facilities can be used on the database and also on the audit trail if it can be accessed as a normal object of the DBMS. The data-selection capabilities of the query language can then be used to find information such as "Who modified field x at a given time of day?" Although questions have been raised about the auditor's ability to retain independence while relying so heavily on vendor and client software, use of the DBMS may provide the only practical way to extract data.

What to look for

Once the data has been extracted, the auditor can:

- *Check control information.* Control totals, hash totals, and any other control information can be verified.

- *Check semantic-integrity constraints.* (In Chapter 8 this was called a time T4 check.)

- *Check the data with an independent source.* The data can be checked against the real-world object it represents (inventory, for example). It can be checked against related data kept by a different department or even by another company. Another node in a distributed system may also keep redundant data that can be used for checking.

9.7 DEVELOPING RELIABLE APPLICATION SYSTEMS

Even with the best of DBMS support, a great deal of responsibility rests with the application system for ensuring that the application meets its specifications, follows enterprise policy, and does not provide openings for fraud on the part of either system developers or end users. In this section we discuss the development of reliable application systems, considering:

- characteristics of reliable systems, and
- the system development process.

Our emphasis is on technical rather than administrative techniques and on software rather than user interfaces or hardware. It should be stressed, however, that people who have analyzed system development from an audit viewpoint feel that *programming* is often overemphasized. It is only one part of the process. Although the principles of reliable software also apply to system software (such as the DBMS or operating system), problems specific to systems software are deferred to the next two chapters.

9.7.1 Reliable and Secure Systems

Reliability has been defined in [10] in terms of two properties: *correctness* and *robustness*. A correct system properly performs its intended functions and does nothing else. A robust system continues to operate reasonably even in the face of irregular conditions, such as hardware failure or bad input data. A reliable system thus has high *system integrity*. We can see that reliability is a necessary condition for most kinds of security and for data integrity.

9.7.2 Principles of Reliable Software

Modularity

Modularity has been defined [33] as *purposeful structuring*. That is, the structure of a modular system makes it easier to attain goals such as modifiability or reliability. The components of such a structure are called *modules*. The idea is to decompose an extremely complex system into parts that are small enough to be understood. Some of the issues that arise in this context are:

- the nature of the structural relationship of modules, such as hierarchical;

- the best method of decomposing into modules, taking into account *module strength* (relationships within the module), *module coupling* (relationships between modules), and optimum module size;
- defining the interfaces between modules.

Figure 9.11 shows a hierarchical structure of modules for an accounts payable application. In a hierarchical structure, a lower-level module cannot use a higher-level one. Some approaches to modularity start with *processes* and then consider data; others reverse that emphasis.

Modular approaches may eventually make it possible to design systems out of an inventory of standard "replaceable parts" analogous to the parts used by hardware designers. This would have many advantages for reliability, since these standard parts could be more thoroughly tested and understood.

Abstraction

Abstraction is a good way to achieve modularity. Abstraction means extracting the essential properties of some component of a system, omitting nonessential detail. This principle is most often applied to the description of a component as seen by other components that use it. The module that computes item extended price (in Fig. 9.11) is seen by the

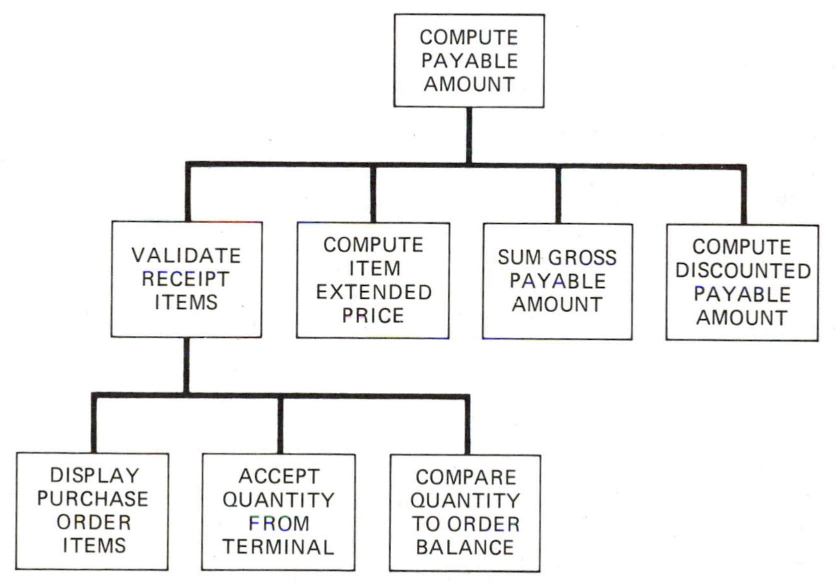

Fig. 9.11. Hierarchical modular structure (from Stay [39]). [Reprinted by permission from *IBM Systems Journal.* Copyright 1976 by International Business Machines Corporation.]

module that uses it only in terms of its function. When that module changes internally, no change is needed in the modules that use it, as long as it continues to support the same abstraction. This is an example of *procedural* abstraction [36]. A *data abstraction* also would be seen by components that use it only in terms of its behavior.

Least privilege

The policy of least privilege (introduced in Chapter 5) applies to software components as well as to users. In this context it has two aspects: *information hiding* and *access rights*. Each module hides its inner workings from other modules, revealing only those properties used by the other modules. These other modules have no "need to know" the inner workings. Information hiding is a way of enforcing abstraction. A module may consist of certain data structures and also the procedures that have access rights to those structures. Other procedures cannot access that data. Programming language features can support this least-privilege principle.

Confirmability

It is important to design software from the beginning in ways that will help us to determine whether it is correct. This principle is discussed further in connection with program testing.

9.7.3 The System Development Process

The system development life cycle

Most disciplined approaches to application system development assume some kind of *life cycle*. A typical set of stages for the life cycle is:

- Analysis of needs,
- Specification,
- Architectural design,
- Detailed design,
- Implementation and component testing,
- System test,
- Operation,
- Maintenance and modification.

At control points in the cycle auditors can check on the security and integrity of the system being developed, as well as on the progress of development. There is also a trend toward including auditors in the design team, but there is a question whether this can be done in a way that does not compromise later audits of the system.

Various techniques have been introduced to improve the quality (and efficiency) of system development. Some of these are organizational or procedural (such as the chief-programmer team, or design and code inspection). Others are automated tools. We mention here three major topics: system-description tools, programming languages, and program-testing techniques.

System description

The specification and design stages of the life cycle are too often carried out without any systematic computer aid. Even where documentation is computer-maintained, this is often done in a nonuniform way. A better approach is to use a computer-aided design system, which allows designers to describe the system and to analyze the description. One such system is PSL/PSA [42]. PSL (Problem Statement Language) is based on an entity-relationship information model. Systems are described in terms of *objects* (entities), *properties* of objects (attributes), and *relationships* between objects. Figure 9.12 shows the major aspects of a PSL description. PSA (Problem Statement Analyzer) analyzes the description, detecting errors, omissions, and inconsistency. PSA produces reports that give considerable insight, showing, for example, which processes use which data, or showing the hierarchies of objects. System-description tools contribute to reliability by detecting errors in the logic of the design and by preventing mechanical errors.

Programming-language support for reliability

Appropriate design and use of programming languages can significantly enhance reliability. The use of high-level languages reduces error by reducing the amount of detail that must be managed. Well-designed languages prevent errors by being simple and uniform in structure. Lan-

PSL description
System input/output flow
System structure
Data structure
Data derivation
System size and volume
System dynamics
System properties
Project management

Fig. 9.12. Aspects of PSL system description.

guages provide varying degrees of support for *static analysis,* thus allowing errors to be found without executing the program.

One very helpful feature is the *typing* of variables, which allows the compiler to catch many programming errors. Some languages (Pascal, for example) provide a set of built-in types (such as INTEGER or CHAR) and also allow the programmer to define new types. The compiler can then detect an illegal operation on a type or an attempt to assign a variable of one type to a variable of another type.

Languages can also support modularity, abstraction, and access rights. It should, of course, be possible to compile modules independently. Languages such as Modula [44] and ADA [32] enforce information hiding by allowing modules to declare which of their variables are visible outside the module, and which outside variables they use. It is interesting that the languages with the most reliability support were not designed for database applications but rather for highly reliable real-time systems. There is certainly a need to apply the same concepts to the typical database environment.

Abstract data types

An *abstract data type* (ADT) [14] is a class of objects characterized by a set of operations that provides the only means for creating and manipulating those objects. For example, the ADT named Queue might be manipulated by the operations ADD (which adds an item to a queue) and REMOVE (which removes an item). Users of the ADTs have no way of knowing how the data objects are represented or how the operations are implemented. That information is hidden. ADTs support the principles of modularity, abstraction, and information hiding. Abstract types are defined in a representation-free way—algebraically, for example. Since this kind of definition removes nonessential detail, it is easier to understand; since it is formal, it helps in verifying correctness of a design. The specifications can also aid in achieving and verifying correctness of the representation.

Abstract types can be used without any support from the programing language. With such support, however, it is possible to *encapsulate* the representation of both the data structures and operations. Some programming languages (for example, Simula) allow users to define new ADTs, which can then be used along with the built-in types.

Building on such languages, Jones and Liskov [19] have proposed language extensions to control the kinds of access allowed to data objects. With this scheme, access-control restrictions are stated explicitly in programs and enforced by the compiler. The programs thus become both more reliable and more understandable (since their rights are explicitly stated.) An ADT has a set of *rights,* which is equivalent to the set of allowed operations. Each program variable corresponds to an ADT and also has a set of rights, which are declared in the program. These rights must be included in the rights of the ADT. All uses of the variable can be checked by the compiler for both type compatibility and access correctness.

Program testing

Program testing is a crucial part of several phases of the life cycle. The goal of testing is to arrive at correct programs; that is, programs that do not contain errors. In large part, therefore, testing is directed at uncovering errors [27, 28]. There are two main classes of errors. First, the program may not behave as its specifiers intended, because they did not understand the application, or because they specified the program incorrectly, or because the specifications were misunderstood. That is, the program does not meet its *functional specifications*. Secondly, the program may fail to meet its *design specifications*. It may implement the right functions, but inefficiently, or with incorrect algorithms, or with coding errors.

Most software testing effort goes into maintenance rather than the initial testing. Maintenance is necessary to correct the two types of error and also to make improvements in both function and design. Changing programs tends to introduce new errors. It is therefore necessary to do *regression testing*; that is, to repeat the tests performed at initial testing and subsequently. This means that test cases and testing procedures must be very systematically maintained. The techniques we discuss are beginning to provide some help with this very difficult problem.

Many errors can be detected without any execution of the program. This static analysis can be done by people (as in structured walkthroughs), by compilers, and by more sophisticated tools not currently available in compilers. The errors or possible errors that a static analysis can detect include variables not initialized, code segments that can never be reached, variables set but not used, the use of undefined variables, and mismatched types. Static analysis uses the concept of a *control-flow graph,* which represents all possible control paths through a program. The nodes of the graph are statements or groups of statements, and the edges represent control flow.

Static analysis fails to detect many errors, but it takes very little tester time [12]. Static analysis and the flow graph are also useful in planning dynamic testing. Commonly used dynamic methods are to traverse every edge at least once, or to traverse each path from the setting of a variable to its use. These techniques are time-consuming, however, and do not catch all errors. The most effective test cases are constructed using knowledge of the program and the application and intuition about which kinds of errors are likely. These cases usually test at least all boundary conditions. Once a good set of test cases has been constructed, they and the procedures for running them must be maintained and used for regression testing.

A promising technique still in the research stage is *symbolic execution,* which combines aspects of both static analysis and dynamic testing. The program is executed (interpretively), but *symbols* are used as values in place of the usual data values. A program tester can derive quite a bit of information from symbolic execution without having to develop any test data. Symbolic execution can also help in the preparation of efficient test data and can serve as a tool in another program-validation technique, formal proof of correctness, which is discussed in Chapter 11.

The tracing and mapping techniques used by auditors are examples of *program instrumentation* [15], where the program is manipulated in some way to produce information beyond its normal outputs. Such information might be, for example, counts of the number of times each node or edge of the control-flow graph is encountered. Program instrumentation can also support the monitoring of program variables or the testing of assertions about them [40], directed by statements such as:

```
MONITOR NUMERIC RANGE (X)
```

or

```
ASSERT (X > I).
```

9.8 DBMS SUPPORT OF AUDIT AND CONTROL

In this section we consider what characteristics the DBMS needs in order to support audit and control. First, the system must be credible; it must have high reliability or integrity, so that auditors can trust both its controls and its modes of accessing the data for auditing. There must be some way to *authenticate* the DBMS: to determine whether the system that is running really is the system described in the specifications. Another requirement is for people who are not primarily database experts to understand the operation of the DBMS, as well as the application systems that are produced on it. To this end, the DBMS needs clean design and clear documentation.

Many of the DBMS features needed for audit and control have already been discussed in this or previous chapters. They include:

- *Semantic integrity support.* This support can be used to implement controls on the "results of processing." As indicated earlier it may also assist in verifying data input.

- *Flexible access control.* Access rules allow responsibility to be separated and ensure that the areas of responsibility are well defined in terms of the transactions and data objects that a person can use.

- *A generalized audit trail.* The events to be recorded can be specified in access or integrity rules, and the contents of the audit trail can be controlled by auxiliary procedures specified in those rules.

- *Protection for the production program library.*

- *An integrated data dictionary.* A repository for descriptions of all system objects—their structure, their relationships, and their use, as well as any access and integrity constraints—is valuable for understanding the system and for establishing and verifying controls.

- *Scheduling facilities.* The DBMS could support follow-up on errors by rescheduling a controls check at intervals until the error is corrected.

9.9 CONCLUSION

In this chapter we have introduced the vitally important topic of auditing and controls as they relate to principles of database security and integrity. We have given a brief survey of the many approaches to developing reliable software. Finally, we have drawn conclusions about what DBMSs must provide to support auditing and controls.

EXERCISES

9.1. Assume that you are an administrator for a company that uses a transaction-conflicts matrix to separate responsibility. The matrix is represented by a table named CONFLICT with columns T_1 and T_2. A row of this table with the value ('TA', 'TB') means that TA conflicts with TB. Assume also that access rules are stored in a table named AUTHORITY with columns S (subject) and O (object). Write an integrity rule for AUTHORITY that prevents transaction conflicts. Use SQL syntax. [*Hint.* Define a view that is the join of AUTHORITY with itself on SUBJECT.]

9.2. Using the extended model of Chapter 6, define an access rule such that, for objects in data class 'C', administration of these objects requires that a majority of administrators agree and administrator 'A' does not disagree ('A' has veto power). If the request does not attain the required majority, then procedure 'P1' is invoked; if 'A' disagrees procedure 'P2' is invoked; and in both cases procedure 'P3' is also invoked.

9.3. Relate the concept of an atomic transaction (discussed in Chapter 8) to the principles of abstraction and information hiding.

REFERENCES AND BIBLIOGRAPHY

1. B. Allen, "The biggest computer frauds: Lessons for CPAs." *Journal of Accountancy* **143,** 5 (May 1977), 52–62.
2. "An Analysis of Computer Security Safeguards for Detecting and Preventing Intentional Computer Misuse." Nat. Bureau of Standards Special Publication 500–25 (January 1978). Nat. Bureau of Standards, Washington, D.C.
3. "Audit Considerations in Electronic Funds Transfer Systems." American Institute of Certified Public Accountants, New York, 1978.
   Reviews the regulatory and legislative environment of EFT systems and suggests changes implied by EFT for the controls described in [4].
4. "The Auditor's Study and Evaluation of Internal Control in EDP Systems." American Institute of Certified Public Accountants, New York, 1977.
5. H. Baruch, "The Foreign Corrupt Practices Act." *Harvard Business Review* **57,** 1 (Jan–Feb 1979), 32–50.
6. L. A. Bjork, Jr., "Generalized audit-trail requirements and concepts for data base applications." *IBM Systems J.* **14,** 3 (1975), 229–245.
   Presents a model of an audit trail, including the concept of time addressing, which adds the time dimension to the values stored in the database, allowing reference to past versions of data. The contents of an audit trail are defined in detail, and some possible architectures are considered.
7. J. I. Cash, A. D. Bailey, and A. B. Whinston, "A survey of techniques for auditing EDP-based accounting information systems." *The Accounting Review* **LII,** 4 (October 1977), 813–832.
8. R. E. Fairley, "Tutorial: Static analysis and dynamic testing of computer software." *Computer* **11,** 4 (April 1978), 14–23.
   A very readable introduction to modern methods of testing, covering both static and dynamic techniques.
9. E. B. Fernandez and H. Kasuga, "Data Control in a Distributed Database System." IBM Los Angeles Scientific Center Report G320–2693, Sept. 1977.
10. P. Freeman, "Software reliability and design: A survey." Reprinted in [43], 75–85.
11. R. Fried, "Monitoring data integrity." *Datamation* **24,** 6 (June 1978), 176–181.
    Describes how one organization uses periodic scans of databases or files to determine how well they meet integrity criteria. Different user-oriented reports on the condition of data are produced for the different users of a database.
12. C. Gannon, "Error detection using path testing and static analysis." *Computer* **12,** 8 (August 1979), 26–31.
13. H. M. Gladney, "Administrative control of computing service." *IBM Systems J.* **17,** 2 (1978), 151–178.

Describes general principles for the administration of computing resources. The need for accountability of actions and the importance of auditing are emphasized. Several of these principles were incorporated in the design of RACF.

14. J. Guttag, "Abstract data types and the development of data structures." *Comm. ACM* **20,** 6 (June 1977), 396–404.

15. J. C. Huang, "Program instrumentation and software testing." *Computer* **11,** 4 (April 1978), 25–32.

16. IBM Corporation, "Data Security Controls and Procedures—A Philosophy for DP Installations." IBM Form No. G320-5649-01. White Plains, N.Y., March 1977.
    A management-oriented overview of tools and procedures to promote security. Among the chapters are Interface Controls (e.g., journaling); Traditional Classes of Control (Organizational, Personnel, Operational, Development); Functional Duties; Plans and Programs.

17. E. G. Jancura, *Audit and Control of Computer Systems.* Petrocelli/Charter, New York, 1974.

18. E. G. Jancura and F. L. Lilly, "SAS No. 3 and the evaluation of internal control." *Journal of Accountancy* **143,** 3 (March 1977), 69–74.

19. A. K. Jones and B. H. Liskov, "A language extension for expressing constraints on data access." *Comm. ACM* **21,** 5 (May 1978), 358–367.

20. L. I. Krauss and A. MacGahan, *Computer Fraud and Countermeasures.* Prentice-Hall, Englewood Cliffs, N.J., 1979.
    A practical management-oriented guide to protection against computer fraud.

21. R. C. T. Lee, J. R. Slagle, and C. T. Mong, "Towards automatic auditing of records." *IEEE Trans. Software Eng. SE-4,* 5 (Sept. 1978), 441–448.

22. W. C. Mair, D. R. Wood, and K. W. Davis, *Computer Control and Audit.* Institute of Internal Auditors, distributed by Q.E.D. Information Sciences, Inc., Wellesley, Mass., 1978.
    A standard text on EDP auditing.

23. E. C. Maxson and N. R. Lyons, "Designing the next generation of auditing software." *The Internal Auditor* **35,** 6 (Dec. 1978), 73–83.
    Proposes an audit command language, which could be translated to a programming language such as COBOL and then compiled to run on various DBMSs.

24. W. B. Meigs, E. J. Larsen, and R. F. Meigs, *Principles of Auditing.* R. D. Irwin, Inc., Homewood, Illinois, 1977.
    A standard textbook on auditing.

25. T. L. Miller, "EDP . . . A matter of definition." *The Internal Auditor* **32,** 4 (July/August 1975), 31–38.

26. N. Minsky, "Cooperative authorization in computer systems." *Proc. IEEE COMPSAC 77 Conf.*, 729–733; available from IEEE.

27. G. J. Myers, *Software Reliability: Principles and Practices*. Wiley, New York, 1976.

28. G. J. Myers, *The Art of Software Testing*. Wiley, New York, 1979.

29. A. J. Neumann, "Features of Seven Audit Software Packages—Principles and Capabilities." Special Publication 500–13, Nat. Bureau of Standards, Washington, D.C., July 1977.

A survey, oriented to the computer professional, of features of some generalized audit packages. A summary of the U.S. General Accounting Office Auditing Standards is also provided.

30. R. L. Patrick, "Performance Assurance and Data Integrity Practices." Report PB–276 400, Nat. Bureau of Standards, Washington, D.C., January 1978.

31. W. T. Porter and W. E. Perry, *EDP Controls and Auditing*. Wadsworth Publishing Co., Belmont, Calif., 1977.

32. "Preliminary ADA Reference Manual." *SIGPLAN Notices* **14,** 6 (June 1979), Part A.

33. D. A. Ross, J. B. Goodenough, and C. A. Irvine, "Software engineering: Process, principles, and goals." Reprinted in [43], 62–72.

34. Z. G. Ruthberg and R. G. McKenzie (Eds.), "Audit and Evaluation of Computer Security." Nat. Bureau of Standards Publication SP 500–19, Washington, D.C., October 1977.

Report of a 1977 workshop that brought together experts in auditing and computing.

35. G. M. Scott, "Auditing the data base." *Canadian Chartered Accountant* **III,** 10 (October 1978), 52–59.

Suggests two possible solutions to the "crisis" in audit software:

1. For packages to directly access the database storage, bypassing the DBMS. This could be done, for example, by accessing backup dumps of the database.
2. For the packages to retrieve data through the DBMS and for audit functions to be built into the DBMS.

36. K. S. Shankar, "Tutorial: Data structures, types, and abstractions." *Computer* **13,** 4 (April 1980), 67–77.

37. "Special Collection from Workshop on Software Testing and Test Documentation, 1978." *IEEE Trans. Software Eng.* **SE-6,** 3 (May 1980), 236–290.

A collection of six papers on program testing.

38. Statement on Auditing Standards No. 3, "The Effects of EDP on the Auditor's Study and Evaluation of Internal Control." American Institute of Certified Public Accountants, New York, 1974.

The auditing standard for computerized systems. Divides accounting controls into *general controls,* which apply to the overall operation, and *application controls,* which apply to specific tasks. General controls apply either to the "computer service center" (or "information processing facility") or to the system-development process [41].

39. J. F. Stay, "HIPO and integrated program design." *IBM Systems J.* **15,** 2 (1976), 143–154.

40. L. G. Stucki and G. L. Foshee, "New assertion concepts for self-metric software validation." *Proc. 1975 Int. Conf. on Reliable Software,* 1975, 59–71.

41. "Systems Auditability and Control Study." Institute of Internal Auditors, Altamonte Springs, Florida, 1977.

This comprehensive survey of auditing and control practices was prepared by SRI, administered by the Institute of Internal Auditors, and supported by a grant from IBM. Intensive interviews were conducted at 45 selected enterprises in the U.S., Canada, Europe, and Japan, and several hundred organizations were surveyed by questionnaire. The practices surveyed do not reflect a database orientation. The conclusions include:

- Top management is responsible for overall internal control, and users should have operational responsibilities. (Currently, control is often entrusted to the data processing organization.)
- Internal auditors must participate in the development of new information systems to ensure that audit and control features are included.
- Current EDP audit tools and techniques are inadequate.

42. D. Teichroew and E. A. Hershey, "PSL/PSA: A Computer-Aided Technique for Structured Documentation and Analysis of Information Processing Systems." Reprinted in [43], 195–202.

43. *Tutorial on Software Design Techniques* (Second ed.), IEEE Computer Society, Long Beach, Calif., 1977.

44. N. Wirth, "Modula: A language for modular multiprogramming." *Software–Practice and Experience* **7,** 1 (1977), 3–35.

10 Enforcement Design

10.1 INTRODUCTION

According to the model of Chapter 6, enforcement of access control consists of:

- detection of the access request,
- analysis of this request,
- checking the authorization for the request, and
- allowing, denying, or modifying the request in the light of the check.

Enforcement also includes mechanisms that prevent any of the steps in this process from being bypassed or subverted. In short, enforcement is concerned with ensuring that security policy, reflected by the access rules, is correctly implemented within the computing system.

In this chapter we first discuss principles of design for secure systems. These principles apply to both the DBMS and the operating system that supports it. We then present an overview of some of the various design choices for enforcement in the DBMS itself. We follow this with a description of authorization and enforcement as proposed or implemented in a number of DBMSs. Finally, information-flow control is discussed. The basic security mechanisms that the DBMS relies on the operating system or hardware to provide are described in the next chapter.

10.2 DESIGN PRINCIPLES FOR SECURE SYSTEMS

Simplicity

A simple system, with *economy of mechanism,* is more likely to be implemented correctly and has a better chance of being validated by thorough auditing or proof.

Open design

The design should not be secret. Any secrecy is in passwords or keys and not in the mechanism itself. An open design can be scrutinized by many experts and can inspire trust on the part of users.

Fail-safe defaults

If a user or component of the system fails to state some option, the default option should always be on the side of safety. This is an application at a more detailed level of the principle that a closed system is more secure than an open system.

Least privilege

We argued in Chapter 5 that the principle of least user privilege was a sound policy for database security. Least privilege is also relevant for system design in two very important ways. First, the design should support the least privilege policy for users. Second, the same principle can be applied to components of the DBMS and the operating system. A number of benefits accrue from giving program components only those privileges they need to perform their specific functions.

- *Confinement of errors*. If a component contains an error, the effect of that error is more likely to be limited. For example, an erroneous procedure with unlimited privileges could completely corrupt main and secondary storage. By limiting the memory that the procedure can access, we can confine the effects of error. Confinement facilitates testing, since there is a much better chance of finding the origin of an error, and simplifies recovery.

- *Maintenance*. It is easier to judge the effect on the system as a whole of a modification to one component if the privileges (and therefore the capabilities) of that component are explicitly restricted.

- *Trojan horse problem*. It is difficult to ensure that programs that have not been developed in-house do not contain code that manipulates data in unauthorized ways. The source code may not even be available for checking. Such programs should execute with minimum privileges.

- *Proof of correctness*. Much of the effort in proving a program correct is spent in showing that certain things cannot happen. Restriction of privileges limits what a program can do and therefore aids proof of correctness.

Least common mechanism

A *common mechanism* has been defined [27] as one that operates on behalf of many users and that could lead to a security flaw if it operated improperly. It is a good design principle to minimize the amount of code that all users depend on for security.

Separation of responsibility

We saw in Chapter 9 that separation of responsibility among people is a good control principle. The same principle applies to enforcement mechanisms. If two enforcement mechanisms must "agree" before access to some object can occur, the chance of security breach is reduced.

Hiding existence of data

Users should be given no more information about the structure or content of the database than they are entitled to view. The *existence* as well as the *contents* of other data objects should be hidden. This has been called the concept of the invisible database [15].

Straightforward correspondence of design levels

Security is enhanced if mappings between different levels of design are simple.

We have discussed principles of *security,* but a system design also must satisfy a number of other criteria, such as usability and performance. In the following sections we discuss some of the major design alternatives for the DBMS.

10.3 DETECTION AND ANALYSIS OF ACCESS REQUESTS

Validation of a database access request is at the heart of the enforcement procedure. We have described conceptually how an access request, represented as (s, O, t, p), is validated against access rules. We have said little, however, about how the system discovers that a request is being made, or identifies its components.

10.3.1 Types of Requests

The exact form of an access request depends on the language and DBMS being used. There are three basic ways to specify an access request in a general-purpose programming language.

One is to call a DBMS routine, passing parameters that indicate the nature of the request. For example, a PL/I program accesses an IMS database by calling a routine named PLITDLI.

A second approach is to extend the programming language to include the DML statements. Extensions to COBOL based on DBTG's work are described in the 1976 *CODASYL COBOL Journal of Development* [7]. Two proposals [9, 34] extend PL/I for database access. Both of these proposals employ *direct reference;* that is, items in the database are directly manipulated, rather than being moved into and out of work areas.

In the third approach, the DML is embedded in the programming language. For example, in System R, SQL statements may be directly embedded in either COBOL or PL/I programs. With an extended language or an embedded DML, programs either are processed by an extended compiler or are first processed by a *precompiler,* which converts the DML statements into statements that can then be processed by the regular compiler. A fourth possible approach is to use a self-contained database-oriented language.

10.3.2 Intent Analysis Time

An access request must be evaluated by the DBMS in order to determine the set of data occurrences to be operated upon. If validation is to be performed at execution time, the identity of the requester (program or user) is known, thus allowing the complete access request (s, O, t, p) to be determined.

To some extent a database system can analyze requests before they are actually issued. This "early" analysis can be very important for both security and efficiency. There are many different times when this analysis can be performed. We consider three:

1. compile time,
2. view-binding time (which may be at compile time or later), and
3. open time.

In all three cases only the set of *potential requests* can be determined. Some of these may not actually occur on a particular execution of the program.

Compile-time analysis has been implemented [8] for a situation where compile-and-execute was the normal mode of operation. This meant that the user was known at compile time and that access rights could be checked at that time. In general, however, analysis of a program to detect potential requests does not occur at the same time as validation of the requests. In the LASC proposal [35], a program is analyzed at compile time and a record (called the *data access list*) is made of the program's data-access properties. This analysis needs to be done only once, until the program is changed. Requests can be analyzed in some detail because of direct-reference language facilities. Compile-time analysis cannot, in general, determine the particular data occurrences that will be accessed because, while the predicate can be detected, it cannot be evaluated. Compile-time analysis therefore determines the potential (O, t) pairs. In some circumstances the subject may also be determined. For example, the subject may be either the user invoking the compilation or the application program itself.

The view mechanism allows some information to be determined about a program's potential set of access requests without an analysis of the program. For example the CODASYL subschema specifies the record types and sets that may be accessed. The PSB in IMS specifies the segment types and the corresponding allowed access types. It is of course necessary to check at some time that the program requests are compatible with the view definitions and any existing access rules. With System R this can be done at precompile time if the views and rules have already been defined. In contrast, in IMS the checking must be performed at execution time, because the call parameters can be set up during execution. It is therefore possible for an IMS program to fail at execution time because it requests an operation that has not been specified in its PSB.

In CODASYL, before a program can access the database all the relevant areas must first be opened. The potential set of records and sets that the program may access can be determined at this time.

10.4 ACCESS VALIDATION

10.4.1 Access Validation Time

Once the access request has been determined, it must be validated against the access rules. This validation takes place at the *access validation time* (AVT). The AVT can range from the time that the request is analyzed to the time that it is executed. Validation entails first checking for the existence of a rule identified by the (s, O, t) of the request and, second, evaluating the predicate p in the rule. These two steps may be done at different times. The predicate itself may also be partially evaluated at a number of different times. For example, consider the rule:

```
(s1, EMP, READ, p)
```

where p is:

```
TERMINAL_ID = 'X12' AND JOB = 'CLERK'
```

(JOB is an attribute of the relation EMP.)

The predicate can be considered as two partial predicates p_s and p_d. Predicate p_s can be evaluated at logon time when the terminal identification becomes known to the system. Evaluation of p_d must be postponed to the time when the request is executed. Only then will it be possible to determine whether the particular tuples requested have JOB attribute values equal to 'CLERK'. An exception occurs when the predicate in the request can be evaluated, because, for example, it specifies a value for JOB. For example, an SQL request might be of the form:

```
SELECT * FROM EMP
 WHERE JOB = 'MANAGER'
```

Thus the predicate in the access rule is always false for the request. For the request

```
SELECT * FROM EMP
 WHERE SAL > 10000
```

it is not known whether the access-rule predicate will be true for any occurrences of EMP without examining their contents at execution time.

In general, the result of an access validation (AV) can be considered as the conjunction of the results of a number of *partial-access validations* (PAV) [14]. That is,

$$AV = \prod_{i=1}^{n} PAV$$

By performing the partial validations as early as possible, the execution time overhead for a transaction or program can be reduced. Figure 10.1

	Compile time	View-binding time	Load time	Execution time
Intent analysis	C,D	B		A
Content-independent validation	D		B,C	A
Content-dependent validation				A,B,C,D

A: Generalized programs using a DML not amenable to compile-time analysis and potentially having access to the complete database.
B: Programs using a DML not amenable to compile-time analysis but accessing the database through restricted views.
C: Programs using a DML allowing compile-time analysis.
D: Programs as in C but with a customized load module for every user group.

Fig. 10.1. Intent analysis and validation times.

summarizes, for different types of programs, the earliest times that intent analysis and validation can be performed.

10.4.2 Timing Problems

Consider two operations performed in sequence. If the first operation is a check for the validity of the second operation, then a change might occur between these two events that invalidates the check. In the context of operating systems this time interval has been called TOCTTOU (time of check to time of use) [25]. If no mechanism exists to detect this situation and redo the check, an unauthorized operation may be permitted. The larger the time interval between the access validation and the request execution, the higher the probability that the result of the validation is no longer valid. For example, an access rule may be changed by the DBA so as to deny an access that was previously authorized. Ideally, any access validation (partial or total) performed using the old rule should be redone, if the change in security policy is to be correctly enforced. This is certainly reasonable when the validation has been performed at compile time but may cause considerable overhead if the validation has been performed during execution of the program. In System R, for example, the basic unit of enforcement is a transaction, which can include several access operations. Revocation of access rights is delayed until completion of any transactions that use those rights. Additionally, as the TOCTTOU increases, there is more chance that the result of the checking will be improperly modified unless it is well protected.

10.4.3 Architectural Level for Enforcement

In Chapter 7 we argued that basic access rules should be *specified* at the conceptual level with the possibility of more restrictive rules being specified at the external level. We now consider the possible levels within the database architecture at which validation can be performed.

Enforcement at the conceptual and external levels

Here the request is specified in terms of external-level objects, and rules are at both external and conceptual levels. A possible validation procedure is:

1. The request (s, O, t, p) is checked against the external-level rules. If a matching rule (with the same s, O, and t) exists containing a data predicate, p_d, this is combined with the request predicate giving an *effective request* (s, O, t, $p \wedge p_d$).

2. The effective request is mapped according to the external schema definitions into a request at the conceptual level. (The mapping may result in a *sequence* of requests at the conceptual level.)
3. Each of these conceptual-level requests is checked against the conceptual-level rules. If the corresponding rule does not exist, the request is denied. The request predicate is again modified by conjoining any data predicate in the rule.
4. The modified request is executed.

Performing validation at different levels, while providing additional flexibility, can cause execution-time overhead. It may therefore be desirable, for efficiency reasons, to consolidate the rules at one level. There may, however, be no need to consolidate when a significant amount of validation is performed prior to execution.

Enforcement at the internal level

Another possible approach is to store the access rules at the internal level in the form of *access-control lists*—one for each object. Each list consists of all the (s, t, p) tuples associated with the object. Depending on their form these lists may be stored either with the directory or with the object itself. For example, if there is no data predicate and the object is a relation that is stored as a file, then the access-control list can be associated with the directory entry for that file. Enforcement is then the responsibility of the operating system. Multics is an example of such an implementation. (The access-control list concept could also be used for rules maintained at the external or conceptual level.)

Content-dependent control may sometimes be implemented by storing the access-control list with index entries [13]. For example, consider access rules authorizing managers to READ the rows of the EMP relation that represent the employees they manage. If there is an index on the attribute MGR, an access-control list can be associated with each manager entry in the index. This approach has the advantage that a request can be rejected before the unauthorized data is brought into main storage. However, it does require that there be no access path to the data (such as a sequential search through the file) other than through the index.

Enforcement at the storage level

Another possibility for implementation of content-dependent control is to attach the access-control list to each data item occurrence so that it acts as a *tag*. This method is extremely wasteful of secondary storage but has the advantage that the TOCTTOU is minimized. If the tag also contains the logical name of the item, an additional advantage is that access of the correct physical location can be verified. Tagged data is more feasible when using the multilevel security policy, especially if there are only a few security levels.

Choice of enforcement level

The choice of the level at which to maintain the authorization rules depends on many factors. Two important considerations are:

- the time when the request is mapped to lower levels, and
- the time when validation is performed.

For example, if validation is to be performed at compile time, the rules should not be maintained at the storage level. Alternatively, if the request is mapped to the internal level at compile time, it would be inefficient to maintain rules at the external level for execution-time checking.

10.5 IMS

This and the next few sections provide overviews of the authorization schemes of several DBMSs and describe how each system enforces access control. Figure 10.2 gives an overview of IMS access control for online transactions. We consider an IMS system with RACF.

10.5.1 Types of Authorization

IMS has two basic types of authorization:

1. Views of the database to which programs can be given access. These views are defined by DBAs [Fig. 10.2, (1)] in the form of PSBs and placed in a PSB library. Job-control statements are used to associate a program with a particular PSB.
2. Explicit access rules (called *security statements*) written by authorizers (2). These rules provide the following types of authorization:
    - Terminal to program or command function (called terminal security). This specifies which application programs and system commands can be invoked from specific terminals. (It is important to control the use of certain commands because of their impact on security and integrity. For example, they can be used to change security specifications, initiate database recovery, or bring the system down.)
    - Password to program or command function (password security). This requires users to provide passwords in order to enter trans-

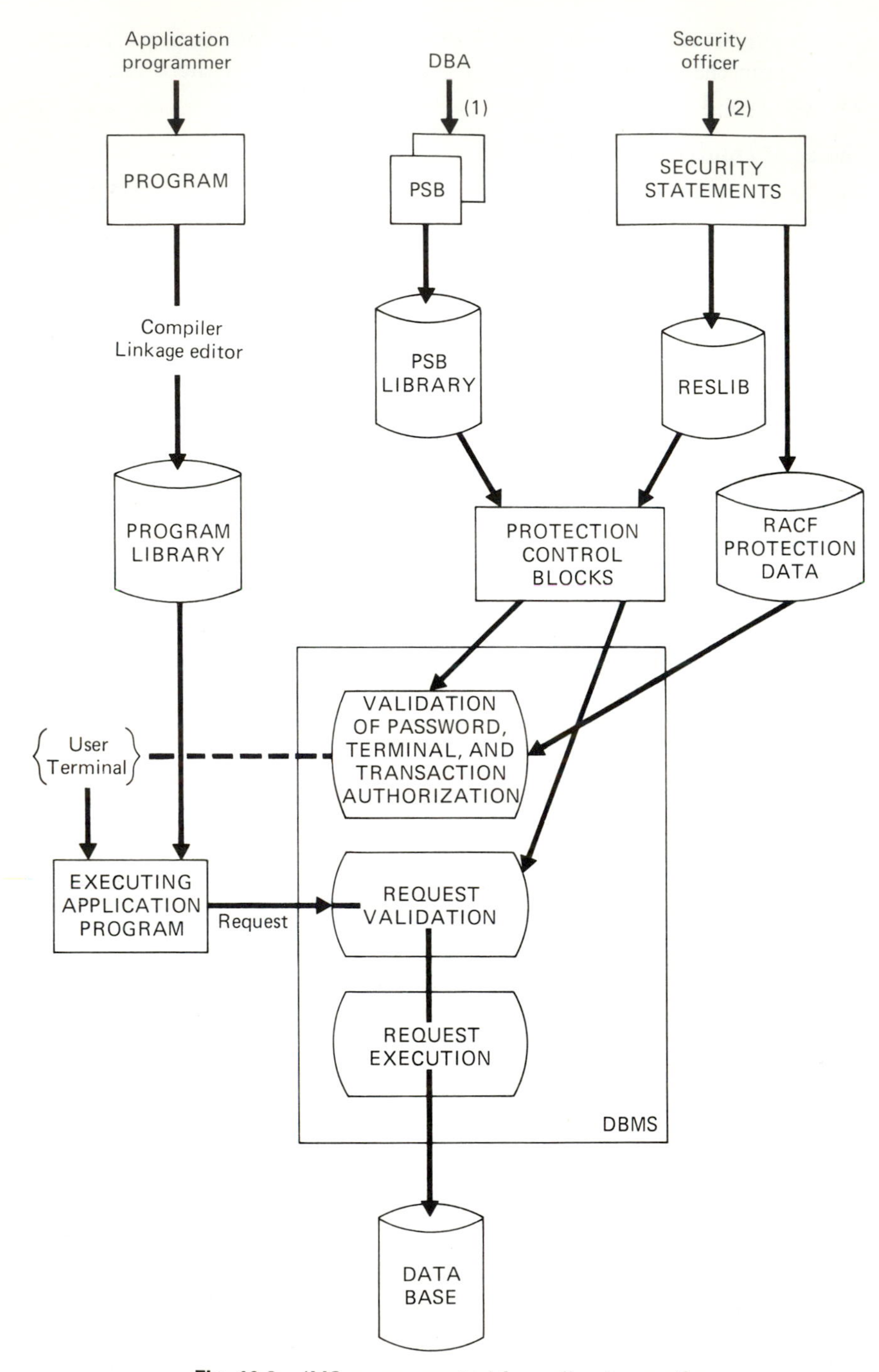

Fig. 10.2. IMS access control for online transactions.

actions or commands. The individual parameters of commands can also be protected by passwords.

- User to program. This authorizes a user to invoke a specified program.
- Region to Application Group. An *Application Group* is a set of resources which can include transactions, PSBs, and logical terminals. (A region is an operating system concept defining an environment in which application programs execute.) This type of authorization allows the Application Group to be used from a specified region.

Authorization data for IMS is stored in a number of different data sets: the PSB library, the ACB library (which contains the various protection control blocks), and a library (RESLIB) containing the load modules produced by the utility that processes the security statements. These load modules contain some of the explicit rules in the form of tables. Other rules are maintained by RACF in its data sets. All these data sets must be protected (for example, by using the facilities of RACF) against improper modification by other programs running on the same system.

10.5.2 IMS Requests and Validation

IMS uses a *call* mechanism for access requests. From PL/I programs, for example, IMS is invoked by a statement of the form

```
CALL PLITDLI (P1, P2, P3, P4, P5)
```

where the parameters specify the following:

P1	The number of parameters in the CALL statement;
P2	The requested DL/I database function (GET NEXT, INSERT, DELETE, or REPLACE);
P3	The PSB;
P4	The work area that contains or will receive the segment;
P5	The search argument, which is used to identify the segment type and occurrence to be accessed.

Let us see how the information in this call relates to our model of a request as (s, O, t, p). The subject in this case is the program, since it is programs that are authorized to access specific data. The object is defined by parameters P3 (specifying the PSB) and P5 (specifying the segment type). Parameter P5 also may provide a predicate. Parameter P2 provides the access type.

The request is analyzed entirely at execution time, and all validation is done at that time. Since the parameters could be set up by the program just prior to executing the call, it is not possible to analyze IMS calls before execution time. Validation involves comparing the segment type and operation against those specified in the PSB. If the request is invalid, the access is prevented, and an error indication is returned to the calling program. Certain types of access violations are logged. (Since requests are validated against a PSB, representing a view, they are validated at the external level, before being mapped to other levels.)

10.6 IDMS

10.6.1. Authorization

IDMS authorization is based largely on program access to views. A subschema defines a view that is a subset of a database defined by a schema. The subschema selects certain areas, records, and sets and may also omit portions of records. Each program uses exactly one subschema, but any number of programs may use a subschema. If a subschema carries an "any-program" option, any program may use that subschema. Schemas without this option may be used only by programs explicitly *registered* for the schema. IDMS does not explicitly control the use of programs by users, although database procedures can provide this and other types of control.

A program must declare its subschema usage. The following PL/I example states that the program being compiled (named ENROLL) uses a subschema named CLASS_RECORDS, which is a subset of the schema named REGISTRAR.

```
DECLARE (CLASS_RECORDS SUBSCHEMA, REGISTRAR SCHEMA,
   PROGRAM ENROLL);
```

A subschema description can carry PRIVACY LOCKs specifying how its various components may be used. The lock (with values YES or NO) specifies the allowable usage modes for an AREA and the DML operations that are allowed for a RECORD. (Since these restrictions apply to all programs that use the subschema, they are integrity constraints rather than access rules in the terminology of this book.) Database procedures can be associated with specific DML functions on specific record types, by use of the CALL option on the record description. These procedures can be used for data-dependent access control, for password checking, for transformation or encryption of the data, or for specialized audit trails.

10.6.2 Enforcement

A DDL processor processes a subschema description, producing control tables that are maintained in a central data directory and used for later checking. Registering a program for a subschema also results in entries in the data directory.

A COBOL or PL/I program communicates with IDMS by means of DML statements embedded in the program. The DML processors enforce access control at compile time, checking to see whether the subschema exists and whether all DML statements appearing in the program are authorized for the subschema. If any violations are detected, the compilation is prevented.

Checking of programs written in other languages (for which there is no DML processor) occurs at run time. Database procedures may also be invoked at run time.

10.7 LASC PROPOSAL

The LASC proposal [35] illustrates the approach of performing access validation as early as possible. One of the system goals is to provide security with reasonable performance by moving many security and data-management functions away from execution time to earlier points during program preparation.

Figure 10.3 gives an overall view of application program preparation and execution. Assume that application views and access rules have been defined. The subjects in these rules correspond either to applications or to a combination of user class and application. The programmer writes the program in a language with DML extensions and then invokes an extended compiler, supplying the name of the application for which the program is being compiled. For each view used by the program, the extended compiler invokes a *Checker* component, which determines whether the application is authorized to use the view.

The extended compiler produces, in addition to an application object program (the *A-program*), an analysis of all data accesses made by the program. This *Data Access List* is the input to an *Access Generator* component, which invokes the Checker to determine what different types of access can be made to each data object by user classes authorized for the application. The Access Generator produces a tailored *D-program* (tailored to the needs of this particular program) that contains code to perform only authorized data access. The D-program also contains code to do checking of content-dependent access rules. Since the user classes may differ in authorization, the D-program may be generated in more than one configuration. The Access List and D-program are retained by the system and catalogued by sensitivity to data objects and access rules.

If access rules or certain aspects of the data description change so as to invalidate a D-program, the D-program is regenerated from the Access List. (The original source program is not used, and the A-program is still valid.)

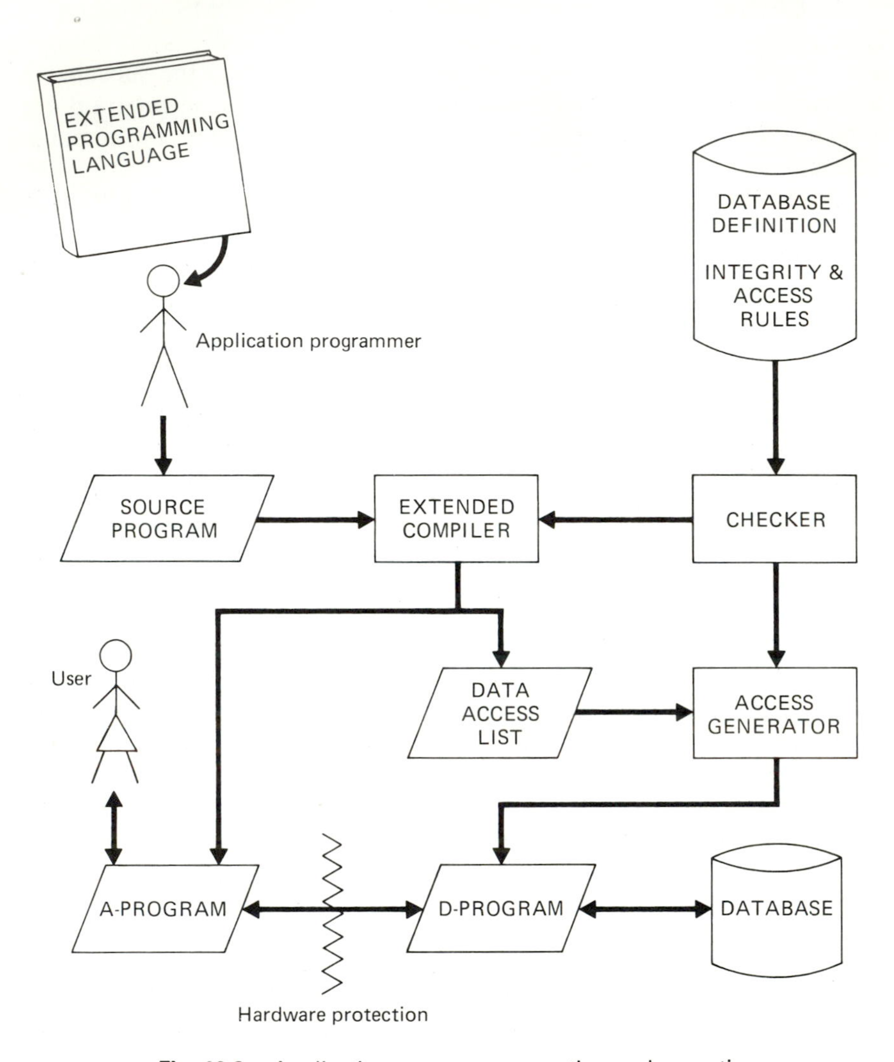

Fig. 10.3. Application program preparation and execution.

Programs always execute in the context of an application and a user class. At execution time, the A-program has limited communication with the D-program; it issues high-level calls that are served by its companion D-program. The operating system and special protection features (discussed in Chapter 11) ensure that only D-programs can access the database and that the results of the early checking are not altered before they are used, or bypassed at execution time.

10.8 SYSTEM R

10.8.1 Authorization

System R access requests are written in the SQL language. SQL can be used by itself as a query language, or SQL statements can be embedded in PL/I or COBOL programs. We consider here primarily this second type of usage. SQL access types include SELECT, INSERT, DELETE, and UPDATE.

The System R approach to authorization [12] is that the creator of an object initially has all rights (called privileges in System R) on that object. The creator may then grant some or all of these rights to other users. A grant may, at the grantor's option, permit the grantee to further grant the privileges to other users. (This grant option corresponds to the "copy flag" of the model of Chapter 6.) Grants may be revoked, leaving the authorization state of the system as if the grant had never been made. More details on this delegation of authority are given in Chapter 12.

Authorization is to entire tables for all access types except UPDATE, which is to columns. System R relies on a view mechanism for achieving fine granularity of access control. Views, in conjunction with UPDATE access to columns, provide field-level control as well as the equivalent of content-dependent control.

System R treats certain operations in a special way. These are operations that use system resources (operations such as creating new tables, or allocating space in the database) or that perform sensitive administrative functions.

Any user with *resource authority* may define a new table. Any user may also define a view using any SQL query, and this user's rights on the view are constrained in the following way:

1. *View semantics*. Certain operations may not be performed on some views; for instance, an UPDATE cannot be performed on a view that is constructed from a join or materializes a function (such as an average).

2. *The definer's privileges on the underlying tables*. A user who has SELECT but not UPDATE access to a table has only SELECT access to any view defined from that table. If the view combines several tables, the user's privileges are constrained by the intersection of his or her privileges on these underlying tables. Also, privileges on views are grantable to other users only if the corresponding rights for the underlying tables are also grantable.

10.8.2 Enforcement

System R makes heavy use of early checking, as part of a more general approach of doing all processing as early as possible [5]. A program containing SQL statements is precompiled to produce two things: a modified source program and an *access module* (analogous to the LASC D-program). The SQL statements in the source program are replaced by calls to the access module. All database access code is encapsulated in the access module, which is tailored to a specific application program. In a sense, the access module implements a highly tailored set of views. The "author" (the user who precompiles the program) receives RUN access to the program. RUN privilege is given even if the author does not have all the privileges needed for all the SQL statements; the access module is marked to indicate which sections are not checked, and these are checked at execution time—if they are executed. For statements explicitly in the program, authorization is checked for the author; for statements indicating a query to be provided by the user at execution time, checking refers to that user's rights. The author may grant RUN access to other users, but only if the author *does* have all the necessary privileges with GRANT option.

RUN authorization is checked only when the program is initially invoked. Content-dependent control is enforced at execution time. When System R runs under an operating system with the necessary support, the user's program (analogous to the LASC A-program) and the access module are protected from one another at execution time by System/370 protection features.

This early-checking approach must include a way to determine whether any privileges have changed between the time of checking and the time the program is invoked. Changes in privilege do not affect transactions that are already in progress. This policy is implemented by locking. At the beginning of each transaction, the access module locks its own description in the system catalogs. This means that no change that would affect the module can occur until the transaction ends and the description is unlocked.

Whenever a privilege is revoked, the system catalogs are searched to determine which access modules are affected. Those modules are marked invalid. When an invalid access module is next invoked, it is regenerated automatically. (This is possible because the access module contains the original SQL statements.) If, for some SQL statements, the author lacks a privilege with GRANT option, all RUN grants to the program are revoked. The author retains RUN privilege, but (as with the original generation) may be unable to execute certain statements.

10.9 INGRES

The INGRES relational DBMS introduced a way to implement fine-grained access control, using a technique called *query modification*. INGRES provides two modes of interaction with the database:

1. a high-level query language, QUEL, and
2. QUEL statements embedded in programs written in the "C" language. (C is the language used with the UNIX operating system [28].)

A QUEL *interaction* includes a RANGE statement and one or more statements of the form:

Command (target list) [WHERE qualification]

For example, consider the relation EMPLOYEE, with attributes NAME, SAL, MGR, and DEPT. A query to retrieve the names and salaries of all employees whose manager is JONES would be:

```
(Q1)  RANGE OF E IS EMPLOYEE
      RETRIEVE (E.NAME, E.SAL) WHERE E.MGR = 'JONES'
```

where E is a tuple variable that ranges over the EMPLOYEE relation. Query Q1 retrieves all tuples of EMPLOYEE that satisfy the qualification (predicate).

In INGRES a centralized DBA is responsible for the creation and destruction of all shared relations and also for all authorization. No mechanism for the delegation of this responsibility exists. This centralized approach was chosen in order to simplify database administration and the system design.

Unlike IMS and System R, INGRES protects base relations rather than views. The INGRES designers originally felt that protection through views would be inconvenient for their query-language users. Since certain combinations of access rights cannot be expressed as a single view, users would have to try a sequence of views to find all the data they were entitled to access. In retrospect, however, the designers concluded that protection of views would have been cleaner [32].

Access rules (called *protection interactions*) are written by the DBA in QUEL. For example,

```
(Rule 1)  RANGE OF E IS EMPLOYEE
          PERMIT E TO JONES FOR
          RETRIEVE (E.NAME, E.SAL, E.MGR)
             WHERE E.DEPT = 'D1'
```

Access rules may also be specified for maintenance operations: APPEND, DELETE, and REPLACE. The rules are stored in a directory

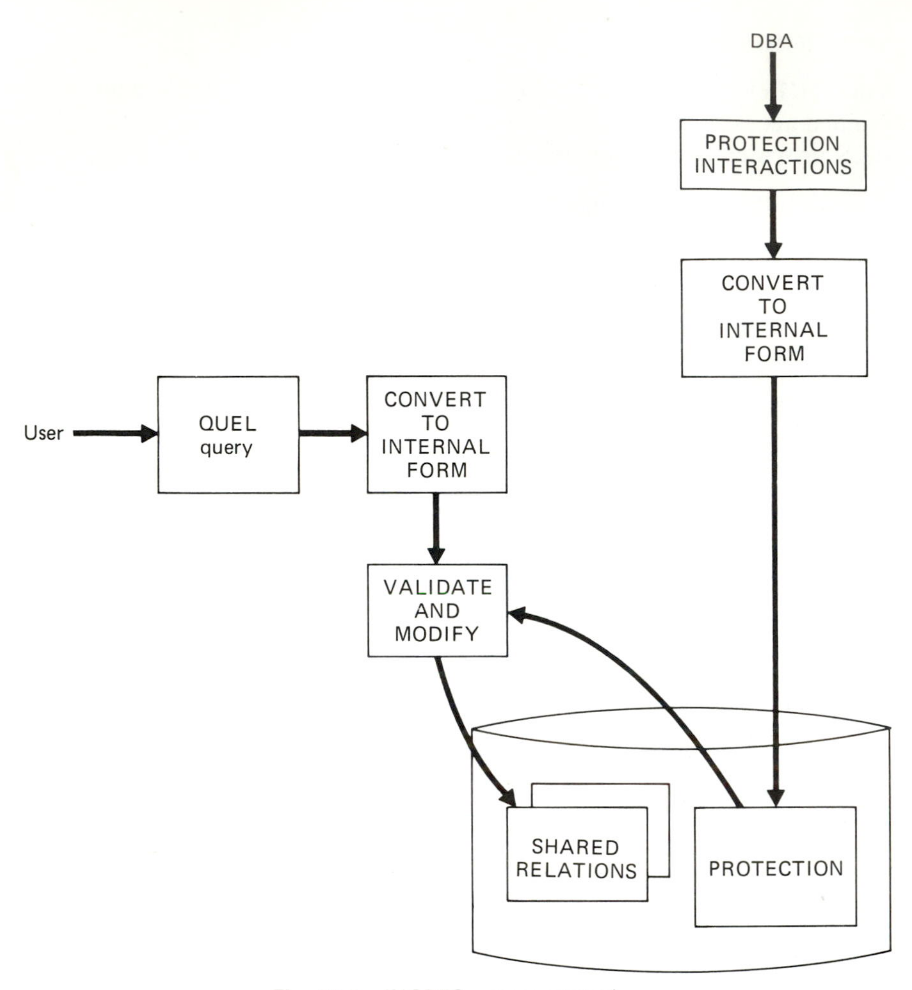

Fig. 10.4. INGRES access control.

relation named PROTECTION (see Fig. 10.4). The predicates are not stored in their original form, but are converted into an internal tree-structured form.

INGRES requests are analyzed and validated completely at execution time, one statement at a time. For the query user there is no compilation, so no possibility of compile-time analysis. Compile-time analysis and validation might be possible for QUEL statements embedded in C programs, but this is not done.

Let us see how query Q1, issued by user Jones, is affected by Access Rule 1. The rule predicate (E.DEPT = 'D1') is conjoined (ANDed) with

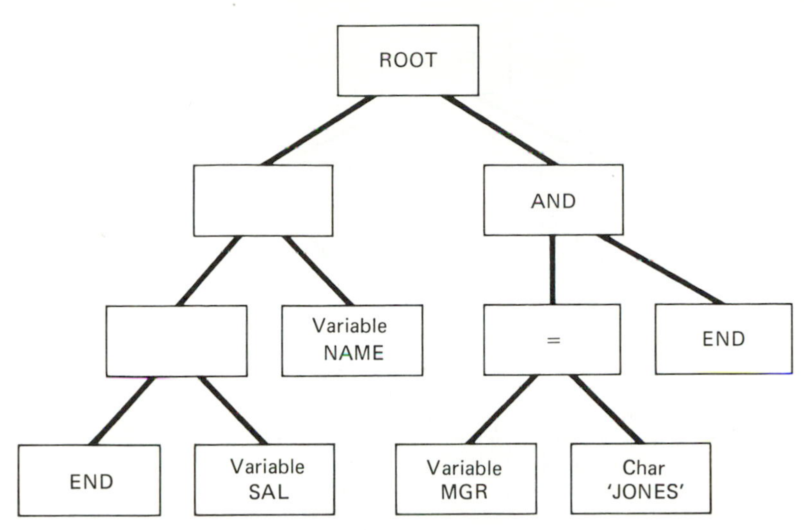

Fig. 10.5. Query tree.

the predicate of the original query (E.MGR = 'JONES'). This is done by appending the stored tree representing the access-rule predicate to the tree representing the request predicate. Figure 10.5 shows the tree for query Q1 and Fig. 10.6 the tree for the modified query. The lefthand side of each tree specifies the attributes to be retrieved and the righthand side the qualifications.

Now consider the following *set* of rules about Jones's access to EMPLOYEE.

(*Rule 2*)
```
RANGE OF E IS EMPLOYEE
PERMIT E TO JONES FOR
RETRIEVE (E.NAME, E.DEPT, E.MGR)
   WHERE E.DEPT = 'D1'
```
(*Rule 3*)
```
PERMIT E TO JONES FOR RETRIEVE (E.NAME, E.SAL)
   WHERE E.MGR = 'JONES'
```
(*Rule 4*)
```
PERMIT E TO JONES FOR RETRIEVE (E.SAL)
   WHERE E.SAL < 100000
```

Which rules would be used on the following request?

```
(Q2)  RETRIEVE (E.NAME, E.SAL)
```

Before answering this question, we describe a simplified version of the INGRES *access-control algorithm* for any RETRIEVE request R.

1. Find all attributes in the target list or the request predicate. This set is called S.
2. Find the set T of access rules with RETRIEVE as the access type and

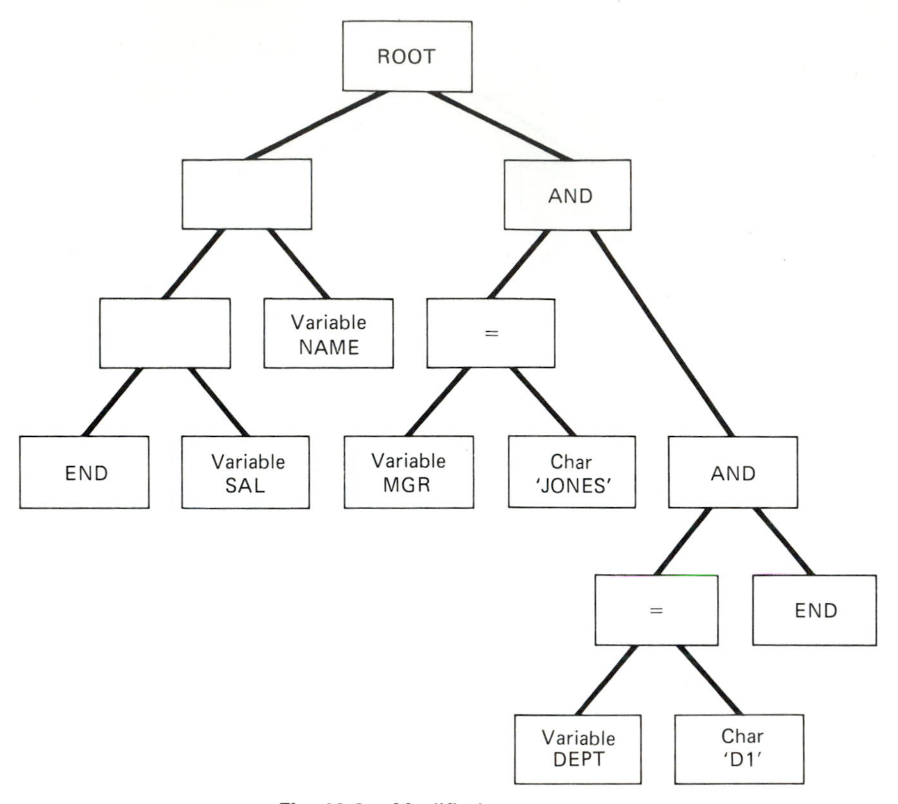

Fig. 10.6. Modified query tree.

with a target list containing *all* attributes in S. If there is no such rule, deny the request.

3. Ignore any access rules in T whose target lists contain the target lists of other rules in T. Call the resulting set T′. That is, find the smallest target lists that cover the request R. Call the predicates of the remaining rules $P_1, \ldots, P_n$.
4. Replace the request predicate, P_r, by P_r AND (P_1 OR P_2 OR . . . OR P_n).

The resulting query can now be executed normally.

What this algorithm means is that all rules relevant to the request are first located. It is then assumed that rules are well nested; that is, Rule A is more restrictive than Rule B if Rule B authorizes access to a subset of the attributes in Rule A. Only the most restrictive rules are retrieved for the query modification.

For request Q2 the set S is {NAME, SAL}, so only Rule 3 contains all attributes of S. Jones is allowed to see NAME and SAL only for her employees, even though she can see NAME for all employees in department D1. The modified query is:

```
(Q2') RETRIEVE (E.NAME, E.SAL) WHERE E.MGR = 'JONES'.
```

Now consider another request:

```
(Q3)  RETRIEVE (E.NAME).
```

Both Rule 2 and Rule 3 apply (are in set T′), since both include the NAME attribute, and neither rule includes the attributes of the other. Their predicates are ORed before being ANDed with the request predicate (absent in this example) to give

```
RETRIEVE (E.NAME) WHERE E.DEPT = 'D1'
          OR E.MGR = 'JONES'.
```

Finally, consider the request

```
(Q4)  RETRIEVE (E.SAL)
```

Here {T} = {Rule 3, Rule 4}, but {T′} = {Rule 4}, since Rule 3 includes all the attributes of Rule 4. So the modified request is:

```
RETRIEVE (E.SAL) WHERE E.SAL < 100000.
```

The authorization mechanism of INGRES has been compared to that of System R by McLeod [24].

10.10 A KERNEL DESIGN FOR A SECURE DBMS

The *kernel design* approach developed at UCLA [11] aims at a verifiably secure DBMS through retrofit of security controls into an existing system.

The general approach of using a DBMS security kernel also applies to a DBMS designed from scratch. If security-relevant code is scattered throughout the DBMS, then the whole system must be correct to ensure security; there is a great deal of common mechanism. If, however, all security-relevant code could be isolated in a DBMS security kernel, security would depend only on the correctness of the DBMS kernel and of the underlying operating system and hardware. If a kernel approach were also used for the operating system, then only the two kernels would need to be correct. If the kernels are simple and small, it may become feasible to prove the code correct using program-verification methods [16]. To illustrate the kernel approach, we describe the UCLA design. While this design has been applied to securing an INGRES system, the approach may be applicable to other DBMSs.

Figure 10.7 illustrates the high-level design of the UCLA system. The Data Management Module (DMM) is the noncertified, non-security-related part of the DBMS. The only security requirement of the DMM is

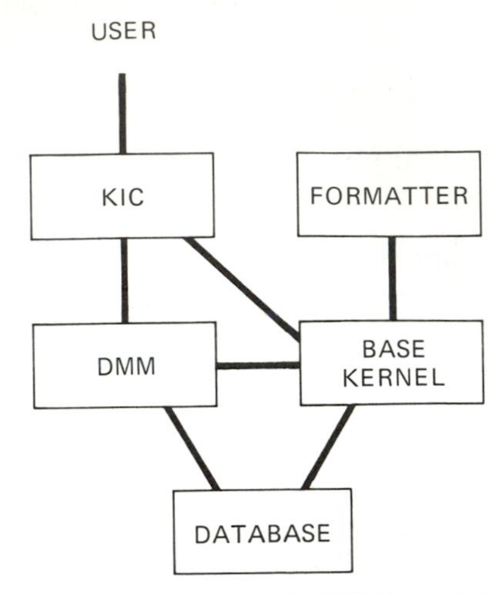

Fig. 10.7. UCLA secure INGRES kernel design.

that it be isolated in its own execution environment, so that users cannot directly retrieve data from it. The kernel consists of two parts: the Kernel Input Controller (KIC) and the Base Kernel (BK).

The KIC takes a user request, parses it, and retains for itself the type of command and the logical name of the requested data objects (for example, the attribute or relation name). It translates the external-level names used in the request to conceptual-level logical names. It checks the legality of the request against the access rules, which are maintained by the BK. It then passes the request to the BK, along with the user identification that is provided by the secure operating system.

The user request is also passed to the DMM, which performs all the usual DBMS functions, finally preparing, for example, a read command specifying the physical location of the data to be accessed. That command is passed to the BK, which must verify that the user is allowed to access the data in that location (as the DMM is potentially untrustworthy). This verification is performed by mapping the physical location back to the logical name, a process that is possible because each data item carries a tag indicating its logical name. As only the BK is allowed to modify the database, the reliability of the tag is guaranteed. The BK therefore reads the data specified in the command and checks the tag against the logical name passed to it by the KIC. Note that the BK needs to check only operations that return results to the user and not intermediate operations (since the DMM is confined). If the tag is correctly matched, and the data is in final form for the user, the data is passed directly back to the user. This means that while users are guaranteed to receive only data to which they are authorized, their queries may still be wrongly answered if the DMM is in error.

The data may have to be mapped to a program view before being returned to the user. The correctness of this operation is not necessary from the security point of view and can be performed by a noncertified module—the data formatter. However, the data passed to the formatter must not be leaked to unauthorized users. The formatter must therefore be confined by the operating system.

To summarize, the main advantages of this kernel approach are:

- Certification of security is possible.
- It is possible to retrofit security to an existing insecure DBMS.

There are a number of potential and actual disadvantages:

- Only content-independent access control can be supported.
- The KIC could be quite complex, depending on the level of user interface provided by the system.
- Tagging increases the amount of secondary storage required.
- Performance could be degraded.
- A significant portion of a practical DBMS is concerned with integrity and recovery. Further research is required to determine how much of this code must be included in the kernel.

10.11 ENFORCEMENT OF MULTILEVEL SECURITY IN DBMSs

In this section we consider possible ways that a DBMS might enforce the multilevel security policy. In all cases it is assumed that an underlying operating system provides multilevel security at a file level. Most of these operating systems are based on the concept of a *reference monitor,* which has the following properties:

- It is invoked on every access by a subject to an object;
- It implements the multilevel security policy;
- It is tamperproof and uncorruptible; and
- It is small enough to be verified correct.

The reference monitor is generally associated with an operating-system kernel; we will discuss this in Chapter 11.

Most attempts to implement a secure multilevel DBMS have mapped the DBMS security requirements into those provided by the operating system. This means that no security enforcement code is required in the DBMS itself and therefore that only the operating-system kernel need be certified correct to ensure that the multilevel policy is correctly enforced.

If the DBMS must implement the reference monitor, then it is necessary to verify that:

- the DBMS kernel is correct, and
- the operating system prevents modification or bypassing of the DBMS kernel by users of the system.

In general, this is a more complex task than proving that the operating-system kernel is correct, so we restrict our discussion to the first approach. The major design decision in the implementation of multilevel enforcement in DBMSs is the granularity of classification. We will look at possible alternatives, using the relational model as an example [29].

10.11.1 Classification by Relation

In this case a complete relation is assigned a security level. If each relation is stored as a separate file, all accesses to the database are controlled by the operating system. No security-relevant code is required in the DBMS. However, this approach may result in the overclassification of some data because the items in a relation may have different security levels. The security level of the relation will correspond to the highest security level among all the items.

10.11.2 Classification by Row

If different rows of relations have different levels, then the rows can be distributed over a *set* of files, each file containing rows of the same security level but from possibly different relations. For example, the rows of a personnel relation may be classified by the clearance level of the employee. Directories are split in the same way, and only users who are cleared for top secret can access the top secret directory. Figure 10.8 illustrates a possible database including directories. Once again only the operating system is required to monitor data access.

10.11.3 Classification by Column

The columns of a relation may vary in level. In such a case overclassification can be prevented by storing columns in separate files, with several columns of the same security level residing in the same file to improve performance. The operating-system kernel again handles all security checking.

Figure 10.9 illustrates the case where the salary column of the EMPLOYEE relation is considered top secret while the employee's name is unclassified. Note that the key of the employee relation must appear in both files so that a row can be reconstructed.

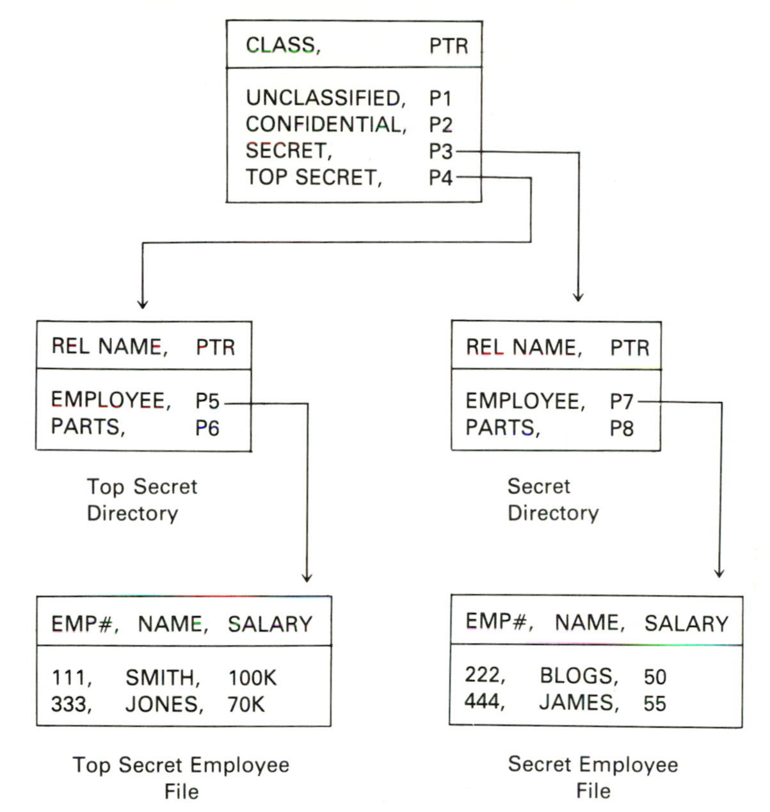

Fig. 10.8. Protection of classified data by row. [From Schaefer [29]. Reprinted by permission of North-Holland Publishing Co.]

Direct pointers linking all column entries for the same row are not allowed because of the * principle. In order to create the pointer that points from data of a low classification to data of a high classification, it would be necessary to obtain the address of the high-classification data. This requires a high-classification process, which is then prevented from writing the pointer in the low-classification area. Pointers from high to low classification would be left dangling when a low-classification process deleted a low-classification item.

10.11.4 Content-dependent Classification

While content-dependent classification results in the minimum overclassification of data, it goes beyond the security capabilities of operating systems. The reference monitor must therefore be implemented in the DBMS. Verification of the system becomes much more difficult.

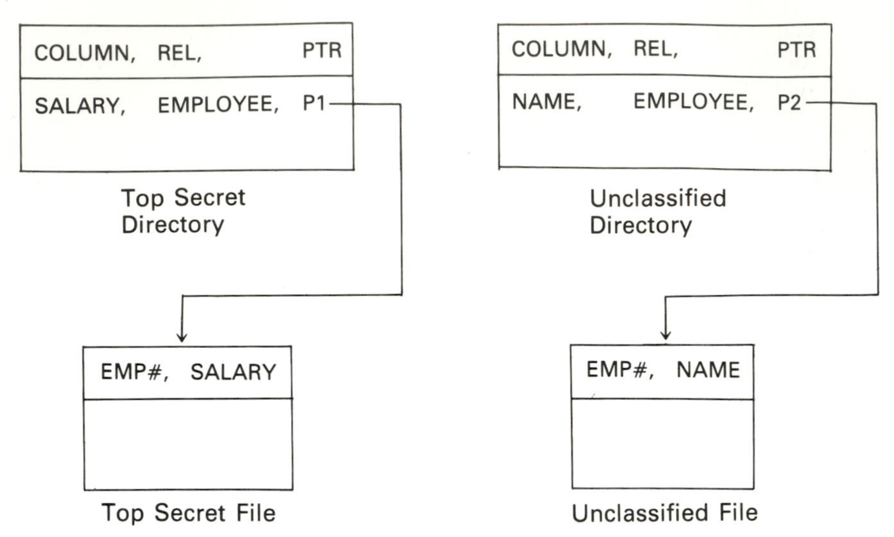

Fig. 10.9. Protection of classified data by column. [From Schaefer [29]. Reprinted by permission of North-Holland Publishing Co.]

10.11.5 Multilevel DBMS Designs

A number of multilevel DBMSdesigns have been proposed. SDC [15] developed a model and design of the security-related portions of a DBMS using an underlying secure Multics operating system [30]. In order to avoid security-relevant code in the DBMS, this design stores each column of a relation in a segment that has a single security level. The DBMS operates as part of a user's process and has no privileges that are not also afforded the user.

I. P. Sharp [20] investigated the design of kernel primitives to support the implementation of a family of secure DBMSs. The study recommended that each relation be assigned a single security classification.

MITRE designed a secure INGRES system to run on the MITRE Secure UNIX operating system [37]. A relation is again assigned a single security classification.

Two problems of multilevel systems that remain to be solved are [38]:

1. The *efficient protection* of small objects. Restricting relations (or even columns) to a single classification can cause a serious classification problem.
2. *Design of the user interface* in such a way that the user is not greatly hindered by the security features. For example, a terminal user may wish to update a low-level relation while reading information at a high

security level. If a display screen has multiple, independently controllable windows, each window can be used for a different security level [1].

10.12 DATABASE MACHINES

An architectural possibility of great interest is the assignment of the DBMS to a separate processor. This *database machine* (DBM) can be used as a back-end processor for a host machine or as a free-standing processor connected to a network or to a set of terminals (Fig. 10.10). A DBM could serve a back-end processor to multiple main processors, thus providing a way for them to share data. The DBM can be a conventional processor or can be specially designed. Partial approaches, such as self-managed storage hierarchies and intelligent controllers [6] are also possible, but are not considered here. We discuss here three DBM designs which have security or integrity as major objectives; other DBM work is surveyed in [23].

10.12.1 Security and Integrity Advantages of Database Machines

Even if implemented with conventional processors, DBMs present inherent security advantages because of their structure. Since the DBM is clearly the only access to the data, it can check all requests for compliance with access rules. Penetrations of the host operating system do not provide paths that could bypass checking, as would be possible in a conventional system. However, if the host can be subverted to allow a violator to impersonate a legitimate user, the DBM is not essentially more secure, unless the DBM has its own means to authenticate the requests.

When specialized processors are used, security overhead can be reduced by the use of hardware to support some of the security functions. If the DBM is a multiprocessor, security functions can be performed in parallel with other DBMS functions, thus enhancing performance (this is also possible in a conventional multiprocessor). However, the separation of functions brings the problem of efficient communication between these functions. If not managed carefully, intercommunication overhead could offset the performance gains due to parallelism.

Hardware support and multiprocessing can also be used to improve performance of concurrency control and semantic integrity checking. Recovery advantages are possible because of the existence of at least two separate machines, which can provide some desirable redundancy. For example, both the DBM and the host could keep logs. If a host crashes, the DBM can undo any changes made by active transactions from the

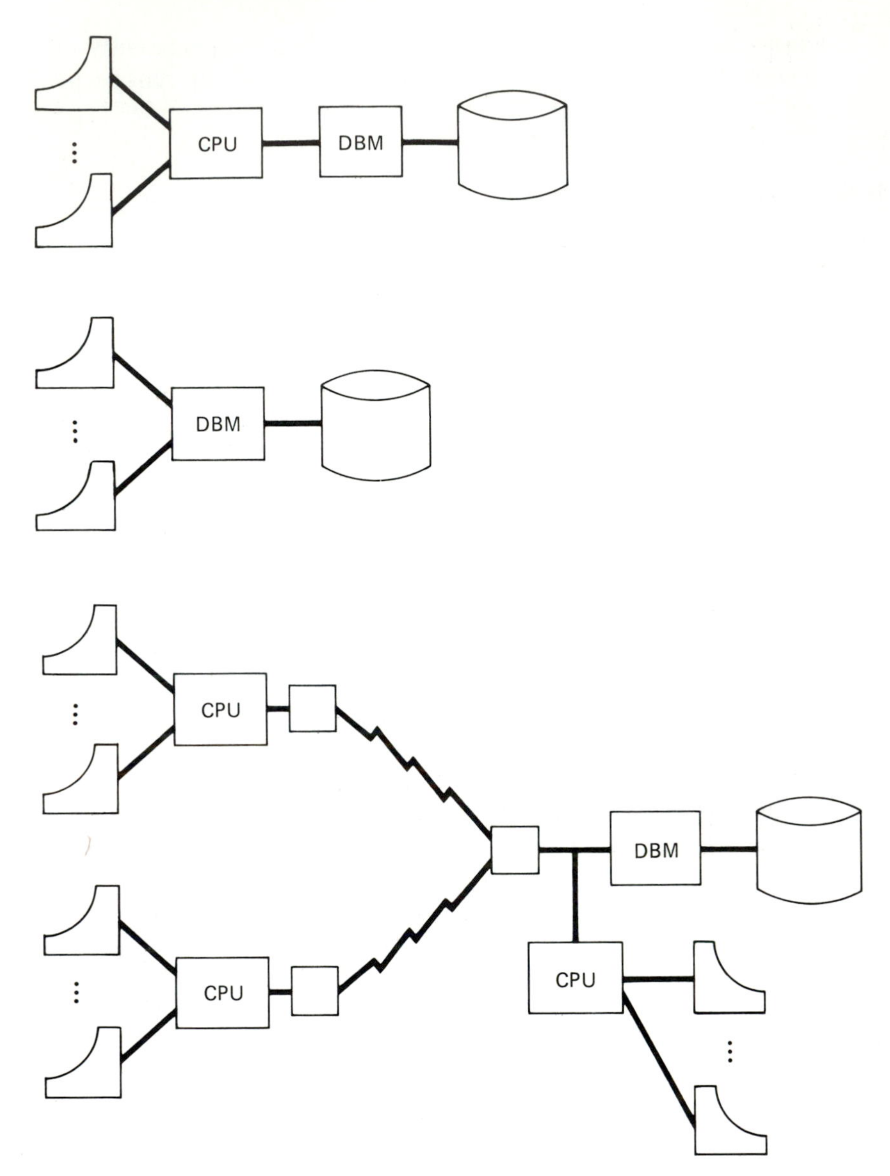

Fig. 10.10. Use of database machines.

failed host and continue processing requests from other hosts. If the host detects that the DBM has failed, then it can stop sending requests to it, and initiate recovery actions, such as redoing the transactions that were active when the DBM crash occurred.

10.12.2 Some Architectures for Database Machines

Ohio State University

This proposed DBM [3] was consciously designed to support security; in fact, the security mechanism was the first part to be designed. The DBM supports a lower-level model, concerned with directory and storage organization and access paths, which could be used to implement relational, network, or hierarchic models. Special hardware is used. The architecture is shown in Fig. 10.11. The DBCCP translates requests into lower-

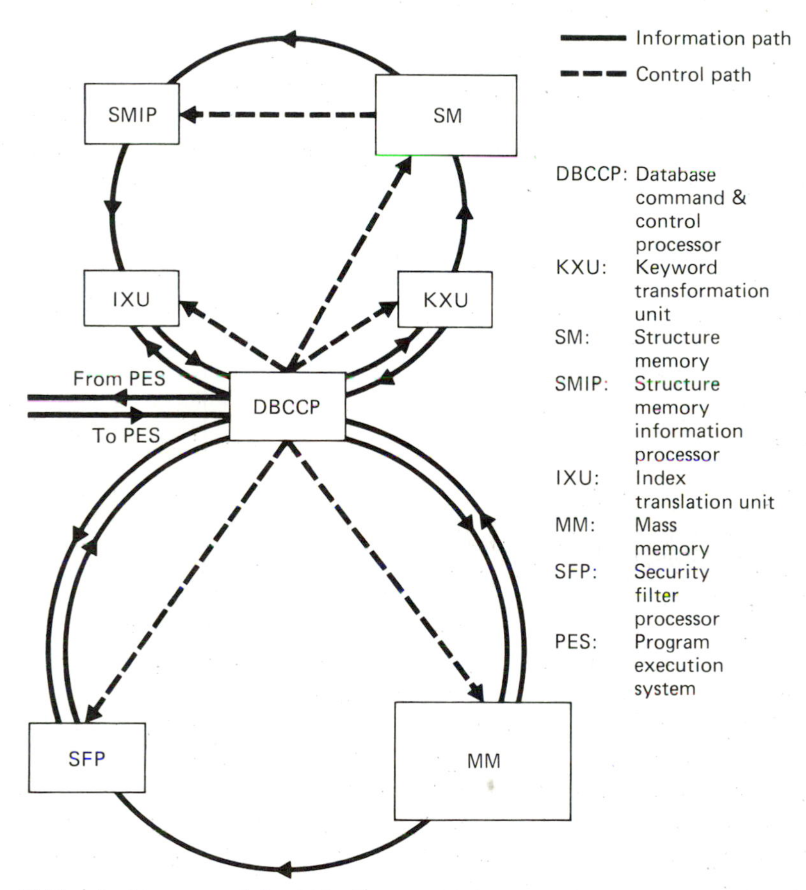

Fig. 10.11. Architecture of the Ohio State DBM. [From Reference 3. Copyright 1978, Association for Computing Machinery, Inc., reprinted by permission.]

level operations and coordinates the actions of the other components. The MM contains the database, and the SM contains the directory.

The DBCCP physically groups records of files into *security atoms*, on the basis of the values of prespecified security attributes. The DBCCP also maintains a table for each user, specifying the user's capabilities for each file. (These are originally provided by the host.) The DBCCP checks each request against these capabilities. A finer level of protection than the security atom can also be chosen for a file. In that case, each record is passed to the SFP for checking. When a query is satisfied, each record is tagged with the user id and file name before being passed to the host.

MULTISAFE

This DBM, designed at Virginia Polytechnic Institute [36] is a multiprocessor that uses parallelism to improve performance and security checking. The architecture is based on the idea of assigning different processing units and memories to the three basic functional units of a secure system:

- the user and application modules,
- the data storage and retrieval module, and
- the security module.

(This division corresponds to a similar division of software modules [21] for the purpose of decreasing sensitivity of compile-time checking.) The separation of processing and isolation of memory contributes to security. A specialized security processor improves performance for security enforcement. Flexibility is achieved by using multiple access-decision times.

MUFFIN

This DBM is designed to execute a distributed version of INGRES [31]. One of the main objectives is resiliency (ability to survive certain hardware failures without crashing and without data loss). Conventional processors are connected in a special type of multiprocessing configuration (Fig. 10.12). Each processor is either an A-cell (application program cell), or a D-cell (database cell). These cells have their own memories and are connected into "pods" by a high-speed bus. Pods are connected to other pods through lower-speed communication links. The database is stored in D-cell memories, and D-cells accept only messages containing QUEL commands. There is no physical protection of data objects, since only the DBMS runs on the D-cell. Query modification is performed on the A-cell.

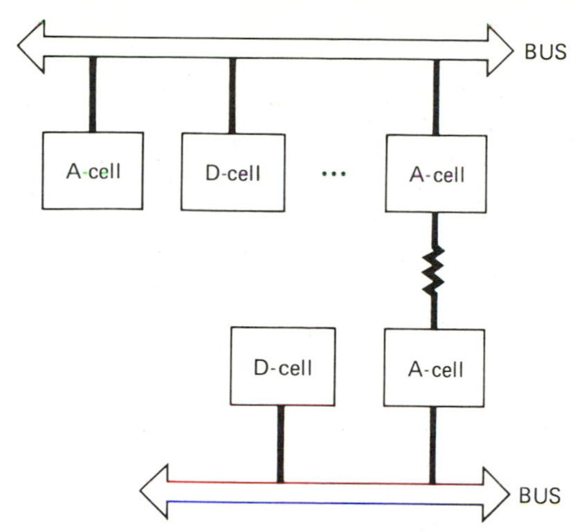

Fig. 10.12. Architecture of the MUFFIN system.

10.13 SUMMARY

This chapter first introduces some design principles of general value. It then deals with the method and the time for detecting and analyzing a request for data. This time is significant for both the security and the efficiency of an enforcement design. Similar issues regarding the time of validation of the request are then discussed. The architectural level of the access rules also has an impact on the design. Validation at various levels is described. The enforcement designs of several DBMSs are then described, and their design choices discussed. Finally, a relevant architectural approach, which assigns the DBMS functions to a special processor or database machine, is considered.

EXERCISES

10.1 Compare the approach of giving users access to base objects (relations, fields, . . .) as opposed to access to views. Indicate the advantages and disadvantages of each approach, considering the viewpoints of ease of administration, system overhead, and user convenience.

REFERENCES AND BIBLIOGRAPHY

1. S. R. Ames, Jr., "User interface multilevel security issues in a transaction-oriented data base management system." *Proc. of Symposium on Computer Security and Integrity,* IEEE 77CH1204-7C, 1977; 120–124.

2. F. Bancilhon and N. Spyratos, "Protection of information in relational data bases." *Proc. 3rd Int. Conf. on Very Large Data Bases,* 1977, 494–500.
Proposes a model of security that describes the information in a database by a set of propositions and their truth values. The objects to be protected are the truth values of certain propositions. A query violates the security of a protected proposition if the answer modifies the user's knowledge about the truth value of this proposition. The model is used to evaluate some protection mechanisms, including query modification. (See Chapter 13 for an application of similar ideas to statistical databases.)

3. J. Banerjee, D. K. Hsiao, and R. I. Baum, "Concepts and capabilities of a database computer." *ACM TODS* **3,** 4 (Dec. 1978), 347–384.

4. R. H. Canaday *et al.*, "A back-end computer for data base management." *Comm. ACM* **17,** 10 (Oct. 1974), 575–582.
The first systematic study of the DBM idea. A DBM was implemented at Bell Labs that supported a DBTG-like interface. A discussion of the advantages and disadvantages of the approach (as resulting from this study) is given.

5. D. D. Chamberlin *et al.*, "Support for Repetitive Transactions and Ad hoc Query in System R." IBM Research Report RJ2551, San Jose, Calif., May 1979.

6. G. A. Champine, "Trends in data base processor architecture." *Proc. 1979 COMPCON Spring,* 69–71. Available from IEEE.

7. CODASYL Programming Language Committee, *COBOL Journal of Development* (1976).

8. R. W. Conway, W. L. Maxwell, and H. L. Morgan, "On the implementation of security measures in information systems." *Comm. ACM* **15,** 4 (April 1972), 211–220.

9. C. J. Date, "An architecture for high-level language database extensions." *Proc. 1976 ACM-SIGMOD Int. Conf. on Management of Data,* 101–122.

10. P. J. Denning, "Fault tolerant operating systems." *ACM Computing Surveys* **8,** 4 (Dec. 1976), 359–390.

11. D. Downs and G. J. Popek, "Data base management system security and INGRES." *Proc. 5th Int. Conf. on Very Large Data Bases* (Oct. 1979), 280–290.

12. P. P. Griffiths and B. W. Wade, "An authorization mechanism for a relational database system." *ACM TODS* **1,** 3 (Sept. 1976), 242–255.

13. E. Gudes, H. S. Koch, and F. A. Stahl, "Security in a multilevel structured model of a data base." *The Computer J.* **22,** 4 (1979), 303–306.

14. H. R. Hartson, "Dynamics of database protection enforcement—A preliminary study." *Proc. of First IEEE Int. Computer Software and Applications Conf.,* COMPSAC 77, 349–356.

15. T. H. Hinke and M. Schaefer, "Secure Data Management System." Report TM–(L)–5407/007/00, System Development Corporation, Santa Monica, Calif., June 1975.

16. C. A. R. Hoare, "An axiomatic basis for computer programming." *Comm. ACM* **12,** 10 (Oct. 1969), 576–583.

17. "IDMS Database Design and Definition Guide." Cullinane Corporation, Wellesley, Mass., 1977.

18. "IDMS Programmer's Reference Guide." Cullinane Corporation, Wellesley, Mass., 1977.

19. IBM Corporation, "IMS/VS Version 1 Application Programming Reference Manual." IBM Form No. SH20–9026.

20. G. Kirkby and M. Grohn, "The reference monitor technique for security in data management systems." *Data Base Engineering* **1,** 2 (June 1977), 8–16.

21. T. Lang, E. B. Fernandez, and R. C. Summers, "A system architecture for compile-time actions in databases." *Proc. 1977 ACM Annual Conference,* 11–15.

    Proposes the segregation of access modules into three components: an *application module* including the program processing actions, a *data access module* with the program's database interactions, and a *data control module,* with the authorization and semantic integrity verification code. The advantages of the approach with respect to sensitivity to change are discussed.

22. B. H. Liskov, A. Snyder, R. Atkinson, and C. Schaffert, "Abstraction mechanisms in CLU." *Comm. ACM* **20,** 8 (August 1977), 564–576.

23. F. J. Maryanski, "Backend database systems." *Comp. Surveys* **12,** 1 (March 1980), 3–25.

24. D. McLeod, "A framework for data base protection and its application to the INGRES and System R data base management systems." *Proc. of First Int. Computer Software and Applications Conf.* (COMPSAC 77), 342–348.

    This paper introduces a set of requirements for protection in a database environment. These include: *variable granularity* of access rules, control of access to *derived* information, limiting access to *operations,* and the ability to distribute authority. INGRES and System R are then discussed in terms of these criteria.

25. W. S. McPhee, "Operating-system integrity in OS/VS2." *IBM Systems J.* **13,** 3 (1974), 230–252.

26. N. Minsky, "Intentional resolution of privacy protection in database systems." *Comm. ACM* **19,** 3 (March 1976), 148–159.

    Proposes a type of control intermediate between access control and information-flow control. The use of the database variables presented to an application program by a subschema is controlled by a set of rules that restrict the possible operations.

27. G. J. Popek, "A principle of kernel design." *AFIPS Conf. Proc.* **43,** 1974 NCC, 977–978. AFIPS Press, Montvale, N.J., 1974.

28. D. M. Ritchie and K. Thompson, "The UNIX timesharing system." *Comm. ACM* **17,** 7 (July 1974), 365–375.

29. M. Schaefer, "On Certain Security Issues Relating to the Management of Data." In *The ANSI/SPARC DBMS Model,* D. A. Jardine, (Ed.). North-Holland, 1976, 131–146.

30. M. D. Schroeder, D. D. Clark, J. H. Saltzer, and D. H. Wells, "Final Report of the Multics Kernel Design Project." Report TR-196, MIT Laboratory for Computer Science, Cambridge, Mass., June 1977.

31. M. Stonebraker, "MUFFIN: A Distributed Data Base Machine." Memorandum No. UCB/ERL M79/28, Electronics Research Lab., University of California, Berkeley, May 1979.

32. M. Stonebraker, "Retrospection on a database system." *ACM TODS* **5,** 2 (June 1980), 225–240.

33. M. Stonebraker and E. Wong, "Access control in a relational data base management system by query modification." *Proc. 1974 ACM Annual Conference,* 180–186.

34. R. C. Summers, C. D. Coleman, and E. B. Fernandez, "A programming-language extension for access to a shared data base." *Proc. ACM 1975 Pacific Regional Conference,* 114–118.

35. R. C. Summers and E. B. Fernandez, "A System Structure for Data Security." Report G320-2687, IBM Los Angeles Scientific Center, April 1977.

36. R. P. Trueblood and H. R. Hartson, "A Working Paper on the Development of Multiprocessor Architectures for Supporting Secure Database Management." Report CS78007–R, Computer Science Dept., Virginia Polytechnic Institute, Blacksburg, Va., Sept. 1978.

37. B. N. Wagner, "Implementation of a Secure Data Management System for the Secure UNIX Operating System." AD–A056902, The MITRE Corp., Bedford, Mass., July 1978.

38. J. P. L. Woodward, "Applications for multilevel secure operating systems." *AFIPS Conf. Proc.* **48,** 1979 NCC, 319–328. AFIPS Press, Montvale, N.J., 1979.

11 Protection Mechanisms

11.1 INTRODUCTION

In the previous chapter we described some DBMS mechanisms that can be used to enforce the data-sharing security policies of an enterprise. These mechanisms in turn depend for their correct functioning on operating-system and hardware *protection mechanisms,* which are the topic of this chapter.

Some of the protection mechanisms that we describe support software reliability as well as security. While software reliability is a desirable *end* in itself, it is also a *means* to support system security. For example, unless the request validation mechanism performs correctly, security policies will not be reliably enforced. Of course, reliable hardware is needed as well. This relationship between protection mechanisms and database security is illustrated in Fig. 11.1.

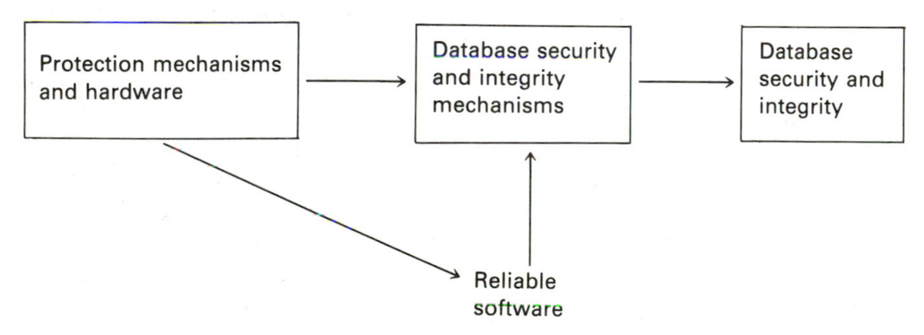

Fig. 11.1. Database security and reliable software.

11.2 THE DBMS AND THE OPERATING SYSTEM

In general there is a separation of responsibility between the operating system and the DBMS. The operating system protects large containers of information, such as files or even volumes, while the DBMS provides a finer granularity of protection. The DBMS may also make finer distinctions among subjects, with the operating system treating the entire DBMS as a single subject. Since the dividing line between the DBMS and the operating system is not always well defined, assigning mechanisms to one category or the other is to some extent arbitrary.*

11.2.1 Security Requirements for the Operating System

In order to ensure database security, a DBMS needs a secure operating system on which to run. At a minimum, the operating system (OS) must [12]:

- Prevent modification of the DBMS and the user programs.
- Protect data in memory.
- Protect the database from access by programs other than the DBMS.
- Perform correct physical I/O. If the DBMS makes an I/O request for data from a certain disk address and the OS returns data from another address, then a security violation may occur. Writing to an incorrect address could cause both integrity and security violations.
- Authenticate DBMS users.

In addition, DBMSs may also require that the operating system provide the following security features [19].

- *Correct compiler.* If some of the security enforcement is done at compile time, the parts of the compiler involved with security must be correct.
- *Correct values of the system variables.* If the system provides access control based on predicates involving system variables (time of day or terminal number, for example), the OS must provide correct environmental information.
- *Secure communication.* When users access the database via telephone lines, the operating system must provide reliable and secure

* This assumes the DBMS to be built on top of the operating system; security functions may also reside in components used by both the DBMS and the operating system.

communication. Security may be compromised by wiretapping. The use of microwave links makes interception of information even easier. Encryption is the usual solution to this problem.

11.2.2 Integrity Requirements

Operating-system mechanisms also support database integrity in a number of ways.

- *Concurrency control.* With an online DBMS multiple users access shared resources. Mechanisms in the operating system (locks, for example) are designed to synchronize such use of shared resources.

- *Support for transaction management.* Since most DBMSs are built on operating systems that do not provide transaction management, this function is typically in the DBMS. Since, however, some transaction management services (such as scheduling and message queueing) are also needed for non-DBMS programs, there is some justification for providing these services in the operating system.

- *Logging.* Logging of system events is often performed by the operating system for accounting and performance reasons. The database recovery log or the audit trail may be combined with the system log for efficiency although this might cause security and integrity exposures. An alternative is to maintain separate logs but avoid duplication of function by using the same log management functions in the operating system.

- *Other support for restart and recovery* such as checkpointing.

- *Efficient and secure invocation of auxiliary procedures.* The use of auxiliary procedures in current DBMSs is limited because the operating system does not provide the necessary support. For example, INGRES does not allow auxiliary procedures because the only efficient way to use them would be to call them from the query-modification routines, in which case they would execute in the same UNIX process as the INGRES nucleus and would have access to all relations.

11.3 PROTECTION PROBLEMS

To a very great extent, protection problems arise because a common set of hardware resources concurrently supports a number of different streams of activity, which may be executing on behalf of different users. The shared resources include the processor, the memory, and external storage such as disks. The streams of activity are called *processes* or sometimes *tasks*. The hardware of a computing system provides certain features that are used by the operating system to control access to resources. These hardware features, together with the software in the operating system that uses them, comprise the *protection system*.

Much of the work on protection problems deals with a situation where arbitrary programs, possibly written in machine language, use a wide variety of operating-system functions. This is a worst-case situation. The typical DBMS usually presents a more restricted user interface. It may, for example, accept requests only in a high-level query language. Nevertheless, many aspects of the worst-case situation remain. For example, the potential may exist for user programs to access DBMS files without using the DBMS.

A technique often used to uncover flaws in a protection system is the *penetration experiment* [1]. A small group of people who are very familiar with the system (sometimes called a *tiger team*) postulates potential flaws and then attempts to use the flaws to gain control of the entire computing system or to bypass a particular protection mechanism. Certain generic classes of flaw turn up in many systems. For example, the time-of-check to time-of-use problem (TOCTTOU) described in Chapter 10 appears here with much shorter times. A parameter passed to the operating system may be changed in the few microseconds after it is validated and before it is used. One reason this is possible is that there are concurrent processes. Another reason is that multiple processes have access to the same memory locations. An important class of such processes performs I/O concurrently with execution, through I/O channels or direct memory access. Other flaws derive simply from the complexity of the operating system's design and resulting errors of design or implementation.

Figure 11.2 depicts some of the protection problems associated with the DBMS and the database. Only the DBMS can be allowed to access the database directly. Any attempts by application programs to do so must be prevented, because this would allow DBMS security to be completely bypassed. Application programs should also be unable to modify DBMS code, since they could thus circumvent the security mechanism in the DBMS. They must not have uncontrolled access to the DBMS buffers; these may contain data from the database for which the programs have no authorization. We can therefore think of the database and DBMS as forming a subsystem that must be protected from attacks by other programs in the system. Mechanisms in the operating system and hardware are required to create this *protected subsystem*. As a first step, we can isolate this subsystem completely from all non-database application programs. However, some communication between the DBMS and the database application program is obviously needed in order to allow database requests to be made and satisfied.

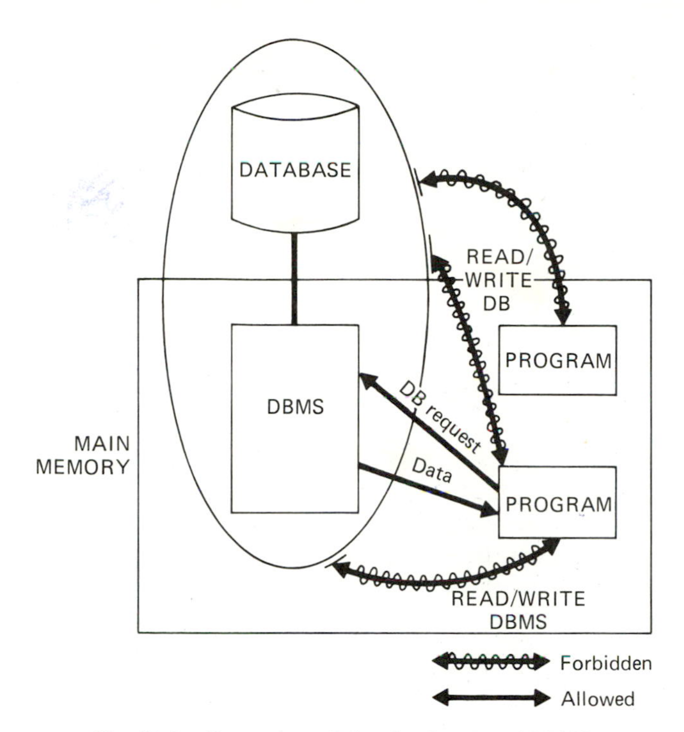

Fig. 11.2. Protection of the database and DBMS.

The protection requirements can be extended to include the protection of one application program from another and also the protection of an application program and its own files from the DBMS itself. More extended requirements—for control of information flow—are discussed in Section 11.7.

11.4 PROTECTION MATRIX

The access matrix model described in Chapter 6 is capable of representing a wide range of database authorization policies. It is not surprising (since this model derives from a similar model for operating-system protection) that a matrix model can also be used at the operating-system level to represent protection specifications. We will call it a *protection-matrix* model to distinguish it from the database access-matrix model. A subject (a row) is an active agent in the system, such as a process. Objects (columns) are resources known to the operating system, and can be software (such as programs, procedures, and files) or hardware (such as

SUBJECTS \ OBJECTS	Application A	SELECT procedure	File X	File Y	Database
Application A		CALL	READ	READ WRITE	
SELECT procedure					READ WRITE
Process B	ENTER				

Fig. 11.3. Protection matrix.

memory, terminals, and disks). For each subject/object pair the corresponding entry in the matrix is the set of accesses that the subject is permitted to the object. In Fig. 11.3, which shows a simplified example of a protection matrix, application program A has direct access to its private files X and Y but not to the database. However, it can call the SELECT procedure of the DBMS, which does have READ access to the database. Note that the SELECT procedure appears as both a subject and an object in the matrix.

We can now define the *protection domain* of a subject as the set of access rights the subject has to objects in the system. This domain is described by the entries in a row of the matrix. The protection matrix can represent the principle of least privilege by allowing arbitrarily small protection domains to be defined. By small we mean the minimum set of rights (access/object pairs) that a subject needs to do its job. Unlike the database access-control matrix, the protection matrix will vary dynamically as a process executes. For example, if application program A invokes a general routine SORT to sort File Y, then SORT must be given the right to READ File Y. However, this right is required only for this particular invocation. To handle this in the model, we introduce the concept of a *copy flag* associated with each right. When the copy flag is on, the right may be passed on to other routines when they are called.

We saw that it is possible at the database level to *encapsulate* authorized accesses in program load modules. This means that it is only necessary to control who invokes which modules at execution time. However, at the operating-system level, the situation is more unpredictable and complex, especially in the area of data sharing. Unless the applications of the system are relatively static (as in the case of an office system where user programming is kept to a minimum), it is not possible to compile or link the complete system at one time. Some execution-time implementation of the protection matrix is therefore required.

11.5 MECHANISMS

We now discuss in very general terms some of the mechanisms that are used to support the least-privilege principle and the protection-matrix model.

11.5.1 Modes of Privilege

The hardware may provide multiple *modes* (sometimes called *domains* or *states*) of the processor. The different modes have different privileges, primarily in what instructions they can execute. System/370, for example, has two modes: *problem* and *supervisor*, and the PDP 11/45 has three domains: *user*, *supervisor*, and *kernel*. Certain System/370 instructions (I/O, for example) can be executed only in supervisor mode. With only two modes, however, the granularity of protection is coarse and the rights of different portions of the operating system cannot be independently granted.

A generalization of the mode concept is the concept of hierarchical *rings* of privilege [62]. As shown in Fig. 11.4, rings resemble the layers of

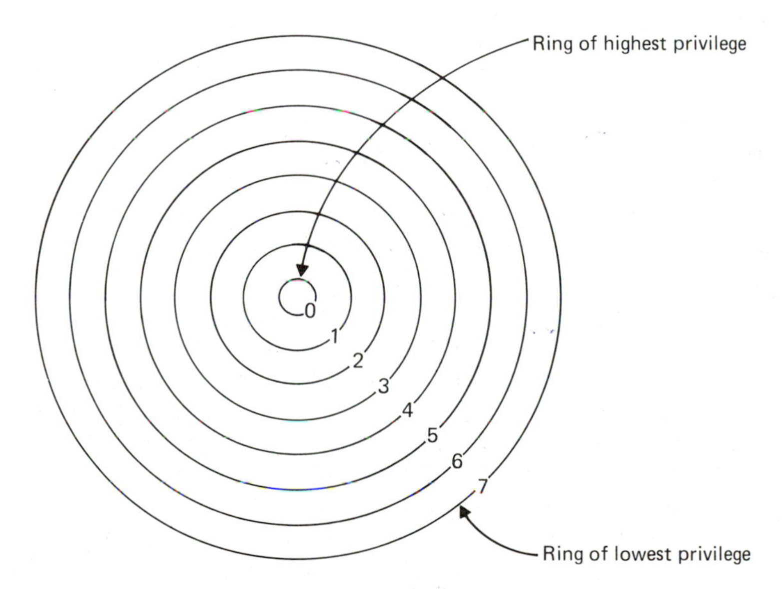

Fig. 11.4. Multics rings of protection.

an onion, where the center has the highest privilege and the outside of the onion has the lowest privilege. Each process is associated at any moment with a state or ring, and the processor enters that state when the process goes into execution. Using rings of privilege, while we could protect the database from the application program, we could not protect the application's private files from the DBMS. The protection matrix does allow this policy to be represented. In Fig. 11.3, for example, application A can access the database only indirectly through calling the DBMS, while the DBMS cannot access Files X and Y belonging to application A.

11.5.2 Gates

In order to support the concept of protected subsystems, it is necessary to control entry into the subsystem, restricting it to specified entry points. If an application program could enter the DBMS routines at any point, it could bypass the DBMS security mechanisms. A gate is a mechanism, usually implemented in hardware, which enforces entry-point constraints.

11.5.3 Memory Protection

The path to any object is almost always through memory. Memory locations contain either the object itself or some other data that is needed to find the object. Protection of objects thus often reduces to memory protection.

One simple form of memory protection uses *locks* and *keys*. Memory is divided into blocks, and a lock is assigned to each block. The CPU at any moment has a "protection key" that is part of the processor status, and writing is allowed only if the protection key matches the lock. The number of different keys is often quite limited, however, and this restricts the flexibility of the lock-and-key mechanism.

A more flexible kind of protection is provided by a *base-limit register*. The first part of this register specifies the lowest memory address that can be accessed (at least in user mode) and the second part specifies the highest address. (See Fig. 11.5.) The base is also used for relocation. By setting the base-limit register, the operating system can control what memory is available to the current process.

Most computing systems now rely heavily on *virtual memory* for memory protection. A typical virtual memory consists of one or more *segments*, where a segment is a linearly addressed sequence of cells (such as words or bytes). The segments are usually divided into units called *pages*, which are individually mapped to frames of real memory or to locations on external storage. A segment table specifies what segments are available to the process that is executing (see Fig. 11.6) and can also

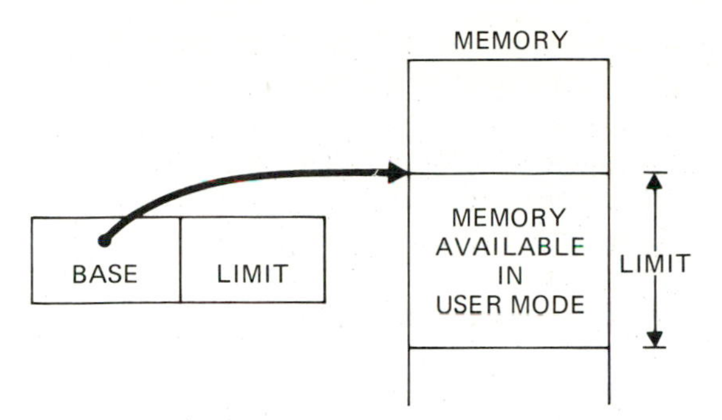

Fig. 11.5. Base-limit register.

define what type of access is allowed to the segment. All other memory is inaccessible to the process. The segment-table entry gives the address of a *page table* from which the real address of a page is found. Special hardware, such as an associative memory, is used to speed the translation to real addresses. The segment table can also define what type of access is allowed to the segment.

Memory can be protected in a different way by *tagging* each piece of memory according to the type of information it contains. For example, instructions and data can be tagged differently, so that a programming error can never cause data to be executed. Tagging can be used to distinguish protection information (such as segment tables) from ordinary data, and it has other applications [20].

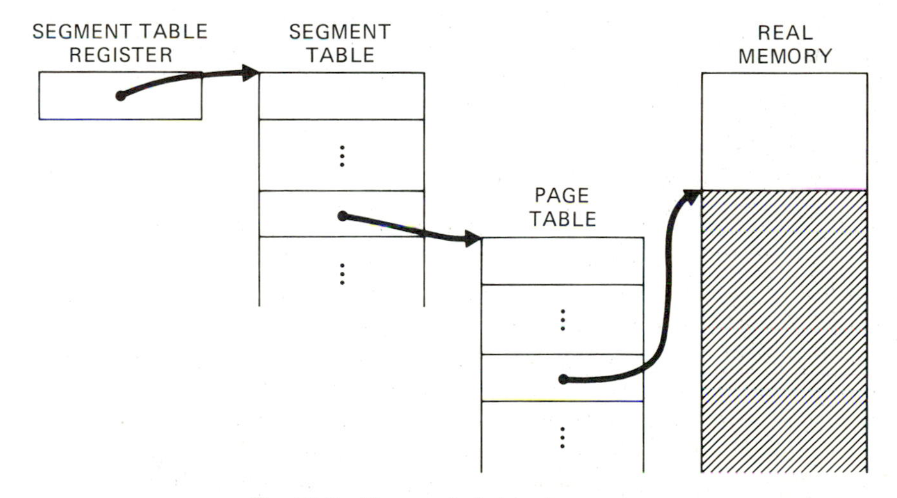

Fig. 11.6. Segmented virtual memory.

I/O is often the weakest link in memory protection. A protection key can be assigned to an I/O operation, in the same way that the CPU has a key. This I/O key must match the lock of the blocks of memory involved in the I/O. Virtual-memory hardware is sometimes used to mediate all I/O as well as references by the CPU. Another mechanism (software or microcode) scans a channel program before it is executed to ensure that all memory it refers to is accessible to the process that initiates the channel program. (This method has certain deficiencies, since some channel programs can be modified during execution.) Another possibility is for I/O to be mediated by special micro- or miniprocessors, sometimes with all data being buffered in their memory until the I/O is complete.

11.5.4 File Protection

While the protection matrix represents in a uniform way the protection of all system objects, many operating systems handle file protection in a different way from memory protection. Two common mechanisms for controlling access to files are passwords and access rules. These are designed to control file *sharing* but can also be used to enforce file *isolation*.

Passwords

The password mechanism of VSAM [30] provides an example of how passwords are used to protect files. (The other important use of passwords, to authenticate users, is discussed in Section 11.8.) Passwords may be defined for individual data sets, indexes, and catalogs. There are different passwords for various types of access:

- *Full access*. This master password allows all types of operation on the data set, index, or catalog associated with it. Using this password to gain access to a catalog gives the ability to delete data sets and to alter password information and any other information contained in the catalog.
- *Control access*. This password allows access to a more physical level than is normally allowed.
- *Update access*. This password allows the user to retrieve, update, and insert or delete records in a data set. It allows entries in the catalog to be redefined but not deleted.
- *Read access*. This password allows only retrieval of records in data sets and catalogs.

These access types are ordered, so that a higher-level password implies the right to all operations permitted by lower levels. If only a lower-level password is defined, all higher-level passwords are given the same value.

Password protection is defined using the VSAM definition control language. Passwords are normally supplied by the application program, which means that, since the password probably is contained in the program, the program must then be protected. However, computer operators and terminal users may be given the opportunity to supply a password not provided by the program. A prompting code may be used so that the operator does not have to know both the name of the data set and the password. A data set definition can specify how many incorrect password tries are allowed. If this number is exceeded, a log record is written to indicate a possible security violation.

One serious problem with passwords is that there is no efficient way to withdraw rights from one of many users. Another serious problem is keeping the password secret. The password for a DBMS file will usually either be coded into the DBMS program or entered by an operator or initial invoker of the DBMS system. In both cases the possibility of password leakage exists.

Access rules

A more secure method is to specify access rules as for database access, but at the file level under control of the operating system. Much of what has been said for database access rules can apply to file access rules, with the difference that the object is a file or group of files, and there is no predicate. RACF [31] may be used with VSAM to provide access rules instead of password protection. No user of the system (except the DBMS) would be allowed to access the database. In this way only the authorized users of the DBMS can access the database. Access-rule protection is often implemented as an access-control list, which may be stored in the directory entry for a file or may be stored as a series of independent and free-standing statements [70].

Protection of external storage

The hardware usually provides some help to the operating system in protecting external storage. For example, tapes cannot be written unless a plastic ring is inserted into a groove in the tape reel. Disk drives may have switches that can be set for read-only use. A command to a disk device can be used to establish a range of allowable disk addresses for subsequent commands in the same sequence. This allows the operating system to ensure that user-written I/O commands do not access data outside the file being accessed. If external storage is included as part of a single-level storage system, then the same mechanism used to protect main storage extends to the external data [57]. Protection mechanisms based on tagging the different types of external data are also useful to ensure correct transfer of information between the CPU and external storage (Section 11.6.2 describes one such mechanism).

11.5.5 Capability Mechanisms

An approach that seems to promise an efficient implementation of the protection matrix and hence small protection domains is based on the concept of *capabilities* [9, 16]. A capability can be thought of as a *ticket* specifying an *object* and an *operation*. Possession of the ticket by a subject provides proof that the subject is authorized to perform the operation on the object. A list of capabilities (called a *C-list*) is associated with each subject; the C-list represents a row of the access matrix.

A subject, if authorized to do so, may pass one of its capabilities to another subject. This is required when a process wants to allow a common shared procedure to access one of its private files. For good performance, the protection authorizations for an active process must be kept in a form that can be checked quickly and efficiently. A C-list contains just this information.

It is essential to prevent a process from improperly modifying, copying, or generating capabilities. *Tagging* and *partitioning* are two hardware mechanisms for maintaining the integrity of capabilities. With tagging, bits in each word and in the processor registers indicate whether or not the contents are a capability. System 250 [14] built by the Plessey Company in the United Kingdom, uses the partitioning approach. Each segment is designated at creation as containing either capabilities or data. In addition there is a set of processor registers for data and a set for capabilities. Data can be copied only into data segments and registers, while capabilities can be copied only into capability segments and registers. IBM's System/38, on the other hand, uses tagging [28]. The tagging approach is more flexible, since a single object can include both data and capabilities.

A number of problems remain unresolved in the capability approach. One is the great difficulty of controlling and auditing what capabilities have been given out, and consequently of revoking them [23]. These capabilities may be scattered throughout the system. The problem can be controlled somewhat by adding a copy flag to the capability and by the use of indirect capabilities, where a capability must use another capability to reach the actual object and this direct capability can be destroyed to revoke all delegated access to the object.

11.5.6 Access-Control Lists

These problems of capabilities can be avoided by checking at execution time to see whether a subject is on an *access-control list* for some object (typically a segment). Such a list indicates the type of access allowed each subject that can access the object. Making this check at each memory reference is not practical, so a compromise approach is to use the access-control list only when the segment is first bound into the subject's domain and then to create the appropriate capabilities that allow efficient access subsequently. This mixed approach is used in Multics.

11.5.7 Virtual Machines

The term *virtual machine* is used in different ways. One meaning is the environment presented by the operating system to its users, which is different from the bare real machine. The term *abstract machine* is also used in this sense. The operating system provides a machine that is easier to use (and more secure) than the real machine. This machine typically consists of a set of *abstract objects,* such as processes and segments.

A slightly different concept is a virtual machine system, where a *virtual machine monitor* creates multiple replicas (virtual machines) of some computing system on one real system. Each virtual machine behaves exactly like the real machine; each can run a different operating system. (See Fig. 11.7.) The files and programs of one user can be isolated from those of other users. A virtual machine facility has the advantage that most of the operating-system functions are in the virtual machine and thus are not involved in isolating the users. This is an example of the principle of least common mechanism. Also, the interface between the

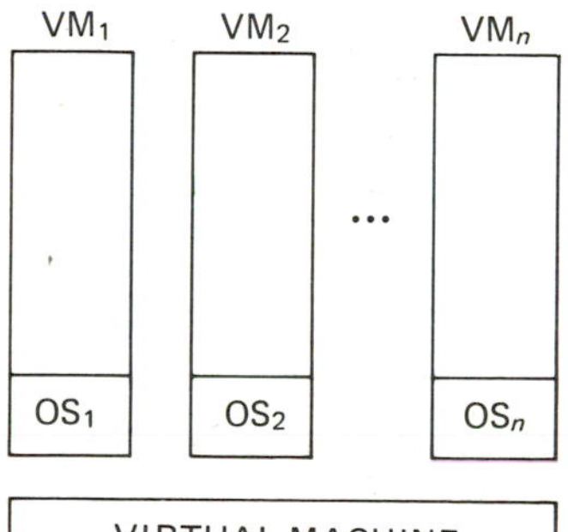

Fig. 11.7. Virtual machine system. [From Attanasio [2]. Reprinted by permission from IBM Systems Journal. Copyright 1979 by International Business Machines Corporation.]

virtual machine monitor and the virtual machines is simple and well-defined, which enhances security.

11.5.8 Interpretation

A protection mechanism that is generally used for reasons other than protection is *interpretation.* An interpreter is a program that analyzes and executes statements written in a high-level language, such as APL [22]. The interpreter provides a kind of virtual machine. Program development is usually easier in interpreted languages. Interpretive execution is more secure for two reasons. First, the user-written program never executes on the bare machine, so it cannot possibly execute security-sensitive instructions or directly call on the supervisor. Second, an interpreted language tends to diverge further from machine-oriented concepts than a compiled language. Variables, for example, do not map as directly to bytes or words of storage.

11.6 SEVERAL PROTECTION SYSTEMS

11.6.1 System/370

IBM System/370 hardware supports two domains or states: supervisor and problem. The current state is determined by a bit in the program status word (PSW). Supervisor state can be entered through a Supervisor Call (SVC) instruction or as the result of an interrupt. In supervisor state, all instructions are valid. In problem state, instructions that affect system integrity are not valid. These include I/O instructions and instructions that control memory protection and virtual memory. Basic memory protection is provided by associating a *key in storage* with every 2048-byte block of storage and by a CPU protection key in the PSW. The key in storage contains four *access-control* bits, a fetch protection bit, and two bits used for other purposes. WRITE access to memory is allowed only if the CPU key is zero or matches the access-control bits. READ access is allowed if either the keys match or the fetch protection bit is zero. For I/O, the key associated with the I/O operation is used instead of the CPU key.

System/370 supports virtual memory through address-translation facilities that are used in different ways by different operating systems. MVS [60] uses them to create multiple address spaces. Each region has a separate address space, and there is no direct way for a program running in one region to read or write data in another region.

With virtual memory, the protection key mechanism becomes available for other uses, and it is used in MVS to distinguish domains of privilege. Keys 0 through 7 are used for the operating system, with only the most privileged parts using key 0. A *key-switch* technique is used to prevent a user program from tricking the operating system into violating protection for it, and also to prevent passing of user data masquerading as system data, such as control blocks for I/O. An operating-system component switches to the key of its caller while performing work for it, thus restricting the protection domain. A special System/370 instruction allows this switch to be done efficiently.

When these facilities are used by an online IMS system, the IMS control program resides in a *control region,* and application programs reside and run in separate *dependent regions* (Fig. 11.8). IMS is thus protected against application programs, and they are protected against each other. The data sets for the databases are allocated to the control region in such a way that they are unavailable to other programs that might attempt to use them.

When an application program issues a DL/I call, IMS code residing in its region issues an SVC to communicate to the control region. Other SVCs are used by the control region to transfer data to and from the dependent region. The data buffers are located in the control region and are thus inaccessible to application programs. Other mechanisms (such as password protection or RACF) are required to prevent application programs directly accessing the database files when these are not allocated to the IMS control region.

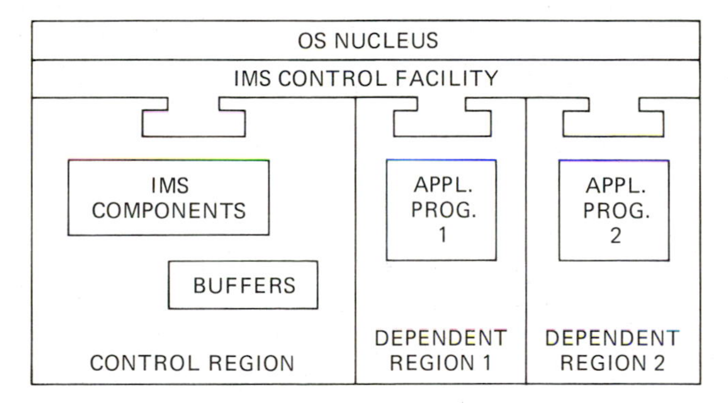

Fig. 11.8. Protection environment of IMS.

11.6.2 LASC Proposal

For the LASC system (described in Chapter 10), three types of extensions to the System/370 protection system were proposed: new states of privilege, memory tagging, and protection of data transmission [18]. The first two of these extensions support the execution of A-programs (application programs) and D-programs (tailored data-access programs). A-programs execute in *application state,* D-programs in *utility state,* and the supervisor in supervisor state. Figure 11.9 shows the allowed state transitions.

To access the database, an A-program invokes its D-program partner with a utility call (UC). At compile time, each UC in the A-program is assigned an integer and a *transfer vector* is generated that specifies all allowed D-program entry points. This vector is loaded at execution time into a protected area of storage. The argument of a UC indicates which entry point in the transfer vector is to be used. This gate mechanism ensures that only authorized calls on the D-program succeed and that control passes to the right location. The D-program issues SVCs to obtain operating-system services. Since the A-program is not allowed to issue SVCs, one potential source of system penetration is removed. The I/O supervisor accepts database I/O requests only from utility state, thus ensuring that only D-programs access the database.

Memory protection is extended to differentiate between the data and instructions of A- and D-programs. The matrix in Fig. 11.10 shows the allowed operations as a function of execution state and information type.

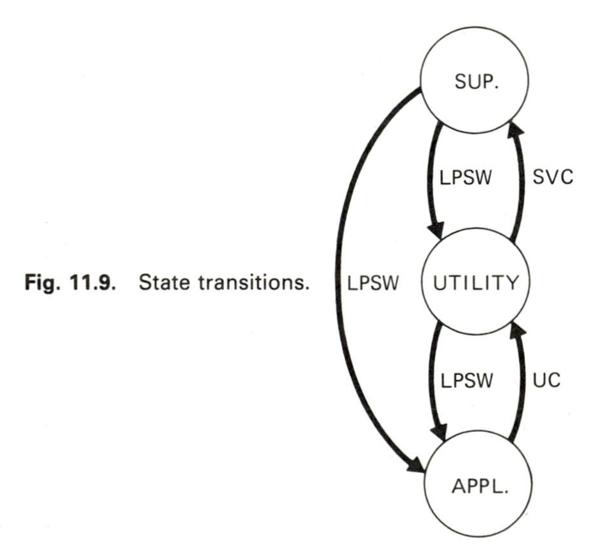

Fig. 11.9. State transitions.

STATE	A-data	A-inst	D-data	D-inst
A	READ STORE	EXECUTE	—	—
U	READ STORE	READ	READ STORE	EXECUTE
S	NO RESTRICTION	NO RESTRICTION	NO RESTRICTION	NO RESTRICTION

Fig. 11.10. Allowed operations.

In application state, A-program instructions can be executed and A-program data can be read and stored. This means that an A-program cannot execute its own (or any other) data and cannot alter its instructions. In utility state, D-program instructions can be executed and both A- and D-program data can be read and stored. This allows the D-program to move data to and from the A-programs. D-programs are also allowed to read A-program instructions to allow passing of inline parameters. In supervisor state there are no restrictions.

These mechanisms provide execution-time protection of the results of the compile-time analysis and the access generation. In order to also protect these results on external storage, as well as to control their use, we can distinguish functionally different areas of external storage and establish rules governing information flow between external storage and memory. The following categories could be used for example:

1. supervisor programs;
2. read-only utility programs (compilers, processor libraries, utilities);
3. writable utility programs (including D-programs);
4. the system database (including database descriptions and access rules);
5. A-programs; and
6. the application database.

Each record of external storage is categorized by a protected identifier stored with the record.

It is then possible to define, by means of a matrix, which operations are allowed for each category of external storage, as a function of the category of memory providing or receiving information. Such a matrix would specify, for example, that A-programs could be read only into application instruction areas and written only from system data areas.

11.6.3 Multics

Multics [57] is an example of a system that was consciously designed to provide a high degree of security and reliability. In Multics all storage (main, memory, and external) is organized as named segments, and the segment is the unit of protection. A segment can contain either data or procedures. Since a file is a segment, file protection in Multics can use the memory-protection mechanisms. A Multics process is usually associated with an end user and is identified by a unique number. In the database context we can imagine that the end user is invoking a database application program combining a number of procedures. Eventually one of these procedures will call a DBMS procedure, which in turn may call other DBMS or operating-system procedures. The user can build protected subsystems by grouping procedures into segments that can then be protected from one another.

Associated with each process is a *descriptor segment,* which is a vector of segment descriptor words (SDWs) providing addressability to all the segments accessible to the process. The directory system, which has been mentioned in previous chapters, is used to locate a segment when it is first referenced by a process. The directory entry for a segment contains an access-control list specifying which users can access the segment and what their rights are. If the requested access is authorized, the segment is added to the user's virtual memory by adding the appropriate SDW to the user's descriptor segment.

Multics uses rings of privilege. Since the structuring of the rings of privilege is hierarchical, ring 5, for example, has all the privileges of rings 6 and 7 plus additional privileges specifically associated with ring 5. Throughout its life a process may execute with any or all of the rings of privilege. At any moment, however, the process has a single ring number.

Ring brackets are associated with each accessible segment as shown in Fig. 11.11. READ and WRITE privileges are always associated with a ring bracket starting at ring 0. In the figure, for example, the *READ bracket* is defined as ring 0 to ring 4. This means that, if the process is currently executing in ring 0, 1, 2, 3, or 4, then it may READ the segment. Similarly, if it is executing in ring 0, 1, 2, or 3, it may WRITE into the segment. The *CALL bracket* is defined as rings 5 and 6. This means that

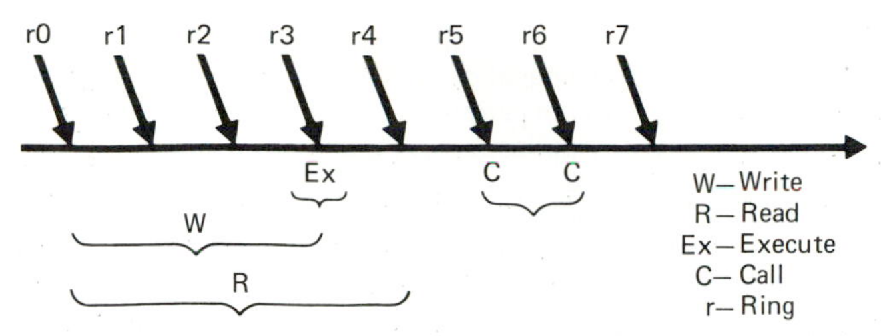

Fig. 11.11. Segment privileges.

only when the process is executing in ring 5 or 6 can it CALL this segment. Finally, when the segment is being executed, the process is in ring 3. Of course not every segment can be called, read, and written. Flags indicate which of these modes are allowed. A list of legal entry points is also associated with the ring bracket information.

Initially all the information is stored in the access-control list. However, when the segment is first referenced, the information is copied into the SDW for the segment. For every subsequent access by the process the SDW alone is checked by hardware to determine whether the access is authorized.

Figure 11.12 gives an example of how rings of privilege may be associated with the execution of a process that accesses the database. The operating-system routines run with the highest privilege in rings 0 and 1, the DBMS runs with the next highest privilege in rings 2 and 3, and the application code runs in rings 4 to 7. The operating system is thus protected from all other routines and the DBMS is protected from the application program code. The operating-system routines running in ring 0 are protected from those running in ring 1. Similarly, the DBMS and application program can be partially protected against themselves. The database segments have READ/WRITE brackets of ring 0 to ring 2, thereby preventing less privileged DBMS routines and all application code from accessing the database directly.

While the Multics grain of protection is not arbitrarily small, it is certainly finer than that allowed in two- or three-state machines. One of the problems of small protection domains is the overhead incurred every time a process enters a new domain. In Multics this efficiency problem was tackled by providing hardware support for the implementation of CALLs to protected subsystems.

While Multics was an important step forward in providing secure systems, the hierarchical structuring of privileges does not solve the problem of cooperation between mutually suspicious subsystems. For example, in Fig. 11.12 the private files of the application program are

r7	Application
r6	Application
r5	Application
r4	Application program and files
r3	DBMS
r2	DBMS and database
r1	OS
r0	OS

Fig. 11.12. Rings of privilege for a DBMS.

accessible to the DBMS even though this is not functionally required. According to the principle of least privilege, the DBMS should be denied access to them. Capability systems solve this problem and also support a finer granularity of protection.

11.6.4 CAPS System

The Cambridge University CAPS computer [27, 45, 71] provides very detailed capability protection. The basic unit of protection is a segment, which can be as small as six words. All access to a segment is through capabilities.

Capabilities are stored in capability segments. At any moment a process can have access to up to 16 capability segments. These represent its protection environment. Any word in memory is addressed as (c, co, o), where (c, co) is the *capability specifier* (capability segment and offset), and o is the word's offset in its segment. One special segment (called the Process Resource List, or PRL) represents the process and specifies the maximum set of resources available to any *protected procedure* in which the process might execute.

Each capability in a capability segment points to an entry in the PRL; the capabilities at any moment thus constitute a selection from the process's total set of resources (see Fig. 11.13). Each capability also contains a base and limit and an *access status*. The access status consists of five bits, three for *data access* (read, write, execute) and two for *capability access* (read, write). No capability may have both types of access; that is, there are data capabilities and capability capabilities. The access status is enforced by the addressing hardware.

Capabilities can be copied or *refined*. The REFINE instruction copies the capability with a reduction of privilege. This allows, for example, giving access to part of a segment, while also eliminating write access. The protection environment is changed when a protected procedure is called by an ENTER instruction, or left by a RETURN. These instructions change the set of active capability segments.

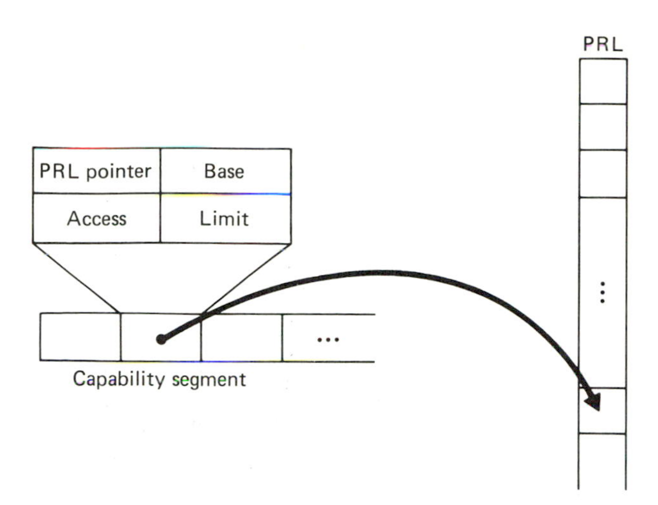

Fig. 11.13. CAPS capability and Process Resource List.

A *capability unit* provides hardware support. It interprets capabilities that are used for segment reference, and it stores capabilities that have been evaluated by a microprogram. (Evaluation transforms a capability into a form that the hardware can interpret.) If the referenced segment is not in main memory, the evaluation fails. The capability unit can hold 64 evaluated capabilities in a memory that can be searched very rapidly, using the capability specifier as a key. Capabilities that are invalidated because of an ENTER or RETURN remain in the memory, but will not satisfy a search until reenabled by another ENTER or RETURN.

The entire CAPS operating system is implemented as a set of protected procedures. While a protected procedure executes, certain capability segments play special roles. These include:

- The *program capability segment,* which contains those capabilities the procedure needs regardless of which process is using it. These include capabilities for segments of program code.
- The *interface capability segment,* which represents the procedure's workspace associated with the using process (called the *stack* in other systems).
- The *argument capability segment,* containing arguments passed from the calling procedure.

CAPS also uses *software capabilities,* which are protected by the same hardware mechanisms but are *interpreted* by software rather than hardware. They can be presented to a protected procedure as proof of authorization to use some of its services. In this way software capabilities allow the system to do its work with fewer but more general protected procedures, with a consequent saving in overhead.

The CAPS filing system is based on the concept of *preserved capabilities*. The system can preserve any capability by placing in a directory segment information that allows the capability to be reconstructed at a later time. Different access rights to the shared objects are implemented through different capabilities for the objects.

11.6.5 VM/370

VM/370 (Virtual Machine Facility/370) [63] provides multiple virtual System/370 systems, each with virtual I/O devices. VM/370 has two main components: the control program (CP) and the operating system (CMS) that runs in a virtual machine. It is the control program that creates the virtual machines. These can run essentially any software that runs on a real System/370. When VM/370 is used to support a DBMS (such as one version of System R), isolation is achieved by running the DBMS and all users in separate virtual machines, as shown in Fig. 11.14. The "firewall" in the figure indicates that no direct communication between virtual machines is allowed. Thus the database and DBMS code are protected from all users of the system. However, some communication between virtual machines is necessary. An application must be able to pass a database request to, and receive a response from, the database virtual machine. In addition, if a number of database user virtual machines execute concurrently, the DBMS must be able to partially serialize their execution in order to preserve database integrity.

Various means for communication between virtual machines have been developed. They involve shared segments [25] or communication through virtual I/O channels, or a request-queuing mechanism [33]. It is important for these mechanisms to be implemented in a secure and controlled way, so that the inherent security of the VM facility is not undermined. With any of these methods, one *serving* virtual machine, such as the DBMS machine, can provide service to a number of *client* machines. Certain performance problems arise with such an approach, primarily because every protection domain change is also a process switch. (This is so because a virtual machine is not only a unit of isolation but also a unit of scheduling.) A different approach [2] is to make available a second, more privileged domain within a single virtual machine. This domain is invoked through "virtual instructions" that behave much like real instructions and that are able to share segments in a very secure way.

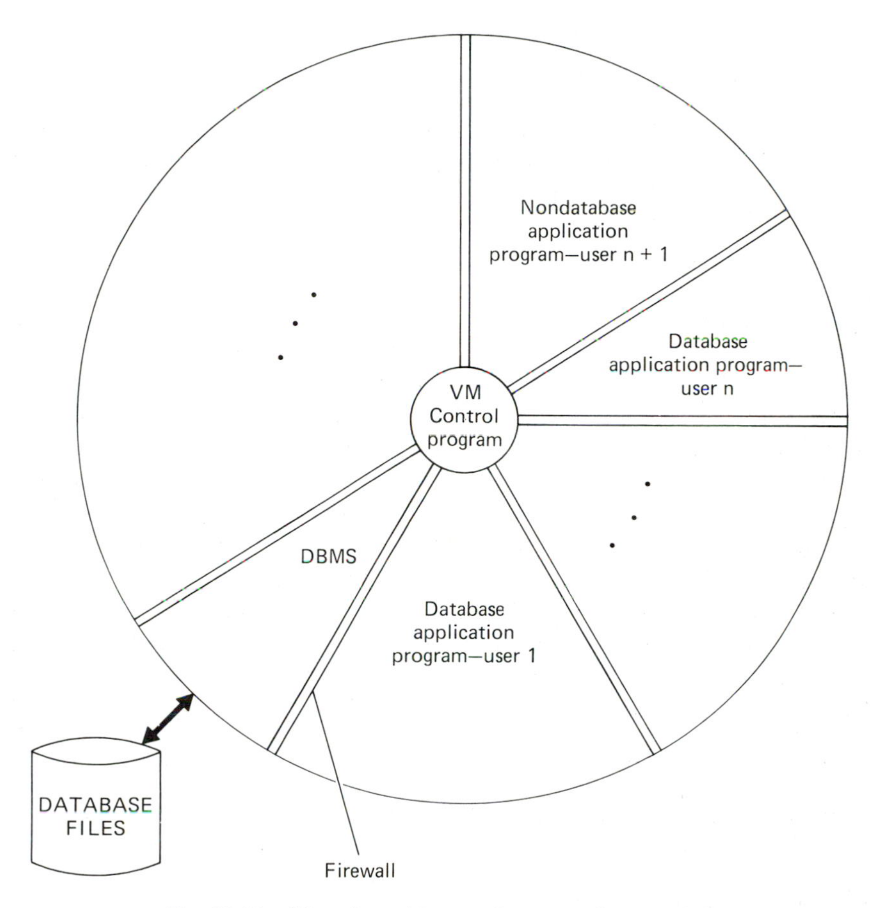

Fig. 11.14. Virtual machine environment for a DBMS.

11.7 INFORMATION-FLOW CONTROL AND TRUSTED OPERATING SYSTEMS

The mechanisms and systems discussed so far focus on access control and do little to control information flow. Yet, as we have seen, certain security policies demand some control over information flow. For this reason, the U.S. Department of Defense (DoD) has sponsored research and development in operating systems to support its security policy [68].

Traditionally this policy has been implemented by *periods processing,* where a computing installation is dedicated for a period (several hours perhaps) to one security level. Then it is cleansed (all storage volumes removed, memory cleared) and given over to another security level. This is obviously not the best way of operating. Service is denied to users, valuable computing resources are idle, and, perhaps most important, multilevel operation is restricted. That is, a user cannot flexibly access data at different levels in the same period. (Read-only switches on disk drives do make possible read access to lower levels and write access to a single higher level.)

It was also felt that there was a need for certifiable security. Merely correcting security flaws was not enough; it was necessary to have confidence based on something other than testing and experience, and appropriate design techniques could produce this trust. The research was therefore directed at trusted operating systems that could support multilevel operation. One of the main outcomes of this work is the *kernel approach* to secure operating systems.

11.7.1 Kernel Approach

A kernel design localizes in a small portion of the operating system all functions essential to security. The idea is that, since the kernel is relatively small and simple, there is a potential for certifying it as correct—through formal proof, exhaustive analysis and testing, and penetration attempts.

One very clean definition of a kernel is the following: There is some antagonist who is allowed to supply all of the operating system but the kernel; even under those conditions the system correctly implements security policy. A different definition is used more frequently, however. The kernel concept developed from the idea of a reference monitor that checks all accesses, and sometimes the kernel *is* essentially this reference monitor. To repeat from Chapter 10, a reference monitor is:

- complete (mediates all access),
- isolated or tamperproof,
- verifiable by formal proof.

There are really two aspects to the kernel approach: the methodology and the structure of the design. The methodology involves first formally specifying the security policy. The multilevel model of Chapter 6 usually serves this function, with a process serving as subject. The next step is to formally specify the design, at some fairly high level, and special languages have been developed for this purpose. The implementation is then done in a programming language that is suited to proofs. Most of the languages that have been used are derivatives of Pascal.

Proof of correctness has two steps:

1. Proof that the design correctly implements the formally stated policy, and
2. Proof that the implementation correctly implements the design.

(Of course, more steps could be used, with a proof at each stage that a more detailed design correctly implements the less detailed design.) It should be emphasized that correctness is proved only with respect to the formally stated security policy. The system could operate incorrectly in other ways and still be formally secure. To date, mainly designs have been proved, and few implementations. Programs that verify theorems are used to help in this task. Program proof has turned out to be very difficult. In fact, some researchers have concluded that program proving can never give the kind of certainty that mathematical proofs do [5]. One reason is that the proofs are too long and complex to compel agreement about their validity. Also, the correctness of the implementation depends on the correctness of the compiler and of the microcode and hardware.

Even if we accept this view, however, the kernel approach remains valuable. For one thing, the *design* is potentially verifiable. Also, the formal specification results in cleaner, more carefully considered designs. And the concept of localizing security function is still valid.

Kernel design structure generally involves the following elements:

- an explicit process concept,
- explicit segmentation of memory,
- domains of privilege.

The kernel (according to our first definition*) includes two elements: those security functions used by all processes (the kernel according to the second definition) and *trusted processes,* such as those that handle logon, or accept authorizer commands.

11.7.2 Kernel Designs for Trusted Operating Systems

We now review some major efforts in trusted operating systems: KSOS, UCLA Secure UNIX, and KVM. Although all are kernel designs, they differ significantly from one another.

KSOS

The Kernelized Secure Operating System (KSOS) [39] grew out of work at the MITRE Corporation and is being implemented by Ford Aerospace and Communication Corporation for the PDP 11/70. (Another version is

*Sometimes called a *trusted computing base* [46].

being developed by Honeywell for its hardware [3].) KSOS provides a user interface very similar to that provided by UNIX. This interface is provided by a KSOS component called the UNIX Emulator, which transforms user calls into sequences of calls to the kernel. The kernel is designed to eventually support other interfaces as well.

The function of the kernel is to implement certain objects and to mediate all access to them. The objects are: processes, segments, files, devices, and file subtypes. Accesses are checked for compliance with DoD policy and also for a simple form of discretionary control. Because the hardware does not provide enough protection, all I/O must be handled by the kernel. The KSOS system structure is shown in Fig. 11.15. KSOS is written in the Modula language [73], which was chosen in part because it supports the process concept.

User mode	User programs	Untrusted nonkernel security-related software	
Supervisor mode	UNIX EMULATOR		Trusted nonkernel security-related software
Kernel mode	SECURITY KERNEL		

Fig. 11.15. KSOS structure. [From Reference 39, by permission.]

UCLA Secure UNIX

The UCLA system [50, 67] differs from KSOS in supporting a different and possibly more general security policy. This policy is not built into the kernel, but is implemented by a policy manager that maintains the protection data. The system provides a large number of labels, called *colors*. Each file can be labeled with a number of colors, and each user has a *color list*. Access is allowed only if the user's color list covers the file's color list. The process profile (which determines what access is currently allowed) specifies a subset of the user's color list.

The kernel implements a few abstract objects—process, page, device, and capability—and about a dozen primitive operations on these objects. The access rights of a process are represented by a capability list that is maintained by the kernel. Only the kernel can execute privileged instructions. A process contains two address spaces: one for an operating system interface (analogous to the KSOS UNIX emulator) and one for application code. Calls to UNIX from the application are interpreted by the interface, which issues kernel calls.

System security depends on the kernel and also on two trusted processes: the policy manager, and a process that authenticates users and maintains the association between users and the processes that represent them.

A UCLA kernel operation behaves like a machine instruction, in that it is not interruptible and I/O instructions are never issued during it. This is in contrast to KSOS, where a process can be suspended while it is in the kernel. One reason for the UCLA choice is to facilitate verification, since verification of parallel programs is much more difficult. The different implications for hardware requirements of the two approaches are discussed in Section 11.7.3.

KVM/370

KVM/370 (Kernelized VM/370) [24] retrofits an existing operating system for security.

The standard VM/370 Control Program (CP) might well be regarded as a kernel, since it is relatively simple and since it mediates all I/O and all sharing. KVM essentially introduces another level of kernelization. It splits the functions of the VM/370 control program (CP) into two parts: security-relevant and not. Security-relevant code either executes privileged instructions or accesses global system data, i.e. data that crosses security levels. The security-relevant code goes into a kernel that provides only primitive virtualization and mediation of all I/O. The remaining code is in the Non-Kernel Control Program (NKCP). The kernel supports a *set* of NKCPs, each of which supports all the virtual machines at a specific security level. Since only the kernel runs in real supervisor state, the NKCPs cannot perform real I/O and therefore cannot compromise security.

The subjects for KVM are the individual NKCPs. Thus the kernel protects each virtual machine from other virtual machines at different levels, but not from other virtual machines at the same level.

The overall structure is shown in Fig. 11.16. The kernel and trusted processes execute in real supervisor state. A set of ''semitrusted'' processes also have access to global system data, but they execute in real problem state and can use only virtual addresses. Each NKCP has access to system data only for its own level, and each user virtual machine is controlled by the NKCP for its level.

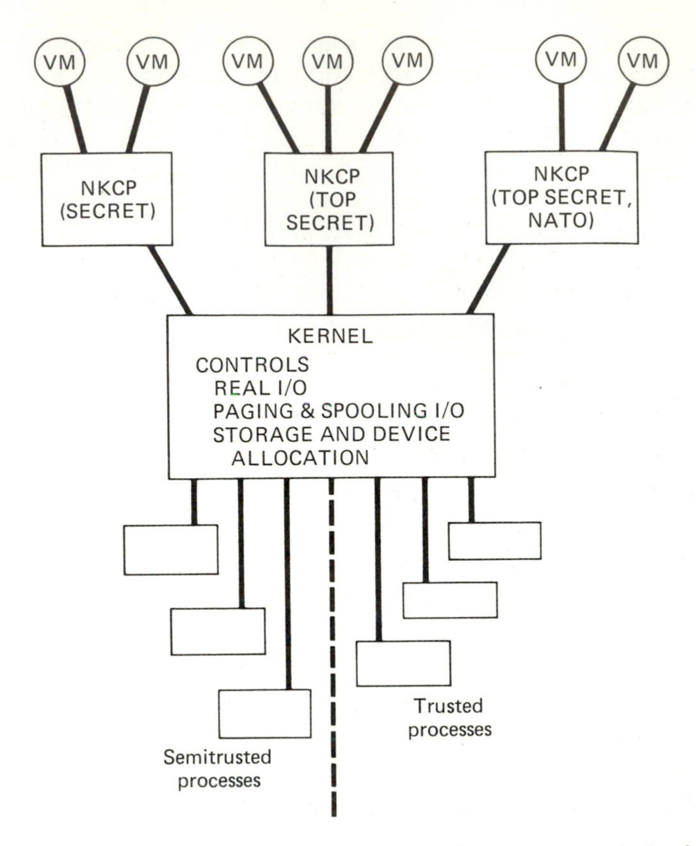

Fig. 11.16. KVM structure. [From Reference 24, by permission.]

11.7.3 Hardware Requirements for Kernel Designs

Certain hardware features are needed to support the kernel approach. One can look at the three attributes of a reference monitor and translate each into a corresponding hardware requirement [4]. One, each memory access must be checked by some mechanism, such as virtual-memory hardware. Two, isolation of the kernel must be provided. Some systems use a domain of privilege, such as the kernel domain of the PDP 11/45. The kernel can also be isolated by being implemented in microcode so that it becomes an extension of the hardware. This is realistic if the kernel is small and simple. The UCLA system is designed for a possible firmware implementation. A hardware capability mechanism can also provide kernel isolation. The third attribute—verifiability—is enhanced if the hardware provides good support for the process concept, so that implementation of processes by the kernel is quite simple.

In addition to these requirements, the following hardware features are desirable:

- gates for interdomain calls,
- argument validation, such as keeping an unforgeable record of the domain of any argument passed across domains, or the key-switch instruction used by MVS,
- independent control for different types of access (read, write, execute),
- efficient switching of process and domain.

Conversely, if one is designing a kernel for existing hardware, the characteristics of this hardware, even if the basic required support is provided, have an effect on the way the kernel is to be implemented [51].

11.7.4 Other Approaches to Information-flow Control

Multilevel operating systems control information by what has been called "extended access control" [8]. That is, each data access is checked to ensure that the simple security and * properties are not violated. Since information can flow only upward in level, the result is that data tends to be overclassified. This problem can be alleviated somewhat by letting the security level of a process rise during execution as a function of the levels of data that it has read. The level of the process at any moment is then a *high watermark* [69]. It is argued, however, that an operating system cannot be secured in this way, since all its outputs would have to be classified as high as any of its inputs.

An alternative method is to examine each program statically in order to determine exactly how each input flows to each output. Each flow can then be checked for consistency with the system's flow policy [7]. (As we saw in Chapter 6, both explicit and implicit flows must be considered.) The methods that have been proposed for this static certification have not yet been put into practice. Their generality is limited in that they cannot handle variables whose security classes change, or inputs that can have different classes at different times.

Both static analysis and run-time access control deal with *legitimate* channels of information flow; that is, the information flows along the normal paths of the system. A much harder problem is to control flow of information along *covert* channels. Any sharing of a finite pool of re-

Levels
User environments
User input/output
Procedure records
User processes
User objects
Directories
Extended types
Virtual memory (segmentation)
Paging
System processes and input/output
Basic operations (e.g., arithmetic)
Real memory
Capabilities and interrupts

Fig. 11.17. PSOS hierarchical levels.

sources provides such a channel. An example is the response time of a time-sharing system. By controlling its own rate of usage of the CPU, a process can convey information to another process, which can observe the real time needed for some computation. Covert channels in a time-sharing system can have a surprisingly large bandwidth.

11.7.5 PSOS—A Capability Approach

PSOS [17] is a design for a "provably secure" operating system, which can support a wide range of different security policies. The only specific hardware assumed is a tagged architecture for implementing capabilities. The system is structured as a hierarchy of levels; the functions at one level depend only on functions at the next lower level. These levels are shown in Fig. 11.17. The lowest level implements capabilities.

The PSOS design methodology and the structure of the design are intimately related. The methodology divides the development of the system into the following stages:

(S0) The interface visible to users is defined. It is then structured as a set of modules, each of which manages a particular type of object.

(S1) The modules are arranged into a hierarchy.

(S2) The functions performed by each module are formally specified. Following methods developed by Parnas [49], each function is either an O-function (which changes the state of its module), a V-function (which returns a value characterizing the module state) or an OV-function (which does both). Each O- or OV-function is specified as a set of effects on the state and a set of exception conditions that cause a call on the function to be rejected. These specifications, written in a language called SPECIAL, do not reflect any implementation decisions.

(S3) A mapping function is written for each module that characterizes its state in terms of the states of lower-level modules. These mappings make explicit how a module's data structures are represented in terms of lower-level modules. For example, a segment would be represented as a sequence of pages.

(S4) Programs are written to implement the functions.

For each of these stages, appropriate verification is done, for both correctness and security.

11.8 AUTHENTICATION

Whether the system provides access control or information-flow control, authentication of users is fundamental for security. The DBMS usually relies on the operating system to perform this function, to avoid duplication.

When users log onto a system, they must first identify themselves. In turn the system authenticates them; that is, it determines whether the specified identity is correct.

There are three basic approaches to authentication, which use:

1. something the person *knows,*
2. something the person *has,* or
3. something the person *is.*

The first group includes passwords; the second, machine-readable badges and keys; the third, physical characteristics of the person, such as voice or fingerprints.

While the third approach is theoretically the most secure because of the uniqueness of personal characteristics, these methods are not yet in widespread use. The second approach has the disadvantage that the cards or keys may be lost, and this loss may go unnoticed for some time. The cards or keys may also be illegally copied. Passwords [74] are the most widely used of the techniques.

Passwords should be easy to memorize in order to avoid the need for written copies. However, users should not be allowed to choose their own passwords because knowledge of the user often means that only a few intelligent guesses are required to determine the correct password. (The security threat here can be minimized by allowing only a certain number of unsuccessful logon attempts.) Because a password should also be changed frequently, it may help to generate passwords automatically. Multics [57], for example, generates a random, eight-character password which has English-like characteristics, so it is both pronounceable and easy to memorize. The user has the option of rejecting the password and requesting another. UNIX requires its users to choose passwords that satisfy length and character-set constraints [43]. Constraints and automatic generation can make passwords easier to guess, however.

A user is authenticated by comparing the user-provided password with the one stored in a table in the computer. An important issue in the use of passwords is the protection of this *password table*. One possibility is to rely on the protection facilities of the operating system. If more security is needed, a better approach (again used in Multics) is to use a hard-to-invert transformation on the password before storing it in the password table (see Section 11.9.6). Encryption can be used to prevent the password from being detected by the tapping of the communication lines connecting the terminal with the host machine.

It is essential not to display or print the password entered by the user. If the hardware does not allow deactivation of the printer, then a background of overstruck characters can be used.

If authentication is performed only at logon time, there is a danger that the user may leave the terminal for a period without first logging off, thus enabling someone else to gain access to the system. One solution to this problem is for the system to log out a user automatically if there is no activity for a defined length of time.

Mechanisms are also required to prevent users from being tricked into divulging their passwords by user-written programs that simulate the logon procedure. This technique is a form of *spoofing*. A spoofing program typically sends the initial screen of the logon procedure to a terminal and then waits for someone to log on. When this happens, the logon procedure is simulated until the password is entered and read by the spoofing program. At this stage an error can be generated (or simulated), thereby forcing the terminal user to restart the logon procedure—this time the correct one. The terminal user therefore succeeds eventually in logging onto the system and is unaware that the password has been compromised. In order to safeguard against this kind of attack, special *break characters* can be included in the initial logon request. When such a character is recognized, control is passed to the authentication routines irrespective of the apparent destination of the message. Another sound practice is to report the time of the last logon at each logon. While this does not prevent security violations, it does aid in their detection.

With switched lines it is also necessary for the terminal user to verify the identity of the computer, and for the computer to reauthenticate the user on a reconnect after a line drop. Encryption can be used for the mutual authentication of terminal user and computer.

11.9 ENCRYPTION

Data encryption is a rapidly evolving area. Once of interest only to governments for the protection of their military and diplomatic communications, encryption has become, through the increasing use of the computer, important for business in general. In this section we briefly review the implications of data encryption for database security. See [35, 52, and 64] for more detailed surveys of the field in general.

Encryption involves the encoding of data to hide its true content from unauthorized persons. Encryption mechanisms provided by the operating system or hardware can support database security in a number of ways. For example,

- Data in the database can be encrypted to restrict its access to certain users or to protect against unauthorized access through theft of disk packs.
- Information transmitted to a remote terminal can be encrypted to protect against illegal interception, such as wire-tapping.
- Password tables can be stored in encrypted form in the computer.

A *cipher system* consists of

- an algorithm—*the encryption and decryption procedures*—which remains constant, and
- a cryptographic key, K, selected from a large set of possible keys.

The algorithm is usually public knowledge, while the particular key used is kept secret. We can represent the encryption of a *plaintext* P by an encryption procedure E using a key K to produce a *ciphertext* C as:

$$C = E^K (P)$$

With a conventional cipher system such as the NBS data encryption standard (DES) [41], the plaintext is recovered by a decryption procedure, D, using the same key (Fig. 11.18):

$$P = D^K (C)$$

In DES a 64-bit block of plaintext is encrypted using a 64-bit key, producing a 64-bit block of ciphertext. As eight bits of the key are used for parity checking and the encryption algorithm possesses a symmetry with respect

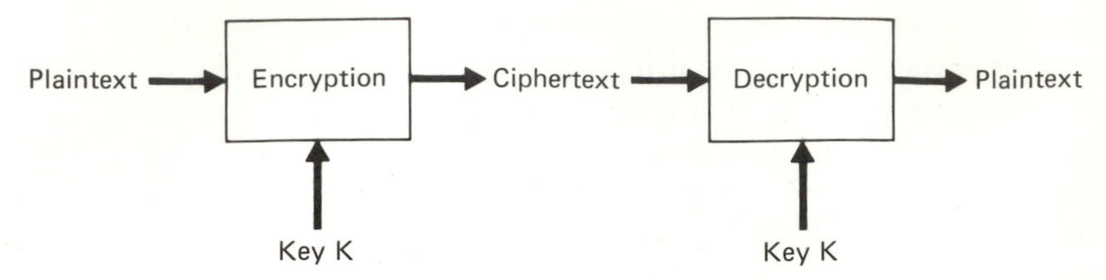

Fig. 11.18. Encryption and decryption.

to complementation, there are 2^{55} possible keys. Figure 11.19 illustrates encryption and decryption using the DES.

The job of the cryptanalyst, who is assumed to have full knowledge of E and D but not K, is to produce a best estimate of the plaintext P, given the ciphertext C. While in some cases it may be possible for the cryptanalyst to produce the correct P without having first found K, breaking a cipher system usually means finding a scheme that is capable of determining K.

One can classify the attacks on a cipher system by a cryptanalyst in increasing order of strength as follows [10]:

1. *A ciphertext-only attack.* The cryptanalyst possesses substantial amounts of ciphertext but does not know the corresponding plaintext.
2. *A known-plaintext attack.* The cryptanalyst possesses substantial quantities of ciphertext and the corresponding plaintext.
3. *A chosen-plaintext attack.* The cryptanalyst can choose and submit unlimited plaintext and examine the resulting ciphertext. Cipher systems are most vulnerable to this type of attack. For example, a simple alphabetic-substitution cipher could be immediately broken by submitting a plaintext consisting of the letters A to Z.

In order for a cipher system to be secure, it must be able to withstand a chosen-plaintext attack by a cryptanalyst with knowledge of the encryption and decryption procedures. Cipher systems can sometimes be broken by techniques other than exhaustively trying all possible keys. For

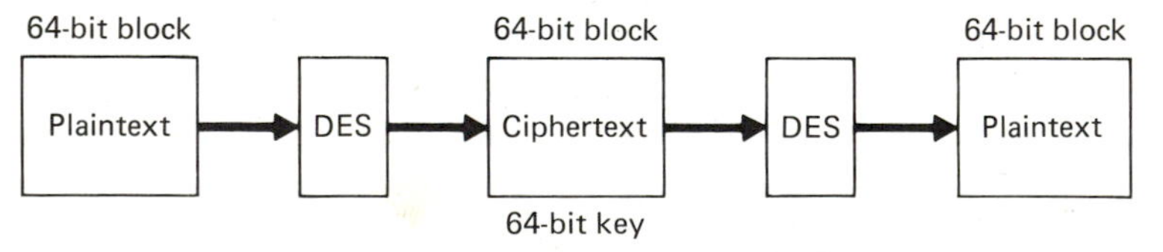

Fig. 11.19. Data Encryption Standard.

example, a simple substitution cipher for the English alphabet has 26 possible keys. This means that it is computationally infeasible for an analyst to try all keys, even using the fastest computer. However, redundancy in the English language means that in practice a message of more than twenty-five letters can be broken by making use of, for example, letter-frequency distribution. In the ideal encryption algorithm, the statistical structure of the input language will *not* show through into the encryption language. The only ciphers that are *unconditionally secure* are those that use nonrepeating keys, where each symbol of the key introduces at least as much uncertainty as is removed by a symbol of the cipher. However, the use of one-time keys in most situations is infeasible. The requirements for a *practical* secure encryption algorithm are:

1. No method of recovering the key is known other than trying all possible keys.
2. Trying all possible keys is not economically feasible.

While the first requirement cannot be proved for the DES, no alternative method of key recovery has been discovered after many person-years of investigation. Testing all possible keys of the DES appears not to be economically feasible with current hardware.

As the encryption algorithm is public knowledge, security achieved through encryption ultimately depends on the secrecy of the key. Mechanisms for protecting the key vary, depending on the purpose for which encryption is being used.

11.9.1 Hardware Support

Encryption is a time-consuming process when performed by software. One of the advantages of having an encryption standard is that hardware implementations of DES are available. These single-LSI-chip implementations are both cheap and fast (up to one megabit of text per second).

11.9.2 Key Distribution for Communication Security

We now consider the problem of transmitting a message securely between two nodes of a network over a potentially insecure channel, using a cipher system. (By insecure we mean an intruder can intercept, change, and add messages on the channel.) Before transmitting a message the two nodes must first agree upon the key to be used for encrypting the message. Clearly the sending node cannot transmit the key over the insecure channel in plaintext form to the receiving node. There are three approaches to this key-distribution problem.

Special key channel. A separate, more secure channel is used to distribute keys (Fig. 11.20). This could be a special communication link but most frequently it would be a trusted courier, or even registered mail or telephone. Security can be improved by splitting the key into two or more pieces and sending these in separate ways.

Hierarchic key systems [38]. Here keys are of two types: *data-encrypting keys* and *key-encrypting keys*. Data-encrypting keys are generated dynamically and used to encipher messages, while key-encrypting keys are used to encipher other keys. Key-encrypting keys can be of two types: *primary* or *master* keys, which protect data-encrypting keys and other key-encrypting keys, and *secondary keys,* which are used only to encipher data-encrypting keys. Data-encrypting keys are distributed through the communication links encrypted using a key-encrypting key. These latter are distributed by a special key channel.

For a centralized system, communication occurs between a terminal and the host computer. The host in this case establishes the new data-encrypting key for each session and transmits it to the communicating terminal encrypted using the secondary key for that terminal. The keys for each terminal in the system can be stored in encrypted form in the host, using the master key. This means that only one key needs to be protected. A host-based protocol has been described in [13], which satisfies the criterion that no key appears in plaintext form outside the *encryption facility*. The encryption facility is defined as the inaccessible area containing the master key and the encryption algorithm.

Centralized key control can also be used for key distribution in a network [44]. One node in the network is designated the *key distribution center* (KDC). Suppose node A wishes to establish a connection with node B, and A and B have encryption keys K_a and K_b, known only to themselves and the KDC. In order to establish a session key and authenticate themselves to each other, they execute the following procedure.

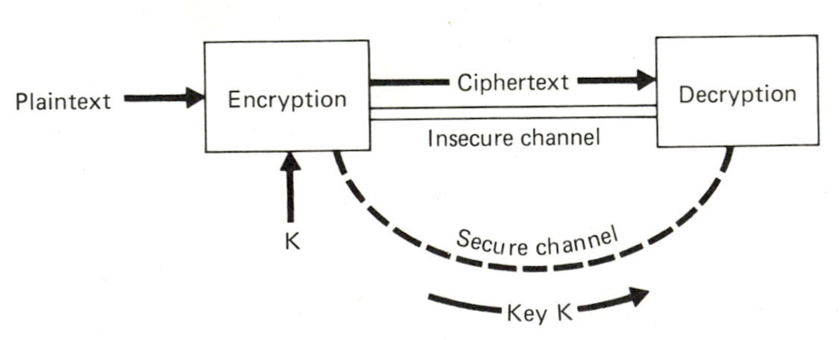

Fig. 11.20. Communication over an insecure channel.

1. A sends to the KDC a message encrypted under K_a requesting a session with B. The request also contains a random number identifier, id.

$$E_{K_a} (B + id)$$

2. The KDC returns to A a message encrypted under K_a containing the following:

   - a session key K_S,
   - the original request from A, thus protecting against replay of earlier messages or modification to the current request,
   - the session key K_S, and A's identity, encrypted under K_b.

$$E_{K_a} (K_S + B + id + E_{K_b} (K_S + A))$$

3. A sends the message $E_{K_b} (K_S + A)$ to B.
4. B sends a random-number identifier id′ encrypted under K_S to A to check that message 3 is not a replay.

$$E_{K_S} (id')$$

5. A performs a preestablished function on the identifier and returns the result to B, thus proving there has been no replaying of earlier messages.

$$E_{K_S} (f (id'))$$

A similar protocol works for *distributed* key control where every node serves as a KDC.

Public key systems. In this approach [55], encryption and decryption are performed with two distinct keys, K and K′. Computing K′ from K is computationally infeasible using current algorithms and hardware. The encryption key K can therefore be made public and placed in a public directory without compromising the decryption key K′. Anyone wanting to send a message to A encrypts the message with A's public key K_A. A is the only person who has K'_A and therefore the only person who can decrypt the message.

If E_A and D_A are the encryption and decryption procedures using A's public and private keys, respectively, then:

$$C = E_A (P)$$
$$P = D_A (C)$$

Initially the public key systems were considered to be superior to hierarchic key systems; however, it has been shown that the key distribution protocols are similar for the two approaches [44]. This is because, while a *secret* exchange of keys is no longer required, an *authenticated* exchange of keys is still required. The number of protocol messages exchanged is very similar. A clear superiority with respect to security has not been found for either method, since security depends on the implementation and on administrative procedures.

11.9.3 Digital Signatures

In a network environment where important messages are transmitted, there must be a way to provide digital signatures, equivalent to the signatures found on paper documents. The functions of these signatures are threefold:

1. They guarantee to the recipient of the message and to a third party that the message originated with a given sender; i.e., they provide authentication.
2. They do not allow the sender to later disavow messages sent.
3. They prevent the recipient from forging messages for some illegal purpose. Both conventional encryption algorithms and public-key algorithms can be used as the basis for digital signatures [44].

If the public key procedures E and D have the additional property that $P = E(D(P))$, then a message sent from A to B can be signed by A in the following way: A first applies the private decryption procedure D_A to the message before encrypting with B's public encryption procedure:

$$C = E_B (D_A (P))$$

B decrypts the message by applying the private procedure D_B, followed by the public procedure E_A. Only A could have sent the message because only A knows D_A.

A problem (which also applies to the other methods) is that, if the secrecy of the encryption key is compromised, then the validity of all messages carrying this signature is put in doubt. This would allow a user to disavow previous messages by saying that the key was compromised.

11.9.4 Levels of Network Encryption

An important issue in a secure network is the architectural *level* at which encryption occurs. On one extreme we have *link encryption,* where encryption occurs at each physical link between two nodes.

At a higher level, encryption is performed at the host systems, and messages are encrypted only once in the network (this is sometimes called *node-to-node encryption*). This approach allows different logical channels sharing the same link to be isolated from each other by assigning different encryption keys (we call these channels *cryptographic paths*).

An even higher level requires encryption to be performed at the individual processes that are communicating with each other (this is sometimes called *end-to-end encryption*).

Figure 11.21 illustrates these three approaches. In link encryption two keys, K1 and K2, are needed to send a message from Node 1 to Node 2. Encryption and decryption are performed at each end of a link (usually with cryptographic hardware devices). In node encryption the front-end processor for Node 1 does the encryption and the front-end for Node 2 decrypts the message. Intermediate nodes only act as switches and only one key is needed. In end-to-end encryption, a sending process encrypts a

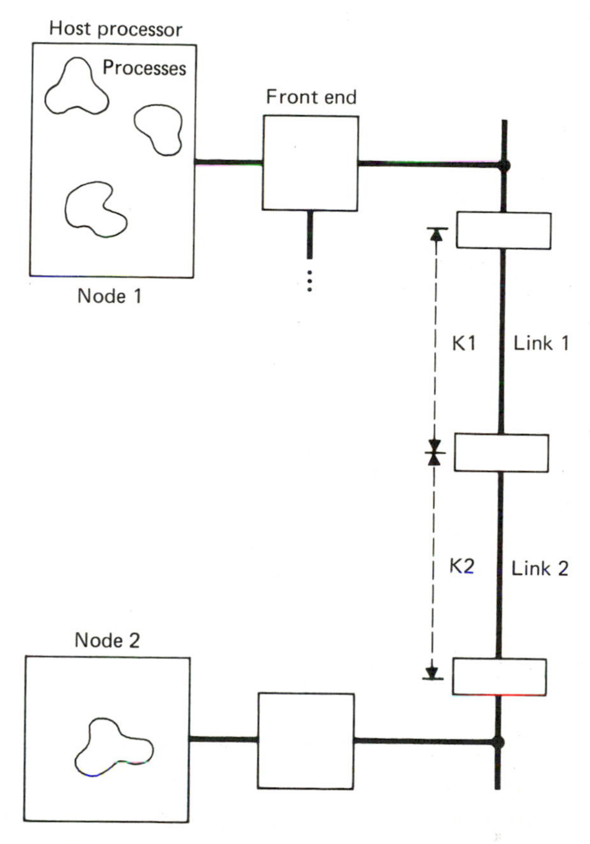

Fig. 11.21. Levels of encryption for a network.

message (using a software algorithm or special hardware integrated into the host), and the receiving process decrypts it.

In principle, end-to-end encryption is the most secure. This is because the need for trusted software is reduced when higher levels are used (the lower levels deal only with encrypted text and cannot tamper with it). However, the number of processes is normally higher than the number of processors and this, in turn, is higher than the number of links. This means that the number of protected entities is higher for the higher levels, and the number of key pairs to be distributed is correspondingly larger. Furthermore, performance will be affected since, if encryption is performed at a high level, there is little room for the front-end processors to do any extra processing, such as formatting or data compression. These depend on statistical properties of the message to be effective, and those properties are hidden once the message is encrypted.

IBM's Systems Network Architecture (SNA) [40] provides end-to-end encryption. SNA defines a *system services control point* (SSCP) as the control function for all communications activity within a *domain* (a portion of the network). Tables in the SSCP describe the configuration and characteristics of its domain, including cryptographic capabilities. One of the tables specifies the master keys associated with each cryptographic path within the domain. These master keys are encrypted with the master key of the SSCP. For communication between SSCPs it is necessary to exchange data keys securely. A secondary key is used to encrypt the data keys.

11.9.5 File Encryption

Protection against loss of portable memory devices such as tapes and removable disk packs can be achieved by encryption. One possibility is for each disk and tape drive to be equipped with its own encryption mechanism and key. The advantage of this approach is that the encryption is transparent to users: all data stored is automatically encrypted and all data read is automatically decrypted. However, in the case of a drive failure, files must be capable of being read by another device. This would require the ability to retrieve and alter keys, making it difficult to protect their security.

An alternative is for the user to keep the key and present it to the system every time access to the file is required [34]. While this may be acceptable for personal files, it is a poor solution for a shared database with many different users, since the key would have to be very widely distributed. A third possibility is that the same host encryption facility used for communication could be used to store all file keys, again in encrypted form. There must be some way of retrieving these keys if the host fails and a backup machine is required to process the files.

File compression is used in some DBMSs to save storage and reduce I/O time. Encryption could be performed together with compression, with little additional overhead [32].

The use of file encryption may soon become more widespread, as reduced hardware costs begin to allow many users to have personal computers. These will be linked to shared facilities that provide storage for large files, as well as shared software. Denning [6] has proposed that all personal data that is communicated to a shared *central facility* (CF) be encrypted by the user's public key. It can then be decrypted only by the user's secret key, which exists only in an encryption device at the personal computer. In particular, the CF has no way of deciphering this data. If the user borrows software from the CF (a compiler, for example), any Trojan horse within that software would have no way of passing plaintext outside the personal computer. Users can communicate through the CF by exchanging public keys and enciphering the messages with the recipient's key. (A switch on the encryption device selects either the user's public key or an alternative key that can be set by a program.) Sharing of confidential files is done by way of copies, each sent enciphered with the public key of the authorized recipient. (Some criticisms and modifications of the Denning design can be found in [47].)

Another possibility [26] is to encrypt different levels of a multilevel database architecture or the mappings between these levels. This could prevent "sneak" paths to the database (paths not under the control of the DBMS).

11.9.6 Encryption Support for Authentication

As discussed earlier, hard-to-invert transformations (called *one-way-ciphers*) can be used to protect password tables. Two types of transformations are discussed in [15] and [53]. The DES can also be used in this way, as shown in Fig. 11.22. The password is used as the key to the encryption procedure with any plaintext input. The plaintext does not have to be kept secret because knowledge of plaintext and ciphertext does not allow the password to be determined. A further improvement can be obtained by modifying the internal tables in the DES chip [43]. This mechanism only protects the password directory from theft. It does not protect against a wiretapper intercepting the password in plaintext form. Protection against wiretapping in the authentication procedure can be achieved, for example, by requesting the user to send the date and time encrypted in the user's personal key. This requires encryption support in the terminal. The

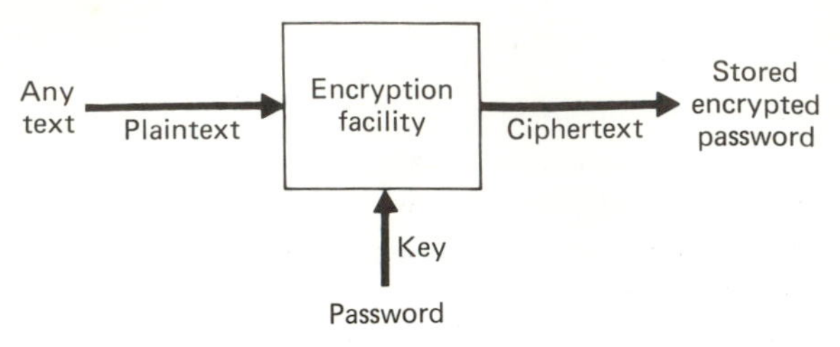

Fig. 11.22. Password table.

host must then decrypt the message by trying all possible user keys. The protocol of [44] using key distribution centers performs authentication as well as key distribution and protects against both wiretapping and theft of tables.

11.9.7 Conclusions

It is important to realize that encryption alone cannot solve all data-security problems. While encryption is sufficient to provide secure data transmission and authentication, its application to the controlled sharing of data in a database is less clear. Encryption cannot prevent destruction of data, and other mechanisms are required to provide functions such as content-dependent control. Additionally, as data must be processed in plaintext form within the computer, protection mechanisms are required in the operating system.

11.10 SUMMARY

Security in a DBMS depends ultimately on the environment provided by the operating system and the computer hardware. Elaborate security measures in the DBMS are useless if, for example, an operating-system flaw permits the database files to be accessed directly. We started by listing the security and integrity requirements that the DBMS expects the OS and hardware to provide, and some of the possible threats coming from that environment. Using the protection matrix as a reference model, we discussed several access mechanisms. These include domains of privilege, gates, and specialized mechanisms to protect main memory and external storage, as well as more general approaches such as capabilities, access-control lists, virtual machines, and interpretation. We then showed how the mechanisms are used in several systems, including IBM's System/370, a proposal of the IBM Los Angeles Scientific Center, Multics, the Cambridge CAP system, and VM/370. The concept of kernel

systems that control information flow, an
OS, UCLA Secure UNIX, KVM/370, PSOS)

nction which the OS usually provides for the
d some possible approaches were considered.
ique that can be applied at all levels, from
ection to network link protection. Its basic
elements were ... as well as some applications to specific protection problems.

EXERCISES

11.1. How might some of the mechanisms described in this chapter be used to solve a TOCTTOU problem arising from concurrent I/O?

11.2. The System/370 has two modes of privilege for the processor. What additional mechanisms are used in System/370 hardware and software to provide a finer granularity of protection?

11.3. The "tagging" approach to capabilities is more flexible than the "partitioning" approach. What are some disadvantages of the tagging approach?

11.4. Name some protection mechanisms whose primary purpose is something other than protection.

11.5. Discuss the problems that must be solved in applying encryption to protect data in the database.

REFERENCES AND BIBLIOGRAPHY

1. C. R. Attanasio, P. W. Markstein, and R. J. Phillips, "Penetrating an operating system: A study of VM/370 integrity." *IBM Systems J.* **15,** 1 (1976), 102–116.

   The results of an IBM–SDC joint study, which uncovered in a systematic way security flaws in the design or implementation of VM/370 (version of Feb. 1973). They found that VM's main strength was its simplicity and the small size of its code, while its worst vulnerability was the I/O system (complex due to the need to simulate the standard 370 I/O interface).

2. C. R. Attanasio, "Virtual control storage—Security measures in VM/370." *IBM Systems J.* **18,** 1 (1979), 93–110.

3. C. H. Bonneau, "Secure Communications Processor (SCOMP)." *Proc. 2nd Seminar on the DoD Computer Security Initiative Program,* Jan. 1980, S1–S4.

   Honeywell's SCOMP (Secure Communications Processor) is modeled on KSOS, and was developed for use by the Defense Department. SCOMP uses a Level 6 minicomputer with a security kernel written in Pascal.

Special hardware implements a Multics-like ring structure, instructions allow fast context switching for processes.

4. E. L. Burke, "Secure Minicomputer Architectures." Report M76– MITRE Corp., Bedford, Mass., October 1976.
5. R. A. DeMillo, R. J. Lipton, and A. J. Perlis, "Social processes and proofs of theorems and programs." *Comm. ACM* **22,** 5 (May 1979), 271–280.
6. D. E. Denning, "Secure personal computing in an insecure network." *Comm. ACM* **22,** 8 (August 1979), 476–482.
7. D. E. Denning and P. J. Denning, "Certification of programs for secure information flow." *Comm. ACM* **20,** 7 (July 1977), 504–513.
8. D. E. Denning and P. J. Denning, "Data security." *Comp. Surveys* **11,** 3 (Sept. 1979), 227–249.
9. J. B. Dennis and E. C. Van Horn, "Programming semantics for multiprogrammed computations." *Comm. ACM* **9,** 3 (March 1966), 143–155.
10. W. Diffie and M. Hellman, "New directions in cryptography." *IEEE Trans. on Information Theory* **IT–22,** 6 (Nov. 1976), 644–654.
11. E. W. Dijkstra, "Cooperating Sequential Processes." In *Programming Languages,* F. Genuys (Ed.). Academic Press, New York, 1968.
12. D. Downs and G. J. Popek, "A kernel design for a secure data base management system." *Proc. 3rd Int. Conf. on Very Large Data Bases,* Tokyo (Oct. 1977), 507–514. Available from ACM and IEEE.
13. W. F. Ehrsam, S. M. Matyas, C. H. Meyer, and W. L. Tuchman, "A cryptographic key management scheme for implementing the data encryption standard." *IBM Systems J.* **17,** 2 (1978), 106–125.
14. D. M. England, "Architectural Features of System 250." In Infotech *State of the Art Report on Operating Systems,* 1972.
15. A. Evans, Jr., and W. Kantrowitz, "A user authentication scheme not requiring secrecy in the computer." *Comm. ACM* **17,** 8 (August 1974), 437–442.
16. R. S. Fabry, "Capability-based addressing." *Comm. ACM* **17,** 7 (July 1974), 403–412.
17. R. J. Feiertag and P. G. Neumann, "The foundations of a provably secure operating system (PSOS)." *AFIPS Conf. Proc.* **48,** 1979 NCC, 329–334. AFIPS Press, Montvale, N.J., 1979.
18. E. B. Fernandez, R. C. Summers, T. Lang, and C. D. Coleman, "Architectural support for system protection and database security." *IEEE Trans. on Computers* **C–27,** 8 (August 1978), 767–771.
19. E. B. Fernandez and C. Wood, "The relationship between operating system and database system security: A survey." *Proc. of the Computer Software and Applications Conf.* (COMPSAC), Nov. 1977, 453–462. Available from IEEE.

    Makes a case for separating DBMS security from OS security, lists security features to be provided by the OS, and surveys the requirements of some existing or proposed systems.

20. E. A. Feustel, "On the advantages of tagged architecture." *IEEE Trans. Comput.* **C–22,** 7 (July 1973), 644–656.
Proposes that all data elements be self-identifying by means of a tag, and presents the advantages of this type of architecture for operating systems, languages, and hardware design.

21. I. Gat and J. P. Considine, "An Architecture for a Controlled Information-Flow Facility in RACF." IBM Research Report RC 7334, Yorktown Heights, N.Y., Feb. 1978.
Applies to RACF the ideas of the Generalized Capability Vector Machine [56]. This model would allow RACF to support controlled information flow. Additionally, a way of dealing with the TOCTTOU problem in this environment is discussed.

22. L. Gilman and A. J. Rose, *APL—An Interactive Approach.* Wiley, New York, 1974.

23. V. D. Gligor, "Review and revocation of access privileges distributed through capabilities." *IEEE Trans. on Software Eng.* **SE–5,** 6 (November 1979), 575–586.

24. B. D. Gold *et al.*, "A security retrofit of VM/370." *AFIPS Conf. Proc.* **48,** 1979 NCC. 335–344. AFIPS Press, Montvale, N.J., 1979.

25. J. N. Gray and V. Watson, "A Shared Segment and Interprocess Communication Facility for VM/370." IBM Research Report RJ 2450, San Jose, Calif., Jan. 1979.

26. E. Gudes, H. S. Koch, and F. A. Stahl, "The application of cryptography for data base security." *AFIPS Conf. Proc.* **45,** 1976 NCC, 97–107. AFIPS Press, Montvale, N.J., 1976.

27. A. J. Herbert, "A Hardware-Supported Protection Architecture." [71, Appendix 1].
Design of a new protection architecture for the CAP computer. The extended facilities include the protection of abstract objects.

28. IBM Corporation, General Systems Division, "IBM System/38—Technical Developments." Form No. G580–0237, Atlanta, Ga., December 1978.

29. IBM Corporation, "IBM Virtual Machine Facility/370: Introduction." Form No. GC20–1800–9, Poughkeepsie, N.Y., March 1979.

30. IBM Corporation, "OS/VS2 Access Method Services." Form No. GC26–3841, San Jose, Calif., 1978.

31. IBM Corporation, "OS/VS2 MVS Resource Access-Control Facility (RACF). General Information Manual." Form No. GC28–0722–4, Poughkeepsie, N.Y., 1978.

32. Informatics Inc., "SHRINK/2—Generalized File Compression/Encryption System." Canoga Park, Calif., 1979.

33. R. M. Jensen, "A formal approach for communication between logically isolated virtual machines." *IBM Systems J.* **18,** 1 (1979), 71–92.

34. A. G. Konheim *et al.,* "The IPS Cryptographic Programs." *IBM Systems J.* **19,** 2 (1980), 253–283.

35. A. Lempel, "Cryptology in transition." *Comp. Surveys* **11,** 4 (Dec. 1979), 285–303.

36. R. E. Lennon, "Cryptography architecture for information security." *IBM Systems J.* **17,** 2 (1978), 138–150.

Shows the implementation of cryptographic measures in IBM's SNA; in particular key management, the establishment of communication sessions, and file security.

37. S. M. Matyas, "Digital signatures—An overview." *Comp. Networks* **3,** 2 (1979), 87–94.

38. S. M. Matyas and C. H. Meyer, "Generation, distribution, and installation of cryptographic keys." *IBM Systems J.* **17,** 2 (1978), 126–137.

39. E. J. McCauley and P. J. Drongowski, "KSOS—The design of a secure operating system." *AFIPS Conf. Proc.* **48,** 1979 NCC, 345–351. AFIPS Press, Montvale, N.J., 1979.

40. J. H. McFadyen, "Systems network architecture: An overview." *IBM Systems J.* **15,** 1 (1976), 4–23.

41. National Bureau of Standards, "Data Encryption Standard." FIPS Pub. 46, U.S. Dept. of Commerce, Washington, D.C., January 1977.

42. R. C. Merkle, "Secure communications over insecure channels." *Comm. ACM* **21,** 4 (April 1978), 294–299.

Proposes a way to transmit keys using an insecure channel. The idea is to send (to the recipient of the key) N puzzles (a puzzle is an encrypted message that can be deciphered by brute force). The sender selects the size of the key so that each puzzle requires O (N) operations to decipher. Each puzzle contains an identifier and a different key (to be used in subsequent communication between the sender and the receiver). When the receiver breaks the puzzle, it sends the puzzle ID back to the sender, who now knows what key will be used. An intruder attempting to determine the key must break puzzles at random until the one with the right ID is found. Therefore the effort of the intruder to determine the key is $O(N^2)$.

43. R. Morris and K. Thompson, "Password security: A case history." *Comm. ACM* **22,** 11 (Nov. 1979), 594–597.

44. R. M. Needham and M. D. Schroeder, "Using encryption for authentication in large networks of computers." *Comm. ACM* **21,** 12 (Dec. 1978), 993–999.

45. R. M. Needham and R. D. H. Walker, "The Cambridge CAP Computer and its protection system." *Proc. 6th Symposium on Operating Systems Principles, 1977. Op. Sys. Rev.* **11,** 5 (1977), 1–10.

46. G. H. Nibaldi, "The trusted computing base." *Proc. 2nd Seminar on the DoD Computer Security Initiative Program,* Jan. 1980, O1–O6.

47. "On secure personal computing." Technical Correspondence, *Comm. ACM* **23,** 1 (January 1980), 35–39.

48. E. I. Organick, *Computer System Organization—the B5700–B6700 Series.* Academic Press, New York, 1972.

49. D. L. Parnas, "A technique for software module specification with examples." *Comm. ACM* **15,** 5 (May 1972), 330–336.

50. G. J. Popek *et al.,* "UCLA Secure UNIX." *AFIPS Conf. Proc.* **48,** 1979 NCC, 355–364. AFIPS Press, Montvale, N.J., 1979.

51. G. J. Popek and C. S. Kline, "Issues in kernel design." *AFIPS Conf. Proc.* **47,** 1978 NCC, 1079–1086. AFIPS Press, Montvale, N.J., 1978.

Discusses the effect of design constraints on kernel architectures. These constraints include: security policies, system functions, hardware, and performance. This discussion is followed by a set of principles of kernel design, possible hierarchies of secure code (kernels, trusted process, decomposition of trusted processes into subkernels, and distrusted software), internal kernel architecture, and the confinement problem.

52. G. J. Popek and C. S. Kline, "Encryption and secure computer networks," *Comp. Surveys* **11,** 4 (Dec. 1979), 331–356.

A good survey of key management, network encryption protocols, digital signatures, and the relative merits of conventional versus public-key encryption methods. The integration of cryptography in the ARPA network is discussed.

53. G. B. Purdy, "A high-security log-in procedure." *Comm ACM* **17,** 8 (August 1974), 442–445.

54. D. P. Reed and R. K. Kanodia, "Synchronization with eventcounts and sequencers." *Comm. ACM* **22,** 2 (Feb. 1979), 115–123.

55. R. L. Rivest, A. Shamir, and L. Adleman, "A method for obtaining digital signatures and public key cryptosystems." *Comm. ACM* **21,** 2 (Feb. 1978), 120–126.

56. H. J. Saal and I. Gat, "A hardware architecture for controlling information flow." *Proc. of the 5th Annual Symp. on Comp. Architecture,* 1978, 73–77. Available from IEEE (Cat. No. 78CH1284-9C).

A model of a Generalized Capability Vector Machine is developed. The paper provides a correctness proof of the behavior of this machine in controlling information flow and enforcing *memoryless execution.* (Memoryless execution is the invocation of a program which, after performing a computation on behalf of some invoker, does not keep any illicit account of the data input to it or produced by it.)

57. J. H. Saltzer, "Protection and the control of information sharing in Multics." *Comm. ACM* **17,** 7 (July 1974), 388–402.

58. J. H. Saltzer and M. D. Schroeder, "The protection of information in computer systems." *Proc. IEEE* **63,** 9 (Sept. 1975), 1278–1308.

59. J. H. Saltzer, "On digital signatures." *Op. Sys. Rev.* **12,** 2 (April 1978), 12–14.

60. A. L. Scherr, "Functional structure of IBM virtual storage operating systems. Part II: OS/VS2–2 concepts and philosophies." *IBM Systems J.* **12,** 4 (1973), 382–400.

61. M. D. Schroeder, D. D. Clark, J. H. Saltzer, and D. H. Wells, "Final Report of the Multics Kernel Design Project." Report TR–196, MIT Laboratory for Computer Science, Cambridge, Mass. (June 1977).

Describes work done toward redesigning Multics to use a security kernel that supports the multilevel model. Problems with Multics that are addressed include complex and circular dependencies in its design.

62. M. D. Schroeder and J. H. Saltzer, "A hardware architecture for implementing protection rings." *Comm. ACM* **15,** 3 (March 1972), 157–170.

63. L. H. Seawright and R. A. MacKinnon, "VM/370—A study of multiplicity and usefulness." *IBM Systems J.* **18,** 1 (1979), 4–17.

64. G. J. Simmons, "Symmetric and asymmetric encryption." *Comp. Surveys* **11,** 4 (Dec. 1979), 305–330.

65. M. J. Spier, T. N. Hastings, and D. N. Cutler, "A storage-mapping technique for the implementation of protective domains." *Software—Practice and Exp.* **4** (1974), 215–230.

A domain here is a dedicated memory space for a given process. Processes executing in some domain can make calls to other domains to execute there under control of another process; the call's target is an approved gate of the called domain. This paper describes a storage-mapping technique and a call/return mechanism implemented in a PDP–11/45.

66. R. C. Summers and E. B. Fernandez, "A System Structure for Data Security." Report G320–2687, IBM Los Angeles Scientific Center, April 1977.

67. B. J. Walker, R. A. Kemmerer, and G. J. Popek, "Specification and verification of the UCLA Unix security kernel." *Comm. ACM* **23,** 2 (Feb. 1980), 118–131.

68. S. T. Walker, "The advent of trusted computer operating systems." *AFIPS Conf. Proc.* **49,** 1980 NCC, 655–665. AFIPS Press, Arlington, Va., 1980.

69. C. Weissman, "Security controls in the ADEPT-50 time-sharing system." *AFIPS Conf. Proc.* **35,** 1969 FJCC, 119–133. AFIPS Press, Montvale, N.J., 1969.

70. M. V. Wilkes, *Time-Sharing Computer Systems* (Second ed.). Macdonald/American Elsevier Computer Monographs, New York, 1972.

Chapter 5 contains a lucid development of the capability concept as a generalization of base-limit registers. Chapter 8 discusses control of file access, in particular the mechanism developed by A. Fraser for the Cambridge University multiple-access system.

71. M. V. Wilkes and R. M. Needham, *The Cambridge CAP Computer and Its Operating System.* Elsevier North Holland, New York, 1979.

72. S. Winkler and L. Danner, "Data security in the computer communication environment." *Computer* **7,** 2 (Feb. 1974), 23–31.

73. N. Wirth, "Modula: A language for modular multiprogramming." *Software—Practice and Experience* **7,** 1 (1977), 3–35.

74. H. M. Wood, "The use of passwords for controlling access to remote computer systems and services." *AFIPS Conf. Proc.* **46,** 1977 NCC, 27–33. AFIPS Press, Montvale, N.J., 1977.

12 Security and Integrity in Distributed Database Systems

12.1 INTRODUCTION

An increasingly important approach to the design of database systems involves *distribution* of the data and processing throughout a network—either local or remote. Distributed systems can improve reliability and performance, provide greater local autonomy, and allow incremental growth of the system. While there are also problems associated with them—such as management control, communication costs, greater hardware investment, new integrity problems, and different security considerations—distributed systems are increasingly common.

In this chapter we first discuss the general architecture of distributed database systems and then survey their special security problems including decentralized authorization. Database integrity in a distributed system is also considered.

12.2 THE ARCHITECTURE OF DISTRIBUTED DATABASE SYSTEMS

12.2.1 Distribution of the Database

The database may be distributed in physically separated *nodes,* or *sites,* each containing processing capability. The distance may be very great, or only tens of meters; many of the same problems arise in the two situations, but the solutions may differ because data transmission is faster and less expensive in local networks. Nodes are joined by physical *links,* each one of which can act as a set of logical communication *channels.* A technique frequently used is *packet switching,* where the link is for the exclusive use of a message during a prescribed time. The physical link can be a wire circuit or a microwave or radio circuit. Different types of links are characterized by their bandwidth and transmission delay. The network may obey some structured set of interconnection principles. One example is IBM's SNA [20], and other well-known disciplines are used in DECNET and in the ARPA network [12].

In a *distributed database system* (*DDS*), each node may contain a database or portions of a database. A DDS can be represented by the generic architecture of Fig. 12.1. We define a distributed *integrated* system as one where application programs are written as though there were a *single* centralized database, so that the programs are independent of where the data is physically stored. (This is called *location transparency.*)

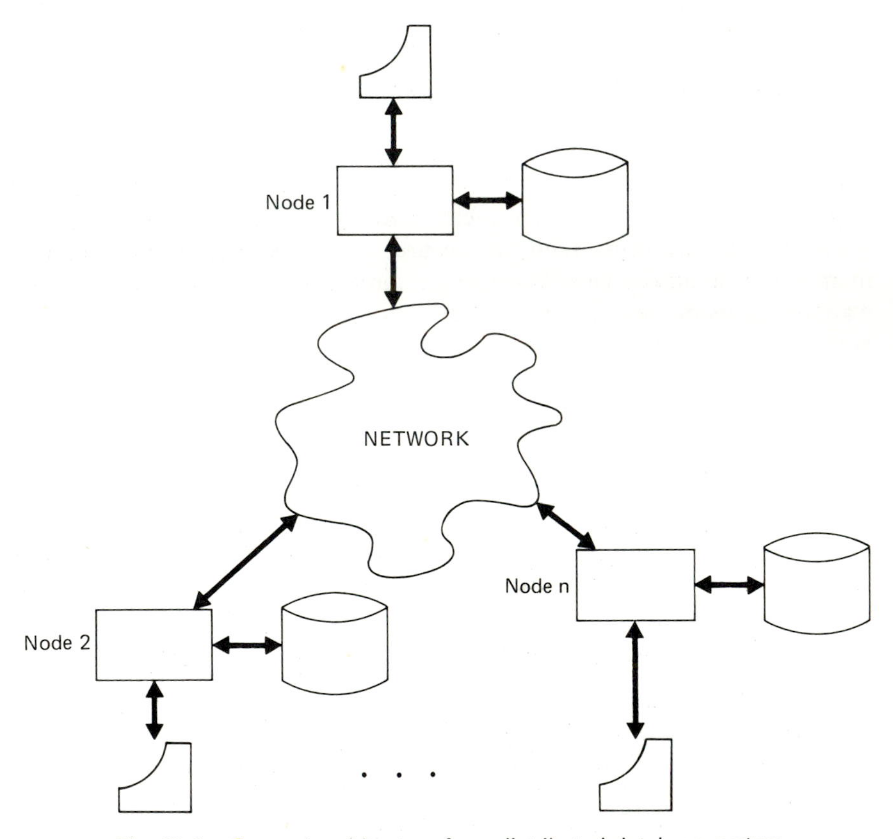

Fig. 12.1. General architecture for a distributed database system.

In a homogeneous system, the same type of DBMS resides at each node. Some of the additional problems that arise when the nodes are heterogeneous are discussed in [23]. Although we concentrate on integrated systems, the problems discussed also arise in less integrated networks, and many of the same principles apply.

Distributed database systems can also use the multilevel architecture discussed in Chapter 3. We can think of a DDS as described by a set of *local conceptual schemas*, which together constitute a *global conceptual schema*, describing data in a unified way across the network. A directory or catalog contains the different schemas plus information required for security and integrity.

The distribution of data can take two basic forms:

1. The database is divided into *disjoint* sets, each of which is a unit for physical distribution;
2. The database is divided into *overlapping* sets, which are physically distributed.

The first approach results in a *partitioned* database and implies nonredundancy of data. As compared to a centralized database, a partitioned database can reduce message traffic and improve response time if most of each transaction's data requirements can be satisfied locally. The second approach results in a *replicated* database, with redundant data. It can provide benefits in reliability and availability. Performance may also be improved if most of the actions on the database are retrieval only. In its extreme form the replicated approach could mean that all nodes contain copies of all the data. However, this *fully replicated* database is clearly impractical for large databases.

Assume that we have six files, F1 to F6; then Fig. 12.2 shows an

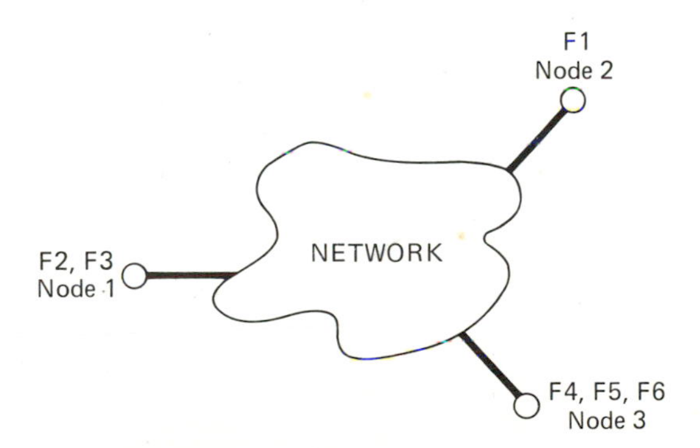

Fig. 12.2. A partitioned database.

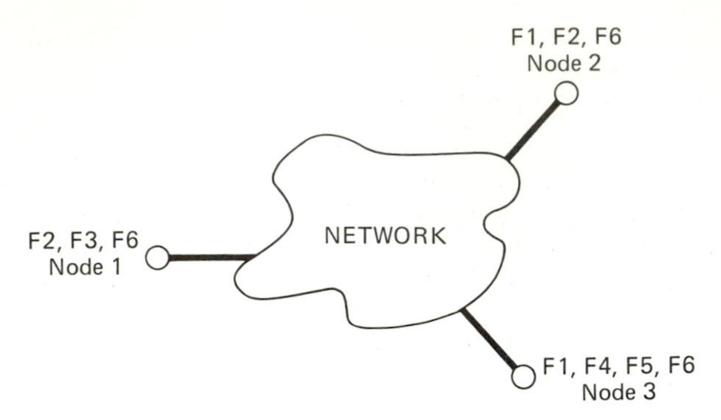

Fig. 12.3. A replicated database.

example of a partitioned database, while Fig. 12.3 shows a replicated database. Whichever approach is taken, the *unit* of distribution can vary. At one extreme (as in the two previous figures), only entire files are distributed across the network; at the other extreme we can distribute *fragments* of some data structure. Figure 12.4 shows a fragmentation for a relational database, where the relation is broken along both row and column boundaries.

Data distribution can imply *distributed query evaluation,* where pieces of data from different nodes must be put together to satisfy a single query [1, 27]. The problem of efficient query processing in this environment differs from the centralized case because of two new factors:

PERSONNEL

NAME	AGE	POSITION	MNGR	DEPT	SALARY	EXPER
	PERS-1		PERS-2		PERS-4	
		PERS-3				

Fig. 12.4. Fragmentation of a relation.

1. There is a considerable processing delay in communicating between the nodes, and
2. There is more opportunity for parallel processing.

The solutions depend on whether the data must be distributed according to some criterion (for example, branch offices of a bank maintain data about their own customers), or whether the data can be placed so as to optimize query evaluation. This *optimal file placement* problem has been studied using linear programming methods [27].

12.2.2 Extended Transaction Concept

The concept of transaction can be extended for the DDS environment [31] to provide the programmer and the user with the following types of transparency:

- Location transparency: All the data appears to be at one node.
- Replication transparency: All the data appears as stored once at a single node.

The following types of transparency continue to be provided, as in a centralized system.

- Concurrency transparency: Each transaction appears to be the only activity in the system.
- Failure transparency: Either all the actions of a transaction occur or none of them occur. Once a transaction occurs, its effects survive failures.

If a system could provide such transparency it would be as easy to use as a centralized system.

12.2.3 Security of a Distributed System

It is important in a distributed system that either all sites implement the same level of security controls, or the more secure sites take account of the lesser security of other sites when validating requests. The controls at a specific site become irrelevant if information at that site is readily available to other sites that do not have effective security controls. Network processors which, for example, handle tasks associated with packet switching pose additional security threats. The programs in these processors must be trusted unless end-to-end encryption is used. On the other hand, distributed systems can enhance security by allowing the physical isolation of sensitive data, by separating sensitive data into pieces which individually are meaningless, and by allowing sites to check on one another. Some of the security controls and mechanisms discussed in Chapters 9, 10, and 11 apply to distributed systems, and additional security problems specific to distribution are treated in this chapter.

12.3 DECENTRALIZED AUTHORIZATION

The term *decentralized* refers here to the way the authorization function is divided among a number of administrators. This decentralization of function can occur for a centralized database, but is essential when the database is distributed. Despite its importance the problem of decentralization of authorization has received little attention, the only systematic work being the schemes proposed for System R [13] and for DB1 [2], and in work done at IBM's Los Angeles Scientific Center [33]. Although all this work assumes a relational database, the same basic approaches apply to other models.

12.3.1 System R

In System R the owner of a table may grant various access rights to other users. The owner also has the option of permitting the grantee to further grant the acquired rights to other users. If owner A wishes to grant user B SELECT and INSERT rights to the ENROLLMENT relation and to allow these rights to be passed on, A enters the following statement:

```
GRANT SELECT, INSERT ON ENROLLMENT TO B WITH GRANT
OPTION;
```

Any user who has granted a privilege may subsequently REVOKE it, as in `REVOKE INSERT ON ENROLLMENT FROM B`. The state of the system after the revocation is as if the grant had never been made.

Consider the grants of a specific privilege on a specific table. The grants may be represented by the sequence

$$G_1 \ldots G_i \ldots G_j \ldots G_n$$

such that $i < j$ implies G_i was granted at an earlier time than G_j. If G_i is now revoked by the command R_i then

$$G_1 \ldots G_{i-1}, G_i, G_{i+1} \ldots G_n, R_i$$

is formally identical to

$$G_1 \ldots G_{i-1}, G_{i+1} \ldots G_n.$$

That is, the revoked grant appears never to have occurred.

As an example consider the following sequence of grants by users A and X:

```
A:  GRANT SELECT, INSERT, UPDATE ON ENROLLMENT TO X WITH GRANT
    OPTION;
A:  GRANT SELECT ON ENROLLMENT TO Z;
X:  GRANT ALL PRIVILEGES ON ENROLLMENT TO Y;
Z:  REVOKE ALL PRIVILEGES ON ENROLLMENT FROM X;
```

This sequence is formally equivalent to removing the first grant from the sequence. Then one of the remaining grants,

```
X:  GRANT ALL PRIVILEGES ON ENROLLMENT TO Y;
```

is not valid since X has no rights on ENROLLMENT. Hence the effect of the revocation is to withdraw rights not only from X but also from Y. The effect of the revocation for this example is shown in Fig. 12.5.

12.3.2 Administrative Approach to Decentralization

A contrasting approach to decentralization allows only *privileged* users to control other users' access to the data. Then special access types such as ADMINISTER may be granted independently from the other rights such as READ or UPDATE. Users who are given ADMINISTER rights to a set of data object occurrences (called a *data class*) become administrators for that class.

In the scheme proposed in [33], data classes are the objects of delegation. Predicates can be used to define *subclasses* of a class. The structuring of classes can be described by a *class structure graph* where nodes represent classes and a directed arc from node i to node j indicates that class j is a member of class i. An administrator of a class D may define subclasses of D and delegate their administration. The various rights associated with the task of administration may be delegated separately or in groups. These rights include:

r1 Right to create, delete, and modify objects in D;
r2 Right to redefine and delete D;
r3 Right to authorize READ access to objects in D;
r4 Right to authorize DELETE access to objects in D;
r5 Right to authorize UPDATE access to objects in D;
r6 Right to authorize INSERT access to objects in D;
r7 Right to recall a delegated right for D.

In order to simplify the administrator commands, macro-access types that include two or more of the above can be defined. In particular *CONTROL,* C, implies r2 to r6, and *ADMINISTER,* A, implies all these rights, except r7. The rights can also be ordered, so that, for example, r1 implies r3.

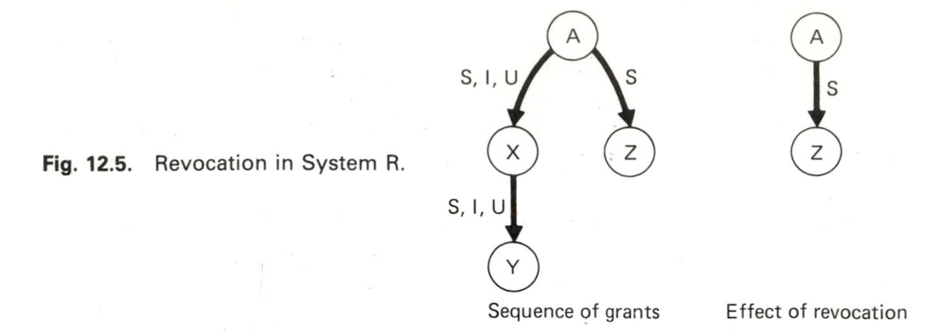

Fig. 12.5. Revocation in System R.

Figure 12.6 shows a sequence of delegations, d1 to d5. Administrator DBA1, having ADMINISTER access to class D1 with the right to delegate, delegates to DBA2 the right to CONTROL class D2 (with right to delegate), and to DBA3 the right to CONTROL D3 (with no right to delegate). DBA2, besides delegating administration right r3 to DBA4, also gives user U1 a set of access rights on view V1 (an object in D2). Revocation works differently for administrative rights, which go back to the delegator, and user rights, which cease to exist. When administrative rights are revoked, the *users* retain their current rights, but these are now controlled by the revoker. Figure 12.7 shows what happens to the graph of the previous figure when CONTROL right on class D2 is revoked from DBA2. If we assume that there is one administrator per class and that a

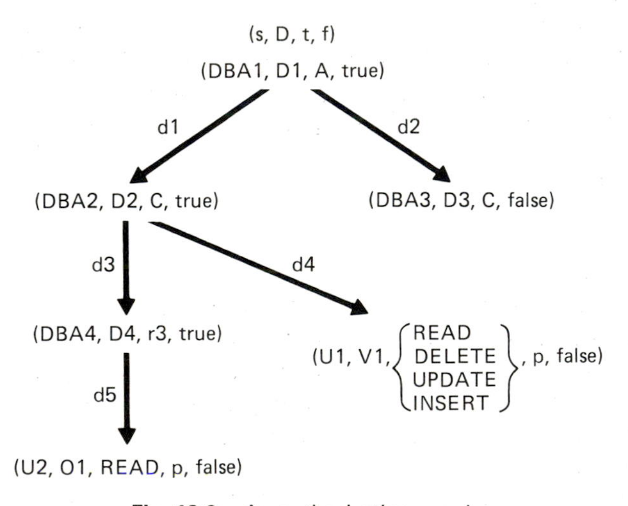

Fig. 12.6. An authorization graph.

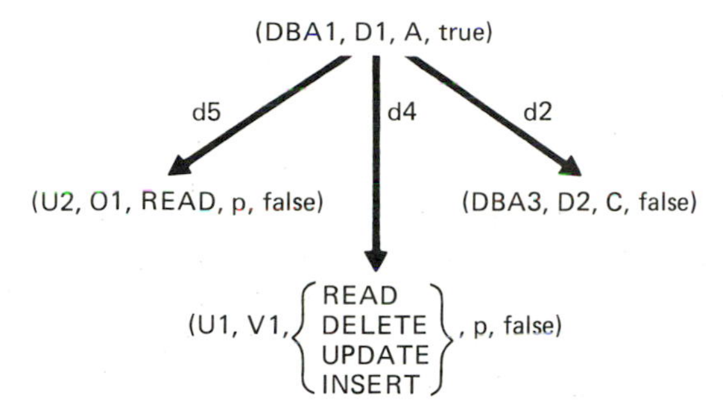

Fig. 12.7. Authorization graph after recall of Class D.

given class can be delegated only once, then the revocation algorithm only needs to maintain the class structure graph.

12.3.3 Comparison of Decentralization Approaches

What is delegated in the administrative approach is not an access right for a given object but rights *to control* that object. The concept of data class allows the scope of these control actions to be limited. In System R, the units of delegation are base relations or views, which are dictated by the semantics of the applications. In the administration approach, a data class is an aggregate defined exclusively for administrative purposes. When the administrative rights of DBA1 are recalled, the users who received access rights from DBA1 do not lose them; the rights are simply now under the control of a different administrator. The only people who lose their rights are those who received administrative rights directly or indirectly from DBA1. The two approaches are compared in Fig. 12.8. The approach followed in DB1 [2], falls between these two; ownership is used but owners are hierarchically structured with respect to their rights.

12.4 DISTRIBUTION OF ACCESS RULES

Much of what has been said in previous chapters about access control also holds true for a DDS. However, for a DDS a decision must be made as to where to store the access rules [32]. One approach is to store each rule at the same node as the data to which it refers. Validation is then performed as in a centralized system (all requests go to the node that contains the desired data and this node validates the request). When data are replicated, the access rules for that data are also replicated. In this case, revocation of an authorization requires every copy of the relevant

LASC	SYSTEM R
Concept of administration.	Concept of ownership.
Delegation only of administrative rights.	Delegation of any rights that have copy flag true.
Unit of delegation is a data class.	Unit of delegation is relational database object (relation, view).
Revocation destroys administrative rights, recaller acquires access rules of recalled data classes.	Revocation has effect of right never having been granted.
Need to keep track of class structuring for revocation.	Need to keep track of all delegations, including time of delegation and delegator.

Fig. 12.8. Comparison of decentralization approaches.

access rule to be deleted. This means that all nodes at which the rule is stored should be in communication at the time of revocation, if the revocation is to take effect immediately.

We have seen that in systems like System R, where compile-time checking is performed, the only rule that needs to be checked at execution time is one giving RUN access to an application program. Following the above approach, this rule would be stored at the node (or nodes) where the application program is stored. This has an implication for revocation when the application program refers to data at more than one site.

For example, consider the case of an application program stored at node A, which references data V1, stored at node B. A user at node B may wish to revoke access rules for V1 or to drop the definition of V1. Both of these actions must be reflected at node A. This means that remote access is required in order to perform an essentially local action. The action may not be allowed if node A is not currently in communication with node B. This loss of local autonomy may be considered undesirable. An alternative approach is *not* to reflect the revocation or redefinition at remote sites but rather to deny access at execution time. This requires execution-time checking for all programs, and conflicts with the efficiency improvements gained by earlier checking.

12.5 NONDISCRETIONARY SYSTEMS

Multilevel security can be supported in distributed environments by enforcing a common security lattice on all sites. In general, a network will contain *secure* and *insecure sites*. A secure site has a secure, multilevel, operating system capable of running untrusted processes at different security levels without violating security policy. An insecure site must run in dedicated mode with all its processes and data at one security level. Since an insecure site cannot be trusted to correctly label its output messages with its security level, receiving sites must assume that all messages they receive from the insecure site are at its dedicated security level. Secure sites may not be authorized to receive all levels of data. For example, a secure justice department computer may not be authorized to receive data from a secure IRS computer.

12.5.1 Communication with Insecure Sites

Some forms of communication are possible with insecure sites. Two insecure sites running at the same dedicated security level can certainly be allowed to communicate freely since no security violation is possible. Similarly, an insecure site and an untrusted process on a secure system can communicate if they are at the same security level. There is a problem however, with communication between insecure sites running at different levels.

For example, we would like site A to be able to read data at site B if A's security level is greater than B's. In a single multilevel computer, a process running at a high security level can be granted read-only access to lower-level data. In a distributed system, however, a high-level process must send a message to a lower-level process on the other site requesting the data. Thus what on the surface is a read-only transaction becomes a read-write transaction. If the high-level process is untrusted, the write violates the rules of the multilevel security model.

A solution to this problem is to duplicate databases with the lower-level site B handling all updates. Each update made by B is also sent to the higher-level site A. There are two drawbacks to this approach. First, A has no control over the amount of duplication. Second, the problems of controlling error and message flow are not solved. These require A to send acknowledgments to B, to request new messages, or, in the case of errors, to request that messages be resent. This cannot be allowed, as a Trojan horse in the communication software of A could encode information by sending fictitious negative acknowledgments to B. A solution illustrated in Fig. 12.9 is to use a secure front-end processor [15] which guarantees to deliver messages to A. No end-to-end acknowledgments are now allowed. Site A still can communicate covertly with B by causing the message store on the front-end processor to become full, but this event can easily be monitored.

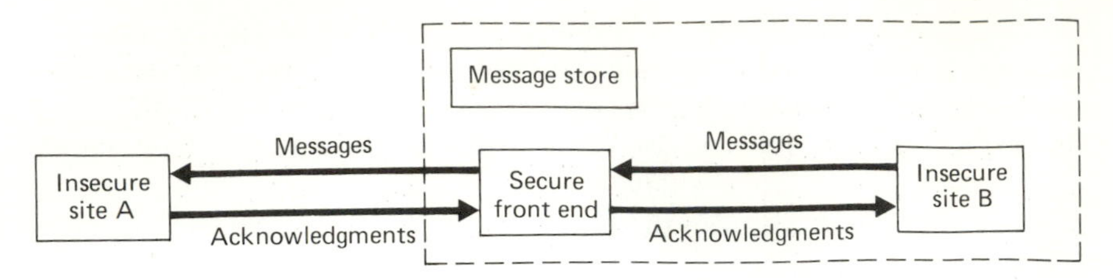

Fig. 12.9. Communication between insecure sites.

12.5.2 Additional Problems

The following problems are discussed in [16].

1. *Proliferation of security levels.* While a few classification levels may suffice for the entire network, each node may need a different set of categories. For example, the different nodes may belong to different organizations. If a given object can belong to multiple categories, then the system potentially needs to support all the possible security levels defined by the classification levels and the combinations of the sets of categories. Even in a system with a few nodes and a few categories per node this number could be impractically large. For example, with eight levels and 20 nodes with five categories each, the number of security levels is 2^{103}. Even fewer levels create a problem because a node might need one process for every possible level. If we assume a packet-switched network, where packets from different levels could be intermixed, the security label for each packet (which specifies its security level) would also be impractically large.

2. *Assignment of categories and clearances.* In nondiscretionary systems, users cannot make decisions about who has access to objects in the system. In nondiscretionary, centralized systems, assignment of levels and categories is made by a system security officer (SSO). In a network, a mechanism is needed that enables a local SSO to define new categories and grant clearances for them to other nodes.

Some possible solutions to these two problems are discussed in [15] and [16]. The number of security levels can be reduced, on the basis of the knowledge that only a few categories are in use at a given time. Processes could be dynamically created as needed. A process would be destroyed when it had received no packets for some time. The size of the security labels can be reduced by taking advantage of the fact that most objects belong to only a few categories. The label could simply list the category numbers, rather than specifying a security level. A local SSO requests a new category for its node from a *network security center,* and also grants clearances for the node's categories through that center.

12.6 INTEGRITY IN A DDS

We consider three important aspects: concurrency control, failure transparency, and the mutual consistency of replicated databases. Very little work has been done on semantic integrity in this environment and we choose not to discuss this issue; it is discussed in [10].

12.6.1 Concurrency Control

The problem of concurrency control in centralized systems was discussed in Chapter 8. In a DDS, this problem becomes more complex because a concurrency-control mechanism at one site cannot instantaneously know what is happening at the other sites.

Many schemes have been proposed to prevent concurrency anomalies in such a situation. One approach [31] is to use the two-phase locking protocol described in Chapter 8. The protocol still works in a nonreplicated distributed database. Each node in the DDS executes actions on its local objects, at the request of a set of transactions, in some serial order. It can be shown that for a distributed system of n nodes the n sequences of actions may be modeled as the execution of a single node executing the same actions in some sequential order. It therefore follows that a two-phase locking protocol that is sufficient to prevent concurrency anomalies in a single node is also sufficient when there are multiple nodes.

Locking may be either centralized or distributed. A centralized lock controller [21] maintains lock tables and detects and resolves deadlocks in a way similar to that described for a centralized database in Chapter 8. With distributed locking, however, deadlock may not be detected locally by any site. For example, Fig. 12.10 illustrates a deadlock situation involving two sites. The deadlock graphs at both sites are acyclic; no site therefore can detect deadlocks. A possible solution is to designate one site as the deadlock detector. Other sites in the DDS periodically send it lists of locks that have recently been requested, granted, or released. Deadlock detection then operates as in the centralized case.

Several schemes have been proposed that use timestamping as an alternative to locking for the synchronization of accesses to a DDS. Reed [24] introduces a *pseudo-time* ordering of events. Pseudo-time must pre-

Transactions	Order of lock requests at each site
	Site 1
T1: Read X	Lock X for T1
Write Y	* Lock X for T2
T2: Read Y	Site 2
Write X	Lock Y for T2
	* Lock Y for T1

* Lock cannot be granted

X Y

Site 1 ⟷ Site 2

Fig. 12.10. Multiple-site deadlock.

serve the real-time ordering of events that are observable outside the system, but does not have to preserve the real-time ordering of events that are nearly simultaneous and not ordered parts of the same computation. The proposal treats a data object as a *sequence of versions* that reflect the changes made to the object over time. (Note the correspondence to the generalized audit trail of Chapter 9.) Updating an object creates a new version, while reading selects the appropriate version (according to an algorithm using pseudo-times). This allows long-running read-only transactions to be processed without delaying other transactions. A unique feature of Reed's proposal is that transactions can be constructed out of previously existing transactions without either modifying the existing programs or requiring that the new transaction know what objects the existing transactions access.

An alternative to locking is also used in SDD-1 [3, 4, 5, 26]. Transactions are grouped (by DBAs, for example) into classes on the basis of their sites of origin and the objects they read and write. Using this information the system can choose at run time a synchronization protocol (based on timestamping) that is just strong enough for the needs of each transaction. It is considered particularly important to do this in a replicated database, since global locking there can be very expensive.

12.6.2 Failure Transparency

We have seen that a transaction appears as an atomic action to the user; that is, it either completes successfully or it has no effect at all. This means that, if there is a failure and the transaction has not been committed, the effects of the transaction must be backed out. Care must be taken in a DDS to coordinate nodes during a commit that involves multiple sites; otherwise some nodes might back out (because of local failure) while others commit successfully. A *two-phase commit* protocol [11, 19] is sufficient to prevent this type of inconsistency. It has not yet been demonstrated that the two-phase commit protocol is practical, however.

As an example, we describe a *linear two-phase* commit protocol involving three sites (Fig. 12.11). We first define the *READY state* for multinode transactions. A transaction enters the READY state after being sent a *PREPARE-TO-COMMIT* request but before responding to the request. The READY state implies that the node will not abort or commit until it receives a request from another node. In the event of a failure at the node, the node must ensure that all effects of the transaction are restored.

We assume in Fig. 12.11 that the transaction is originally entered at node A. When node A has received answers to all its requests for work related to the transaction, it commits the transaction. Node A has a list of all nodes involved in the execution of the transaction and passes the list, together with the PREPARE-TO-COMMIT request, to the next node in the list, node B in our example. Node B then enters the READY state and passes the PREPARE-TO-COMMIT request to node C. Node C, the last node involved, commits the transaction and passes a COMMIT request to

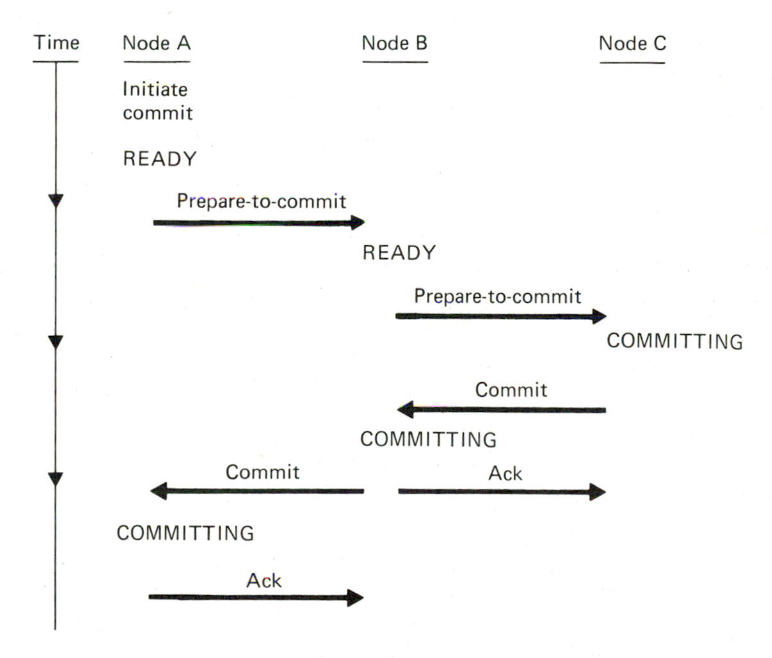

Fig. 12.11. Linear two-phase commit protocol.

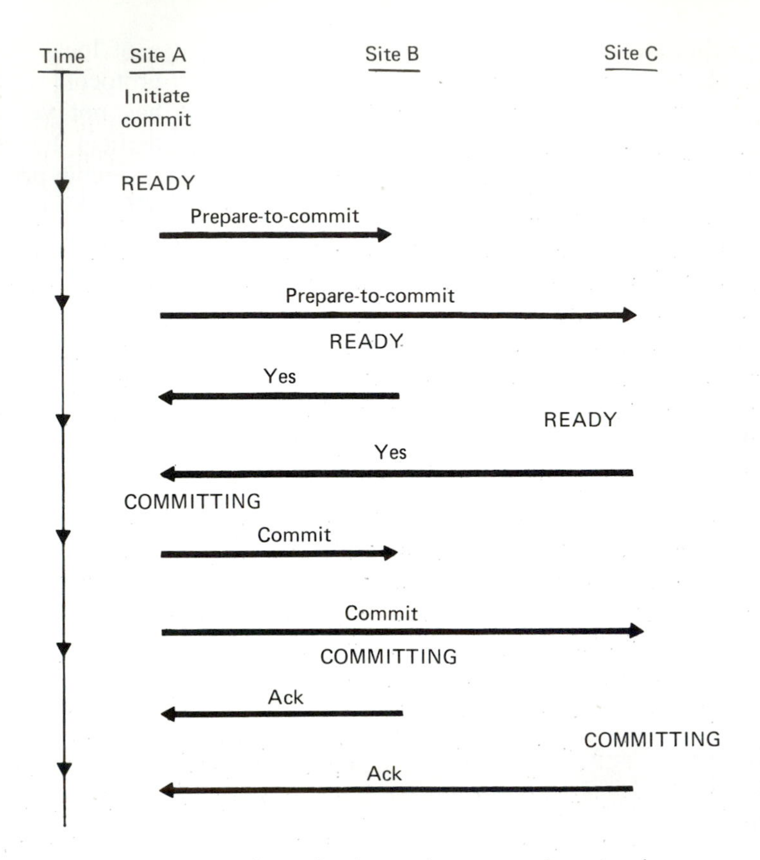

Fig. 12.12. Centralized two-phase commit protocol.

node B. Node B commits and passes a COMMIT request to node A. It also notifies C that it has successfully committed. This is necessary because C's commit messages may have failed to reach node B and must then be resent. Node A finally commits and the transaction is successfully committed. If a node cannot enter the READY state on receiving a PREPARE-TO-COMMIT request, it issues an ABORT request, which propagates in a manner similar to the commit, backing out the effects of the transaction in all the nodes.

In a *centralized two-phase* commit protocol (Fig. 12.12), one site serves as commit coordinator, sending all the PREPARE and COMMIT messages. When a site enters the READY state it sends a *VOTE-YES* to the coordinator. If all sites vote yes, the transaction is committed and COMMIT messages are sent to all sites. Both the linear and centralized protocols ensure that all sites either commit or abort even when messages are lost or sites fail.

Lampson and Sturgis [17] have proposed an algorithm that preserves the serializability of transactions even in the event of certain types of system failures. They start by developing models for physical processors, communications, and storage. Better-behaved *abstract* devices and actions are constructed from those physical devices by eliminating expected types of failure. At the highest level of abstraction, atomic transactions are constructed.

While the main objective of the coordination of updates in a DDS is the preservation of transaction and database integrity, another important goal is site autonomy. Ideally, the failure of a site should not prevent processing of any transaction that does not require data at that site. It has been shown [11] that this goal is impossible to achieve. For example, a transaction that does not need data at a failed site may be waiting for another transaction that is in READY state waiting for a COMMIT or ABORT signal from the failed site. However, good schemes will at least minimize the effect of site or communication failures on the rest of the network. The *polyvalue* mechanism [22] is an example of a scheme that specifically addresses this problem. With the two-phase commit protocol, a communication failure may leave a site in the READY state not knowing whether the transaction updates are to be committed or aborted. In the polyvalue mechanism, when a site is uncertain about the outcome of a transaction, it installs polyvalues in its local database for the results of that transaction. A polyvalue associated with a data item is a set of pairs $<v_i, p_i>$ where v_i is the value of the data item if the predicate p_i is true. For example, if the transaction T_1 updates a data item d_j from v to v′, then if the outcome of T_1 is uncertain, the following polyvalue is associated with d_j:

$$\{<v, \neg T_1>, <v', T_1>\}$$

Since this polyvalue may be read by another transaction and affect the update of other data items, polyvalues will tend to spread through the database with more and more complex predicates. Predicates can be reduced when the outcome of a transaction becomes known. The feasibility of this approach depends on the nature of the applications. Response times must be more important than absolute accuracy in output to the end user. Credit checking and airline reservation are two possible examples.

12.6.3 Replicated Databases

When a database is replicated, it is necessary to ensure that the copies remain *mutually consistent*. Since a maintenance request can be rejected at some site (because it conflicts with other concurrent actions), some discipline is needed to ensure that all sites make the same decision about the request. The simplest discipline, described in the previous section, requires *unanimous consent*. Where the number of sites, n, is large, this discipline becomes impractical, since the probability that all sites are up at any moment tends to zero as n becomes large. A number of update strategies that address this availability problem have been proposed [19].

In the *primary site* approach [29], one copy is designated as *primary* and the rest as *secondary*. All updates are applied to the primary copy and are broadcast to the secondaries at a later time. This approach can be extended to allow for a new primary to be designated on failure of the current primary. Another scheme requires the acceptance of only a *majority* of sites [30]. In both these schemes, concurrency anomalies may occur if care is not taken. For example, if a user wishes to read the most current value, the READ must be directed to the primary site. In the majority update scheme, the READ must be addressed to all sites. One of the advantages of a replicated database is that READs can be satisfied locally. Thus the user must distinguish between ordinary READ requests and MOST-CURRENT-READ requests. It is also necessary to devise schemes that prevent a single transaction from accessing both old and new data.

The *majority consensus* algorithm of Thomas [30] guarantees serializability for a fully redundant DDS using a timestamping protocol. Transactions are assigned timestamps and each stored data item is also tagged with the timestamp of the transaction that updated it most recently. Reads in a transaction are satisfied locally without checking, while writes are deferred until after all sites have voted. As a transaction executes, a write causes the name and new value of the data item to be entered into a list. The names of all data items read and the timestamp of the transaction are also included in the list. When the transaction ends, the list is sent to all sites, which then vote on whether or not to accept the transaction. The vote on transaction T depends on two conditions:

1. The data items read by T have not been modified by another transaction.
2. There is no conflict with any other transaction that has been voted on but not yet committed by that site.

If both conditions are true the site votes YES. If (1) is not satisfied the site votes NO. If (1) is satisfied but (2) is not, then the site should wait until the pending transaction is resolved before voting. However, to avoid deadlock the site votes NO if transaction T is younger than the pending one. If a majority of sites vote YES, the transaction is accepted. This protocol is sufficient to preserve serializability.

12.7 SUMMARY

We started by describing a generalized architecture for a distributed database system. Those additional security and integrity problems introduced by distribution of data were then considered. Additional access-control problems are decentralization of authorization (delegation of administrative control over the data) and distribution of access rules. Systems adopting multilevel security have different types of problems, which are discussed in Section 12.5. Integrity issues include concurrency control, which becomes more complex due to propagation delays, and failure transparency, where the need to coordinate commits involving multiple nodes is a serious problem. The mutual consistency of replicated databases is discussed in Section 12.6.3. Integrity problems in a distributed environment are among the most serious obstacles to the realization of practical DDSs and are the subject of considerable research. Our discussion attempts only an introduction to this important topic.

EXERCISES

12.1. Figure 12.13 shows a graph of grants for a System R table. What rights remain if A revokes the rights granted to B?

12.2. Give an algorithm to delegate administrative rights according to the policy described in Section 12.3.2. Assume that, after a delegation command is entered,

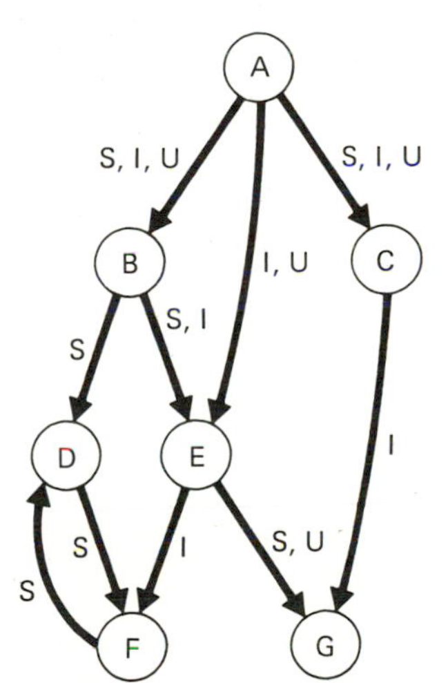

Fig. 12.13. Graph of grants.

the system extracts a request of the form (s,O,t,f), where s is the DBA entering the command, O is the controlled object, t is the type of administrative access delegated (any of r1 to r7), and f indicates whether the recipient of the right can delegate it. The algorithm must check that the delegator has the appropriate authorization. Assume a set of data structures for storing access rules (for example, a set of relations).

REFERENCES AND BIBLIOGRAPHY

1. M. Adiba *et al.*, "Issues in distributed data base management systems: A technical overview." *Proc. 4th Int. Conf. on Very Large Data Bases,* Berlin 1978, 89–110. Available from ACM.

2. J. Arditi and E. Zukovsky, "An Authorization Mechanism for a Data Base." In *Data Bases: Improving Usability and Responsiveness,* B. Schneiderman (Ed.). Academic Press, 1978, 195–213.

   A scheme for delegation of rights that is intermediate between System R and the administrative approach. The set of access rights of a group of users is called a *world.* Users can grant any of the rights included in the worlds for which they have authorization, if they have GRANT option for these worlds. Access types are ordered and a world includes another if it includes all its data units and its access types for them are at least as high. A world can receive rights from only *one* other world; i.e., only subsets of a world are delegated.

3. P. A. Bernstein and N. Goodman, "Approaches to concurrency control in distributed database systems." *AFIPS Conf. Proc.* **48,** 1979 NCC, 813–820. AFIPS Press, Montvale, N.J., 1979.

4. P. A. Bernstein *et al.,* "The concurrency control mechanism of SDD-1: A system for distributed databases (The fully redundant case)." *IEEE Trans. Software Eng.* **SE-4,** 3 (May 1978), 154–168.

5. P. A. Bernstein, D. W. Shipman, and W. S. Wong, "Formal aspects of serializability in database concurrency control." *IEEE Trans. Software Eng.* **SE-5,** 3 (May 1979), 203–216.

6. P. G. Comba, "Needed: Distributed control." *Proc. 1st Int. Conf. on Very Large Data Bases,* 1975, 364–373. Available from ACM.

   Makes a case for the need to decentralize administrative functions in a DBMS.

7. R. Davenport, "Integrity in distributed database systems." *Proc. EURO-COMP 78* (European Computing Congress, London 1978), 751–773. Online Conf. Ltd., Uxbridge, U.K., 1978.

   Discusses some architectural aspects in general terms, and recovery in some detail.

8. M. E. Deppe and J. P. Fry, "Distributed data bases—A summary of research." *Comp. Networks* **1,** 1976, 130–138.

   The state of the art in this field around 1975.

9. R. Fagin, "On an authorization mechanism." *ACM TODS* **3,** 3 (Sept. 1978), 310–319.

10. E. Fong and S. R. Kimbleton, "Database semantic integrity for a network data manager." *AFIPS Conf. Proc.* **49,** 1980 NCC, 261–268. AFIPS Press, Arlington, Va., 1980.

11. J. N. Gray, "Notes on Database Operating Systems." In *Operating Systems—An Advanced Course,* R. Bayer *et al.* (Eds.), Springer-Verlag, 1978, 393–481.

12. P. E. Green, "An introduction to network architectures and protocols." *IBM Systems J.* **18,** 2 (1979), 202–222.

13. P. P. Griffiths and B. W. Wade, "An authorization mechanism for a relational database system." *ACM TODS* **1,** 3 (Sept. 1976), 242–255.

14. Infotech International, Berkshire, England, 1976. *Distributed Systems.* Infotech State-of-the-Art Report.

This is an uneven potpourri of papers that have some relation to the rather ambiguous title. The discussion on distributed databases, while incomplete, provides some helpful views. See *Computer Reviews,* Review No. 33642, for a more detailed analysis.

15. P. A. Karger, "Nondiscretionary Access Control for Decentralized Computing Systems." Report MIT/LCS/TR–179, MIT Laboratory for Computer Science, Cambridge, Mass., 1977.

16. P. A. Karger, "The lattice security model in a public computing network." *Proc. ACM 78 Annual Conf.,* 453–459. Available from ACM.

17. B. Lampson and H. Sturgis, "Crash recovery in a distributed data storage system." To appear in *Comm. ACM.*

18. B. P. Lientz and I. R. Weiss, "Trade-offs of secure processing in centralized versus distributed networks." *Comp. Networks* **2,** 1 (1978), 35–43.

A simulation study of the effect of security on the workload of a network. The workload considered was a mixture of several categories: secure and nonsecure, computation oriented, and I/O oriented.

19. B. G. Lindsay *et al.*, "Notes on Distributed Databases." IBM Research Report RJ2571, San Jose, Calif., July 1979.

20. J. H. McFadyen, "Systems Network Architecture: An overview." *IBM Systems. J.* **15,** 1 (1976), 4–23.

21. D. A. Menasce, G. J. Popek, and R. R. Muntz, "A locking protocol for resource coordination in distributed databases," *ACM TODS* **5,** 2 (June 1980), 103–138.

22. W. A. Montgomery, "Polyvalues: A tool for implementing atomic updates to distributed data." *Proc. 7th Symposium on Operating Systems Principles,* Pacific Grove, Calif., December 1979, 143–149. Available from ACM.

23. E. Nahouraii, L. O. Brooks, and A. F. Cardenas, "An Approach to Data Communication between Different Generalized Database Management Systems." In *Systems for Very Large Data Bases,* Lockemann and Neuhold (Eds.). North Holland, Amsterdam, 1976, 117–142.

24. D. P. Reed, "Implementing Atomic Actions on Decentralized Data." *Preprints for 7th Symposium on Operating Systems Principles.* Pacific Grove, Calif., 1979, 66–74.

25. D. J. Rosenkrantz, R. E. Stearns, and P. M. Lewis, "System-level concurrency control for distributed databases." *ACM TODS* **3,** 2 (June 1978), 178–198.

Describes a model where processes (transactions, in our terminology) are considered to move from site to site according to the location of the data they need. Problems of consistency and deadlock avoidance are discussed, and designs to solve them are presented.

26. J. B. Rothnie *et al.*, "Introduction to a system for distributed databases (SDD-1)." *ACM TODS* **5,** 1 (March 1980), 1–17.

SDD-1, designed and built by the Computer Corp. of America, is the first integrated DDS to be built. This paper provides background needed to understand References 3, 4, and 5.

27. J. Rothnie and N. Goodman, "A Survey of Research and Development in Distributed Database Management." *Proc. 3rd Int. Conf. on Very Large Data Bases,* Tokyo 1977, 48–62. Available from ACM.

28. M. Stonebraker and E. Neuhold, "A distributed data base version of INGRES." *Proc. of the 2nd Berkeley Workshop on Distributed Data Management and Computer Networks,* Lawrence Berkeley Lab., LBL–6416, May 1977, 19–36.

This paper discusses some early design decisions about data and directory distribution for an integrated distributed version of INGRES. Integrity problems are discussed in [29].

29. M. Stonebraker, "Concurrency control and consistency of multiple copies of data in distributed INGRES." *IEEE Trans. on Software Eng.* **SE-5,** 3 (May 1979), 188–194.

30. R. H. Thomas, "A majority-consensus approach to concurrency control for multiple-copy databases." *ACM TODS* **4,** 2 (June 1979), 180–209.

31. I. L. Traiger, J. N. Gray, C. A. Galtieri, and B. G. Lindsay, "Transactions and Consistency in Distributed Database Systems." Report RJ2555, IBM Research Lab., San Jose, Calif., June 1979.

32. S. Winkler and L. Danner, "Data security in the computer communication environment." *Computer* **7,** 2 (Feb. 1974), 23–31.

33. C. Wood and E. B. Fernandez, "Decentralized authorization in a database system." *Proc. 5th Int. Conf. on Very Large Data Bases,* Rio de Janeiro, 1979, 352–359. Available from ACM.

13
Security of Statistical Databases

13.1 INTRODUCTION

Statistical databases typically contain sensitive and confidential information about individuals or enterprises. This information might, for example, be obtained from medical records or from a population census. The purpose of the database is to provide statistical summaries of the information in response to user queries to support activities like economic planning or scientific research. The question that we are interested in examining in this chapter is how to guarantee the confidentiality of the information about any one individual while at the same time being able to provide useful statistical summaries of the data to users. The need for guaranteeing confidentiality is important in a census if people are to be expected to provide confidential information about themselves. In the case of a medical database, the need for confidentiality is extremely important. For example, a political career can be cut short if it becomes public knowledge that a politician was treated for mental illness. Security of statistical databases is a subject of considerable current research; a survey of issues and solutions can be found in [3]. Uses of statistical databases are surveyed in [8].

The problem of securing a statistical database is not solved by the access control mechanisms we have described previously. There we were interested in selectively restricting a user's access to portions of the database. In the statistical case, we can consider that every user has identical access to the complete database (specific authorization restrictions will make the problem simpler, so we consider here the worst case).

The objective here is to prevent individual values of data items from being inferred from the answers to sequences of queries. We say that a database has been *positively compromised* if the value of a particular data item is known, and that it has been *negatively compromised* if it is known that a data item does *not* have a certain value. A database is secure if it cannot be compromised either positively or negatively.

In order to avoid compromise, it is necessary to restrict either the type of queries allowed or the values returned. Without restrictions it is trivial to compromise the database. For example, if a database provides salary statistics of arbitrary subgroups of the population (called the *query set*), then the query:

```
AVERAGE SALARY OF (JONES)
```

would, if allowed, return the exact value of Jones' salary.

Possible restrictions are:

- Limit the minimum and maximum size of the query sets allowed in queries.
- Limit the amount of overlap of query sets used in different queries.
- "Perturb" the values to be returned, so that they are individually inexact, although keeping their statistical properties.

In the following sections we look at ways of compromising databases and examine some of the preventive measures that may be taken.

13.2 COMPROMISE OF A DATABASE

Figure 13.1 illustrates a database containing the results of a hypothetical opinion survey among employees of a company. Answers to questions are given on a scale of 1 to 5. In order to interpret the results meaningfully, some information about the respondent must also be stored. For example, suppose that there is a question:

Would you be prepared to move to a new location for promotion?

Then it would be sensible to store the *present location* of the respondent. In general, there will be some *characteristic information* stored about each individual, as well as the responses to the survey (referred to as data). In this particular example, it is unlikely that the individual's unique identifier (such as name or employee number) is stored in the database. However, in databases where individual records need to be updated by privileged users (such as a medical history database), identifiers would need to be stored.

NAME (Not stored)	SEX	LEV (Job level)	LOC (Work location)	SAL (Salary)	Q1	Q2	Q3
DIAZ	M	60	SF	36	1	2	2
SMITH	F	58	SF	24	3	2	1
JONES	M	56	LA	26	4	2	3
KATZ	M	57	LA	30	3	3	2
CLARK	F	58	LA	28	5	1	4
WONG	F	60	LA	34	1	1	1
WEBB	M	58	SF	32	5	5	5

Fig. 13.1. Opinion survey database.

We assume a specific form for our queries, although the results we describe apply more generally to statistical databases. In the queries a *characteristic formula* C, which is an arbitrary predicate specifying characteristic values connected by the operators AND ($\wedge$), OR ($\vee$), and NOT ($\neg$), is used to determine the subgroup of the population (the query set) for whom the statistics are to be computed. Queries of this type will be written as q(C:F) where q represents a function (such as AVERAGE, SUM, or MEDIAN) of field F of those records that satisfy the characteristic formula. For example, the query:

```
AVERAGE (LOC = 'LA'  :  SAL)
```

calculates the average salary of all employees working in Los Angeles. COUNT is a special case of this type of query, where the field parameter is unnecessary. The query:

```
COUNT (LOC = 'LA')
```

counts the number of employees in Los Angeles.

In the following sections, n is the size of the database.

13.2.1 Restriction on Query Set Size

In order to be able to compromise the database, it is necessary to know some of the characteristics of an individual to start with. This is not unreasonable, since the individual may be personally known. For example, it may be known that Clark is female and works in Los Angeles. It may also, in some situations, be possible to insert a characteristic value (not necessarily true) concerning an individual into the database to allow future compromise.

Suppose that it is known that Smith is female and works in San Francisco. Then the query

```
COUNT(LOC = 'SF' ∧ SEX = 'F') = 1
```

confirms that these characteristics uniquely identify Smith.

In order to find out Smith's salary a number of queries can be tried. The query

```
COUNT(LOC = 'SF' ∧ SEX = 'F' ∧ SAL = 24) = 1
```

provides the information that the salary of Smith is 24. Even if the guess of the salary had been wrong, the database would still have been negatively compromised. In fact it is not necessary to guess since the query

```
SUM(LOC = 'SF' ∧ SEX = 'F' : SAL) = 24
```

directly returns Smith's salary. The reason that we can find out characteristics of Smith so easily is because our query set size is one. A sensible restriction on our DBMS is therefore to respond to queries only where the set size is greater than some integer k. However, restricting query set size to exclude small values is not sufficient because large values close to the size of the database also allow compromise. In order to compromise the database using large query set sizes, we make use of the relationship:

$$\text{COUNT}(C) = n - \text{COUNT}(\neg C)$$

For example, the difference between the two queries:

```
COUNT(LOC = 'SF' ∨ LOC = ¬'SF') = 7
```

and

```
COUNT(¬(LOC = 'SF' ∧ SEX = 'F')) = 6
```

determines the number of females in San Francisco: namely one. When we know that there is only one individual, the difference between the following two queries

```
SUM(LOC = 'SF' ∨ LOC = ¬'SF' : SAL) = 210
SUM(¬(LOC = 'SF' ∧ SEX = 'F') : SAL) = 186
```

provides the salary of Smith. To prevent compromise, the query set size must therefore also be constrained by an *upper* bound, $(n - k)$. The query set size is thus restricted to the range $[k, n - k]$ where $1 < k \leq n/2$. Even this restriction, however, is not sufficient to guarantee security, as we will see shortly.

13.2.2 The Individual Tracker

Schlörer [10] showed how a database could still be compromised using counting queries (even with restricted set sizes) by means of a *tracker*. A tracker involves a set of auxiliary attributes added to the original query. These attributes pad the query set so as to form an answerable query. When the effect of the auxiliary attributes is eliminated from the answer, it is possible to determine the answer to the original query. As an example, assume that the questioner knows that a given individual, I, is uniquely characterized by C. Now decompose C into C1 and C2 such that:

$$C = C1 \wedge C2$$

To ensure that queries with characteristic formulas C1 and $C1 \wedge \neg C2$ are answerable, the following conditions must also hold:

$$k \leq COUNT(C1 \wedge \neg C2) \leq COUNT(C1) \leq n - k$$

The formula $C1 \wedge \neg C2$ is known as the *individual tracker*, T, of I.

The database is compromised by using the following relationship:

$$COUNT(C) = COUNT(C1) - COUNT(T)$$

which can be easily verified by drawing a Venn diagram (Fig. 13.2). Note that both COUNT(C1) and COUNT(T) are answerable directly, even though COUNT(C) is not. Clark is uniquely characterized by (LOC = 'LA' $\wedge$ LEV = 58 $\wedge$ SEX = 'F'). The choice of C1 = (LOC = 'LA') and C2 = (LEV = 58 $\wedge$ SEX = 'F') produces an individual tracker that satisfies the above condition.

As COUNT(C1) = 4 and COUNT(T) = 3, they are both answerable. The salary of Clark may then be compromised by first confirming that C is a unique characterization as follows:

```
COUNT(C1) - COUNT(T) = 1
```

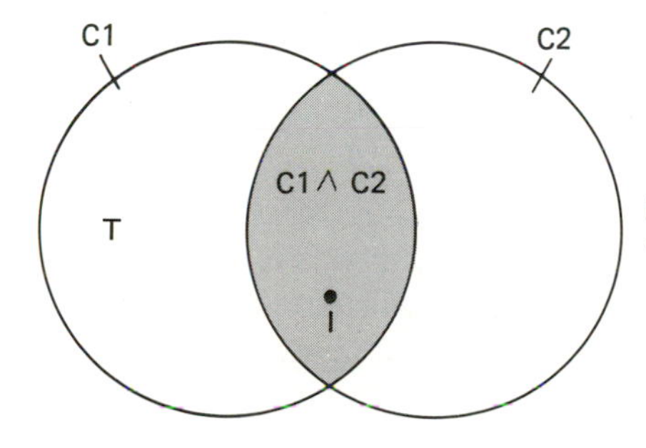

Fig. 13.2. Venn diagram for the individual tracker.

The salary may then be found by subtracting the results of the two summing queries:

```
SUM(C:SAL) = SUM(C1:SAL) - SUM(T:SAL) = 28
```

13.2.3 The General Tracker

A new individual tracker must be found for each person who is to be compromised. It has been shown [4] that a single formula called a *general tracker* can often be found which works for anyone in the database. A general tracker is any characteristic formula T for which the following condition holds:

$$2k \leq \mathrm{COUNT}(T) \leq n - 2k.$$

By symmetry, ¬T is also a tracker.

The strategy for compromise for the case when COUNT(C) < k is:

```
COUNT(C) = COUNT(C ∨ T) + COUNT(C ∨ ¬T) - COUNT(T) - COUNT(¬T)
```

Let us assume that the individuals represented by C are contained in T. Then the first term is equivalent to COUNT(T), which is answerable. The second term includes all individuals not in T plus those in C. For this query to be answerable, the following condition must hold:

$$\mathrm{COUNT}(\neg T) + \mathrm{COUNT}(C) < n - k$$

Hence COUNT(¬T) must be less than n − 2k. By subtracting those in T and those in ¬T, we are left with the individuals in C. Similar arguments apply if the individuals in C are in ¬T or partially in both.

In our example we have a wide choice of general trackers, as is often the case. If we select SEX = 'F' as our tracker, then because COUNT(SEX = 'F') = 3, it is good for any value of k. As

```
COUNT(C ∨ (SEX = 'F')) + COUNT(C ∨ ¬ (SEX = 'F'))
    - COUNT(SEX = 'F') - COUNT(¬ (SEX = 'F')) = 1
```

we confirm again that C uniquely identifies Clark. The salary of Clark is then given by:

```
SUM(C ∨ (SEX = 'F') : SAL) + SUM(C ∨ ¬ (SEX = 'F') : SAL)
    - SUM(SEX = 'F' : SAL) - SUM(¬ (SEX = 'F') : SAL) = 28
```

A similar strategy can be used for the case when COUNT(C) > n − k.

A general tracker always exists if the database contains at least 2k + 1 disjoint classes of individuals, which can be distinguished by characteristic formulas. Even if 2k + 1 classes do not exist, a general tracker can still sometimes be found. In general, the larger the number of classes of individuals, the more useful the database as a source of statistical information. This implies that the more useful the database, the more likely it is to be compromised by use of the trackers.

13.2.4 Difficulty in Finding a Tracker

Schlörer [10] found that in one medical database, 98 percent of the records were identifiable by ten characteristics. This means that an individual tracker may be found in $2^{10} = 1024$ queries. A general tracker can be found in a time proportional at most to n^2. However, if each characteristic value is equally probable, then 99 percent of the distinct possible nonempty query sets will correspond to a general tracker. Thus it is likely that the tracker can be quickly found by simply guessing. In fact, it was found that the number of queries needed to find a tracker is at most $O(\log_2 S)$, where S is the number of distinguishable records in the database [5]. Experiments on a real database showed that a tracker often could be found in one or two queries.

13.3 QUERY OVERLAP

One of the reasons why we could compromise the database was because the query sets overlapped. We now examine the effect of query overlap on the ability to compromise the database. We assume the database is represented by a set of numbers $\{x_1, \ldots, x_n\}$ and that queries can be made about the sum (or average) of any subset of the n values. Consider queries that sum three elements and have an overlap of two elements. Then the following four queries:

$$\begin{aligned} q1 &= x_1 + x_2 + x_3 \\ q2 &= x_1 + x_2 + x_4 \\ q3 &= x_1 + x_3 + x_4 \\ q4 &= x_2 + x_3 + x_4 \end{aligned}$$

can be used to solve for all elements x_i, $i = 1,2,3,4$. For example, $x_4 = (-2q1 + q2 + q3 + q4)/3$. Dobkin *et al.* [6] determined that the lower bound on the number of queries required to determine the element $x_{\ell+1}$ is:

$$1 + (k - (\ell + 1))/r$$

where k is the size of the query set, ℓ is the number of elements known (i.e., $x_1, x_2, \ldots, x_\ell$) with $0 \leq \ell < k - 1$, and r is the number of overlapping elements.

As we might have intuitively expected, the number of queries required for compromise increases with the query set size and decreases with the number of elements known and the amount of overlap. With no overlap there is no compromise.

A corollary of this result is that, if the population of the database, n, is less than

$$\frac{k^2}{2r} + \frac{k}{2} + \frac{(\ell + 1)}{2} - \frac{(\ell + 1)^2}{2r}$$

then the database is noncompromisable.

13.4 QUERIES THAT RETURN A DATABASE VALUE

Queries that return actual database values pose similar problems for security enforcement [6]. Examples are queries that compute the median, maximum, or minimum of a set of values. If we assume that salaries are unique, then the following two queries:

```
MIN (SEX = 'F' : SAL) = 24
```

and

```
MIN (LOC = 'SF' : SAL) = 24
```

allow us to make inferences about an individual: namely, that there is only one female living in San Francisco, and her salary is $24,000. DeMillo *et al.* [2] showed that, even if the database sometimes lies and returns a value that is not the minimum from the query set, the database can still be compromised. We refer the reader to [9] for further details on this subject.

13.5 SECURITY MECHANISMS

We have seen that trackers exist in most databases and can be found using relatively few queries. Even when the database lies, it can be compromised in some cases. The problem of guaranteeing the security of the database is therefore a difficult and subtle one.

INGRES [11], for example, distinguishes between two types of statistical queries: those that apply to all rows in a relation and those that specify a subset of rows. The first type of query is equivalent to specifying no characteristic formula. These queries are answered normally. The second type of query is modified with the relevant access rules in much the same way as a nonstatistical query. This means that, in order to ask a statistical query relating to a set of rows, one must have READ access to each individual row. While this prevents compromise of the database, it is too restrictive for most situations.

Other approaches [1] are:

1. Partition the database, ensuring that all nonempty query sets contain at least one partition [12]. For example, queries could be restricted to refer only to characteristics involving whole groups. A basic problem with this approach is that the partitions may not allow the users to obtain needed information. Additionally, if records are continually being added and deleted, there may be considerable overhead in maintaining partitions.

2. Perturb the data in an unpredictable way, either before or after processing the queries but before passing the result to the user. It is not sufficient to add a zero-mean random value because this can be averaged out by repeating the query a sufficient number of times. Adding a pseudo random value that depends on the data is more secure, but if it is large enough to prevent compromise it may reduce the quality of the statistics to an unacceptable level.

3. Select query sets that are random samples of the original database [7]. For example, the 1960 census was distributed as a 1/1000 sample of the full data with names and addresses removed. However, this approach is applicable only to large databases.

4. Produce audit trails to detect suspicious sequences of queries. While this does not directly prevent compromise, the threat of exposure may deter would-be infiltrators.

Approaches 1 through 3 are most applicable to very large databases; they trade a reduction in the information that can be extracted from the database for a gain in security. We have shown how certain sequences of queries can be used to compromise a database. In order to prove that a database is secure, it is necessary to demonstrate that no method of compromise exists. This is a considerably more difficult task.

REFERENCES

1. R. Conway and D. Strip, "Selective partial access to a database." *Proc. 1976 ACM Annual Conf.*, 85–89.
2. R. A. DeMillo, D. Dobkin, and R. J. Lipton, "Even data bases that lie can be compromised." *IEEE Trans. on Software Eng.* **4,** 1 (Jan. 1978), 73–75.
3. D. E. Denning, "Are statistical data bases secure?" *AFIPS Conf. Proc.* **47,** 1978 NCC, 525–530. AFIPS Press, Montvale, N.J., 1978.
4. D. E. Denning, P. J. Denning, and M. D. Schwartz, "The tracker: A threat to statistical database security." *ACM TODS* **4,** 1 (March 1979), 76–79.
   A clear exposition on the threat of individual and generalized trackers.

5. D. E. Denning and J. Schlörer, "A fast procedure for finding a tracker in a statistical database." *ACM TODS* **5,** 1 (March 1980), 88–102.

6. D. Dobkin, A. K. Jones, and R. J. Lipton, "Secure databases: Protection against user influence." *ACM TODS* **4,** 1 (March 1979), 97–106.

   This paper investigates the effect of query overlap and set size on the ability to compromise the database for average and median type queries.

7. L. J. Hoffman and W. F. Miller, "Getting a personal dossier from a statistical databank." *Datamation* **16,** 5 (May 1970), 74–75.

8. F. Land, "The Integrity of Statistical Data Bases." In "Policy Issues in Data Protection and Privacy." *Proc. Organization for Economic Cooperation and Development Seminar,* June 1974. OECD, Paris, 1976.

9. S. P. Reiss, "Security in databases: A combinatorial study." *J. ACM* **26,** 1 (Jan. 1979), 45–57.

   This paper extends the results of Dobkin, Jones, and Lipton [6].

10. J. Schlörer, "Identification and retrieval of personal records from a statistical data bank." *Methods of Info. in Medicine* **14,** 1 (Jan. 1975), 7–13.

11. M. Stonebraker and E. Wong, "Access control in a relational database management system by query modification." *Proc. 1974 ACM Annual Conference,* 180–186.

12. C. T. Yu, M. K. Siu, and K. Lam, "On a partitioning problem." *ACM TODS* **3,** 3 (Sept. 1978), 299–309.

14 The Future of Database Security

14.1 CHANGING NEEDS AND TECHNOLOGY

In this final chapter we speculate briefly about the future of database security. One thing is certain: Database security will continue to be recognized as an important goal. We can expect to see major transformations of this goal, however, for a number of reasons. First, new uses for databases will impose new requirements. Second, changes in hardware and software technology will eliminate some of the old problems while introducing new ones. Finally, research in database security will discover new problems and begin to solve some of those (such as inference) that are recognized now but as yet unsolved.

Some major new ways of using databases are rapidly imposing new requirements, even as the technology of database security struggles to catch up with current requirements. One major change is the growing use of distributed databases, whose security issues are discussed in Chapter 12. A related development is the growing importance of EFT. Privacy legislation will continue to evolve and will affect new types of enterprises. Office systems offer a whole new set of problems, since their databases consist largely of text and of graphic material, which may be NCI (non-coded information). Text and graphic objects have complex structures and therefore may consist of smaller objects of differing authorization characteristics; but the theory of their structure is not well developed in comparison with the usual type of structured data, and we know of no work specifically addressing the security of text, graphics, and NCI.

The cost of processing power is rapidly decreasing, and that of memory somewhat less rapidly. These changes lead inevitably to different ways of organizing the entire computing and database system. Today's problem of sharing a computing system and a database may be transformed into the problem of sharing a set of databases, since there may be no economic reason to share the computing system. The system that maintains a database may also see a transformation in structure. Doubtless it will include multiple processors that perform different parts of the database access and maintenance task, including access control. One likely eventuality is that such a system never runs arbitrary user-written machine-language programs. If this is the case, many of today's protection problems vanish.

The availability of inexpensive encryption devices opens many new possibilities. The development of ways to use these devices in the protection of databases is still in its infancy.

These hardware developments will be matched by equally important changes in the way applications are written. We can expect much greater reliance on high-level languages, and these languages will evolve toward better support of security. One such development will be languages that are at a higher level than today's languages and are therefore inherently safer. (Such languages are discussed in Reference 2.) Database access functions will be integrated into the languages in a way that will allow static analysis for security purposes. At the very least, it will be possible to determine what objects are accessed by a program, and in what way. It may also be possible to analyze information flow.

14.2 SOURCES FOR THE DATABASE SECURITY ART

We would have liked to describe in this book some "ideal" DBMS with excellent discretionary access control, running on a perfectly secure operating system, and fitting with that operating system in some very coherent way. Unfortunately, no such system exists, so we have used as examples what we consider to be the best approximations to this ideal. We have also described techniques, principles, and guidelines that are not associated with any particular system. The systems and the other results derive from four quite different sources:

- commercial DBMSs,
- auditing and control,
- university and laboratory research, and
- military-oriented research.

Today's commercial DBMSs began with relatively little security provision. In general, these systems catered to carefully tailored applications rather than to ad hoc query, and the application was relied on for security. As it came to be recognized that the DBMS had to assume more security responsibility, security features had to be added in a way that did not obsolete existing application programs. It is not surprising, then, that these systems do not always provide a coherent model of security or adequately support security for all types of users. Commercial systems have been forced, however, to provide good reliability and are generally quite advanced in this respect. Commercial DBMSs will continue to evolve toward better security and toward an appropriate division of security responsibility between the DBMS and the operating system.

Two research systems that have emphasized security—INGRES and System R—both were inspired by the relational model of data, which provided a coherent basis not only for data description and access but also for integrity and security. Efforts of this type are of the greatest importance in advancing the art of database security, because they provide a fruitful interaction of research and practice. Many of the excellent ideas behind commercial systems are never published; certainly they are not widely disseminated during the development process. Theoretical research, on the other hand, is not subjected to the discipline that comes from implementing a system to support real users. Research prototypes have been successful, and can be expected to increase in number. Problems that will receive increased research attention include security of distributed databases, inference, theory of authorization, and architectures for secure database systems.

In spite of all the attention that it is receiving, the field of database audit and control remains little developed, especially as it relates to the DBMS. We can expect to see more people receiving training in both auditing and database systems. The issue of whether auditors can use the DBMS will probably be resolved in favor of the DBMS; if so, support for auditing will be built into the DBMS, and auditing software will exploit DBMS features.

Finally, the secure military systems have shown that it is possible to formally state a security policy and to design at least an operating system to enforce that policy. Moreover, these systems control information flow, something not attempted by the commercial or research systems. We do not yet know whether usable DBMSs can be built on this framework, but at the very least a great deal has been learned about how to structure a system design so that we can have some trust in its correctness.

It is to be hoped that the next decade will see a convergence of these multiple streams of work. Certainly each has much to offer the others. Perhaps the problems of the different environments are not really so different, but only the ways the problems are formulated.

REFERENCES

1. T. Winograd, "Beyond programming languages." *Comm. ACM* **22,** 7 (July 1979), 391–401.

Answers to Selected Exercises

Chapter 5

5.3. Imagine a database containing employee information in a relation EMP (NAME, NUMBER, ADDRESS, SALARY). A clerk in the personnel department could insert records for new employees, filling in the employee's name, number, and address. However, only the employee's manager would be authorized to fill in the salary.

Chapter 6

6.3. We have the following situation:

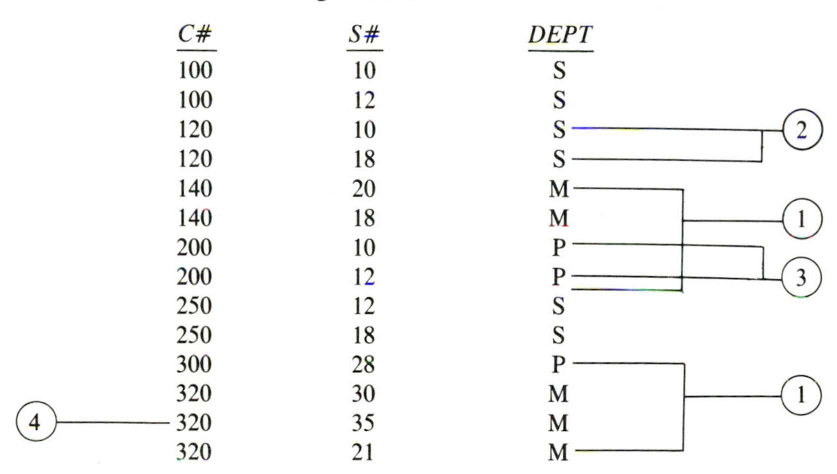

C#	*S#*	*DEPT*
100	10	S
100	12	S
120	10	S
120	18	S
140	20	M
140	18	M
200	10	P
200	12	P
250	12	S
250	18	S
300	28	P
320	30	M
320	35	M
320	21	M

The table indicates (1) the tuples selected to be read by the program request, (2) the tuples authorized to be read by the first access rule, (3) the tuples authorized to be updated (and therefore also to be read) by the second access rule, and (4) the fields authorized to be read by the third and fourth access rules.

The program receives the pairs (C#, S#) : (200, 10), (200, 12), and (320, 35).

6.5. The lattice is given in Fig. ANS. 1. The class-combining operator yields a ≥ level and the union of the categories.

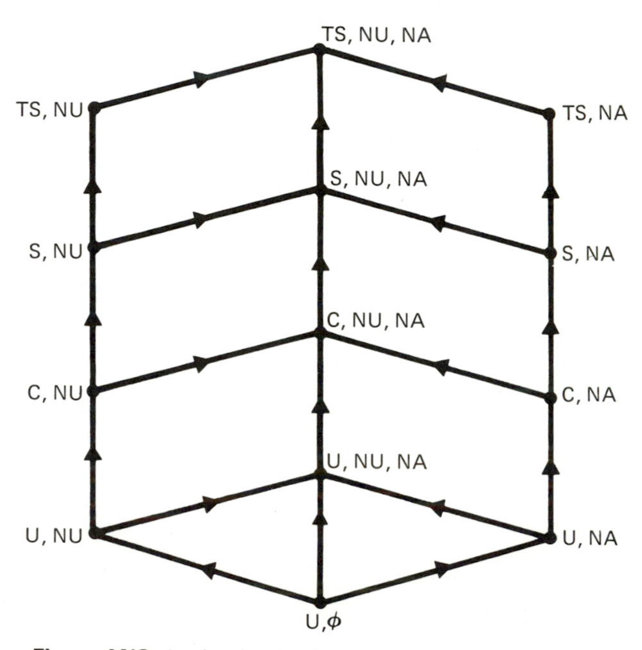

Figure ANS. 1. Lattice for four levels and two categories.

Chapter 7

7.2. The method shown in Fig. ANS. 2 can be used in QBE for any fixed number of levels of management. Figure ANS. 3 shows a more general solution using a

EMP	NAME	MGR	SAL
I.AUTH(P.) JOHN	N	JOHN	S
	Q	M	S
	M	JOHN	
	R	M2	S
	M2	M	

Figure ANS. 2. QBE Authorization.

EMP	NAME	MGR	SAL
I.AUTH(P.)JOHN	SMITH(5L)		S

Figure ANS. 3. Altnerative answer to Exercise 7.2.

proposed *level* operator.† With this solution it is not necessary to know beforehand the number of levels.

In SQL one could define a series of views for each manager, such as:

```
DEFINE VIEW ANNSEMP AS
     SELECT * FROM EMPLOYEE
     WHERE MGR = 'ANN'
DEFINE VIEW ANNSEMP2 AS
     SELECT * FROM EMPLOYEE
     WHERE MGR IS IN ANNSEMP.NAME
...
     GRANT ANNSEMP TO ANN
     GRANT ANNSEMP2 TO ANN
```

7.4. This is an exercise in applying the access rule model. Since there is a rule for every (s,O,t), all rules that apply to the request have the same access type.

7.5. The lattice of Fig. 6.9 can also be seen as a hierarchical class structure, where higher-level classes include lower-level ones. One could define data classes such as Treatment, Financial, and Patient History, and user classes such as Admissions (with access to Patient History and Financial) and Accounting (with access to Financial and Treatment).

Chapter 8

8.1 A rule in this data-control model has the following components:

- s — subject (GENERAL for integrity rules)
- O — object
- t — access type
- p — access-control predicate or semantic assertion
- $(c_1, ap_1) \cdots (c_n, ap_n)$ — where (for integrity rules) any of the pairs can specify the condition and type of integrity checking.

† See Date (Reference 7 of Chapter 3) or M. Zloof, "Query-by-Example: Operations on the Transitive Closure." Report RC5526, IBM Research Center, Yorktown Heights, N.Y., July 1975.

8.4 The orderings and the dependency graphs for the lost update schedules are given in Fig. ANS. 4.

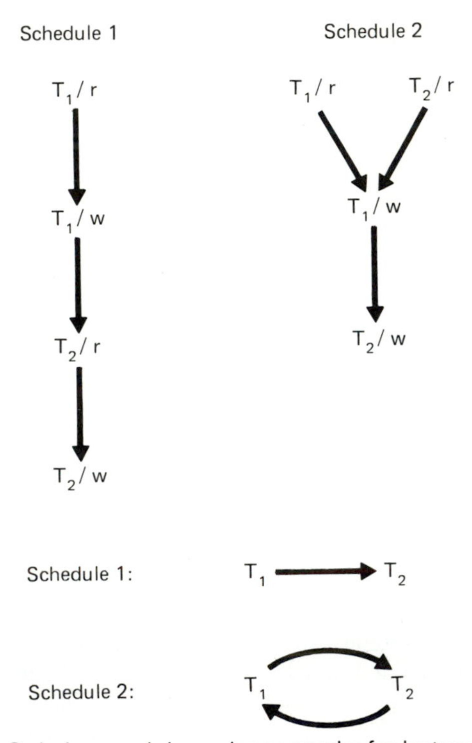

Figure ANS. 4. Orderings and dependency graphs for lost-update schedules.

Chapter 9

9.1 Assume the contents of CONFLICT and AUTHORITY to be as shown.

CONFLICT

T1	T2
TR2	TR3
TR6	TR3

AUTHORITY

S	O
S1	TR1
S1	TR2
S2	TR3
S2	TR2
S3	TR4

We need to find all the pairs of transactions that each subject can access. We use for this the view ALLOBJ defined as shown below. (ALLOBJ is an equijoin on S of AUTHORITY with itself.)

```
DEFINE VIEW ALLOBJ (S, 01, 02) AS
  SELECT *
  FROM AUTHORITY, AUTHORITY.X
  WHERE AUTHORITY.S = X.S
  AND AUTHORITY.0¬= X.0
```

The contents of this view are then:

ALLOBJ	S	O1	O2
	S1	TR1	TR2
	S1	TR2	TR1
	S2	TR3	TR2
	S2	TR2	TR3

The rules that are in conflict are obtained by defining another view, BADRULES:

```
DEFINE VIEW BADRULES AS
   SELECT * FROM ALLOBJ, CONFLICT
   WHERE 01 = T1 AND 02 = T2
```

BADRULES	S	01	02	T1	T2
	S2	TR2	TR3	TR2	TR3

Then the following assertion prevents transaction conflicts.

```
ASSERT A1 ON BADRULES: COUNT (*) = 0
```

9.2 In the access rule make:

s = any administrator,
O = 'C',
t = Administer,
p = MAJ(A, B, . . . , K) $\wedge$ A.

A, B, . . . K are system variables that have the value 'true' if the corresponding administrator indicates agreement. MAJ is a system function that returns a true value if a majority of the input variables are true.

(c1, ap1) = ($\neg$MAJ (A, B, . . . , K), P1),
(c2, ap2) = ($\neg$A, P2),
(c3, ap3) = ($\neg$p, P3).

Chapter 12

12.1. See Fig. ANS. 5 for the remaining rights.

12.2. See Reference 33 of Chapter 12 for a possible solution.

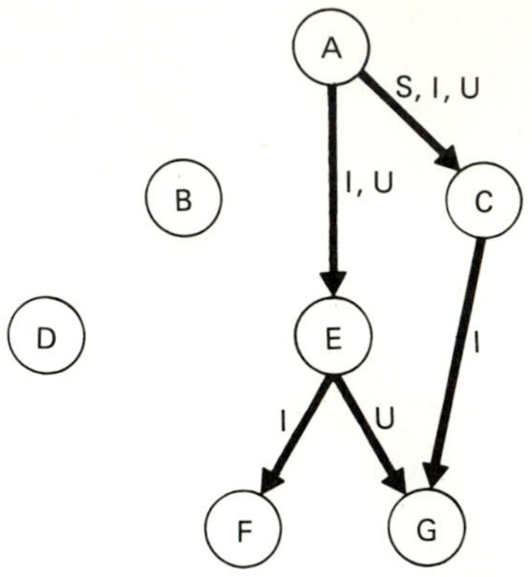

Figure ANS. 5. Rights remaining.

Index